Abolitionism and Imperialism

in Britain, Africa, and the Atlantic

CAMBRIDGE CENTRE OF AFRICAN STUDIES SERIES

Series editors: Derek R. Peterson, Harri Englund, and Christopher Warnes

Derek R. Peterson, ed.
Abolitionism and Imperialism in Britain, Africa, and the Atlantic

Abolitionism and Imperialism
in Britain, Africa, and the Atlantic

Edited by Derek R. Peterson

Ohio University Press • *Athens*

Ohio University Press, Athens, Ohio 45701
www.ohioswallow.com
© 2010 by Ohio University Press

To obtain permission to quote, reprint, or otherwise reproduce or distribute material
from Ohio University Press publications, please contact our rights and permissions
department at (740) 593-1154 or (740) 593-4536 (fax).

Printed in the United States of America
Ohio University Press books are printed on acid-free paper ⊗ ™

18 17 16 15 14 13 12 11 10   5 4 3 2 1

Library of Congress Cataloging-in-Publication Data
Abolitionism and imperialism in Britain, Africa, and the Atlantic / edited by Derek R.
Peterson.
    p. cm. — (African studies from Cambridge)
  Includes bibliographical references and index.
  ISBN 978-0-8214-1901-4 (hc : alk. paper) — ISBN 978-0-8214-1902-1 (pb : alk.
paper)
  1. Slave trade—Great Britain—History. 2. Slave trade—Great Britain—Colonies—
America—History. 3. Slave trade—Africa—History. 4. Antislavery movements—
Great Britain—History. 5. Great Britain—Colonies—History. 6. Imperialism—
Social aspects—Great Britain. I. Peterson, Derek R., 1971–
  HT1162.A26 2010
  326'.809171241—dc22
                              2009033389

Contents

Series Editors' Preface

The University of Cambridge is home to one of the world's leading centers of African studies. It organizes conferences, runs a weekly seminar series, hosts a specialist library, and coordinates the work of the several dozen Cambridge lecturers whose research concerns Africa. With the generous support of the Leverhulme Trust, the center has recently inaugurated the Cambridge/Africa Collaborative Research Programme. Each year the center announces a fellowship competition organized around a particular theme and invites applications from Africa-based scholars. Four or five fellows are brought to Cambridge for six months, during which time they pursue research on separate projects while meeting regularly to discuss their work. At the conclusion of their tenure, the visiting fellows present the fruits of their labors at two conferences, one in Cambridge, the other at a partner African institution.

This book is the first installment in a new Cambridge Centre of African Studies Series, published by Ohio University Press. The series will publish edited volumes arising chiefly out of the body of scholarship generated by the Cambridge/Africa Collaborative Research Programme. These books will highlight the work that young, promising African scholars have composed and refined over the course of their time in Cambridge. The books will also feature the work of European or American Africanists who have offered papers at conferences and seminars convened in Cambridge. Contributors will have been involved in a yearlong conversation about the themes in which each book is engaged. This long period of incubation will, we hope, allow us to produce books that are both thematically coherent and methodologically innovative, full of fresh, cutting-edge research from scholars who are excited about their work.

Academic presses today face growing financial pressures, and it is increasingly difficult to find a publisher for the fruit of collaborative research. We thank the editors at Ohio for their support in fostering a more dialogical, more democratic approach to the production of knowledge about Africa.

Derek R. Peterson
Harri Englund
Christopher Warnes
Cambridge, England

Acknowledgments

This book arises out of a series of lectures convened by the Centre of African Studies at the University of Cambridge in 2007. The series was occasioned by the bicentenary of the Act for the Abolition of the Slave Trade, which was then being celebrated with much pomp and circumstance by Tony Blair's Labour government. The lectures were meant to focus critical scholarly attention on British abolitionism, to illuminate the broader geographic and temporal terrain in which abolitionism took place, and to claim the study of abolitionism as a field for Africa's historians. The lecture series was supported by the Smuts Fund for Commonwealth Studies and the Centre for History and Economics, both of the University of Cambridge. Cambridge's Centre of African Studies subsidized this book's production. My editorial work has been supported by the Leverhulme Trust, whose Philip Leverhulme Prize gave me relief from the demands of teaching. I am most grateful to these organizations for their support.

I am a historian of colonial eastern Africa. At a time when historians are separated as much by their bibliographies as by their research fields, I have had a great deal of reading to do. In learning the scholarship on the eighteenth-century Atlantic world, I've relied particularly on Rebecca Scott, Seymour Drescher, and the anonymous reviewer from Ohio University Press, all of whom offered welcome guidance on the book's intellectual architecture. Jonathon Glassman and John Lonsdale commented on the introduction. Gillian Berchowitz, the press's senior editor, has been a pleasure to work with. Rebecca Peterson has, as ever, been my most lively interlocutor, and I am most grateful to her.

Algiers

D.R.
CONGO
UGANDA
BUNYORO
BUGANDA
MUBENDE Kampala
KENYA
ANKOLE
Lake
Victoria
RWANDA
TANZANIA

Senegal R.
Gambia R.
Sierra
Leone
Gallinas R.
Niger R.
Freetown
Cape Coast
Castle

São Tomé

Kongo R.

Nairobi

Mombasa

São Salvador
Kongo
Luanda
Ndongo

Zambezi R.

Dahomey
Abeokuta
Ouidah
Lagos
Badagry
Porto Novo

TANGANYIKA
Pemba
Tanga
Zanzibar
Island
Zanzibar
Bagamoyo
Dar es Salaam

1,000 km

Cape Town

Introduction

Abolitionism and Political Thought in Britain and East Africa

DEREK R. PETERSON

IN 1931, Zakaliya Lugangwa and sixty-three compatriots wrote to the governor of the British protectorate of Uganda, the Anglican bishop, and the secretary of state for the colonies to complain about the government of Mubende District. Mubende, historically part of the Bunyoro state, had with the backing of British administrators been folded into the kingdom of Buganda in the late nineteenth century. British administrators regarded Buganda's hegemony over the disputed territory as an administrative convenience. Lugangwa and his compatriots, by contrast, argued that Ganda rulers were making them slaves. They catalogued the tyrannies of Ganda government—schools conducted exclusively in the Ganda language, discriminatory rules about land tenure—and cast themselves in a familiar moral drama: "the thing that hurts us most is *Slavery* which has been practiced over us. . . . We wish of the British Government that every country subject to the English Flag should enjoy freedom and that slavery should be done away with. . . . Free us from Bondage in which we are, let us go back to our mother land Bunyoro."[1]

Abolitionism had many advocates in colonial Africa. Activists like Lugangwa used abolitionist language to dramatize the starkly unequal power relations of colonial government and to transform their partisan political interests into a moral problem that demanded attention. In the British mandated territory in Tanganyika, activists of the Tanganyika African National Union drew from rural people's own vocabulary to characterize the cadre of government-appointed chiefs as *utawala wa kitumwa,* a "slave regime."[2] TANU activists argued that national independence would bring *uhuru,* "freedom," conceived both as political sovereignty and as liberation from slavery. Just to the north, in the colony of Kenya, Kikuyu detainees held in government-run camps during the Mau Mau war were similarly representing their situation in an abolitionist framework. In a 1957 petition to the commissioner of prisons, detainees at the Sanjusi Island camp complained over their paltry rations, the hard work they were forced to perform, and their inadequate clothing. "Now we have learned that instead of being detained, the government has turned us to be slaves," they wrote, "for we are employed in the same work as African slaves were employed in America."[3] In 1954 detainees at the Manyani camp wrote to the secretary of state for the colonies, to Jawaharlal Nehru, and to parliamentarian Fenner Brockway to complain that "the Kenya Government wants to make us its slaves. Would you please inquire this of the British Government of our Queen Elizabeth II to help all people . . . not to be made Kenya slaves."[4]

In Uganda, Kenya, Tanzania, and other locales, subject peoples were exerting political leverage over local colonial authorities by representing themselves as slaves. There were other roles in which they could cast themselves. In the kingdom of Buganda, for example, the founder of the separatist African Orthodox Church replied to the Anglican bishop's condescension by comparing himself with "Martin Luther, Calvin, Erasmus, [the] Huguenots, Henry VIII, Parker, Wycliffe, Cranmer, King Edward VI . . . Queen Elizabeth, Wolsey, the Protestant Episcopal Church, Booth, the Scotch church, the old Catholic church of Holland," and other advocates for Christian orthodoxy.[5] His contemporaries in the populist Bataka Party sometimes compared themselves with Oliver Cromwell, highlighting their opposition to the powers that Buganda's king enjoyed.[6] African activists drew on a wide range of historical precedents in order to validate their contemporary political projects. But for people confronting the starkly unequal power relationships that British colonialism cultivated, for prisoners, ethnic minorities, forced laborers, and nationalist politicians, being a slave was good politics. Abolitionist rhetoric was, among other things, a means of making political inequalities look unjust. What abolitionist rhetoric did particularly effectively was dramatize petitioners' plight as exploited subjects, suffering under local authorities' tyranny. By positioning themselves in this way, African entrepreneurs obliged British administrators in faraway London to act in order to uphold British honor. In speaking as abolitionists, Africans on the colonial periphery brought the imperium close to hand.

Historians working within their separate subdisciplines have sectioned off the whole field of moral and political discourse that abolitionist thought supported. There is a vast literature about the politics of eighteenth- and nineteenth-century Britain. There is a separate, equally vast scholarship about slavery and emancipation in the Atlantic world. And there is a growing historiography about colonial Africa's intellectual and political life. What these chronological and geographic partitions obscure are the ongoing uses to which abolitionist symbolism, rhetoric, and ideology could be put. The East African activists who filled British officials' mailboxes with petitions about slavery were not contemporaries of Wilberforce or Clarkson. Neither were they actually engaged in the liberation of slaves. But thinkers in anglophone Africa could nonetheless appropriate the discourse of abolitionism in order to lend moral authority to projects that were secular in character. Anglophone Africa's activists knew William Wilberforce, David Livingstone, and other advocates of British abolitionism through the dozens of vernacular-language biographies that missionaries published. Mau Mau detainees ransacked the slim collection of books available from their camps' libraries and found therein accounts of the slave trade and the struggle against it.[7] African politicians in 1950s Zanzibar composed dozens of essays hymning Livingstone, John Kirk, and other abolitionists, using their rhetoric to dramatize the brutalities of "Arab" slaveholders. Abolitionist discourse helped Zanzibar's African activists configure their political situation in racial terms and gave them a grammar with which to reply to Arab elites' cultural condescension (Glassman, this volume). For these entrepreneurs, British history was close at hand. Their chronological remoteness from the eighteenth century did not make it impossible for these thinkers to position themselves as subjects of abolitionist discourse.

The present volume arises out of a lecture series organized at the University of Cambridge to mark the bicentenary of the Act for the Abolition of the Atlantic Slave Trade. New Labour was in 2007 fighting a deeply controversial war in Iraq, and the Blair government seized on the bicentenary of abolition as an opportunity to stiffen the backs of the British public. The Heritage Lottery Fund disbursed some twenty million pounds to fund public events celebrating abolition. The Royal Mail issued a commemorative coin and a series of stamps. Inspirational biographies describing William Wilberforce's life were published, and a hagiographic film,

Amazing Grace, was released in March of that year (Hilton, this volume). In his November 2006 pronouncement on the bicentenary, Tony Blair publicly expressed his "deep sorrow" at Britain's involvement with the Atlantic slave trade. But against the backdrop of the Iraq war, he also called the bicentenary an opportunity to "increase our determination to shape the world with the values we share."[8] For Blair, the bicentenary was a pedagogic event, an occasion to remind an increasingly skeptical public about imperial Britain's historical role as an agent of civility and human rights.[9]

Abolitionism and Imperialism was conceived as a contrarian effort to challenge the self-congratulatory frame in which the bicentenary of the Abolition Act was being cast. The authors argue that abolition was never a singular achievement for British idealism. They show, rather, that abolitionism was a joint production, authored not by a few British activists but by a cosmopolitan set of actors, working on a disparate set of projects from a variety of positions. The cast of characters was broad. British businessmen were interested in the agronomic potential of West Africa. They promoted free-labor colonies and experimented with crops that might fuel the British economy (Brown and Drescher, this volume). West African rulers, working to keep hold over their polities' demographic and political future, opposed the slave trade where it upset social order (Thornton, this volume). Caribbean planters were in the early nineteenth century experimenting with some of the principles of free labor. The evidence they generated helped abolitionists argue that slave emancipation would advantage the plantation economy (Morgan, this volume). Miners, colliers, and other middling artisans endangered by the inhumane conditions of Britain's new factories put their names to antislavery petitions as an act of protest against industrial capitalism. Working-class radicals identified themselves as "white slaves," and claimed the moral authority of abolitionism for themselves. And parliamentarians worried about the wrath that God was storing up against the British state supported abolition as an act of national absolution (Hilton). For these actors, the moral authority that antislavery conferred assisted projects that were themselves pragmatic. Economic and political entrepreneurs in West Africa, the Caribbean, and in Britain itself hooked into the discourse of abolitionism, using its symbols and its vocabulary to advance their disparate goals. Abolition was formed out of a contrapuntal discourse that crisscrossed the Atlantic.

Seeing abolitionism as a contrapuntal discourse makes it possible to think of the British Empire itself in a new frame: not as a vehicle by which already-established British values were extended to the unenlightened corners of the world, nor still as a hegemonic imposition on subject peoples' cultural and political autonomy, but as an arena of moral discourse. A new cadre of imperial historians has shed light on what Frederick Cooper and Ann Laura Stoler have termed the "tensions of empire," highlighting how, in the transcontinental space opened up by Europe's empires, normative conceptions of religion, cuisine, motherhood, and matrimony were defined and debated.[10] Britain's empire was never simply "out there": it never existed, that is, as a separate political field from Britain itself.[11] During the late eighteenth and early nineteenth centuries, actors in the West Indies and in Africa carried on a long conversation with British activists about labor, rights, and freedom. West Indian planters' racism drove patriots like Granville Sharp to clarify British virtues. Free blacks' commitment to Sierra Leone gave abolitionists evidence to prove the viability of emancipation. William Wilberforce's antislavery rhetoric helped inspire a slave rebellion in Barbados. The empire was the crucible wherein British values were worked out.

This book aims to expand the geographic terrain in which the study of abolitionism is normally conducted. At the same time it illuminates the broader temporal field in which abolitionist thought took place. For abolition was never only an event in nineteenth-century legal history. In Britain's twentieth-century empire, Africans took hold over the discourse of abolitionism in order to bridge the metropole with the colony. Imperial government confronted people in Africa and elsewhere with the challenge of exercising influence over a ruling class that was distant from them. But African activists knew the mailing addresses of the Anti-Slavery and Aborigines' Protection Society, of Fenner Brockway, Clement Attlee, and other liberals. They identified allies that could be mobilized to act on their behalf and filled their mailboxes with petitions and correspondence. Their political strategies produced lines of political connection that were more varied and complex than the hierarchy of superior and subaltern. Activists in Uganda, Kenya, and elsewhere adopted the posture of slavery by highlighting the inhumanity of local conditions. They thereby configured their political situation as a moral problem and compelled British liberals to pay heed.

Abolitionism and the Making of British Identity

The history of abolitionism has very often been composed as advocacy. The earliest work was authored by Thomas Clarkson, whose two-volume history appeared in 1808, the year after Parliament passed the Abolition Act. Clarkson pictured the progress of antislavery as a river. It was fed at its headwaters by the influence of John Wesley and Granville Sharp, and it deepened after 1787, when the Quakers, the Evangelicals, and other groups swelled the movement. In Clarkson's imagery the river reached flood stage in 1807, when with popular support abolitionism overflowed its banks and spilled onto the alluvial plain of Britain's political life.[12] Clarkson's hydrological imagery made a tendentious history look inevitable. It put the opponents of abolition outside the main currents of British history. Writing over one hundred years later, the Cambridge historian G. M. Trevelyan followed Clarkson in representing abolition as the outworking of British ideals.[13] On the centenary of Wilberforce's death, Trevelyan claimed that abolition was accomplished because of "the will and conscience of the people of England," not through the "ordinary machinery of party politics." For Trevelyan the legislative triumphs of 1807 and 1833 had established Britain's moral role as a force for good in the world. "Before [Africa's] exploitation by Europe had well begun," hymned Trevelyan, "the most powerful of the nations . . . had decided that slavery should not be the relationship of the black man to the white." He thus argued that mankind had been "successfully lifted on to a higher place by the energy of good men." Trevelyan's contemporary Reginald Coupland spent his long career composing biographies of David Livingstone, William Wilberforce, John Kirk, and other heroes of British abolitionism.[14] "The lives and works of Wilberforce and the 'Saints' are certain proof," Coupland argued, "that not merely individuals but the common will, the State itself, can rise on occasion to the height of pure unselfishness."[15]

At the high tide of Britain's African empire, the historians Trevelyan and Coupland found in the history of abolitionism evidence with which to fortify the civilizing mission. For the architects of empire in the late nineteenth and in the twentieth centuries, it was the abolitionist project that made Britain uniquely qualified to govern its African subjects. Missionaries and other advocates of empire published dozens of works documenting the accomplishments of the heroes of abolitionism. Today, Cambridge University Library holds 133 titles classified under "Livingstone, David, 1813–1873." Titles such as *David Livingstone: The Great African Pioneer* and *David Livingstone: Light-Bearer to Africa* make Livingstone into a standard-bearer of civility.[16] Other books put Livingstone alongside the makers of British history: one is entitled *Heroes of the Nineteenth Century: Nelson, Napier, Roberts, Livingstone,* and another *Three Martyrs of the Nineteenth Century: Studies from the Lives of Livingstone, Gordon, and Patterson.*[17] But it was not only English readers who were learning about British values through the biographical genre. Africans were invited to apprehend British liberality in the dozens of vernacular-language biographies published by missionary presses. In western Kenya's Luo language, for example, readers of the 1951 collection *Jochir sigendini magadiera* (People who have lived great lives) could learn about David Livingstone alongside Kitty Wilkinson, Mary Scharlieb, Ann Judson, and other Victorian-era philanthropists.[18] As Boyd Hilton notes in this volume, the inspirational tradition of biographical writing persisted to the present. The bicentenary of the Abolition Act, in 2007, saw the publication of no less than eight biographies of William Wilberforce, with titles like *Statesman and Saint, The Man Who Freed the Slaves,* and *The Millionaire Child Who Worked So Hard to Win the Freedom of African Slaves.* The historiography of British liberalism was in its own time composed as biography. Cast as the victory of principle over self-interest, abolitionism was the framework by which Africans and other colonial subjects were taught about their rulers' benevolence.

It was Eric Williams's 1944 book *Capitalism and Slavery* that first punctured the moralistic historiography of abolitionism. Where Coupland and Trevelyan had represented abolition as a victory for idealism over self-interest, Williams attributed the rise of abolitionism to what he called "developing economic forces." Williams argued that the Atlantic slave trade had played midwife at the birth of capitalism, and that capitalism had in turn played pallbearer at slavery's demise.[19] Profits from the slave trade and its allied industries had provided much of the capital that financed industrialization. But by the 1780s, Williams argued, the economy of the British West Indies was in terminal decline, in part because of the loss of the food-provisioning colonies of America. And in England there was a shift in political power, as ascendant industrial capitalists displaced merchant capitalists. The calculus of low profitability and self-interest made it possible for Britain to end the slave trade based on economic, not moral or ideological reasons. "The humanitarians," argued Williams, "could never have succeeded a hundred years before when every important capitalist interest was on the side of the colonial system."[20]

Scholars have filled a library with replies to the Williams thesis in the sixty years since the publication of *Capitalism and Slavery.*[21] Some intellectual historians, like Roger Anstey, sought to rehabilitate the reputation of British liberalism. Anstey calculated that the small profits earned from slave voyages were not enough to suggest "any positive connection between structural change in the imperial economy and abolition."[22] In contrast to Williams's materialist thesis, Anstey argued that antislavery was primarily the fruit of Christian cosmology, of the "powerful idea of benevolence." "It was mainly religious conviction, insight and zeal which made it possible for anti-slavery feeling to be subsumed into a crusade against the slave trade and slavery," Anstey wrote.[23] In his 1975 book Anstey devoted six full chapters, nearly four hundred pages, to the Evangelicals and the Quakers, illuminating the moral, philosophical, and political dynamics of the abolitionist lobby. Other historians, more focused on economics than Anstey, challenged Williams's argument about the slave trade's role in Britain's industrial growth. Stanley Engerman calculated the contributions that the slave trade made to British capital formation and concluded that the trade could have made but little difference in the financing of industrialization.[24] Historian Joseph Inikori worked through the same statistics as Engerman and published a series of books and articles illuminating the slave economy's crucial role in fueling industrialization. Inikori's 2002 book was a catalogue of statistics and graphs demonstrating that Africans, as slaves and as workers, played a central part in England's economy.[25] Like Williams and Inikori, historian Seymour Drescher argued that the slave trade played a significant role in the eighteenth-century British economy. But where Williams argued that the profits from the trade were in decline by the 1780s, Drescher contended there was no decline in the value of the British slave system until well after the abolition of the slave trade.[26] In the first decades of the nineteenth century, during the height of the abolitionist campaign, regions under British control produced 60 percent of the world's sugar exports and 50 percent of its coffee. It is with this evidence in view that Drescher has termed the abolition of the slave trade "econocide," for by it Britain willfully terminated the most dynamic sector of its economy (Drescher, this volume).[27]

The debate over Eric Williams's thesis made economic history into a politically consequential vocation. In tables detailing the revenues that slave plantations earned, in censuses detailing the earnings of slaving voyages, historians looked for evidence by which either to indict abolitionists as self-interested profit seekers or to exonerate them as self-sacrificing idealists. It was David Brion Davis who first charted a path out of this impasse by inviting intellectual history and economic history to join hands. Like Williams, Davis linked the rise of antislavery to the rise of capitalism.[28] But where Williams argued that abolitionism reflected the particular financial interests of industrial capitalists, Davis positioned antislavery within the broader intellectual and moral world that capitalism created. In his 1966 book *The Problem of Slavery in Western Culture,* Davis focused particularly on the Quakers, who played a key role in legitimating bourgeois social relations. With their evangelical allies, they stigmatized the old, external mechanisms of physical constraint and valorized the internal restraint and self-discipline necessary for wage work. Abolitionists sought to free individuals to make rational choices, about God and about their financial interests. Their agenda reached from the slave plantations of the West Indies to the urban slums of London. The antislavery parliamentarian William Wilberforce was also the founder of the Society for the Suppression of Vice. His contemporary Thomas Chalmers, a clergyman, abolitionist, and devotee of Malthus, argued that statutory poor relief should be abolished so that the poor could be made responsible for themselves.[29] Even as they sought to free West Indian slaves from their physical bondage, middle-class reformers also sought to liberate working-class people from moral bondage and financial dependency. In their philanthropic work as in their antislavery advocacy, they argued that social discipline should arise from an internalized moral order.

Davis's latitudinal study of abolitionists' projects makes it possible to think of antislavery neither as an instrument of capitalists' self-interest, nor still as a movement of self-denying idealism, but as part of a broader reorientation in British economic and social life. In their marriages, in business, in religion, and in philanthropy, British people were in the eighteenth century developing mechanisms to hold each other accountable. This societal emphasis of accountability arose, argues historian Thomas Haskell, out of the organizational demands of commerce.[30] Where in an earlier time promises exchanged between individuals were beneath the notice of the courts, in the late eighteenth century contract law emerged as a discrete field of litigation. English courts compelled parties involved in contracts, whether financial or conjugal, to keep their promises. In their married lives, English people were in the eighteenth century eliminating religious sanctions punishing sexual deviance. Where sixteenth-century moralists had called adultery bestial, eighteenth-century novels and periodicals conceptualized sexual infidelity as a violation of the marital contract. Seen in this light, adultery was not a sin against God; it was an offense against the promise that the adulterer had made with his or her spouse.[31] In their sexual conduct, as in their business transactions, English people were keeping their promises and living up to the letter of the law.

The abolitionist project worked by extending the range of social problems for which British people felt themselves accountable. The abolitionists' challenge was to make skeptical people feel that their own reputation was endangered by commerce conducted thousands of miles away, on distant shores in West Africa and the Caribbean. In making British people feel accountable for slave traders' deeds abolitionists drew from the rich historical vocabulary of British citizenship. For the discourse of English citizenship was, in origin and form, abolitionist. Parliamentarians had from the 1620s argued that the English people possessed freedom not as a gift from the king but as a legal right. They complained bitterly when Charles I imprisoned subjects without trial, or imposed taxes without consent. It is "unnaturall," wrote one pamphleteer in 1642, "for any Nation to give away its owne proprietie in it selfe" and thereby "contribute to its owne inherent puissance, meerely to abet Tiranny, and support slavery."[32] Parliamentarians cast the king as a tyrannical slaveholder and represented themselves as chattel, unjustly enslaved. When in 1649 Charles I was beheaded, John Milton, Parliament's secretary for foreign tongues, warned Englishmen never again to consent to the yoke of kingship. "Any form of slavery is shameful to a freeborn man," he wrote, "but for you, after recovering your freedom . . . to wish to return again to slavery, contrary to your destiny . . . will also be both impious and wicked."[33] When on 17 March 1649 the Rump Parliament abolished the office of kingship, they argued that "use hath been made of the regal power to oppress and impoverish and enslave and subject." Two months later, the parliament proclaimed that "the people of England" constituted a "Commonwealth and Free State" governed by the people's elected representatives.[34]

In its conception, the English citizenry was defined in opposition to the figure of the voiceless, maltreated slave. The vocabulary of the English revolution established the terms in which, a century later, abolitionists framed their argument. Abolitionism worked by contrasting hard-won British liberties with the tyranny that the slave trade promoted. The decision in *Somerset v. Stewart* (1772) helped abolitionists make their case. The litigation concerned a young black man, Jonathon

Somerset, the slave of a Boston customs official. While in England he escaped from his owner's custody, then was recaptured and confined on a ship bound for Jamaica. Somerset's godparents, backed by the abolitionist Granville Sharp, brought a suit on his behalf. They argued that Somerset's reenslavement had made England, as Sharp put it, "as base, wicked and Tyrannical as our colonies." To allow slavery in England was to allow the "horrid cruelties . . . perpetuated in America" to "be introduced here."[35] Sharp and his colleagues were dramatizing Somerset's reenslavement as an assault on metropolitan freedoms. They distinguished freeborn Britons from a colonial world dominated by arbitrary power and abject servility. By this contrast they made slavery in Britain look like an abomination. Their argument carried the day: while Lord Mansfield's verdict was ambiguous, it established Somerset's right to go free.[36] The Somerset verdict was expanded into a generalized principle when, in 1778, another judge concluded that a slave brought to England became "as free as any one of us."[37]

Being free was thereby given a particular geography, as a defining quality of the British commonwealth. Abolitionist rhetoric worked by extending the reach of Britain's geographic and moral boundaries. Aphra Behn's novel *Oroonoko,* for example, was published as a play in 1760. It told the story of an African prince, snatched by slave merchants, who contemplates death rather than submission to slavery. One of the play's African characters pricks the slave traders' conscience by asking,

> The Isle which gave thee birth,
> Is mark'd for hospitable Deeds, humane
> Benevolence, extended Charities—
> With ev'ry social Virtue—Is't possible?
> A Nation thus distinguished, by the Ties,
> Of soft Humanity, shou'd give its Sanction,
> To its *dependent* states, to exercise,
> This more than savage Right, of thus disposing,
> Like th' marketable Brute,
> Their Fellow-Creatures Blood?[38]

The play brought British theatergoers face to face with the inhumanity of the slave trade. *Oroonoko* was pushing out the boundaries of British people's accountability even to "dependent states," to the slave dealers that operated in West Africa and the Caribbean. By this geographical extension creative writers made British people feel responsible for slave traders' deeds. In *A Father's Instructions to His Children,* published in 1776, the narrator is "shocked" to tell his readers that "this infernal commerce" was "carried on by the humane, the polished, the Christian inhabitants of Europe, whose ancestors have bled for the cause of liberty, and whose breasts still glow with the same generous flame!"[39] That same year, Granville Sharp's tract *Law of Liberty* trumpeted the fact that "the African slave trade, which includes the most contemptuous Violations of Brotherly Love and Charity, that men can be guilty of, is openly encouraged and promoted by the British Parliament." But the fault lay not only with a few politicians. "The horrible guilt . . . which is incurred by Slave-dealing and Slave-holding is no longer confined to a few hardened individuals . . . but alas! The whole British Empire is involved!"[40]

Men like Sharp were indicting British people as a collectivity, not as selected individuals, for their guilt. They summoned Britons as a polity to stand in judgment for their deeds. The slave trade, went one abolitionist petition in 1792, was a "national disgrace," for it violated Britain's standing as a "free and enlightened nation."[41] As Boyd Hilton argues in this volume, politicians were in the late eighteenth century casting a wary eye on world politics, on the specter of Napoleon's military successes, and finding therein evidence of God's growing wrath. "How shall we hope to obtain, if it be possible, forgiveness from Heaven for the enormous evils we have committed?" Prime Minister William Pitt asked Parliament. "It is as an atonement for our long and cruel injustice towards Africa, that the measure [for abolition] most forcibly recommends itself."[42] If Britons were collectively guilty, they stood also to share in the collective reward that abolition would bring to the nation. The *Leeds Intelligencer* argued that abolition would "raise the true glory and honour of the British empire to an infinitely higher pitch than all the victories of a Marlborough, a Hawke, or an Alexander." "Let no one be afraid of espousing the cause of the Negro," wrote the *Newark Herald* in 1792. " 'Tis the cause of mercy, 'tis the cause of our country—and sooner or later it shall succeed."[43]

Abolitionism worked horizontally, by holding people, by virtue of their membership within the British polity, responsible for slave traders' actions. It was the horizontality of their political imagination that made the abolitionists' project into a popular movement. Where earlier forms of political activism had been small-scale affairs, led by the gentry, abolitionism drew support from thousands of commoners. As many as four hundred thousand people, some 13 percent of the total adult male population of England, Scotland, and Wales, put their name to petitions against the slave trade in 1792.[44] City councils vied with each other in the issuing of proclamations condemning the trade. The city of Leeds, for example, published its 1788 resolution in newspapers in Leeds and York, in *St. James's Chronicle*, and in the *London Packet.* "Let us not, my friends, be backward in so laudable a business," went an editorial in the *Leeds Intelligencer,* "let it not on this occasion be said, that we want either religion or humanity."[45] A boycott of West Indian sugar, organized as a protest at the inhumanity of the sugar plantations, drew the support of as many as three hundred thousand families.[46] And thousands of people purchased Josiah Wedgwood's medallion of a supplicant slave, holding his chained hands aloft, with the inscription Am I Not a Man and a Brother? The medallion, first produced in 1788, was fitted in ladies' hairpieces, printed on coins, and displayed on snuffboxes. In petitions, in proclamations, and in the accoutrements of domestic life, British people were enlisting themselves as patriots, redeeming Britain's reputation on the world stage. By their lifestyles and their rhetoric they affirmed their aversion to tyranny.

Abolitionism was an effort to extend the range of British virtues to places far distant from the islands' shores. Abolitionism cultivated, that is, a symbiotic relationship with empire, as empire was the sphere within which a benevolent government could most readily act.[47] "The principles of justice," argued William Wilberforce in 1807, "are immutable in their nature, and universal in their application; the duty at once, and the interest, of nations, no less than of individuals."[48] By extending Britain's political boundaries, abolitionists sought also to create a one world of labor relations. The late eighteenth century witnessed a variety of experiments, as abolitionists worked out models by which Britain's government could be extended to distant shores. One of the earliest schemes came from Maurice Morgann, who in 1772 published his *Plan for the Abolition of Slavery in the West Indies.*[49] Morgann proposed that the British government should each year purchase several dozen boys and girls from West Africa's slaving forts, send them to England for schooling, and settle them at the age of sixteen in the Pensacola district of the new British province of West Florida. The resulting colony of free Africans would be bound to the British polity not as slaves but as citizens. For Morgann, the abolition of slavery would not compromise

empire. Abolition would place the British Empire on the "sure foundations of equality and justice." In time, the former slaves would "talk the
same language, read the same books, profess the same religion, and be
fashioned by the same laws" as their fellow subjects in Britain. Morgann
was viewing Africans as potential allies, as subjects of the Crown rather
than as property. He envisioned an empire defined by its subjects' shared
allegiance to and veneration for the Crown.

Morgann's project never came to fruition. But his vision of empire—
as a community of subjects, bound together by shared allegiance—shaped a
variety of schemes in West Africa and the Caribbean. The most successful
of them was Henry Smeathman's scheme to establish a settlement for
the castaways of the Atlantic economy—black loyalists, redeemed slaves,
and white craftsmen—in Sierra Leone. Smeathman devised an elaborate plan, modeled after the termite colony, in which each individual's
work would be directed in a rational fashion (Morgan, this volume).
He hoped that the colony would "civilize the country, and gradually
absorb all the petty tyrannies, and change them into subordinate free
states."[50] As the Sierra Leone colony took shape after 1787, the limits of
Smeathman's ambitions became clear: labor was chronically unavailable,
and the investors' capital was quickly expended (Drescher, this volume).
But, as Christopher Brown argues in the present volume, projects like
Smeathman's and Morgann's were important in helping abolitionists
model a world without slavery. By holding out alternatives to slave
labor, entrepreneurs could argue that the abolition of the slave trade
would not compromise Britain's economic position.

In the late eighteenth and early nineteenth centuries, abolitionists
were working to extend the boundaries of the British polity, to compass
ex-slaves and black loyalists as subjects of the Crown. But abolitionists
were not the only ones pushing out Britain's borders. Enslaved people in
the United States and in the West Indies enlisted themselves alongside
abolitionists as advocates for British values and as subjects of the king.
In 1788, at the height of the popular antislavery campaigns that Thomas
Clarkson and others organized, one planter heard Grenadian slaves
proclaim, "Mr Wilberforce for negro! Mr Fox for negro! Parliament for
negro! God Almighty for negro!" (Morgan, this volume). In Barbados,
literate slaves read British and local newspapers aloud to their fellows,
keeping a careful watch on parliamentary debates over slave emancipation. When in 1816 Barbados's slaves rose in revolt, planters argued
that the rebellion originated "solely and entirely in consequence of the

intelligence imparted to the slaves (which intelligence was obtained from the English News papers) that their freedom had been granted them in England."[51] One freedman is reported to have told a group of slaves that "Mr Wilberforce had sent out to have them all freed," but that planters had refused to abide by the new law. West Indian slaves were keeping a careful watch on the news. They made themselves allies of the Crown and got rhetorical leverage with which to hasten the day of their emancipation.

Slaves in the United States were likewise inserting themselves into the transoceanic discourse that abolitionism opened up. In 1830 David Walker, a used-clothing dealer in Boston, published his *Appeal: To the Coloured Citizens of the World,* identifying Englishmen as "the best friends the coloured people have upon earth."[52] Walker and his compatriots had good reason to ally themselves with the British Crown. Canada, a British possession, was a refuge for as many as sixty thousand runaway slaves, defended by the Crown courts against extradition. Black subjects in Canada were therefore Tories, anxious to identify themselves with British values. "Her Majesty's coloured subjects," one advocate proclaimed in 1857, must "resist to the last, every innovation upon Conservative principles of British liberty. . . . Coloured men should become as thoroughly British as they can."[53] Free blacks in the United States likewise lauded Britain's commitment to slaves' liberation. In 1841, Rev. Amos Beman, addressing the Vigilance Committee in New York, described how runaway slaves had escaped the "American eagle—proud and cruel bird" to "stand on free soil, and breathe free air by side of the British lion."[54] African Americans were anglophiles. By standing alongside the British lion, they put distance between themselves and America's cruel slaveholders. In the United States, as in the West Indies, slaves hooked into antislavery discourse and drew Wilberforce and Clarkson into a distant political project. These slaves were pirates. They commandeered British abolitionism and brought its moral authority to bear on their own situation.

Slaves were not the only ones pirating abolitionism into distant seas. Closer to home, antislavery rhetoric and symbolism escaped from the grip of abolitionists and animated contemporary British working-class activism. Reformers seeking to limit working hours, improve factory conditions, and magnify workers' political voice found in the figure of the slave a useful means of illuminating the inhumanity that industrial capitalism was cultivating in Britain. This political strategy was widely adopted in the early 1830s, when campaigners working for the Ten Hours Bill borrowed freely from abolitionist discourse. Petitioners from Manchester, for example, argued that their lack of voting rights was as much a mark of degradation as "the visible brand on the person of a bought and sold negro," while spinners in Stockport claimed to be enduring "all the horrors of a sullen and hapless slavery."[55] A banner commonly carried in working-class rallies depicted a deformed white man with the inscription Am I Not a Man and a Brother?[56] Josiah Wedgwood's famous icon of the supplicant slave gave working-class men and women a means of highlighting the inhumanity of factory labor. "Tell me not of the free labour of a poor famishing artisan, covered in rags and broken in spirit, standing in the presence of an unfeeling, unprincipled Task Master," wrote Richard Oastler in 1833. "This is the freedom that the unprotected British labourer enjoys in his boasted land of liberty."[57] Activists were making the working class look like slaves, and in so doing they made Britain's factories look immoral.

The cross-fertilization of antislavery and factory agitation was more than a rhetorical convenience. For many activists, the reform of factory labor and antislavery were conjoined projects. Richard Oastler, the Clarkson of factory agitation, began his career as an antislavery activist. His friend Henry Whiteley published his best-selling *Three Months in Jamaica* in 1833. It focused both on the "slavery of the poor factory children at home" and on the abusive exploitation of slaves in the West Indies.[58] Rallies organized by the Factory Movement in the early 1830s made no distinction between working-class advocacy and abolitionism: at an 1832 rally in Manchester, for example, the first banner bore the slogan No Infant Slavery. Some working-class radicals argued that antislavery was diverting attention from the more pressing abuses, closer to home. But even antiabolition radicals found antislavery symbolism useful in illuminating the inhumanity of factory discipline. "White men can be sold, and white men are sold, by the week and month all over England," the radical activist William Cobbett told a crowd of workers in 1832.[59] The anonymous pamphlet *The Condition of the West India Slave Contrasted with That of the Infant Slave in Our English Factories* made the comparison most clearly. Published in 1833 and illustrated by the radical thinker Robert Cruikshank, it depicted black slaves as "totally free from the cares, the troubles, the poverty and even the labour and anxieties of the British poor."[60] In his woodcuts, Cruikshank contrasted slaves' favored position with the situation of English workers, depicting the

Woodcut by Robert Cruikshank, from *The Condition of the West Indian Slave Contrasted with That of the Infant Slave in Our English Factories* (London: W. Kidd, c. 1833).

straw-roofed hovels in which factory workers were compelled to live. One particularly awful plate showed two "factory overlookers" beating children, one holding a long pole, the other a cat-o'-nine-tails.[61]

The imagery of slavery was useful for activists like Oastler because it helped transform their controversial political project into a moral problem demanding the public's attention. Stripped of its antislavery cladding, reformers' aims were essentially secular. They objected to the economic and political strictures that limited workers' freedom of choice, and they argued that workers should have a voice in electoral politics. By positioning themselves as abolitionists, activists made the abuses of wage work look like a moral problem requiring a solution. By calling wage workers slaves, working-class thinkers contrasted the liberal values of freedom and self-determination with the injustices of the factory system, and showed that the tyranny of the West Indies was growing on British soil. Their rhetorical strategy made reform seem urgent.

Abolitionism was always more than a parliamentary lobby. Its advocates were working on a variety of projects, from a variety of positions. West Indian slaves sought to hasten the day of their emancipation. Working-class activists sought to alleviate the abuses of the factory system. British Quakers worked to free men to make their own choices about God and about their material welfare. Maurice Morgann and other visionaries cast about for economic alternatives to slave agriculture.

Abolitionism drew these disparate entrepreneurs together. As abolitionists, moral reformers in Britain could help make poor people and slaves alike responsible for their own actions, by removing the external strictures that limited their freedom of choice. As abolitionists, working-class activists could illuminate the inhumanity of the factory system and make its reform seem necessary. As abolitionists, slaves and free blacks could assert their claims to the liberties that British subjects of the Crown enjoyed. As abolitionists, empire builders like Morgann could formulate novel models of community in which people were bound together, not as slaves and owners, but as subjects of the British Crown. All these interests found in the discourse of abolitionism a means to give their controversial, debatable projects moral authority.[62]

Abolitionism opened up a transoceanic sphere of discourse about British values. Its advocates were neither saints nor self-interested profit-seekers. Working from distant positions, they found useful rhetorical and political resources in the discourse of antislavery. In the West Indies, in the southern United States, and in the factories of Lancashire and Manchester subaltern activists took hold over abolitionist discourse in order to bring an idealized Britain close to hand. They sought, that is, to bridge geographic and social space, to elide racial and class differences, and to align disparate people as subjects of the Crown. The power of abolitionist rhetoric was to make people that were subject to political or economic hierarchies—slaves, free blacks, working-class people—look like Britain's responsibility. In their strategic engagements with abolitionist rhetoric and thought, subaltern activists generated moral capital and held the British public accountable.

Abolitionism and Political Advocacy in Colonial Uganda

Once its vocabulary had been established, abolitionist rhetoric and imagery could be pirated abroad to serve projects that were only tangentially concerned with the alleviation of chattel slavery. I here want to explore one distant shore on which abolitionist discourse found a home. East Africa had once been the scene of the thriving slave trade: in the nineteenth century caravans worked by Arab and Swahili merchants had stretched from the Indian Ocean ports at Bagamoyo and Mombasa to the distant hinterlands of the Congo.[63] But by the 1950s the East African slave trade was a memory for partisans to argue over (Glassman, this volume). Their temporal remoteness from the British antislavery movement did not make it impossible for East Africa's political activists to hook into

abolitionist discourse. Minorities in Uganda, suffering under the tyranny of latter-day despots, found in William Wilberforce's rhetoric a
useful means of characterizing their own situation. Uganda's minorities
were not actually slaves. They were enclosed in neotraditional kingdoms
in which legal practice, language, and political authority were defined
by the majority. British administration was deliberately ignorant of the
multilinguistic diversity of Uganda's people. Guided by the philosophy
of "indirect rule," officials reinforced the supposedly traditional preroga-
tives of the kings of Buganda, Bunyoro, Toro, Ankole, and Busoga: they
standardized languages and legal practices, and obliged minorities to abide
by the majority's customs.[64] Minority groups enclosed within Uganda's
kingdoms experienced this form of governmentality as totalitarianism.
They were subject to unfamiliar systems of law, they very often lacked a
voice in local government, and they sometimes were unable to purchase
land. They got leverage over the local legatees of colonial administration by
representing themselves as slaves. Minority activists did historical and
political work to identify themselves as a distinct people, as inheritors
of a culture that was distinct from their rulers'. With the evidence of
their distinctiveness in view, minorities could cast light on the cultural
and political violence they suffered, frame the homogenizing tactics of
indirect rule as tyranny, and position themselves as slaves. In twentieth-
century Uganda, the rhetoric of abolitionism was for minority groups
a powerful strategy of imperial advocacy: it led them to identify their
particular cultural patrimony and gave them a language with which to
make allies in the British metropole.

The Nyoro people living in the borderland between the kingdoms of
Bunyoro and Buganda were particularly skilled at using the grammar of
abolitionism. The Bunyoro kingdom had in the nineteenth century become one of the most innovative and commercially oriented polities in
East Africa. Under *Mukama* (King) Kabalega, Bunyoro's professionalized
armies had successfully pushed the kingdom's boundaries to the east at
the expense of the Buganda kingdom. But in the late nineteenth century British explorers and conquistadors had forged a close alliance with
Kabalega's enemies in the kingdom of Buganda, and in 1890 fourteen thousand Ganda troops backed by British soldiers invaded Bunyoro. During
the eight-year war of attrition that followed, Bunyoro's population was
decimated, its economy was destroyed, and its people were scattered. So
devastating was the assault that Bunyoro's population did not recover
until the mid-twentieth century.[65] When Kabalega was finally defeated,

in 1899, British officials rewarded their allies by allocating a large portion of Bunyoro's southern territory to Buganda's government.

The British strategy for dealing with what Bunyoro's leaders called the "lost counties" was to treat them as an integral part of Buganda. A British officer set the agenda in 1896. As "these provinces became part of the Kingdom of Buganda," he wrote, "so would their native inhabitants become Waganda [people]."[66] Ganda agents were appointed to govern the territories wrested from Bunyoro, while the Ganda language became the official standard for government and the courts. By 1955 the British governor could tell Bunyoro's politicians that "the clock of history . . . could not be turned back." Buganda's government over the lost counties was a fait accompli. The governor would not "accept that there was a great difference between the Banyoro and the Baganda," and recommended that the Nyoro and Ganda peoples set themselves to "learning to live together."[67] British officers and Ganda elites were smoothing over the differences that set Nyoro and Ganda people at odds.

But Nyoro people in the lost counties would not agree to be assimilated into the Buganda Kingdom. In reply to the British demand that they conform to their rulers' culture, the Nyoro minority practiced nativism. They worked, that is, to identify themselves as a distinct people, unjustly governed by a foreign power. The 1930s and 1940s witnessed a wave of historical writings, as political entrepreneurs mined the distant past in order to find evidence of the Nyoro state's distinct character. Bunyoro's king, Tito Winyi, published three historical articles in the *Uganda Journal.* He emphasized the longevity of Bunyoro's ruling lineage and gilded its kingship by describing the royal regalia in great detail.[68] Other historical writers elaborated on Bunyoro's long and glorious history. John Nyakatura, a long-serving government chief, published *Abakama ba Bunyoro-Kitara* (The kings of Bunyoro-Kitara) in 1947.[69] Nyakatura began his book by assuring readers that "Kitara was a very extensive, prestigious and famous kingdom at the height of its power" and argued that the ancient kingdom was in fact the ancestor of Buganda itself. Bunyoro and Buganda were therefore siblings, coequals in politics. Nyakatura made a point of listing the kings of Buganda and of Bunyoro side by side, in columns. Through his historical writing he sought to align Bunyoro's political status with Buganda's.

This glorious but distant history was not enough for the Nyoro people living in the lost counties. They needed hard evidence by which to establish themselves as indigenes, with a prior claim to the disputed territory. Cartography was one vehicle by which they made their case. John Nyakatura's 1947 book began with an excursus into geography: the boundaries of Bunyoro, he argued, had once stretched all the way to Kavirondo, in western Kenya, compassing the whole of Buganda. A map produced by the "Bunyoro Public" association made the point in graphic terms. It represented Buganda's "expansion at the expense of neighbouring areas," highlighting with vivid red ink the vast territory that Buganda had, with British support, wrested from Bunyoro.[70] In 1960 one petitioner told a visiting British commission that, in the lost counties, "the stones, hills, mountains, valleys, hillocks, rivers, streams, trees, grass, the soil itself and even the winds of the air blow hard their horns that they belong to Bunyoro Kitara.... Insects, birds, and animals have locally been and are crying to be returned to their Motherland."[71] For this petitioner, as for other partisan cartographers, the evidence of Bunyoro's rightful government over the lost counties was written on landscape. This cultural essentialism proved both enduring and useful. By late 1963 Bunyoro's government could argue that "the link between us and the Lost Counties is natural; is not man made but God made.... It is he who made the Banyoro as one tribe and gave us a particular land to live in."[72] In their cartographic work, Nyoro entrepreneurs were drawing the lost counties into a foreordained orbit. Their geographic essentialism allowed them to treat the disputed territory as an organic extension of Bunyoro itself.

More than land was at stake in this debate over the government of the disputed territory. Bunyoro's mapmakers were also demographers, enlisting the region's human inhabitants as carriers of an essential Nyoro culture and as subjects of the Nyoro king. Language work proved particularly helpful in establishing the demographic evidence for a Nyoro presence in the lost counties. The British policy was to use Luganda as the language of government: the governor thought that in any case "Luganda and Lunyoro are both Bantu languages with great similarities."[73] But Nyoro population builders could not agree to speak the Luganda lingua franca. John Nyakatura's history book served as the standard for Nyoro orthography and grammar during the 1950s.[74] Nyakatura himself had made several trips to London to press Bunyoro's case over the lost counties, and there he learned his language politics. "Despite their different languages and various dialects," wrote Nyakatura, "the British have one common language—English—to unite them." Like the Welsh, the Irish, and other far-flung residents of Great Britain, Bunyoro's people could constitute an enlarged political sphere by speaking with one voice.

Using the vernacular was therefore a patriotic undertaking. Nyakatura enjoined his readers, "Let us not emigrate from our country," and in the next sentence he encouraged them to "cherish our language and speak it everywhere we go." Greater Bunyoro's political entrepreneurs were putting words in the mouths of the members of their imagined community and anchoring them in position as subjects of the Kingdom of Bunyoro.

By using the vernacular, Nyoro residents of the lost counties generated textual and auditory evidence to establish their unique identity. By speaking like natives, they put distance between themselves and their Ganda rulers and made themselves look like an oppressed people. Nyoro petitioners filled British officials' mailboxes with evidence about Buganda's cultural imperialism. In 1938 the Mubende Banyoro Committee wrote to Uganda's governor to complain that "in every meeting, we are compelled to talk a foreign language such as in courts, in churches etc. In every school, our children are forced to be taught in Luganda. . . . In both birth and baptism registers our children's names are generally reduced to Luganda ones which is a very bad and wonderful habit indeed."[75] Nyoro petitioners represented Buganda's efforts at cultural assimilation in the lost counties as totalitarianism. In a 1955 meeting with the British governor, the chief judge of Bunyoro cited census data as evidence of Bunyoro's claim over the counties. Seventy percent of the people in one of the lost counties were Nyoro, he argued, while only 21 percent were Ganda.[76] These statistics allowed Nyoro petitioners to represent the counties' population in monochromatic terms. In a letter in the *Uganda Argus,* four editorialists argued that "most of us in this district are Banyoro one hundred percent and have been so for centuries, and naturally our outlook is Kinyoro."[77] In 1955 the Bunyoro government asked politicians in Uganda's legislative council to adopt a motion protesting that the "natural culture of the people in [the lost counties] is in fact being destroyed."[78] And by 1961 a tract could describe Buganda's government over the lost counties as "foreign rule." "God created us and put us in those counties which are our heritage," went the tract. "It is a shame to the British and the Baganda who should very well know their responsibility with regard to human rights."[79] With their unique language on their tongues, the entrepreneurs of the lost counties could position themselves both as indigenes and as an oppressed people. Their cultural, linguistic, and historical work generated evidence by which Nyoro politicians represented Buganda's government over the lost counties as a denial of human liberty.

Abolitionist discourse gave Nyoro petitioners the grammar with which to draw British officials onto their side in this dispute over governance. The rhetoric of abolitionism helped Nyoro politicians transform a political dispute into a moral problem that demanded action. In his 1931 petition (above), Zakaliya Lugangwa and his sixty-three colleagues named themselves "the natives of the Mubende counties" and addressed the governor as "the Peace and Civilizer in the Uganda Protectorate, a country over which the Union Jack waves."[80] With the governor's role in view, Lugangwa and his colleagues could meaningfully announce that "*Slavery* has been practiced over us since [the lost counties] were cut off from Bunyoro Kingdom and added to Buganda." Lugangwa proved his case by contrasting an old order of cultural self-possession with the new, debased world in which he and his colleagues lived. Before "being cut off," he wrote, "we had inheritable lands; we had our own language, Runyoro; we had power in our country; we had honour and we could get everything that comes out of our country at ease." But under Ganda overlordship Luganda, not Lunyoro, was used in schools and in courts, and "so we are slowly turned into Baganda, this shows the presence of slavery." Moreover Nyoro were obliged to "buy their land from Baganda overlords." "This shows we are slaves," wrote Lugangwa, "for we are badly treated on our own native soil." Lugangwa and his compatriots were calling themselves oppressed victims of Ganda tyranny. The petitioners concluded by asking "the British Government that every country subject to the English Flag should enjoy freedom and that slavery should be done away with."

Nyoro petitioners used abolitionist rhetoric to remind British officials of their moral duties and to oblige disinterested administrators to take an active role in upholding British honor. Nyoro petitioners were burdening British officials with evidence of their oppression and obliging them to act. In 1938 sixty-six signatories from the Mubende Banyoro Committee petitioned the governor to complain that "1. we lost the rights in our mother country 2. we lost the power in our mother country 3. we lost the dialect language 4. we are slaves." Like Zakaliya Lugangwa and his colleagues, the 1938 petitioners represented the imposition of Ganda language in the lost counties as a mark of Buganda's cultural imperialism. "We are afraid [that] this slavery [will] touch to our poor children as well as our grand children," they lamented. With the issues so clearly drawn, British government should feel itself compelled to act in the favor of an oppressed people. The 1938 petitioners asked for "the *just* kindness of the British government to order . . . that we may be set free from slavery."[81] Other petitioners similarly invited British officials to follow William Pitt's lead. "We are under the same flag and serve the same government of His Majesty the Great King of England, George," wrote an anonymous petitioner in a 1933 letter to the secretary of state for the colonies.[82] "We are to be treated in the same way as other races that are near us, to make us equal to the other parts of the Protectorate."

Nyoro petitioners were ventriloquizing abolitionists' voices. They were addressing the British governor with words and phrases that Wilberforce, Clarkson, and their colleagues had first worked out. Nearly two hundred years after Maurice Morgann and other British abolitionists had first conceptualized the British Empire as an assembly of subjects, united in their shared loyalty to the king, abolitionists in western Uganda were illuminating the unequal politics that indirect rule promoted. Nyoro petitioners framed the political situation in the lost counties in such a way as to make the region's residents look like slaves. And by drawing officials' eyes to the Union Jack fluttering over the Uganda Protectorate, entrepreneurs contrasted British ideals with the evidence of local inequalities. Like Wilberforce and the abolitionists of the eighteenth century, Bunyoro's petitioners were extending the range of issues for which British people felt themselves accountable. In reminding Uganda's administrators of their membership within Britain's empire, they laid out a path of action for colonial officials to follow.[83]

Nyoro activists' rhetoric of abolitionism was conceived as a strategy of imperial advocacy. It depended for its salience on the presumption that government officials could be made to intervene, as Britons, to suppress slavery. But by the late 1950s the efficacy of abolitionist rhetoric was increasingly open to question. Where in the 1920s and 1930s British officials had promoted a "civilizing mission" in Africa, in the 1950s British officials were positioning themselves as advocates of development.[84] Uganda's administration set out to remake the authoritarian institutions that had in an earlier era upheld the politics of indirect rule. They reined in the power of chiefs and kings, and organized local government councils to which Africans could elect representatives. In Bunyoro a parliament was created in 1955, with half the representatives elected by popular vote.[85] The district commissioner welcomed the newly elected members by telling them that "you are here today as representatives of the people of Bunyoro . . . you are acting on behalf of your fellow citizens."[86] In 1958, Ugandans for the first time elected representatives to sit on the colonywide legislative council. And in 1962 the new nation of Uganda declared its independence. Its national anthem, carefully edited by President Milton Obote, had as its first verses "Oh Uganda! May God uphold thee, / We lay our future in thy hand. / United, free, / For liberty / Together we'll always stand."[87]

But how could Milton Obote and other leaders of Uganda be moved to act for the principles of liberty, freedom, and unity? What did minorities in the lost counties and in other parts of Uganda's national territory lose in their country's independence? A few days after the swearing in of Bunyoro's first elected parliament, in 1956, editorialist W. Kaikuru wrote to the *Uganda Argus* to compare the residents of the lost counties with slaves. "Individual slavery ceased to be legal and we are all happy about it," he wrote.[88] But where in the 1930s and 1940s Nyoro petitioners could frame their situation as an offense against British honor, in the 1950s they had to appeal to more abstract, blandly universal notions of fraternity and equality. "Uganda can only be united if the principles of justice, equality and liberty are respected," wrote Kaikuru. "The citizens of Uganda who are interested in Uganda as a whole are eager to see this thorny problem put right." There were, even in the 1950s, appeals to the duties that Britain owed its subjects.[89] But as the Ugandan nation took the place of the British imperium, so too did subject minorities find their vocabulary of claim-making to be radically delimited. For Uganda's new African government was not obliged to uphold Britain's promises. Uganda's politics were majoritarian, and Milton Obote was not honor bound to liberate subject minorities. Bunyoro's activists were therefore obliged to take matters into their own hands. In the 1930s Nyoro petitioners had illuminated their unique cultural heritage in order to oblige British officers to defend their interests. In the 1960s Bunyoro's cultural politicians lost their British audience. What had been conceived as a strategy of imperial advocacy became, in the 1960s, a form of racism. The Mubende Banyoro Committee's 1961 flyer highlights the absolutist character of their discourse: "Objective: Lost counties to be returned to their master. . . . *GOD KNOWS THAT WE ARE BANYORO.* The Baganda, you yourselves prove us that we are Banyoro from in and out, and perpetually shall be Banyoro."[90] A 1963 statement from the chairman of the "Bunyoro-Kitara public" was equally strident: "the people of the lost counties," he said, "are pure Banyoro, and there is no doubt that they themselves know that they are Banyoro. Therefore imposing Buganda rule on them . . . means that Uganda's independence to Bunyoro does not mean anything."[91]

There is a discursive line linking the 1930s cultural politics of abolition-ism with the aggressive, racist politics of the 1960s. In the 1930s Bunyoro's activists standardized languages, did historical research, and made them-selves look like a unique people. Their cultural work identified them as slaves, kept down by the tyranny of Buganda, and made them allies in the British metropole. In the 1960s these stereotypes were used to enlist Bunyoro's people as militant defenders of their homeland. In 1961 Nyoro residents of the lost counties began a campaign of disobedience against their Ganda rulers. Letters distributed by Nyoro activists urged that "all Banyoro . . . must fight the Baganda until they leave their counties." Residents were told not to pay taxes to Buganda, and coffee planta-tions owned by Ganda farmers were cut down in nighttime raids.[92] The palace that the king of Buganda had built in one of the lost counties was burned down in July.[93] In the latter part of 1961 arsonists targeted homes owned by Ganda farmers living in the disputed region. Late that year the Bunyoro parliament declared the lost counties to have "reverted to Bunyoro and [are] thus known as Bunyoro territory."[94] By 1963 a low-level guerrilla war had broken out in two of the lost counties. Nyoro observ-ers reported that Buganda's government had moved hundreds of Ganda ex-servicemen into the disputed territories. They encamped around the tomb of one of Bunyoro's kings, saying that the Nyoro had no rights to bury their dead on Ganda land.[95] Several people were killed, whether by Ganda soldiers or Nyoro guerrillas. In 1964 the issue was put to a referendum, and two counties, Buyaga and Bugangaizi, were handed over to Bunyoro. At the ceremony marking the handover in Bugangaizi, the seven thousand attendees listened to a long history lesson given by the grandson of the Nyoro chief who had once ruled the county.[96]

Uganda's national independence closed off a line of discourse by which minorities could get leverage over their rulers. As subjects of the British Empire, Nyoro entrepreneurs had open to them a powerful vehicle of claim making. British officials were obliged to act to suppress slavery. Their theory of imperial government, structured by late-eighteenth-century debates over citizenship, burdened British officials to act as agents of emancipation. Subject groups in western Uganda, as elsewhere in anglophone Africa, could therefore position themselves as objects of mercy and invite British rulers to act as abolitionists. This was a strategy of representation, a theatrical event that required Nyoro people to play out a role. Entrepreneurs had to configure their language, their cul-tural life, and their history to differentiate themselves from their Ganda overlords. They had, that is, to represent themselves in racial terms, as a distinct, identifiable people. The power of abolitionist discourse was to cast the complicated, interwoven relationship between Nyoro and Ganda people in moral terms, to make rulers look like tyrants and subjects like slaves. By this representational work subaltern abolitionists made Ganda government over the lost counties look unjust, and invited British officials to act in their favor.

But subaltern activists could not, as citizens of independent Uganda, oblige their rulers to pay heed. Citizenship was a passport to political rights, not a vehicle for claiming social and economic justice. As anthropologist Harri Englund has observed about contemporary human rights discourse in Malawi, "new freedoms entail new prisoners."[97] Uganda's government was legitimated by electoral ritual, not by its humanitarian role. Its agents were representatives of the majority. To exercise influence, Uganda's peoples needed to group themselves into constituencies, establish a majority in particular tracts of territory, and gain electoral representation on the national stage. Where in the 1930s Nyoro petitioners could move British officials by the evidence of their oppression in the hands of Ganda overlords, in the 1960s they needed to compete with Buganda for political leverage over Milton Obote's government. It was this competitive politics that drove the violence that gripped Uganda in the mid-1960s. In the 1930s Nyoro people did historical research, spoke the vernacular, and established their distinct identity in British officers' eyes. In the 1960s their strategy of imperial advocacy was translated into a vehicle of political violence.

This book is an effort to expand the temporal and geographic frame in which the history of abolitionism is conceived. The authors argue that abolitionism was more than an outworking of British liberals' idealism. Abolitionism was a theater in which a variety of actors—slaves, African rulers, Caribbean planters, working-class radicals, African political entrepreneurs, Christian evangelicals—played a part. This varied cast of characters was not working from a script authored in London. The Atlantic was an echo chamber in which abolitionist symbols, ideas, and evidence were generated from a variety of vantage points (Morgan, this volume). This book highlights the range of political and moral projects in which the advocates of abolitionism were engaged, and in so doing it joins together geographies that are normally studied in isolation.

The book begins with John Thornton's chapter, which illuminates the ethical grounds on which the leaders of three states in western Africa—Kongo, Ndongo (in modern-day Angola), and Dahomey—found it possible to participate in the Atlantic slave trade. Seen from the position of the ruling caste, the trade in slaves was a means to extend authority over refractory peoples and defend themselves against external enemies. Western Africa's political leaders objected to the commerce in slaves when it outran their control and undermined social order. For western Africa's rulers, argues Thornton, the trade in slaves was not a moral problem that demanded a resolution. It was a pragmatic vehicle of polity building. Britain's eighteenth-century rulers were no less pragmatic about the slave trade. But where western Africa's leaders saw the slave trade as a routine means of political consolidation, British parliamentarians had by the early nineteenth century come to see the trade as morally compromising. In his chapter, Boyd Hilton builds on his earlier work concerning Britain's eighteenth-century intellectual culture to show how abolitionism grew out of British people's religious sense that God was standing in judgment on their nation.[98] The evidence was before them, in the loss of the American colonies, in Napoleon's rise, and in other contemporary events. Parliamentarians therefore abolished the slave trade as an act of atonement, an effort to reconcile their collective guilt with divine standards.

But while Christian eschatology lent abolitionism urgency and conviction, antislavery activists could not be religious ideologues. Neither was their movement purely a British affair. The chapters by Christopher Brown and Philip Morgan show how much the abolitionist project owed to actors in western Africa and the Caribbean, who provided material evidence and rhetorical fuel for British activists to draw upon. Brown's essay focuses on western Africa, where in the eighteenth century abolitionists experimented with a number of "free-labor" schemes meant to expand British enterprise. At Cape Coast Castle in the early eighteenth century, in Senegambia in the 1760s, and in the colony of Sierra Leone, entrepreneurs of the Royal Africa Company tried out new crops and novel forms of labor organization. The evidence they generated, argues Brown, allowed activists to model alternatives to slave agriculture and gave them means to show that abolition would not undermine the British economy. Hardheaded abolitionists were gathering evidence from a variety of sources. Philip Morgan's essay casts light on the diverse set of actors whose ideas about labor organization and human liberty resonated around the Atlantic world. In the West Indies, planters were in the late eighteenth century encouraging slaves to work for their own gain. Planters were disposed against abolition. But by encouraging slaves to marry and bear children, by giving them provision grounds, and by offering them incentives for piecework, planters generated hard evidence that abolitionists could use to illuminate the economic and social benefits of free labor. Free blacks were likewise generating evidence by printing testimonials and other propaganda documenting the inhumanity of the slave trade. Rebellious slaves in St. Domingue weakened France's Caribbean economy, making abolition seem commercially feasible to British entrepreneurs. And the leaders of independent Haiti corresponded with British abolitionists, sending them information about the island's demography and economy.[99] The evidence for abolitionism was generated from a range of sources, from West Indian planters, slaves, visionaries, and other entrepreneurs working on disparate projects.

Even as activists in Britain, western Africa, and the Caribbean worked to end the slave trade, they also extended Britain's imperial reach. But as Seymour Drescher's chapter shows, abolitionism was never simply an instrument advancing Britain's political self-interest. Drescher focuses on Sierra Leone, established in the late eighteenth century as a utopian experiment in free labor. By the 1830s the colony's declining fortunes had convinced British businessman that further imperial ventures in western Africa were doomed to fail. For the first three-quarters of the nineteenth century, therefore, British interests in Africa were markedly circumscribed: a spectacular military intervention in Algiers (1816) was of a purely humanitarian character; while the antislavery patrol off western Africa's shores did nothing to extend Britain's territorial domain. Drescher concludes that imperialism was the "last thing on the minds of British policy makers" during the period of the suppression of the slave trade. But British authorities' aversion to empire building in West Africa did not spring from a fervent regard for African states' sovereignty. As Robin Law shows in his chapter, British jurisprudence had in the early nineteenth century recognized African states as sovereign under international law, and British policymakers had constructed elaborate treaties with African rulers in order to suppress the slave trade. But by the 1840s policymakers had come to regard African states as unworthy of the protection of international law because they lacked the civilized credentials of other modern states. Military men were therefore free to meddle in African states' private affairs, intruding, for example, to engineer a succession dispute in Lagos in 1851–52. Britain's role as an agent for the suppression of the slave trade, Law argues, lent moral authority to its self-interested interventions in other polities' affairs. The abolitionist project thereby cleared the legal and political barriers to the partition of Africa.

The concluding chapter, by Jonathon Glassman, expands the book's geographic and temporal reach. Twentieth-century Zanzibar was a world away from the eighteenth-century Atlantic. But the discourse that British abolitionists, West Indian slaves, and other entrepreneurs authored resonated in Zanzibar and shaped its politics. Colonial Zanzibar's Arab elite learned about the history of slavery from missionary schoolteachers, whose lessons contrasted the chattel slavery of the Atlantic with the comparatively more humane forms of enslavement practiced in the Arab world. From their missionary school teachers, and from contemporary pan-Arabist newspapers, the Arab intelligentsia learned to apprehend their political world in racial terms, to contrast their cultural sophistication with the barbarism of "African" mainlanders. In the 1950s the "African" partisans of the Afro-Shirazi Party replied to Arab elites' scorn by emphasizing the British roots of Zanzibar's civilization. They represented themselves as chattel abused at Arab slave dealers' hands and published dozens of essays recounting how David Livingstone and other abolitionists had freed them from bondage. In Zanzibar, as in the lost counties of Bunyoro, abolitionist discourse invited subaltern activists to represent their political situation in racial terms. When violence broke out in 1961, Glassman argues, its "African" protagonists acted to repay the historical indignities they thought they had experienced in Arab slave dealers' hands. Abolitionist rhetoric helped subaltern nationalists consolidate their racial identities and led them to right the wrongs of an imagined past.

In twentieth-century eastern Africa and in eighteenth-century Britain, abolitionist discourse was useful because it cast hierarchical political and economic relationships as moral abominations. Until the late eighteenth century, British citizens had accepted the slave trade as a commonplace of their nation's economy. But from 1772 onward Granville Sharp and other abolitionists argued that Britain's hard-won liberties were endangered by the practice of colonial slavery. In sermons, pamphlets, Wedgwood medallions, and other media, they brought Britons face to face with the inhumanity of the slave trade and made slavery look like a stain on

Britain's reputation. In their own time, abolitionists' tactics were pirated into a novel sphere by working-class radicals, who used antislavery imagery to cast factory discipline in moral terms. They compared factory managers with plantation overseers and cast workers as maltreated slaves. Radicals thereby made workers' economic situation look morally compromising, a blight on British liberty. Subaltern nationalists in twentieth-century Zanzibar and Uganda confronted social and political hierarchies that denied them a voice in government. They valorized their own history, cast themselves as maltreated slaves, and worked up the political and moral wherewithal to take up arms as righteous militants. British reformers, working-class radicals, East African nationalists, and other entrepreneurs used the figure of the slave to cast their partisan activism in moral terms, as a struggle for human liberty.

The British abolitionist movement opened up a sphere of discourse about the rights that different categories of subjects enjoyed and the responsibilities that rulers owed them.[100] Abolitionism made the British Empire into a sphere of moral argument, where British, African, and other identities were defined and debated. Saying that the British Empire was a sphere of moral argument does not mean that Africans were not also involved in other discourses. Africans conducted vernacular-language debates over civic virtue and political authority more vigorously than the extramural class of English-language advocacy.[101] Neither does seeing empire as a moral unit mean that there was a steady push to bring subject peoples within a universalistic, egalitarian conception of polity. As Robin Law's chapter reminds us, the abolitionist project could reinforce Britons' chauvinistic sense of superiority. What the study of abolitionism allows historians to do is to conceive of empire as its Caribbean, African, and British protagonists saw it: as a theater where lines of discourse tied disparate groups together, and in which activists could take up a character and oblige others to act.

Notes

1. Hoima District Archives (hereafter cited as HDA), file with no cover, Zakaliya Lugangwa et al. to Governor, 1 December 1931.

2. Steven Feierman, *Peasant Intellectuals: Anthropology and History in Tanzania* (Madison: University of Wisconsin Press, 1990), chaps. 8, 9.

3. Kenya National Archives, JZ 7/4, Detainees at Sanjusi Island to Commissioner of Prisons, 7 May 1957.

4. Kenya National Archives, JZ 7/4, John Gitiri to Secretary of State for the Colonies, 5 September 1954. See also Derek R. Peterson, "The Intellectual Lives of Mau Mau Detainees," *Journal of African History* 49, no. 1 (2008): 73–91.

5. Church of Uganda Provincial Archives (hereafter cited as CUPA), file 02, Bp 8/1, Reuben Sparta to J. Willis, 21 April 1935.

6. Carol Summers, "Grandfathers, Grandsons, Morality, and Radical Politics in Late Colonial Buganda," *International Journal of African Historical Studies* 38 (2005): 427–48.

7. J. M. Kariuki, *"Mau Mau" Detainee: The Account by a Kenya African of His Experiences in Detention Camps, 1953–1960* (Nairobi: Oxford University Press, 1963), 110.

8. "PM's article for the New Nation newspaper (27 Nov. 06)," at http://www.number10 .gov.uk/output/Page10487.asp.

9. Not everyone followed Tony Blair's lead. Alongside New Labour's celebration of British virtues there were a series of exhibitions—at the National Maritime Museum in Greenwich, at the International Slavery Museum in Liverpool, and at the Museum of London—that focused on the inhumanity of the slave trade and highlighted the profits that the slave economy generated for British capitalists. For an analysis highlighting the place of abolitionism in Britain's national memory, see J. R. Oldfield, *Chords of Freedom: Commemoration, Ritual and British Transatlantic Slavery* (Manchester: Manchester University Press, 2007).

10. The reference here is to Frederick Cooper and Ann Laura Stoler, *Tensions of Empire: Colonial Cultures in a Bourgeois World* (Berkeley: University of California Press, 1997). India's historians, not Africanists, have pioneered the scholarship I refer to here. The scholarship includes Peter van der Veer, *Imperial Encounters: Religion and Modernity in India and Britain* (Princeton: Princeton University Press, 2001); Gauri Viswanathan, *Outside the Fold: Conversion, Modernity, and Belief* (Princeton: Princeton University Press, 1998); Nicholas Dirks, *Castes of Mind: Colonialism and the Making of Modern India* (Princeton: Princeton University Press, 2001); Tomoko Masuzawa, *The Invention of World Religions, or, How European Universalism Was Preserved in the Language of Pluralism* (Chicago: University of Chicago Press, 2005). An early Africanist contribution is John Comaroff and Jean Comaroff, *Of Revelation and Revolution,* vol. 1 (Chicago: University of Chicago Press, 1991).

11. As argued in Frederick Cooper, *Colonialism in Question: Theory, Knowledge, History* (Berkeley: University of California Press, 2005). See also Duncan Bell, *The Idea of Greater Britain: Empire and the Future of World Order, 1860–1900* (Princeton: Princeton University Press, 2007).

12. Thomas Clarkson, *The History of the Rise, Progress, and Accomplishment of the Abolition of the African Slave-Trade,* 2 vols. (London: Longman, Hurst, Rees, and Orme, 1808), summarized in Christopher Brown, *Moral Capital: Foundations of British Abolitionism* (Chapel Hill: University of North Carolina Press, 2006), 4–8.

13. G. M. Trevelyan, "Wilberforce: The Centenary of a Warrior," *Times* (London), 29 July 1933, 13.

14. Reginald Coupland, *Livingstone's Last Journey* (London: Macmillan, 1947); Coupland, *Wilberforce: A Narrative* (Oxford: Clarendon Press, 1923); Coupland, *The British Anti-slavery Movement* (London: T. Butterworth, 1923); Coupland, *Kirk on the Zambezi: A Chapter of African History* (Oxford: Clarendon Press, 1928).

15. Reginald Coupland, *The Empire in These Days: An Interpretation* (London: Macmillan, 1935), 268.

16. Society for Promoting Christian Knowledge, *David Livingstone: The Great African Pioneer* (London: SPCK, 1885); George Annesley, *David Livingstone: Light-Bearer to Africa* (London: Macmillan, 1956).

17. George Smith, *Heroes of the Nineteenth Century: Nelson, Napier, Roberts, Livingstone* (London: Arthur Pearson, 1899); Elizabeth Rundle Charles, *Three Martyrs of the Nineteenth Century: Studies from the Lives of Livingstone, Gordon, and Patterson* (London:

Society for Promoting Christian Knowledge, 1906). For an analysis of this literature, see Timothy Holmes, *Journey to Livingstone: Exploration of an Imperial Myth* (Edinburgh: Canongate, 1993).

18. *Jochir Sigendini Magadiera* (People who have lived brave lives) (London: Macmillan, 1951).

19. A formulation borrowed from Thomas C. Holt, "Explaining Abolition," *Journal of Social History* 24 (Fall 1990): 371–78. Woodcut by Robert Cruikshank, from *The Condition of the West Indian Slave Contrasted with That of the Infant Slave in Our English Factories* (London: W. Kidd, c. 1833).

20. Eric Williams, *Capitalism and Slavery* (Chapel Hill: University of North Carolina Press, 1944), 136.

21. A useful introduction to this subliterature can be found in Barbara Stolow and Stanley Engerman, eds., *British Capitalism and Caribbean Slavery: The Legacy of Eric Williams* (Cambridge: Cambridge University Press, 1987); and in "Symposium on the Life and Writings of Eric Williams," *Journal of African American History* 88, no. 3 (2003).

22. Roger Anstey, *The Atlantic Slave Trade and British Abolition* (London: Macmillan, 1975), 47.

23. Roger Anstey, "The Pattern of British Abolitionism in the Eighteenth and Nineteenth Centuries," in *Anti-slavery, Religion and Reform,* ed. Christine Bolt and Seymour Drescher (Folkestone: Dawson, 1980), 20.

24. Stanley Engerman, "The Slave Trade and British Capital Formation in the Eighteenth Century: A Comment on the Williams Thesis," *Business History Review* 46, no. 4 (1972): 430–43. Engerman's thesis is restated in David Eltis and Stanley Engerman, "The Importance of Slavery and the Slave Trade to Industrializing Britain," *Journal of Economic History* 60, no. 1 (2000): 123–44.

25. Joseph Inikori, *Africans and the Industrial Revolution in England: A Study in International Trade and Economic Development* (Cambridge: Cambridge University Press, 2002). Another historian who builds on Williams's economic analysis is Robin Blackburn, *The Making of New World Slavery: From the Baroque to the Modern, 1492–1800* (London: Verso, 1997).

26. Seymour Drescher, *Econocide: British Slavery in the Era of Abolition* (Pittsburgh: University of Pittsburgh Press, 1977); Drescher, "The Decline Thesis of British Slavery since *Econocide,*" *Slavery and Abolition* 7, no. 1 (1986): 3–24; Drescher, "Capitalism and Slavery after Fifty Years," *Slavery and Abolition* 18, no. 3 (1997): 212–27.

27. See also David Eltis, *Economic Growth and the Ending of the Transatlantic Slave Trade* (New York: Oxford University Press, 1987).

28. David Brion Davis, *The Problem of Slavery in Western Culture* (Oxford: Oxford University Press, 1966). See also Davis, *The Problem of Slavery in the Age of Revolution, 1770–1823* (Ithaca: Cornell University Press, 1975).

29. Quoted in Patricia Hollis, "Anti-slavery and British Working Class Radicalism in the Years of Reform," in *Anti-slavery, Religion and Reform: Essays in Memory of Roger Anstey,* ed. Christine Bolt and Seymour Drescher (Folkestone: Dawson, 1980), 304.

30. Thomas Haskell, "Capitalism and the Origins of Humanitarian Sensibility," *American Historical Review* 90, no. 2 (1985): 547–66. Haskell's work is debated in Thomas Bender, *The Antislavery Debate: Capitalism and Abolitionism as a Problem in Historical Interpretation* (Berkeley: University of California Press, 1992).

31. David Turner, *Fashioning Adultery: Gender, Sex and Civility in England, 1660–1740* (Cambridge: Cambridge University Press, 2002).

32. Henry Parker, *Observations* (1642), quoted in Quentin Skinner, *Renaissance Virtues,* vol. 2 of *Visions of Politics* (Cambridge: Cambridge University Press, 2002), 296.

33. John Milton, *Populo anglicano defensio* (1651), quoted in Skinner, *Renaissance Virtues,* 305.

34. Quotations from Skinner, *Renaissance Virtues,* 286.

35. Quotations from Brown, *Moral Capital,* 96–97.

36. See Seymour Drescher, "Free Labor versus Slave Labor: The British and Caribbean Cases," in *The Terms of Labor,* ed. Stanley Engerman (Stanford: Stanford University Press, 1999); Drescher, *The Mighty Experiment: Free Labor versus Slavery in British Emancipation* (New York: Ox ford University Press, 2002).

37. Lord Chief Justice Alvanley, quoted in David Waldstreicher, *Runaway America: Benjamin Franklin, Slavery, and the American Revolution* (New York: Hill and Wang, 2004), 198–202.

38. Quoted in J. R. Oldfield, *Popular Politics and British Anti-slavery: The Mobilisation of Public Opinion against the Slave Trade, 1787–1807* (Manchester: Manchester University Press, 1995), 26–27. The play was published in several versions. A contemporary edition can be read as Aphra Behn, *Oroonoko,* ed. Janet Todd (London: Penguin, 2004).

39. Quoted in Oldfield, *Popular Politics,* 23.

40. Quoted in Brown, *Moral Capital,* 181–82.

41. Quoted in Oldfield, *Popular Politics,* 116–17.

42. See Boyd Hilton, *The Age of Atonement: The Influence of Evangelicalism on Social and Economic Thought, 1785–1865* (New York: Oxford University Press, 1992).

43. Quotations from Oldfield, *Popular Politics,* 116–17.

44. Ibid., 114; Seymour Drescher, *Capitalism and Antislavery: British Mobilization in Comparative Perspective* (Houndmills, Basingstoke: Macmillan, 1986).

45. Quoted in Oldfield, *Popular Politics,* 104.

46. Ibid., 57.

47. Andrew Porter, "Trusteeship, Anti-Slavery, and Humanitarianism," in *The Oxford History of the British Empire,* vol. 3, *The Nineteenth Century,* ed. Porter (Oxford: Oxford University Press, 1999), 198, 204.

48. Quoted in Drescher, "Free Labor."

49. Described in Brown, *Moral Capital,* chap. 4.

50. Quoted in ibid., 315.

51. H. McD. Beckles, "Emancipation by Law or War? Wilberforce and the 1816 Barbados Slave Rebellion," in *Abolition and Its Aftermath: The Historical Context, 1790–1816,* ed. David Richardson (London: Frank Cass, 1985), 80–104. Rebellious slaves in the Caribbean very often claimed that a distant king had freed them. See Laurent Dubois, *Avengers of the New World: The Story of the Haitian Revolution* (Cambridge, MA: Harvard University Press, 2004).

52. David Walker, *Walker's Appeal . . . to the Coloured Citizens of the World* (1830), quoted in Van Gosse, "As a Nation, the English Are Our Friends: The Emergence of African American Politics in the British Atlantic World, 1772–1861," *American Historical Review* 113, no. 4 (2008): 1003–28.

53. H. Ford Douglass, quoted in Gosse, "African American Politics," 1013.

54. Quoted in Gosse, "African American Politics," 1021.

55. Quoted in Seymour Drescher, "Cart Whip and Billy Roller: Antislavery and Reform Symbolism in Industrializing Britain," *Journal of Social History* 15, no. 1 (1981): 3–24 (quotation, 8).

56. Hollis, "Anti-slavery."

57. Richard Oastler, *Facts and Plain Words* (1833), quoted in Hollis, "Anti-slavery."

58. Described in Drescher, "Cart Whip."

59. Quoted in Cedric Robinson, "Capitalism, Slavery and Bourgeois Historiography," *History Workshop Journal* 23, no. 1 (1987): 122–40.

60. Quoted in Hollis, "Anti-slavery."

61. See Marcus Wood, *Blind Memory: Visual Representations of Slavery in England and America, 1780–1865* (New York: Routledge, 2000), 273.

62. This argument is derived from Brown, *Moral Capital,* epilogue.

63. The most recent scholarship on the East African slave trade includes Henri Médard and Shane Doyle, eds., *Slavery in the Great Lakes Region of East Africa* (London: James Currey, 2007); Jeremy Prestholdt, *Domesticating the World: African Consumerism and the Genealogies of Globalization* (Berkeley: University of California Press, 2007); Jan-Georg Deutsch, *Emancipation without Abolition in German East Africa, c. 1884–1914* (Oxford: James Currey, 2006). Important older studies include Edward Alpers, *Ivory and Slaves in East Central Africa: Changing Patterns of International Trade to the Later Nineteenth Century* (London: Heinemann, 1975); Abdul Sheriff, *Slaves, Spices and Ivory in Zanzibar: The Integration of an East African Commercial Empire into the World Economy, 1770–1873* (London: James Currey, 1987); and Patrick Manning, *Slavery and African Life: Occidental, Oriental, and African Slave Trades* (Cambridge: Cambridge University Press, 1990).

64. See Kristin Mann and Richard Roberts, eds., *Law in Colonial Africa* (Portsmouth, NH: Heinemann, 1991); Martin Chanock, *Law, Custom, and Social Order: The Colonial Experience in Malawi and Zambia* (Cambridge: Cambridge University Press, 1985); Mahmood Mamdani, *Citizen and Subject: Contemporary Africa and the Legacy of Late Colonialism* (Princeton: Princeton University Press, 1996).

65. This paragraph is largely derived from Shane Doyle, *Crisis and Decline in Bunyoro: Population and Environment in Western Uganda, 1860–1955* (Oxford: James Currey, 2006), chap. 3.

66. Public Records Office, Kew, CO 536/1789, Berkley to the Marquis of Salisbury, 19 November 1896.

67. HDA, "District Council" file, minutes of meeting in secretariat, Entebbe, 5 October 1955.

68. "K.W.," "The Kings of Bunyoro-Kitara," pts. 1–3, *Uganda Journal* 3 (1935): 155–60; *Uganda Journal* 4 (1936): 78–83; *Uganda Journal* 5 (1937): 53–69. See also J. Willis, "A Portrait for the Mukama: Monarchy and Empire in Colonial Bunyoro, Uganda," *Journal of Imperial and Commonwealth History* 34, no. 1 (2006): 105–22.

69. J. W. Nyakatura, *Abakama ba Bunyoro-Kitara* (1947; repr., Kisubi: Marianum Press, 1999).

70. HDA, "Local Government Policy, Lost Counties" file, "Kingdom of Buganda, showing its expansion at expense of neighboring areas," [1961].

71. CUPA, file 02, Bp 211/26, P.T. Eribankya to the Relationships Commission, 6 October 1960.

72. HDA, "Local Government Policy, Lost Counties" file, press release, September 1963.

73. Public Records Office, CO 822/1738, Crawford to Secretary of State for the Colonies, 2 July 1957.

74. HDA, "Language, Orthography" file, B. Kirwan, "Empandika y'orulimi rwaitu," 1952.

75. Catholic Church of Uganda Archives, Kampala D.39 f.5, Mubende Banyoro Committee to Governor, 27 April 1938.

76. HDA, "District Council" file, minutes of meeting in the secretariat, Entebbe, 5 October 1955.

77. Joseph Bitaroho, Lababo Isoke, Denis Kasinyo, and Yowana Katutu to editor, *Uganda Argus,* 23 January 1956.

78. HDA, "District Council" file, O. Magezi to chair, Representative Members Organization, Kampala, 14 October 1955.

79. HDA, "Local Government Policy, Lost Counties" file, Byarufu Masobhe to All People in the Lost Counties, 20 November 1961.

80. HDA, file with no cover, Zakaliya Lugangwa to Governor, 1 December 1931.

81. Catholic Church of Uganda Archives, D.39 f.5, Mubende Banyoro Committee to Governor, 27 April 1938.

82. HDA, file with no cover, anonymous petitioner, Hoima, to Secretary of State, 1933.

83. Their rhetorical tactics had real effects. In 1962 a visiting delegation from the Privy Council heard Nyoro advocates lay out the standard argument about British rulers' obligations to their subjects. The presenters documented how Nyoro subjects in the disputed territory had been forced to adopt the identity of their "hereditary rivals and enemies" and argued that it was the "duty of the British government to cure a continuing wrong" before the end of colonial rule in Uganda. The visiting councillors accepted their line of argument and recommended that two counties, Buyaga and Bugangaizi, should be returned to Bunyoro. *Report of a Commission of Privy Councilors on a Dispute between Buganda and Bunyoro* (London: HMSO, 1962).

84. As argued in Frederick Cooper, *Africa since 1940: The Past of the Present* (Cambridge: Cambridge University Press, 2002); Cooper, *Decolonization and African Society: The Labor Question in French and British Africa* (Cambridge: Cambridge University Press, 1996).

85. David Apter, *The Political Kingdom in Uganda* (Princeton: Princeton University Press, 1961), 41.

86. HDA, "District Council" file, DC's speech to Rukurato, 24 February 1956.

87. CUPA, 1 Abp. 157/11, Milton Obote to Archbishop of Uganda, 13 September 1962.

88. W. Kaikuru, in *Uganda Argus,* 28 February 1956.

89. See, for example, Joseph Bitaroho, Lakabo Isoke, Denis Kasinyo, and Yowana Katutu, in *Uganda Argus,* 23 January 1956.

90. HDA, "Relationships Commission" file, Bunyoro Kitara Public to Makerere Schoolmaster, 11 February 1961.

91. HDA, "Political Parties" file, statement by E. Kiiza, 29 January 1963.

92. HDA, "Local Government Policy, Lost Counties" file, "Freedom Ddembe," 25 July 1961.

93. *Uganda Eyoyeria,* 12 July 1961.

94. HDA, "Local Government Policy, Lost Counties" file, Clerk of the Rukurato, memorandum, 15 October 1961.

95. HDA, "Tombs of the Bakama" file, DC, Bunyoro, to Administrator, Buyaga and Bugangadzi, 7 August 1963.

96. HDA, "Local Government Policy, Lost Counties" file, no title, [January 1965].

97. Harri Englund, *Prisoners of Freedom: Human Rights and the African Poor* (Berkeley: University of California Press, 2006), 4.

98. Hilton, *Age of Atonement.*

99. See David Geggus, "Haiti and the Abolitionists: Opinion, Propaganda and International Politics in Britain and France, 1804–1838," in *Abolition and Its Aftermath: The Historical Context, 1790–1916,* ed. David Richardson (London: Frank Cass, 1985), 113–40; Gelien Matthews, *Caribbean Slave Revolts and the British Abolition Movement* (Baton Rouge: Louisiana State University Press, 2006).

100. As argued in Cooper, *Colonialism in Question,* chap. 6.

101. Feierman, *Peasant Intellectuals;* John Lonsdale, "The Moral Economy of Mau Mau: Wealth, Poverty, and Civic Virtue in Kikuyu Political Thought," in *Unhappy Valley: Conflict in Kenya and Africa,* ed. Lonsdale and Bruce Berman (London: James Currey, 1992), 315–504; Derek R. Peterson, "Culture and Chronology in African History," *Historical Journal* 50, no. 2 (2007): 483–97.

ONE

African Political Ethics and the Slave Trade

JOHN THORNTON

ONE OF the great paradoxes of African history, indeed of world history, is the response of African leaders and decision makers to the slave trade. It does not take much work to demonstrate that the slave trade was very damaging to Africa from a demographic point of view, both on a continental scale and on a more limited local scale.[1] Yet it is also obvious that the slave trade could not have proceeded very far had African decision makers, both political and commercial, not cooperated with the European merchants who sought to buy laborers on the African coast. While some scholars have argued that European technical, military, and economic superiority gave them an extraordinary influence in African decision making, and thus in effect they were forced to participate in the trade,[2] I have argued that African leaders were not necessarily forced into the slave trade through their own inabilities, or the inability of their countries to prevent it.[3]

Accepting a position that African political and economic leaders had substantial say in the crucial decisions to sell slaves to Europeans thus necessarily opens another potential line of investigation that has not been widely studied, that is, the ethical reasoning that African leadership employed in their decision. African leaders clearly participated voluntarily in the slave trade, but that does not mean that they did so without recognizing the ethical problems that the trade presented. As a way of exploring the ethical attitudes of the African elites, I would like to study the correspondence of several African leaders who were literate, or who produced a body of literature through literate secretaries in their employ. By looking at the correspondence of those members of the African decision-making elite who recorded their ideas, we can begin to penetrate their ideas about the ethics of the slave trade seen from the African side.

These leaders include, from west-central Africa, King Afonso I (r. 1509–42) of Kongo; Queen Ana de Sousa Njinga Mbande (r. 1624–63) of Ndongo, and later of Ndongo-Matamba; and King Garcia II (r. 1641–61) of Kongo; and from West Africa the rulers of Dahomey, particularly Adondozan (r. 1797–1818). Scholars have already used this body of material to explore African reactions to the slave trade. The correspondence of Afonso I, for example, is often cited as an example of an African monarch confronting the slave trade.[4] Likewise, Queen Njinga has occasionally been held up as a leader who opposed the slave trade, and perhaps in reaction to this, she is often backhandedly vilified as nothing more than a slave trader when documents show that she, too, participated willingly in the trade.

This examination reveals that all these African rulers led societies that recognized an institution of slavery, and thus they accepted the legal possibility that an individual could have a bundle of rights over another person that surpassed those of any other community or the state. These rights, moreover, could be alienated to any other person by sale. This institutional framework made the slave trade possible and smoothed its way along, and it explains why it is preferable to more complex definitions of slavery in terms of lineage rights, or based on methods of exploitation. These features of African social structure certainly can explain why African leaders did not actively resist the sale of people as slaves, and it must be invoked in their defense when they are accused of being European dupes for doing so. But simply recognizing that the making, holding, use, and sale of slaves were legally permissible did not mean that the slave trade did not pose ethical problems for African leaders. They felt strongly that there were legal limits to who could be enslaved and when. In many cases they felt that the Portuguese and other Europeans violated these limits, and moreover that these violations were a manifestation of greed and pride, two serious political sins. The question was not with the institution of slavery itself but in establishing a proper order of enslavement and an orderly slave trade.

King Afonso (1509–42) and the Slave Trade

Afonso's reign is critical because it illuminates the situation of African rulers at the very start of the Atlantic slave trade. Afonso is best known for being an African ruler who opened his country to European religion and culture, and his project of engagement with Europe is sometimes held as having been undermined by the slave traders.[5] It has been suggested that the legal framework of Kongo changed as a result of the European demand for slaves and that the study of Afonso's interaction with Portuguese and other slave dealers can allow us to see how overseas trade altered benign, domestic institutions of slavery. Under the stress of overseas demands, it is argued, African slavery changed from a less intensive or nonexistent slave system to a more exploitative one aimed at foreign commerce. In her well-researched book, Anne Hilton proposes that slavery was relatively underdeveloped in Kongo at the time of the European arrival. Afonso, she contends, was lured to enter the slave trade through his desire to obtain European goods and services, for which he produced no suitable alternative products. Although he ultimately realized his error, he was too late to prevent a major reshaping of Kongo into a slave-raiding and slave-producing state, with serious negative consequences.[6] J. E. Inikori has subsequently used Hilton's analysis to argue that Kongo fits as a general case study in which slavery was transformed by European contact into a more virulent and negative system.[7] In this way, he has reworked and renewed Walter Rodney's celebrated thesis of the 1960s, which argued that African leaders' participation in the transatlantic slave trade transformed the institution in their own countries.[8]

The case of Afonso is particularly arresting, because a significant portion of what we know about early Kongo in general, as well as the character of the slave trade, comes from his lengthy correspondence with Portugal. Indeed, until 1550, Kongo shares with Songhai the unusual situation in Atlantic African history of being known to scholarship primarily through documentary sources of African origin and not the writings of travelers, slave traders, or other outsiders.[9]

What a close examination of Afonso's letters reveals, however, is that Kongo probably did have a well-developed system of legal slavery at the time of its first contact with Portugal, and that the trade in slaves was always acceptable under Kongolese law. However, it must be said that our knowledge of Kongo's institutions in the roughly twenty years between contact and Afonso's first letters is very limited. Although the Portuguese first visited Kongo in 1483, the early exchanges were purely diplomatic and exploratory, and almost undocumented.[10] As late as 1490, Kongo was so poorly known in Portugal that the king ordered his officers in São Tomé to send a condemned prisoner to Kongo to spy on it.[11] Presumably, if there were some regular commerce before that, such extreme measures would be unnecessary. The spy was needed to provide intelligence for the main mission to Kongo, in 1491. From that point onward, it is probably safe to say that there was regular interchange between the two countries.

It is not clear exactly when Kongo began exporting slaves; certainly European merchants based in São Tomé were buying them in exchange "for things of little value" before 1502, when this trade is mentioned in a legend on the Cantino Atlas.[12] The numbers of purchased slaves may not have been great; Duarte Pacheco Pereira's account of Kongo, describing the situation before 1506, mentions the trade in slaves but characterizes it as being of "little quantity."[13] One way in which Portuguese acquired slaves, perhaps the most important, was through mercenary service in Kongo's wars. Instructions given to Gonçalo Rodrigues, sent by the Portuguese king Manuel I to Kongo in 1509 at the head of a royal mission, tell him to accept any gifts that the king might give him for his military services, "from captives that the said Manicongo [king of Kongo] makes in this war or in whatever service God gives you."[14] It is quite possible that the earlier royal mission of 1491 also obtained slaves in this way and that its experience shaped the language of the later instructions.[15] Certainly the 1491 mission fought in a war, and in his letter to King Manuel of October 1491, the Kongo king João I Nzinga a Nkuwu specifically states that he had "nothing to give in exchange for the ships and people" from Portugal who served him in war, but he makes no mention of slaves being taken or given.[16] It is possible that, somehow, the Portuguese managed to introduce a new form of slavery in this period, along with the practice of selling slaves in markets. But it seems unlikely—Portuguese residents in Kongo were very few in the period, and there does not seem to be any way they could introduce major changes in Kongo's laws and institutions. Rather, it seems much more likely that the description in Afonso's letters after 1509 reflects the situation at the time of contact.

Afonso's letters frequently deal with slavery and include some commentary on the slave trade as it developed. It is quite clear that Afonso, and probably Kongo law in general, had little problem with the holding of slaves, their alienation by sale or gift, or their export from the country. In his earliest extant letter, written on 5 October 1514, Afonso provides important information about these legal matters in the course of complaining to King Manuel about the behavior of some Portuguese in Kongo.[17] The letter is of crucial importance, it is one of the earliest documents we have that comments on slavery, and certainly it is the earliest we have that supplies information of this sort from a Kongolese source. It also clearly contradicts those scholars, like Anne Hilton, who maintain that Kongo's constitution and legal system forbade either the making or export of slaves.[18]

The letter regularly refers to gifts of slaves. Around 1509, for example, Afonso gave Gonçalo Rodrigues fifty slaves, and subsequently he sent another fifty slaves to Fernão de Mello, donatory of São Tomé, and to his wife. Perhaps a year later, he sent "many slaves" to the king and queen of Portugal; later still he made another gift of slaves to them and to de Mello, all before 1512. He even gave twenty slaves to Estevão Jusarte simply for being de Mello's cousin.[19] But these gifts were matters of state, perhaps, and might be viewed as special circumstances.

More significantly, Afonso also noted the possibility of slaves being purchased in Kongo, which would have been impossible without the existence of a local market for such purchases, and indeed without a well-established local custom of buying and selling enslaved people. For example, some of the priests who came in 1508 disappointed Afonso when they bought "some pieces [*peças,* an accounting unit of slaves] which are slaves." Afonso was not upset with the priests because they were buying slaves but because they ignored his plea that they not buy females. Afonso's concern in this matter was not that females ought not to be enslaved but that the priests were taking sexual advantage to the detriment of the status and prestige of the church. Thus, Afonso's central complaint was that Father Pero Fernandez made one of these women pregnant, creating a scandal.[20] At just about the same time as the priest was scandalizing Afonso, masons who arrived in 1509 to construct new buildings for the king were taking the wages that Afonso paid them and buying slaves on the market. Each one is said to have purchased "15 or 20 pieces." Here again, the fact that the masons were buying slaves was not the grounds for complaint, but rather that their commercial activity and general laziness slowed their progress in the work of construction and training of Kongolese masons.[21]

Afonso also gave a Portuguese official named Christovão d'Aguir enough money to buy twenty-seven slaves around 1510 or 1511, which apparently he also was able to obtain on local markets. Similarly, most of the officers sent with the mission of 1512 to Kongo began to "buy pieces," even though Afonso had ordered, in accordance with an agreement he had made with the king of Portugal, that only a royal factor would be allowed to do so.[22] In short, it was perfectly possible for private persons from Portugal to purchase slaves in Kongo, and presumably to export them, as the implications of Afonso's use of the term *pieces* suggests. Kongo law must have recognized this. Already, slavery was not strictly in the hands of the state.

Afonso was prepared to export slaves on his own behalf, not simply to give them away to people he considered worthy, for he gave João Fernandes twenty slaves to buy cloth for him in Portugal around 1510. Soon thereafter, he gave more slaves to one of his cousins, Pedro Afonso, both for his support as a student in Portugal and to buy clothes for Afonso while he was there. When around 1512 or 1513 he sent some twenty-two of his young relatives to Europe to study, he included slaves for their support, adding extras in case some of the slaves should die.[23] In about 1512 two Portuguese serving in Kongo, Diogo Bello and Manuel Cão, carelessly allowed "a hundred and some" slaves to escape while being exported to the coast. The escapees went on a rampage, making the country look "as if there had been the great destruction of a war," but Diogo Bello was unconcerned because, Afonso said, "he had bought them with our money," and this on Afonso's account.[24] Three years later he would ask King João III for permission to purchase a ship of his own, which he certainly intended to use to transport slaves, since he requested that if it were impossible to purchase a ship, he wanted to "be able to load a certain number of pieces without paying customs."[25] Afonso's letter was full of complaints, yet his grief was not about the purchasing or disposing of slaves; it was that he was cheated, that work was paid for but not done, or that priests neglected their vows. Nothing in this letter suggests that the custom of buying or exporting slaves was new, or that it was something introduced by the Portuguese, as if the presence of a handful of European merchants could somehow change Kongo law in fifteen or twenty years.

In the same letter, Afonso did, however, provide important insights on the function of slavery in Kongo and its early relationship to the export trade, in describing a war he conducted against Munza, known only as a nobleman of the Mbundu region, around 1512 or perhaps 1513.[26] Afonso's primary complaint about the conduct of the war was that the Portuguese served him poorly in it. Many were reluctant to join him in a campaign against an opponent who, Afonso maintained, had started the war by attacking the Kongo province of Mbamba. Afonso's account makes it clear that he intended to be served by the people he captured as slaves, both at home and to meet overseas expenses. Some he sent out to Portugal on his own account—some as gifts to the king or others—and some he retained in Kongo, presumably for local service.

In sum, all these letters suggest that at the time of its contact with Portugal, Kongo already had an institution of slavery. Not only did the Kongo elite themselves use slaves as part of their labor force (though they surely had other means to an income as well), but they were prepared to buy and sell them on the market. By the early sixteenth century, and probably from before then, they were also prepared to allow these people to be exported. We have no reason to believe that people were the only exports Kongo had, or that its kings controlled, and thus, as Hilton maintains, Afonso was forced by economic necessity to export slaves.[27] Duarte Pacheco Pereira mentions copper, ivory, and cloth as commodities that were being exported by 1506, and Afonso's letter of 1514 pairs many of his gifts with "manilhas" of copper, sometimes in the thousands. Later, in 1526, Afonso mentions sending ivory to meet the expenses of students.[28] Indeed, as we have seen, Afonso usually paid the Portuguese who served him or were resident in the country in money, with which they could and did purchase whatever they would on local markets, including slaves. That the money in question was the local shell currency, called *nzimbu*,[29] is proved by the units Afonso mentions: in 1516 he gave Álvaro Lopes four *kofu*s to purchase slaves for the king of Portugal, and after buying twenty-five people, he was left with six *lufuku*s in change.[30]

Afonso did, however, have reason to complain about the slave trade, and in approaching this complaint we begin to understand where African rulers would draw the line between legitimate business and unacceptable behavior. In 1526, Afonso sent two letters of complaint to Portugal, writing in an explicitly hostile manner about the way the slave trade was affecting his country. On 6 July he complained, "Our kingdom is being lost in such a way that we must apply the necessary remedy." The problem was the unregulated activities of Portuguese merchants in the country, who dealt in "prohibited items" and whose shops were set up "all throughout our Kingdom and Lordship in great abundance." This had caused, Afonso contended, some of his vassals to rise up, as they had things in greater abundance than he did. Not only this, but "every day the merchants carry away our people [*nossos naturales*], sons of our soil and children of our nobles and vassals and our relatives" who were being kidnapped, secreted away, and stolen by "thieves and people of low condition" driven by the desire to have "your things." Fearing that the country would be "depopulated," he proposed to King João III that he send no more merchants or merchandise to Kongo, but only support the church with priests and bread and wine for the sacraments, because it was "our will that there be no trade in slaves in our kingdoms."[31]

Afonso returned to this theme on 18 October. After repeating many of the earlier complaints about the stealing of free people (including nobles), Afonso noted that they were hidden, branded, and kept in irons. The thieves were "our people"—that is, Kongolese—who took them away at night and sold them to Portuguese merchants, without Afonso's own guards knowing about it. The thieves were not Portuguese; they were guilty only of not asking enough questions about who was free and who was not. Afonso proposed a completely new solution to the problem in order, he wrote, "to do Justice [and] restore the free to their liberty." Instead of demanding that Portugal stop the slave trade, as he had proposed three months earlier, Afonso now announced that henceforth no slaves would be sold without an inquest of his officials, and none would be exported without his knowledge and consent. Anyone who failed to account for the enslavement of those they sought to export stood to have their cargo confiscated.[32]

The problem that Afonso was addressing was threefold. First, he was concerned about his noble subjects having wealth, rising against him, and being even more powerful than he was because of their dealings with the Portuguese. It is likely that he was specifically concerned about the Mbundu lands, to the south, whose territory he had claimed since the very beginning in his royal titles, even though he had constantly fought wars there (at least in 1512 or 1513, 1515, 1517). Portugal had sent a mission to Ndongo, the leading state of the Mbundu area in 1520, no doubt with the goal of establishing a trade in slaves. The mission had failed, but Afonso had managed to rescue the ambassadors and brought them to Kongo just as these letters were being written.[33] In the currently extant documentation this episode is mysterious, but one logical interpretation is that Afonso had played a role in causing the mission to fail and was reasserting his authority over Ndongo's trade. If there were other rebellions, they are unknown to us.

The second problem was that of private persons, of "low condition," engaging in robbery and carrying off free people, and on occasion, even nobles, secretly in the dead of night. Clearly this was a local security issue, or it might refer to those poorly integrated territories like Mpan-zulumbu, located on the banks of the Congo River just inland from the coastal province of Soyo. In 1516 Afonso complained that a ship cap-tained by Cristovão de Coimbra had bought some four hundred slaves from the Mpanzulumbu region (probably just inland from the mouth of the Congo River).[34] The region was regarded as enemy territory, and Afonso saw this as a hostile act. In 1517, Mpanzulumbu raiders had captured gifts that the king of Portugal had sent him, and such raiding might easily have also netted slaves for sale from Kongo.[35]

Finally, Afonso's complaints might have simply been to justify fiscal reform, even if he had evidence that occasional rebellion or kidnap-ping had taken place. By forcing the Portuguese merchants in Kongo to go through this inspection process, he could centralize them and prevent smuggling and tax evasion. The complaint that people were being stolen could be simply a pretext to dress a fiscal reform in the cloth of justice. Certainly the effect of his proclamation would be to place fuller jurisdiction over everything the Portuguese did in Kongo, and undoubtedly to tax and control them more fully. Precisely how the Portuguese community in Kongo would be governed was an important issue. Would they be centralized under a captain appointed in Portugal, as Portuguese kings generally preferred, or would they be allowed to go freely anywhere they pleased, as many of them preferred, or, finally, would they be controlled, but by Afonso, as he clearly preferred?[36]

In any case, the letters of 1526 necessarily reflect on Afonso's attitude toward the slave trade. Did Afonso, clearly a supporter and participant in the export of slaves in 1514, change his mind about the trade after a further dozen years' experience with it? And did he then change his mind back three months later? Was this because he was now so depen-dent on the foreign trade and the slave trade in particular that he could not escape from it, and that he realized his dependence in the three months between his July and October letters? What seems likely, on the whole, is that Afonso never opposed either the idea of the slave trade or slavery, but was concerned when it seemed to fall out of his control and that of his state, through either the activities of rebels or of bandits or the uncontrolled actions of foreigners. As long as it was his army conducting his wars that captured slaves, and as long as enslaved people were being sold on royally supervised markets, he was content with the institution. If these conditions were not met, he was prepared to ban it, or at least to reestablish his control over it.

One matter is quite clear: the dire consequences that Afonso predicted for Kongo did not come to pass, at least not in the years immediately following this correspondence. Afonso died leaving Kongo intact and united. Indeed, Kongo's centralized power, at least over its central districts, grew in the following years, reaching its peak in the mid-seventeenth century. The issue of the slave trade was to emerge after the establishment of a Portuguese colony in Angola after 1575.

Queen Njinga and the Slave Trade, 1624–56

Even as Afonso I was grappling with the control of the slave trade, Portuguese traders were visiting his southern neighbor of Ndongo. Indeed, it is quite possible, as has already been suggested, that Afonso's complaints concerning Portuguese merchants violating his regulations and sovereignty in 1526 were directed at those dealing in Ndongo. Certainly, these Portuguese contacts with Ndongo involved slave trading, for Afonso's successor Diogo conducted an inquest into the slave trade in 1548 that concluded that merchants based in Kongo were being ruined by competition from other merchants based in Ndongo. In this inquest Diogo was clearly not opposed to the functioning of the slave trade, which was well organized and extensive, but only to the lack of shipping for carrying off the thousands of slaves that departed.[37]

Ndongo, however, did not initially produce a literate class and a correspondence that would allow us to explore the institution of slavery in its early history and its relationship to the slave trade from their own perspective, as is possible with Kongo. Although there were Portuguese official missions to Ndongo as early as 1520, it was not until the Portuguese founded their colony of Angola, in 1575, that we have detailed accounts of Ndongo society and its relations with Portugal. Our first observations about Ndongo society were therefore written only in the 1580s, after half a century of contact and trade by outsiders, by the Jesuit missionaries who accompanied Paulo Dias de Novais. They described a complicated system of servile groups, including two groups that would come to be called slaves in Portuguese-language writing. The first group was the *kijiko*s, captives who had been settled on lands and were inalienable though servile. The second group was *mubika*s, captives who were liable to resale and had not been settled. It was clearly this second group that was vulnerable to being enslaved, sold, and deported, and they would be described as "peças" or "escravos" when Ndongo rulers did begin writing in Portuguese.[38]

Initially the Portuguese donatory, Paulo Dias de Novais, cooperated with Ndongo's rulers, especially in their wars. But after 1579 their relationship was more often one of open warfare. Kongo supported Dias de Novais, and it was the timely intervention of a large force from Kongo in 1580 that saved him in his first war with Ndongo. This war had been fought to a standstill by 1600, but that deadlock was broken in 1618, when the newly arrived governor of Angola, Luis Mendes de Vasconcellos, made an alliance with the Imbangala, dreaded cannibal mercenaries from the south, and used their assistance to crush the kingdom of Ndongo.[39]

Njinga came to power in Ndongo during the terror and confusion of the aftermath of Governor Mendes de Vasconcellos's alliance with the Imbangala and his war on Ndongo. In the years immediately following the storming of Ndongo's capital by Portuguese troops in 1619, the rulers of Ndongo had had to flee to the islands of the Kwanza River to make their new capital. There, amid the ruins of his country, Njinga's despondent brother, Ngola Mbandi, committed suicide, leaving only a child as heir. Njinga stepped into the gap, and with the support of many in the royal court at first declared herself regent of the kingdom and then ruler in her own right. The Portuguese, sensing a further weakness in this irregular succession, placed their full support behind one of her rivals, Hari a Ngola, who claimed that female succession was illegal in the Ndongo constitution and that Njinga had murdered the rightful heir, her brother's seven-year-old son, to make way for her succession.[40] The action precipitated a civil war, which the Portuguese entered in support of Hari a Ngola. The fighting went on intermittently until settled by a treaty in 1656.[41]

Queen Njinga was the first ruler of Ndongo to leave a sizable correspondence, and thus the first to provide us with insights from the inside on her ethical vision. Njinga's correspondence shows her relationship to this essentially slave-capturing Portuguese administration, as well as her own attitude toward the slave trade and slavery. It reveals, as does Afonso's correspondence, that she was accustomed to a slave trade, that it was licit under her laws, as under Kongo's, and that she both held and sold slaves as a matter of course. But like her Kongolese antecedent, she also felt that there were definite limits and rules about who could and could not be enslaved.

Njinga's earliest letter, written in 1624 within weeks after she assumed power and addressed to the governor of Angola, Fernão de Sousa, is no longer extant. It is, however, clear from his summary that Njinga was prepared to deal in slaves. In his summary, de Sousa noted that she told him that he should withdraw Portuguese forces from Embaca, a town founded by Mendes de Vasconcellos as a forward base for his illegal wars of 1618 to 1620. If he consented to this, she would "make markets at Quiçala where they are customarily made" and would "order her [followers] to go to them and to carry pieces."[42] In the same letter, Njinga asked that the Portuguese return her subjects who had been taken away by Mendes de Vasconcellos's campaigns. Some were "sobas," local rulers whose lands were not under Portuguese authority. Others were "quijicos" [kijiko], the serflike dependents sometimes called slaves in contemporary documents.[43] Njinga not only held slaves and other dependent groups; she also sold slaves herself. In 1626 she wrote to Bento Banha Cardoso, the Portuguese commander at Embaca, informing him, "I was sending some pieces to the market of Bumba Aquiçanzo, Aire [Hari a Ngola, her Portuguese-supported rival] came out with his army, and robbed me of thirty pieces of those I had sent."[44] She demanded an immediate restitution and announced the capture of some Portuguese soldiers.

Much later in her life, Njinga did not hesitate to continue in the slave trade, although in this case her cause was not simply economic gain. She was anxious to redeem her sister, Barbara, from captivity in Luanda and to that end had to pay a ransom of slaves to the Portuguese. In a letter of 1655 she complained that she had already paid "infinite pieces" and was yet to get satisfaction.[45] We know that these slaves were war captives, for in a dramatic speech announcing her treaty of peace with Portugal in 1657, Njinga thanked her soldiers for "all the labor that you have suffered in the wars, and now in making slaves to ransom my sister."[46]

Njinga may not have had a philosophical difficulty with holding slaves or selling them, but she certainly did have a desire to set limits to the exploitation of both forms of labor. One of the greatest sticking points in her relationships with Portugal concerned rights over the servile kijikos and mubikas and what should become of them in the aftermath of Portugal's war on Ndongo. Thus Njinga sought to draw these groups to her, and away from the Portuguese, as she saw them as her legal subjects in any postwar treaty. Fernão de Sousa, the governor (1624–30) who had to deal with these disputes, noted this when he received advice at the beginning of 1625 that "our slaves fled to her again, with which she became more powerful and we weaker."[47] These legal wrangles continued even with the pliant Portuguese client Ngola Hari, Njinga's rival, for early in 1627 the Portuguese authorities were told to "petition the king of

Dongo to capture all slaves, quizicos and free people who had fled in the time of war that belong to the king of Angola," as the Portuguese were claiming that these people were their subjects.[48] Ngola Hari was also concerned about his rights over these various servile groups, for he presented a formal complaint in writing to the governor in 1629 concerning "bad captives, the pieces of Dongo," that is, servile people who did not belong to Portugal but to him. Indeed, Portugal wished to claim any people taken by their forces in assaults on Matamba (a neighboring kingdom) or in other operations around the town of Quituchela.[49]

Like Afonso before her, Njinga believed that people could be enslaved illegally, and moreover that it was the duty of the state to insure that proper procedures had been followed. Such concepts are fairly clear in a letter that Njinga wrote to António de Oliveira de Cadornega, the Portuguese settler and historian, in 1660. The contents of the letter to which she was responding are unknown, but it complained that slaves that Cadornega had purchased through traveling commercial agents, called *pombeiros,* had run away (or been stolen) in Njinga's territory and she had not recovered them. She responded to his query with her own complaints, that the pombeiros had not sufficiently inquired as to who was free and slave, and that she was now harboring many people who had been wrongly enslaved.[50]

Other elements in Njinga's correspondence of this early period give further insight into the meaning of slavery to Kimbundu-speaking people writing in Portuguese. The term used for the most vulnerable servile group in Ndongo, *mubika,* rested on a root that meant domination, as this meaning is reflected in the use of the root in the catechism of Kimbundu, written shortly after Njinga took power and published in 1642. In this text, God's law is rendered from this root, as in *ubic'ae* (*ubika ae*), an abstract form of the noun built on the root that in another noun class meant slave. Hence, when writing to Portuguese authorities she sometimes referred to herself as a piece (*peça*), or slave, as she did in her letter to the captain of the fort of Embaca of 13 November 1627, in which she described herself as his "daughter and piece."[51] And in an order sent to authorities in the nearby state of Mbondo in late December 1627, Njinga declared that her rival Ngola Hari was "her piece."[52] In the early months of 1630 two other rulers in Ndongo were uncertain about which lord they should obey, but they were certain that they "did not have to serve him who is a piece with them."[53] Clearly this did not mean that any of these people literally regarded themselves as the slave of one or another authority, but did intend to convey that they were prepared to accept some authority from them, much as one might accept authority from God without, however, yielding too much in temporal life.

Garcia II's Denunciation of the Slave Trade, 1643

As Njinga was struggling against the Portuguese and their Imbangala allies, Kongo was drawn into the fray by Governor João Correia de Sousa. Although Correia de Sousa was eager to seek reconciliation with Ndongo during his term in office, he conducted a major campaign, using the same Imbangala allies that had defeated Ndongo, against Kongo interests. The campaign first overcame the district of Kasanze, a Kongo vassal region located near Luanda, and then in a surprise move, Correia de Sousa shifted his forces northward, finally invading southern Kongo. In 1622 the Portuguese-Imbangala army met a small Kongo force at Mbumbi, in Mbamba province, and defeated it. A number of Kongo nobles were killed in the action, and the Imbangala were alleged to have eaten them.

Pedro II, who had just become king of Kongo at the time, was outraged and protested to Rome and Madrid concerning the invasion. More significantly, he also wrote to the States-General of the Netherlands inquiring about the Dutch West India Company, which had recently formed with the idea of attacking Spanish and Portuguese shipping. In his letter to the States-General, Pedro proposed an alliance that would allow a Kongo army to attack Luanda by land while a Dutch force came in by sea. The initial attempts of the Dutch to follow up on the plan were stalled by changes in Kongo's politics, but eventually the plan came to fruition.[54]

In 1641 a Dutch fleet of the West India Company under Admiral Cornelis ("Pegleg") Jol captured Luanda, forcing the Portuguese colonists to withdraw from the city, first to their farms along the Bengo River, and finally to their interior city of Masangano. A number of African powers took this reversal of Portuguese fortunes as an opportunity to reopen issues of control of Angola, among them Garcia II of Kongo (r. 1641–61), who quickly asserted Kongo's alliance with the new Dutch presence against the Portuguese, chiding them for not moving more forcefully against the Portuguese after the fall of Luanda.[55] In February 1643, Garcia, who had himself been educated at the Jesuit College in Kongo's capital of São Salvador,[56] wrote to the rector of the Jesuit order in Luanda regarding the situation in Angola. After noting that rebellions had plagued the Portuguese and hindered their war against the

Dutch, he continued by writing, "therefore there can never be peace with this Kingdom [Angola]." This was "because in place of gold, silver, and other things which serve as money in other places, the trade and money are pieces [slaves], which are not gold nor cloth, but creatures." His particular problem with the trade in slaves was apparently ultimately political. "Our disgrace," Garcia observed, "and that of my ancestors is that in our simplicity we gave place to that from which grows all the evils in our kingdoms, and above all that there are people who affirm that we were never lords of Angola and Matamba. The inequality of arms has caused us to lose all, as where there is force, right is lost."[57]

Like Afonso, Garcia was not necessarily opposed to slavery or the slave trade. Just three days earlier, Garcia had sent some slaves to the Dutch governor of Brazil as a gift, probably as compensation for that country's efforts against the Portuguese, as the terms of the original Kongo-Dutch agreement had stipulated that Kongo would pay the Dutch.[58] Moreover, Garcia was certainly not dependent on the slave trade. Dutch sources noted that Kongo was not a particularly big supplier of slaves, and those that were exported from Kongo ports were enslaved further in the interior.[59] Garcia's understanding of the slave trade was that the greed of the Portuguese had caused them to contend that Kongo was never lord of Angola or Matamba and, moreover, that the application of force had made this so. In writing this, Garcia was placing the Portuguese colonization of Angola in the context of the slave trade.

The battle of Mbumbi, in 1621, in which Portuguese and Imbangala forces had first invaded Kongo after their victories in Ndongo, had fixed in the minds of Kongo leaders a particular image of the rulers of Angola. Kongo's leaders thought the Portuguese at Luanda were solely interested in war and the slave trade, and in defeating Kongo to take its wealth. Garcia reflected this attitude when he wrote the Dutch governor of Brazil contending that "the nature of the Portuguese is unquiet and given to sowing discord, and they seek all means to put us head over heels and in revolution, and they do all this for their own ends."[60] In justifying his actions to the Jesuit rector some years later, Garcia argued that at the time the Dutch took Luanda, the Portuguese governor was in the process of preparing to invade Kongo. In addition, many of the lesser Angolan nobles, who had been forced by the Portuguese to serve them, were rebelling against them because of their injustice. Garcia linked these tyrannical actions to Portuguese greed. "Before the fall of Luanda to the Dutch," he wrote, "the Governors and residents always had perpetual hatred toward this kingdom [of Kongo], tyrannizing and unjustly capturing Souas [local rulers], demanding every year from them tribute of a quantity of people, who came to give up their own children and wives, with the only end being to enrich themselves."[61]

Kongo harbored runaways for years, perhaps in the same way that Njinga did, contending that the runaways were Kongo subjects unjustly abused by the Portuguese. In 1659, for example, the municipal council of Luanda complained that Garcia II had been harboring so many runaway slaves that the country was ruined, not only from the loss of service of those who had fled but also because the masters could not be sure of the service of the others. The Portuguese authorities feared that Garcia was building an army with them, as many were apparently skilled soldiers.[62]

Garcia's attitude toward runaways probably reflected the larger claim that Portugal's colony of Angola existed for war and slavery and thus represented an upsetting of the normal process of enslavement. To return to a more normal situation, Garcia, like Afonso before him, placed a demand in a proposed treaty with Portugal in 1649 that "there be maintained in various parts of the Kingdoms of Congo and Angola impartial judges to examine if the pieces [peças] which are sold are free or stolen or are truly slaves [escravos]."[63] He linked the evil of the slave trade as conducted by the Portuguese to their avarice rather than any intrinsic nature of the trade. In fact, he prefaced his remarks on the evils of the slave trade by noting, "Nothing is more condemning to people than ambition and pride."[64] This greed and pride had put things out of order, and it was its motivations and excessiveness to which Garcia objected.

Central African rulers controlled states typical of their era throughout the world. Such states were often based on assumptions of power and authority that are no longer fashionable in the modern world. Among these assumptions were the right of governments to tax and take tribute without necessarily delivering any services, judicial systems that unashamedly protected the interests of the rich and powerful, and government that granted little responsibility to the governed. Holding people as slaves, as well as selling these rights, were part and parcel of this larger system of government. Today many of these ideas are repugnant, but it does not then mean that all these rulers were simply cynical manipulators of politics. They had their principles and ethics, even if these were not the same as today. Understanding this system of ethics can help us unravel the explanation of African elites' participation in the slave trade.

The Dahomey Counterexample:
Bloodthirsty Patron of the Slave Trade

The kingdom of Dahomey can offer an interesting comparison with the states and rulers of Central Africa. While Afonso ruminated over the slave trade and Garcia denounced it, the rulers of Dahomey were often regarded as the paragon of a slave-trading state, one founded to forward that trade. Much of Dahomey's negative reputation comes from it having been chosen as a bad example by British abolitionists, and perhaps for that reason its commitment to unrelenting slave raiding has been exaggerated.[65]

But like the Central Africans, the rulers of Dahomey have also left a chain of correspondence in which they speak their own part. This chain begins with a letter written by King Agaja (r. 1708?–40) in 1726 to the king of England, and delivered to him by Bulfinch Lambe, the English trading factor at Ouidah, on Dahomey's coast. Lambe had been captured by Agaja's forces when Dahomey took over Allada in 1724 and held the Englishman prisoner in his capital until 1726. When Agaja released Lambe, he also sent a letter, written by Lambe on his behalf in poorly spelled English to King George I of England.[66] The letter then appears to have languished in the British archives until the height of the abolitionist debate in Parliament, when it was brought forth and submitted in 1789 to the discussion as evidence against the claims of the abolitionists.[67]

Given the circumstances of its creation and publication, it is not surprising that, when it arrived in England and when it was presented to Parliament, the letter was denounced as a forgery. There are nevertheless at least some reasons to accept its authenticity, at least partially since a similar letter seems to have been sent to France (though its contents are known only in summary) at about the same time.[68] Moreover, there are a number of references to letters being written to Europe, and most notably to Brazil, in the following years from Dahomey or its immediate neighbors, suggesting that correspondence was not so abnormal as a single isolated letter might suggest.

Most of the eighteenth-century letters mentioned in Brazilian governors' correspondence are known only in brief summaries—altogether three letters from Agongolo (r. 1789–97), ten from his successor, Adandozan (r. 1797–1818), as well as one from the latter's successor, Gezo (r. 1818–58), are extant in Brazilian and Portuguese archives.[69] These letters, as undoubtedly those of their predecessors, were written by Portuguese or *mestiço* secretaries on behalf of the kings, who were almost certainly not literate. Thus, unlike the letters from Central Africa, which originated from bilingual and literate kings, the Dahomey letters raise a certain number of problems since one can never be certain if the secretary did not slip in personal opinions or evaluations under the guise of writing a letter. One scribe, Francisco Xavier Alvares do Amaral, even inserted a personal note in one of Agongolo's letters in which he referred to the Dahomean monarch as a "barbarian."[70]

While many of the letters deal with the business of the Portuguese fort, as one might expect, or other diplomatic affairs, some do deal directly or indirectly with the slave trade. In Agaja's letter of 1726, for example, he notes that he kept an army "least I should be attacked or surprised from the northward, eastward, or westward" and requests powder and other weapons, which he felt important to his defense.[71] Although the letter was introduced by partisans of the slave trade, who apparently felt it showed the Dahomeans to be militaristic and hence naturally inclined to war and the slave trade, it also shows that Agaja did not consider his attacks on Ouidah to be offensive (and thus to obtain slaves) but rather defensive. In fact, the notion that Dahomey was a beleaguered state required to make constant war to survive is a regular theme in Dahomean discussion of the slave trade.

Perhaps the best-known statement on the slave trade by a Dahomean ruler comes from King Kpengla (r. 1774–89), not in a letter but in a speech reported by Lionel Abson, the English factor at Ouidah and a close associate of the Dahomeans, who was married into the royal family and who, in the opinion of some European visitors, was "more Dahoman than European."[72] The king gave the speech after Abson read and translated pamphlets written in England about the debate concerning the abolition of the slave trade. In response to the suggestion made in Europe that Dahomey made wars solely to capture slaves, the king was reported to observe that while the English were surrounded by the ocean, Dahomey was in the middle of a continent and surrounded by other people, and it was "obliged, by the sharpness of our swords, to defend ourselves from their incursions, and to punish the depredations they make on us . . . your countrymen, therefore, who allege that we go to war for the purpose of supplying your ships with slaves, are grossly mistaken."[73] He concluded, "In the name of my ancestors and myself I aver, that no Dahoman man ever embarked in war merely for the sake of procuring wherewithal to purchase your commodities." He noted that he had killed many thousands of people "without thinking of the market" because these people deserved to die for "policy or justice." The motives for war were not commercial, he contended, for "if white men chose to remain at home . . . will black men cease to make war? I answer by no means." He concluded that "God made war for all the world and every kingdom, large or small, has practiced it more or less, though perhaps in a manner unlike and upon different principles. . . . We do, indeed, sell to the white men a part of our prisoners, and we have a right so to do. Are not all prisoners at the disposal of their captors?"[74]

The speech, quoted as it is by Archibald Dalzel in the context of the slave trade debate, in which he stood on the side supporting the trade, probably was also intended to support the idea that the Dahomeans were committed to constant war and thus prepared to continue the slave trade, especially since in one part Kpengla alleged that he or his predecessors often killed people who could be slaves for religious reasons at the festival known as the Annual Customs. But the larger tenor of this speech, like Agaja's letter, was that he was forced to wage war by political circumstances and that these were his primary motives and not the idea of selling captives, though the sale was his right. His speech undercut the possibility, also present in Agaja's letter, that he depended on firearms and other imported weapons to fight by noting that without guns he would still fight with arrows, clubs, and swords.[75]

While Agaja's letter and Kpengla's speech are both of suspect provenance, the corpus of letters from later Dahomean monarchs found in Brazil and Portugal is less problematic. This correspondence is neither directed at the slave trade nor informed by the debates about it. They confirm, by their very offhandedness, that the Dahomean leadership had no qualms about selling slaves. Agongolo in a letter of 1791, for example, announces the port was open for "ships of the Portuguese nation" and that imported tobacco rolls would be paid for in "good captives"; in a letter of 20 March 1795, he tells the Portuguese that "no one . . . will suffer losses in my port and that anyone who carries silk, worked gold or silver . . . , for this there are captives in excess there, and more of them that can be sold against tobacco and *aguardente* [distilled spirits]."[76]

Adandozan, for his part, asked in a letter of 1800 for "good muskets" and other weapons, "for which I will make good payment in good slaves at the Fort of Your Highness."[77] In 1804 he continued the theme of a beleaguered state by starting his letter by announcing himself as "king of this little Dagomé," then noting that it was "the custom among our nations to capture and seize all that we find in the said conflict," before going on to describe military actions he undertook.[78] The military theme was continued in a letter of 1810, in which he sympathized with the king of Portugal (who had been expelled from his country by Napoleon and was residing in Brazil), noting that he would send an army to assist him if he had access to communication by dry land, and then proceeded to describe several military campaigns in considerable detail as a demonstration of his military prowess.[79]

The relevance of the military detail is subsequently revealed in his observations about the slave trade, for after one victory, "I ordered the great and small sold, . . . and then when this was all done I myself took the title of *Imigôu atunguizâ*, which is given when a man is most valiant." This is then followed by complaints that he had not been properly paid for slaves he had sent to Bahia to be sold.[80] Another letter, written in 1811, was very much like the 1810 letter, particularly in the elaborate descriptions of military actions, but it added that because of the European war, no British or French ships were coming to his ports, and that given this lack of shipping he was turning more fully to Brazil. He proposed that he get his own ship "with cargo for my port, I want to be its captain, so that I will be responsible for the benefit of its cargo, and of it, thus I want to see if it is loss or profit and I the same captain of the ship will say to you how they deal with the whites." Adandozan wished to conduct the trading himself, "as I want my brother to see how I can benefit him with its cargo so that when the ship arrives my brother will have to say that it is well done and that my brother does good business as he took it all on his head." He specifically noted that this ship would be dealing in slaves, for he concluded the section by saying, "All captives that they sell would be old because in this land they never lack service from him who is old."[81]

While Dahomey's ethical approach was radically different from that of the Central Africans, Dahomey also had an underlying ethics. These considerations had to do with war, and ultimately with a just-war concept, one that was often denied by the Europeans who described Dahomey's practice and provide a large body of primary literature. Antiabolitionists who provided evidence on Dahomey did so because they believed that they could sway parliamentary opinion by showing that Dahomey was committed to war for war's sake. While it is possible to read such motivations into Dahomey's actions, the letters, taken by themselves, suggest that Dahomean leaders usually saw their wars as meeting primarily strategic and defensive aims, however self-serving these may seem to a modern generation. Kpengla's speech, which becomes more believable when put by the letters of his successors, stresses this point, and his vehemence in denying the commercial motive becomes more plausible.

We are still a long way from being able to explain the whole of the slave trade in terms of African ethical principles, but these special examples do help us to understand how the elite of African society and its prime decision makers continued the slave trade. For them, it was an aspect of the politics that made their countries function.

Notes

1. There have been several attempts to understand the demographic impact, one of the most thorough being Patrick Manning, *Slavery and African Life: Occidental, Oriental and African Slave Trades* (Cambridge: Cambridge University Press, 1990); on my earlier attempt to assess this (which reaches similar conclusions), see John Thornton, "The Demographic Effect of the Slave Trade on Western Africa, 1500–1850," in *African Historical Demography*, ed. C. Fyfe and D. McMaster, 2 vols. (Edinburgh: Centre of African Studies, University of Edinburgh, 1981), 2:691–720. For a quantified model of local impacts in central Africa, see Thornton, "As guerras civis no Congo e o tráfico de escravos: A história e a demografia de 1718 a 1844 revisitadas," *Estudos afro-asiáticos* (Rio de Janeiro) 32, no. 1 (1997): 55–74.

2. An early and influential attempt to see differential levels of economic development as underlying African participation is found in Walter Rodney, "African Slavery and Other Forms of Social Oppression on the Upper Guinea Coast in the Context of the Atlantic Slave-Trade," *Journal of African History* 7, no. 3 (1966): 431–43; Rodney, *A History of the Upper Guinea Coast, 1545–1800* (Oxford: Oxford University Press, 1970). Some indications of continued support for it are found in Manning, *Slavery and African Life*, 32–37.

3. A case argued in general in John Thornton, *Africa and Africans in the Making of the Atlantic World, 1400–1800*, 2nd ed. (Cambridge: Cambridge University Press, 1998), 43–128.

4. A good and still accessible study is found in Basil Davidson, *Black Mother: The Years of the African Slave Trade* (Boston: Little, Brown, 1961).

5. For historiography up to the early 1980s, and a critique, see John Thornton, "Early Kongo-Portuguese Relations: A New Interpretation," *History in Africa* 8 (1981): 183–204.

6. Anne Hilton, *The Kingdom of Kongo* (Oxford: Oxford University Press, 1985), 21–23, 57–85.

7. Joseph E. Inikori, "Slavery in Africa and the Transatlantic Slave Trade," in *The African Diaspora*, ed. by Alusine Jalloh and Stephen E. Maizlish (College Station: Texas A&M University Press, 1996), 61–64. All the evidence cited comes from Hilton.

8. A convenient statement of the "Rodney debate" is in Joseph E. Inikori, ed., *Forced Migration: The Impact of the Export Slave Trade on African Societies* (London: Hutchinson, 1982), which contains several of the original works and editorial comments by Inikori. The original debate between Rodney and J. D. Fage appeared between 1966 and 1969; other contributions followed as well. Paul Lovejoy has provided a more recent

restatement of this thesis, in *Transformations in Slavery in Africa,* 2nd ed. (Cambridge: Cambridge University Press, 2000), 112–14, 120–25.

9. Some scholars, notably Georges Balandier, questioned the authenticity of Afonso's letters, maintaining that he was not literate and that they were the work of Portuguese scribes who may have shaped his words and thoughts to their, or Portugal's, ends. See Balandier, *Daily Life in the Kingdom of the Kongo from the Sixteenth to the Eighteenth Century,* trans. from the French by Helen Weaver (1965; trans., New York: Pantheon, 1968), 52–55. Even if one denies the explicit references in contemporary sources to Afonso reading and studying texts, the crucial letters were certainly the work of his secretary, João Teixeira, a Kongolese who was chosen for the position because of his loyalty.

10. There are no strictly contemporary records of the first contacts, only retrospective accounts created by the chronicler Rui de Pina, whose primary source was clearly an inquest done among the Portuguese sailors who visited in 1491 and had the king baptized.

11. Commutation of Manuel de Vila Maior, 9 August 1490, in Maria Luísa Oliveira Esteves, ed., *Portugaliae monumenta africana,* 2 vols. (Lisbon: Comissão Nacional para as Comemorações dos Descobrimentos Portugueses, 1995–), 2:56.

12. Armando Cortesão and Avelino Teixeira da Mota, eds., *Portugaliae monumenta cartographica,* 6 vols. (Lisbon: Imprensa Nacional, 1960), 1:12, plates 4–5.

13. Duarte Pacheco Pereira, *Esmeraldo de situ orbis,* ed. Augusto Epiphânio da Silva Dias (1905; repr., Lisbon: Sociedade de Geografia, 1975), book 3, chap. 2, p. 134.

14. Despacho de Gonçalo Roiz . . . 1509, in António Brásio, ed., *Monumenta missionaria africana,* 1st ser., 15 vols. (Lisbon: Agência Geral do Ultramar), 4:61.

15. The instructions for the 1491 mission are no longer extant.

16. Italian translation of an untitled Portuguese chronicle of Rui de Pina, ca. 1492, written from the ship's book and six witnesses shortly after the return of the mission. It is published, with Portuguese translation, in Carmen Radulet, ed. and trans., *O cronista Rui de Pina e a Relação do Reino do Congo: Manuscrito inédito do Códice Riccardiano 1910* (Lisbon: Comissão Nacional para as Comemorações dos Descobrimentos Portugueses, 1992), fol. 98rb, 99rb (foliation of original MS). The author of the letter, probably dictated by João, was undoubtedly the "black who knew the two languages and equally, was experienced in writing both, a black who was beginning to teach the nobles and their children, and many other good and virtuous men," that the ship left there (fol. 98vb). Radulet also published the relevant chapters of the better-known version of Pina's *Crónica del rei D. Joham Segundo* (1515), which was based on this text, in the appendix (p. 152), which does not contain João's letter and other details.

17. Afonso I to Manuel I, 5 October 1514, in Brásio, *Monumenta,* 1:294–323. Afonso wrote an earlier letter shortly after becoming king, explaining his accession (see p. 295); this in turn provided the text for three other letters of 1512 (to the pope, the king of Portugal, and his people) that were written in Portugal for him. See *Monumenta* 1:266–73. These letters do not deal with either slavery or the slave trade.

18. Hilton, *Kingdom of Kongo,* 21. She cites as evidence only Afonso's letter to João III, 18 October 1526, in Brásio, *Monumenta,* 1:489–90, which only makes it clear that Afonso opposed the export of free people who had been illegally captured through robbery. For support Raphael Batsîkama ba Mampuya ma Ndwâla proposes that tradition opposed the export of people and offers the proverb "Mbwa ñzîngi, nkulu ñzîngi. Kimfwetete ka tânu' eñkânda. Emûntu mfumu ka wându' embata, ngo ke bañkatul' eñkânda"—"Just as one cannot crush a tiny ant, it is forbidden to take the life of a servant, less that of a dog. A man is a king, one cannot beat him, just as one cannot beat the leopard" (a free translation). While this proverb clearly opposes the mistreatment or murder of slaves, it cannot tell us much about their sale, or indeed their conditions of labor. Batsîkama

JOHN THORNTON

ba Mampuya ma Ndwâla, *L'ancien royaume de Congo et les Bakongo: Séquences d'histoire populaire* (Paris: L'Harmattan, 1999), 93.

19. Afonso to Manuel, 5 October 1514, in Brásio, *Monumenta*, 1:295, 297, 301, 303.

20. Ibid., 1:300–301. *Pieces* (*peças*) was a term used to indicate the value of a healthy adult slave. As a unit of accounting it was useful in the external slave trade, as other slaves were valued more or less against this standard. Afonso's use of the term here suggests that purchasing slaves for export was possible around 1510.

21. Ibid., 1:304–5, 306. Afonso complained that buying slaves was their regular practice, and he was outraged that they had done but very little work in the past five years (1509–14).

22. Ibid., 1:317.

23. Ibid., 1:303, 305, 312.

24. Ibid., 1:313. Eventually Alvaro Lopes, a Portuguese official whom Afonso had appointed to guard his palace, had to round up the runaways, punishing those who had fled with beating, and those who had killed Manuel Cão with death.

25. Afonso to João III, 26 May 1517, in Brásio, *Monumenta*, 1:404.

26. Afonso to Manuel, 5 October 1514, in Brásio, *Monumenta*, 1:312–15.

27. There is, I think, no reason to credit Anne Hilton's pessimistic view of Kongo's economic weakness driving Afonso to export slaves. See Hilton, *Kingdom of Kongo*, 55–65. In the same section, she reads far too much into the sources on the role of the control of trade as the main means of fiscalization of the state.

28. Afonso to King João III, 25 August 1526, in Brásio, *Monumenta*, 1:484.

29. This money is described in the earliest sources: de Pina, chronicle, ed. Radulet, *Cronista*, fol. 93rb and Pacheco Pereira, *Esmeraldo*, book 3, chap. 2, p. 134 (which gives the name).

30. Afonso to Manuel, 4 March 1516, Brásio, *Monumenta* 1:357. A *lefuku* was a unit of 10,000 shells, and a *kofu* was a unit of 20,000 shells.

31. Afonso to King João III, 6 July 1526, in Brásio, *Monumenta*, 1:470–71.

32. Afonso to King João III, 18 October 1526, in Brásio, *Monumenta*, 1:489–90.

33. Baltasar de Castro to João III, 15 October 1526, in Brásio, *Monumenta*, 1:485–7.

34. Afonso to António Carneiro, 5 March 1516, in Brásio, *Monumenta*, 1:359.

35. Act of Inquistion of Afonso I, 22 April 1517, in Brásio, *Monumenta*, 1:393–7.

36. On the complexities of the government of Portuguese in Kongo see Thornton, "Early Kongo-Portuguese Relations."

37. Inquest into the Trade of São Tomé with Angola, 12 November 1548, in Brásio, *Monumenta*, 2:197–206. The testimony was taken on 7–8 May 1548. Manuel Varela testified that in the space of a bit more than a year, ten to twelve ships had left bearing from four to seven hundred slaves each, but also noting that at least once a small brigantine carried only around two hundred. This suggests a volume of about four to eight thousand slaves per year.

38. Pierre du Jarric, *Histoire des choses plus memorables . . .* , 3 vols. (Bordeaux: S. Millanges, 1608–12), 2[1610]: 79–80 (relying on Jesuit papers he found in Portugal). An earlier but less detailed version is Baltasar Barreira, "Informação acerca dos escravos de Angola," 1582–83, in Brásio, *Monumenta*, 3:228–29. Barreira appears to have written an extensive but no longer extant account of Ndongo's politics and social structure around 1580 that forms the base for many other descriptions.

39. For a full background, see Linda Heywood and John Thornton, *Central Africans, Atlantic Creoles and the Foundation of the Americas, 1585–1660* (Cambridge: Cambridge University Press, 2007), 79–103

40. A full overview of the period, splendidly documented, is Beatrix Heintze, "Das Ende des unabhängigen Staats Ndongo (Angola): Neue Chronologie und Reinterpretation

(1617–1630)," *Paideuma* 27 (1981): 197–273, revised edition in Portuguese translation in Heintze, *Angola nos séculos XVI e XVII*, trans. Marina Santos (Luanda: Kilombelombe, 2007), 277–386.

41. Heywood and Thornton, *Central Africans*, 124–58.

42. Queen Njinga to Fernão de Sousa, ca. dry season, 1624, in de Sousa to Government, 15 August 1624, in *Fontes para a história de Angola do século XVII*, ed. Beatrix Heintze, 2 vols. (Wiesbaden: Steiner, 1985–88), 2:85–86 (also in Brásio, *Monumenta*, 7:249–50).

43. Summaries of same letter in de Sousa to Government, 28 September 1624, in Brásio, *Monumenta*, 7:256; de Sousa to Government, 10 December 1624, in Heintze, *Fontes*, 2:117.

44. Queen Njinga to Bento Banha Cardoso, 3 March 1625 [ed. 1626], quoted in Fernão de Sousa to Gonçalo de Sousa and his brothers, ca. 1630, in Heintze, *Fontes*, 1:244–45.

45. Queen Njinga to Governor-General of Angola, 13 December 1655, in Brásio, *Monumenta*, 11:524.

46. Fr. Serafino da Cortona to Governor-General of Angola, 20 March 1657, in Brásio, *Monumenta*, 12:108.

47. Fernão de Sousa to his sons, [ca. 1630], in Heintze, *Fontes*, 1:241.

48. Ibid., 1:259–60.

49. Ibid., 1:343. Notices of 1629.

50. Queen Njinga to António de Oliveira de Cadornega, 15 June 1660, in Cadornega, *História geral das guerras angolanas (1680–81)*, ed. José Matias Delgado and Manuel Alves da Cunha, 3 vols. (1940–42; repr., Lisbon: Agência-Geral do Ultramar, 1972), 2:172–73.

51. Summary of message of Njinga to Alvaro Roiz de Sousa, 13 November 1627, summarized in Fernão de Sousa to his sons, [ca. 1630], in Heintze, *Fontes*, 1:293.

52. Fernão de Sousa to his sons, in Heintze, *Fontes*, 1:299.

53. Ibid., 1:346.

54. Although the original of the letter is lost, there is a summary of it in the deliberations of the States General, Nationaal Archief Nederland, Staten Generaal, vol. 5751, meeting of 27 October 1623, and in less detail in the diary of Piet Heyn, who was sent to carry out the Dutch part in 1624. Heyn, "Journael van de Brasiliese Reyse, gehouden opt Schip De Neptunus . . . 15 January 1624 tot den 16 July 1625," fols. 24v–25, published (with original pagination) in L. M. Akveld, "Journaal van de reis van Piet Heyn naar Brazilië en West-Afrika 1624–25," *Bijdragen en medelingen van het historisch genootschap* 76 (1962): 144–45.

55. Garcia II to Jan Maurtis van Nassau, 12 May 1642, in Brásio, *Monumenta*, 8:584–87.

56. In 1570 King Álvaro I of Kongo began calling his capital "São Salvador," and all other kings following used this name, until the government of Angola named the city "Mbanza Congo" in 1975.

57. Garcia II to Jesuit Rector, 23 February 1643, in Brásio, *Monumenta*, 9:18.

58. Garcia II to Dutch Governor of Brazil, 20 February 1643, in Brásio, *Monumenta*, 9:15. Pedro II, the original formulator of the arrangement, did not mention slaves among the items he proposed to send as payment.

59. Anne Hilton argues that Kongo had come to depend on cloth production from its eastern provinces to pay for imports. Hilton, *Kingdom of Kongo*, 105–44. Much of her larger argument seems to place too much attention on control of trade as the source of Kongo's revenues, and on the autonomy of provinces within the larger kingdom.

60. Garcia II to Governor of Brazil, 20 February 1643, in Brásio, *Monumenta*, 9:15.

61. Garcia II to Fr. António do Couto, 28 July 1649, in Brásio, *Monumenta*, 10:372.

62. Municipal Council of Luanda to Overseas Council, 29 April 1659, in Brásio, *Monumenta*, 12:231–33.

63. Conditions of Peace, 19 February 1649, in Brásio, *Monumenta*, 10:327.

64. Garcia II to Jesuit Rector, 23 February 1643, in Brásio, *Monumenta*, 9:17.

65. Robin Law, "Dahomey and the Slave Trade: Reflections on the Historiography of the Rise of Dahomey," *Journal of African History* 27, no. 2 (1986): 237–67.

66. The letter is signed by "Trudo Audato Povesaw Daujerenjoa Suvveto Ene-Mottee Addee Pow, a Powlo Cow Hullow Neccressy, Emperor of Dawhomay" and adds as a postscript, "Could I write in my own hand, or explain myself as I would, I should say a great deal, but believe this white man has done it as much as possible," col. 90. This is the only pagination marked in Robin Law's facsimile edition of the relevant section. See Law, "Further Light on Bulfinch Lambe and the 'Emperor of Pawpaw': King Agaja of Dahomey's Letter to King George I of England, 1726," *History in Africa* 17 (1990): 211–26. The spelling irregularities originate from Lambe, not from Agaja.

67. Law, "Further Light," 211–15.

68. Ibid., 222n16.

69. Most letters are in the Arquivo Público do Estado de Bahia (APEB), the Biblioteca Nacional de Rio de Janeiro and the Instituto Historico e Geographico Brasileiro (Rio, IHGB). The materials in Portugal are found in the Bahia section of the Arquivo Histórico Ultramarino. Many have been printed in extenso in the text or footnotes of Pierre Verger, *Fluxo e refluxo do tráfico de escravos entre o golfo de Benin e a Bahia de Todos os Santos dos séculos XVII a XIX,* trans. from the French by Tasso Gadzanis (Rio de Janeiro: Corrupio, 1985). I have cited the Brazilian edition, which gives the letters in the original Portuguese.

70. Agongolo to Maria I, 20 March 1795, published in Verger, *Fluxo,* 289–90.

71. William Cobbett, ed., *The Parliamentary History of England, from the earliest period to the year 1803* (London: T. C. Hansard, 1806–20), col. 85.

72. John Adams, *Remarks on the Country Extending from Cape Palmas to the River Congo* (1822; repr., London: Frank Cass, 1966), 52–55.

73. Archibald Dalzel, *The History of Dahomy, an Inland Kingdom of Africa, Compiled from Authentic Memoirs* (London: Spilsbury and Son, 1793), 218.

74. Ibid., 219–21.

75. Ibid., 219–20.

76. APEB, Secção Colonial, Correspondência Recebida de Autoridades Diversas, Maço 197, caixa 76, doc. 2; Agongolo to Fernando José, n.d. [dated by the archive to 1791]; Agongolo to Governor of Bahia, 20 March 1795, quoted in extenso in Verger, *Fluxo,* 287.

77. Adandozan to Prince D. João de Bragança, [ca. 1800], quoted in extenso in Verger, *Fluxo,* 261.

78. Adandozan to João Carlos de Bragança, 20 November 1804, quoted in extenso in Verger, *Fluxo,* 310.

79. IHGB, lata 137, pasta 62, fol. 1, Adandozan to João Carlos de Bragança, 9 October 1810.

80. IHGB, lata 137, pasta 62, fol. 2v, Adandozan to de Bragança, 9 October 1810.

81. IHGB, lata 137, pasta 62, fol. 7, Adandozan to King of Portugal, [ca. 1811].

TWO

1807 and All That

Why Britain Outlawed Her Slave Trade

BOYD HILTON

IT WOULD seem that many a patriotic lip was licked in anticipation of the bicentenary in March 2007 of the abolition of the slave trade, or, to be more precise, the bicentenary of the act that outlawed Britain's central role in its Atlantic triangle. Appetites had been whetted by the two-hundredth anniversary of the battle of Trafalgar seventeen months earlier, but abolition was more comforting to Blairites in search of a national narrative insofar as its two most acknowledged heroes, William Wilberforce and Thomas Clarkson, could be presented as virtuous idealists, whereas ethically speaking Admiral Lord Nelson had all-too-obvious feet of clay.

And so the plans were laid. An official service of remembrance was to be held in Westminster Abbey. Deputy Prime Minister John Prescott would call for an annual "antislavery" day in honor of Wilberforce, his predecessor as MP for Hull. On Merseyside it was decided to build a £12 million International Slave Museum on the site of docks that had once grown rich on slave-grown sugar. These initiatives were to be accompanied by a plethora of commemorative exhibitions, musicals, dances, plays, television documentaries, and radio dramas, not to mention a number of So Sorry walks, one of which would trace Clarkson's campaigning footsteps over 470 miles.[1] Lo, all these things came to pass, and in addition at least eight books on Wilberforce were published or republished during the calendar year with any number of unctuous titles, subtitles, and chapter headings: "God's Politician," "Statesman and Saint," "The Man Who Freed the Slaves," "The Washington of Humanity," "The Millionaire Child Who Gave Up Everything for the African Slaves."[2] The biggest impact of all was made by Michael Apted's full-length feature film *Amazing Grace.* According to this biopic's promotional Web site, "a nation was blind until one man made them see." Such concentrated glorification of Wilberforce personally, and such belief in the power of human virtue generally, had not been ventured by serious historians and commentators for a very long time, if ever.

However, because exhibitions, books, and films take years to project and complete, it often happens that their intended message may easily be blown aside by the whirligig of public opinion and national mood. The anniversary of abolition certainly struck a chord in the media, but few within the ranks of officialdom and bumbledom can have anticipated the extent to which their intended morality play would be subverted. Most spectacularly, the 27 March service in Westminster Abbey faltered to a momentary halt when Toyin Agbetu, an invited representative of the African pressure group Ligali, rushed up to within twenty feet of the altar (and even fewer of the queen) shouting words to this effect: "You should be ashamed. This is an insult to *us.* The Queen has to say sorry. There is no mention of the African freedom fighters. This is just a memorial for William Wilberforce."[3] Likewise, Diane Abbott led a chorus of condemnation directed against *Amazing Grace,* partly because it "prettified" the slave trade by neglecting to depict any irons or whips or weals, any gore or rapine or mutilation,[4] and partly because, as Agbetu also complained, its concentration on Wilberforce and the politicians led it to neglect the blacks' own agency in revolting against their often terrified colonial masters. A member of the UK-based Global Afrikan Congress went so far as to argue that a "perverted, misogynistic and racist" Wilberforce had done his best to prevent the abolition of slavery (as distinct from the trade) after 1807 because "it could have led to a personal 'loss of privileges' on his part, by denying him his unrestricted access to the group of disempowered Afrikan women whom he used as sex toys."[5]

Such responses on the part of the descendants of the victims of slavery were hardly surprising. More interesting was the extent to which descendants of the slave-owning race seem to have shared their jaundiced perspective. Certainly, most of the broadsheets' public commentary, like most individual blogs and Web sites, concentrated not on abolition but on the trade itself: on its role in making Britain the richest and most powerful country in the world, and in laying the basis for its immense empire; on the likelihood that as many as one million of the eleven million Africans forcibly transported died on the Middle Passage; on unspeakable horrors and cruelties, such as Africans being thrown overboard, either because they were sick or because the vessel they were in was overladen, or because (after 1807) their masters wished to avoid Royal Navy fines. All this, and the relative muteness of voices on the other side, prompted one commentator to suggest that "the national conscience is finally beginning to speak after two hundred years of silence."[6] Another journalist, however, thought the anniversary "almost as divisive and difficult as it was unifying and conciliatory."[7] A third, conscious of all the anger swirling around the subject, admitted that as someone of native British stock she found it impossible not to be angry too. "I try. I listen, read, go to lectures and exhibitions. I still get angry, with myself for feeling both guilty and not guilty, with black friends for not giving me credit for trying."[8]

Undoubtedly the lash was on the other back, and it was only a matter of time before the question of an apology was raised. "A British state that refuses to apologise for a crime on such a gigantic scale as the slave trade merely lowers our country in the opinion of the world," declared the mayor of London.[9] Temperamentally, Prime Minister Blair was more disposed to apologize for acts of God (such as the Irish famine) than for human malfeasance, but he went so far as to offer "deep sorrow," and to make a "historical expression of regret" for a shameful "crime against humanity."[10] Contrition must also have been on the mind of the minister of state at the Department for Education and Skills (Alan Johnson) when he directed that the slave trade should figure on the national curriculum as "a keystone of revamped citizenship education." On hearing of that proposal, Mrs. Thatcher's former press officer Bernard Ingham retorted that "the only thing British kids needed to know about the slave trade was that *we* ended it."[11]

A century earlier, British kids would have learned very little about the slave trade. In 1907 there was almost no official rejoicing with regard to abolition, just a single low-key Abbey service organized by Africans. The *Times* under the management of C. F. M. Bell, a self-styled radical with imperialistic leanings, might have been expected to trumpet past glories, yet it was silent. Three very brief facsimile paragraphs were reprinted from an edition published in February 1807, but there were no editorials and no commentaries. On 13 March 1907 a tiny advertisement in minuscule print informed readers that a committee had been formed for celebrating the centenary of abolition and calling on anyone who was "interested in Africa from an evangelical standpoint" to get in touch. The pedestrian tone of the notice, and the fact that it shared a half column with paragraphs about two other less than portentous "coming events"—an exhibition of gentlewomen's work in Marylebone, and a meeting of the fish trade to protest against the Billingsgate Market's proposed move to Shadwell—indicates that the topic of slave trade abolition was not a hot one. The only references to Wilberforce personally in the *Times* of 1907 concerned his house at Battersea Rise, where the so-called Clapham Sect had once plotted slave trade abolition, and where the British and Foreign Bible Society had been founded. On 20 May the house was reported to be up for sale. No buyers came forward, and on 10 July the local council called on either the local residents or the London County Council to come to the rescue. Twelve days later a public meeting at the borough's town hall resolved that ratepayers should not be asked to shoulder the burden, especially as "the purchase was not warranted by any sentimental considerations." Finally, on 21 November it was announced that Battersea Rise would be demolished. "The movement to secure the building as a memorial of Wilberforce and other leaders of the anti-slavery agitation has failed to secure public support." The tone as well as the content of these reports is testimony to the blanket of public indifference on the topic. Yet it was not the case that Edwardians were indifferent to anniversaries in general. So much is clear from the outpouring of jubilation that had greeted the centenary of the battle of Trafalgar in October 1905. Quite apart from any number of anticipatory events, on 23 October alone there were services and demonstrations of thanksgiving in Westminster Abbey, Trafalgar Square, the Albert Hall, the Royal Horticultural Hall, Earl's Court, the City Temple, and in other metropolitan venues, not to mention similar events at Portsmouth and throughout the country. The *Times,* which devoted scores of pages to these events, hailed Lord Nelson as "the greatest sailor since our world began." "His glorious victory and equally noble death, was celebrated . . . in a spirit of solemn gratitude in every corner of land and sea where the sound of the British bugle is heard. The centenary was honoured not in the spirit of triumph over fallen foes, but in that of recognition that freedom, not for Britons only, but for the civilised world, was won at Trafalgar."[12]

Nelson was clearly regarded as an icon in the first decade of the twentieth century, and just as clearly Wilberforce was not. Perhaps this is not surprising since, apart from a filial and official five-volume *Life,* there had as yet been no biography. W. E. H. Lecky had described the "unweary, unostentatious, and inglorious crusade against slavery" as "among the three or four perfectly virtuous pages comprised in the history of nations," yet he was cool about Wilberforce personally. The latter's career was "by no means without charm," but he had unfairly "eclipsed the memory" of many mute inglorious toilers in the cause, thanks merely to his "considerable social position, very eminent social gifts," and "large fortune." Lecky's mind boggled at the fact that Wilberforce should have considered Sabbath breaking a sin of equal enormity to that of slavery, and he had no time for the evangelical's "morbid, exaggerated, and somewhat effeminate self-consciousness."[13] Likewise, J. L. Hammond singled out the opinion formers Granville Sharp, Zachary Macaulay, and Thomas Clarkson for "veneration and gratitude," but he described Wilberforce as merely "the protagonist of the abolitionists in Parliament."[14] The tide began to turn only with the publication in 1913 of Élie Halévy's exceptionally influential *Histoire du peuple anglais aux dix-neuvième siècle,* which accorded Wilberforce personally, and evangelicalism generally, starring roles in the story of how England had managed to industrialize and urbanize while avoiding revolution. A translation of Halévy's first volume appeared in 1924, and anglophones learned not only that Wilberforce was "a great man" but that Britain, "carried away by an outburst of humanitarian zeal, . . . had acted against her commercial interest and had ruined her colonies for the profit of their rivals." Pious humanitarianism was also the theme of two classic studies by Reginald Coupland in 1923 and 1933.[15] The latter year was particularly significant, being the centenary both of Wilberforce's death and of Britain's second great stab at liberation, the outlawing of slavery throughout its overseas dominions, and it is evident that by then the importance of religious zeal as the driving force of abolition had come to be taken for granted.

This may explain why the subject made much more impact in 1933 than it had in 1907. The *Times* carried several editorials, describing the abolition of slavery as "a stupendous and almost incredible achievement, the conquest, after a struggle lasting nearly 50 years, of selfishness, ignorance, and prejudice on a grand scale by sheer moral and spiritual energy. It was an achievement scarcely, if ever, rivaled in history." Wilberforce had done more than anyone to create the "Victorian faith in a continuous progress of humanity in and to freedom, and to vindicate for politics the sublimity that they had possessed in the eyes of Plato."[16] There were reports of numerous public subscriptions, meetings, processions, and services, including one in the Abbey. In Wilberforce's home town of Hull, there was an exhibition in his honor at which a wax model of the great man, presented by Madame Tussaud's, was serenaded for nights on end with Negro spirituals, while in his adopted home of Battersea, the mayor laid a wreath beneath the tablet that now commemorated the spot where Wilberforce's house had stood until its demolition in 1907.

Perhaps the contrast between attitudes in 1907 and in 1933 is not so very surprising. Edwardians saw little point in celebrating the virtue of abolition given that the British Empire was (as they believed) steeped in virtue from first to last. Abolition was a single straw in a haystack of good deeds. By the same token, they did not see why their great nation should agonize about its role in the slave trade. Freedom, as the *Times* encomium on Nelson had pointed out two years earlier, was to be won by fighting tyrants, not by emancipating lesser breeds. By 1933, however, the year in which Hitler became chancellor, most Britons were conscious that they possessed little military or economic strength, and that the continuance of the empire depended mainly on moral suasion, hence the saliency of antislavery. In the case of the *Times*, there was also a more specific message. Under Geoffrey Dawson's editorship that paper would soon become a leading mouthpiece of appeasement, and Wilberforce appealed so strongly because he could be depicted as "a warrior for peace," someone prepared to sacrifice the national interest to a higher good. A stirring editorial ended by calling for another Wilberforce to arise and broker peace between the snarling nations of Europe. By the same principle, it seems likely that in 2007 the unanticipated prevalence of breast beating over drum beating was prompted by uneasiness over Britain's participation in the second Iraq war, and by a consciousness that the country was currently pursuing an unethical foreign policy.

THE HISTORIOGRAPHY of slave trade abolition has revolved around binary oppositions. Did a few fired-up individuals make all the difference, or were wider social and political forces (in and outside Britain) at play? Were abolitionists motivated by altruistic principles or material self-interest? If the former, was Christian moralism or humanitarian sensibility the driving force, and if the appeal to principle was mere humbug, then was economic greed or a desire for imperial aggrandizement the spur? Because so many people denounced the slave trade at some time or other, and because so many different arguments were used against it, it is impossible to say that this or that motive predominated.[17] What can be attempted is to narrow down the search to those whose agency really made a difference, and in order to resolve that question it is first necessary to consider the chronology of abolition.

Passionate and popular enthusiasm for ending the slave trade blew up very suddenly in 1787. In 1792 Parliament, egged on by the prime minister (William Pitt, the Younger) and the leader of the opposition in the Commons (Charles James Fox), resolved by an overwhelming majority that it should be abolished, but only gradually. From that point on the slaveholders, working through their representatives at Westminster, fought like tigers to prevent abolition, and there were many procedural and legalistic loopholes for them to exploit. The slave owners were also helped by the mood of anxiety that set in after the French Revolution went bad in 1793, with the reign of terror, the guillotining of thousands of aristocratic families, and the execution of Louis XVI. Liberty and equality now seemed less desirable ideals than they had the year before. Soon afterward violent slave revolts in Grenada and St. Vincent sparked off an antiblack reaction, which was cleverly exploited by the West India lobby. (Those historians who emphasize the slaves' own agency in achieving abolition are right to say that the revolts made the long-term viability of the trade more doubtful,[18] but in the short term they made abolition harder to push through Parliament.) And so the opposition rallied, years passed, public enthusiasm waned, Pitt "*said* he was for abolition, but . . . didn't throw himself into it,"[19] and by 1804 Wilberforce, Clarkson, and James Stephen[20] were more pessimistic than ever.

Unquestionably, what brought about the breakthrough was not outside pressure but the incidental fact that in January 1806 Pitt died and Fox's Whig Party returned to office, in a ministry headed by William Grenville, after twenty-three years in opposition. Unlike Pitt, Grenville did "throw himself" into the cause. He at once undertook to push through a bill for the suppression of the *foreign* slave trade (the supply by British slave traders of foreign countries and their colonies and of conquered islands), which according to Clarkson's calculations had amounted to about two-thirds of the whole British trade in peacetime.[21] This measure was carried in May 1806, largely because it appealed to many antiabolitionists, not on moral grounds but because it would serve to promote the war effort. Tactically it was a masterstroke, as the historian Roger Anstey has cleverly explained.

> With the supply of foreigners and conquered islands ended by the 1806 abolition bill, the West Indians were like shorn lambs to the wind of a humanity which now blew cold indeed. For in the situation which Grenville and the abolitionists had so ingeniously contrived—and which is perhaps the harder to discern because one is so conditioned to expect interest to masquerade as altruism that one may miss altruism when concealed beneath the cloak of interest—the mass of independent members of Parliament were ready, against all the evidence of the West Indies' importance to the nation, to act as the children of the later eighteenth century, with its manifest anti-slavery convictions, that they really were.[22]

Grenville's next step was to go to the country. It is worth noting that between 1708 and 1830 no ministries were formed in the wake of a general election, but it was common for newly installed ministries to call an early poll, in order to strengthen their position in Parliament by exploiting the electoral influence available to all governments. Grenville duly called an election in October 1806, as a result of which the number of MPs sympathetic to abolition increased considerably.[23] Just as significantly, the election weakened the support, and so reduced the bargaining power, of the few cabinet ministers who were hostile to abolition, notably Lord Sidmouth and William Windham. Wilberforce's bill to outlaw the domestic slave trade passed its second reading in the Lords by 100–34 on 5 February 1807, and similarly in the Commons by the wholly unexpected margin of 283–16 on the twenty-third. The scale of the majority has created the false impression that MPs were—all of a sudden—overwhelmingly in favor, but it is more likely that, the balance having been tipped in favor by the recent elections, MPs who were "adverse" decided to abstain rather than submit themselves to moral opprobrium. Indeed, it seems that the bill squeezed through a very small window of opportunity because, just six days after it received the royal assent, Grenville fell and the Pittites returned to government under the antiabolitionist Duke of Portland. He too held an instant election, and the outcome was a parliament that would have been less sympathetic to the abolitionist cause. The famous act, like Waterloo, was a damned close run thing.[24]

Most leading abolitionists hoped that the suppression of the slave trade would lead to the end of slavery itself, but they were in a bind, having in many cases only managed to persuade MPs to vote for the abolition of the trade by promising they would leave the wider question alone. That was why, on the eve of abolition, Clarkson objected to the circulation of a campaign engraving that implied a desire to go the whole hog. "You will recollect," he wrote privately, "how often we have been charged with this by our opponents—how frequently we have been obliged to do away [with] the impression by public advertisement."[25] The antislavery cause languished therefore, and did not take off again until the 1820s. Once again the timing of success owed almost everything to the fact that in 1830, after a further twenty-three years in opposition, a Whig government once more came to power. The outlawing of slavery throughout British dominions in 1833 was practically the first thing Lord Grey's government did once it had got its Great Reform Act out of the way. It prompts the reflection that evangelicals like Wilberforce would have done more for their beloved cause if only they had campaigned for the party of Fox and Grey, but unfortunately they were too conservative, not to say reactionary, on every other issue for that to have been possible.

AS POLITICIANS, Grenville, Wilberforce, and Stephen were instrumental in the final act of abolition, but it is fair to ask whether they would have acted at all had it not been for the sudden explosion of popular antislavery sentiment in the late 1780s and early 1790s. Historians often give the impression that this extraordinary phenomenon was all due to the single-handed efforts of Thomas Clarkson, who in 1787 rode tremblingly into Bristol with an intention "to subvert a branch of the trade of the large city"[26] and was then nearly murdered in Liverpool. Immediately afterward he went to Manchester, where somehow he conjured up, apparently out of the blue, a petition signed by eleven thousand people, nearly one-fifth of the local population. It was the first mass petition on any subject and provoked what has been called a spiral of competitive philanthropy in other towns, a spiral that peaked in 1792 with a thirteen-thousand-strong petition from Glasgow. In place after place where antislavery protests were registered, Clarkson seems to have been involved, either by correspondence with his contacts in the localities, or else by personal visitation. He claimed to have interrogated twenty thousand sailors and to have covered thirty-five thousand miles on horseback in just seven hectic years. But for all Clarkson's heroics, he could only have lit the touch paper, in which case there must have been a powder keg waiting to explode.

The anti–slave trade campaign had a very different flavor from the earlier association movement, with its petitions denouncing corruption and bewailing the loss of the American colonies. That had been a raucous, county based, and largely gentry led affair; this was urban, polite, rational, and "popular." Only about 30 percent of Clarkson's signatories in 1788, and only 15 percent in 1792, were members of what might be called the elite—nobles, corporators, or freemen—whereas the normal figure in the eighteenth century would have been more like 80 to 90 percent.[27] Antislavery has therefore been seen as the first stirring of a middle-class consciousness, the start of a long and halting process that ended in the 1830s when the business middle classes established a hegemony in local government and a foothold in national politics. A more modish interpretation praises the movement for inculcating "habits of voluntarism" and so contributing to the formation of "civil society."[28] In the words of a recent and most sophisticated contribution, "anti-slavery sentiment had grown fashionable by the 1780s. It had become associated with politeness, sensibility, patriotism, and a commitment to British liberty."[29] In this context it is relevant that the anti–slave trade campaign was one of the first routes through which women were incorporated into public life. Between 1790 and 1810 about 10 percent of subscriptions to the cause were in a female name, and women were often physically active as well.[30]

However, while antislavery might well have helped create civil society, there are at least two reasons why civil society cannot explain abolition. In the first place there was a loss of momentum. Whereas in each year from 1787 to 1795 between twenty and fifty towns sent in petitions signed by thousands, the only significant petition from a large town in 1806 was from Manchester, and even there the inhabitants were much less enthusiastic than in 1792. Clarkson labored as tirelessly as ever to keep the issue on the boil, but he now worked mainly (and more effectively) behind the scenes, lobbying on committees, preparing legal injunctions, and organizing mass boycotts of rum and sugar.[31] In the second place, it is a stubborn fact that only parliamentarians could abolish the slave trade, and they invariably responded negatively to large-scale demonstrations of public opinion, especially after what happened in France between 1792 and 1794. Indeed, many reformers blamed Fox's invocations of "opinion" for setting back the cause. So that although in retrospect Clarkson seems to be the real hero of the movement,[32] in reality his efforts were almost certainly counterproductive. Wilberforce had long appreciated this, having urged a friend in 1792 to "caution [Clarkson] against talking of the French Revolution. It will be ruin to our cause."[33] Closeness to Pitt was always going to give Wilberforce more influence over policy than Clarkson, who was a friend of Fox.

Even if high politics was all, and the wider movement's influence on events was negative, the question of *why* so many mobilized in the cause remains important. The economic explanation of abolition goes back to Eric Williams's Marxist tract *Capitalism and Slavery* (1944), in which he argued that the religious and humanitarian language so freely deployed was hypocritical. In his view, Britain only abolished the slave trade and then slavery after they had become an economic impediment to a mother country that was rapidly industrializing, and increasingly attached to Adam Smith's doctrine that free-market labor was cheaper, more efficient, and better motivated than slave labor. Williams's general line is still widely cited in public debate, despite its comprehensive rebuttal by many historians, most notably Seymour Drescher, who would seem to have conclusively established a number of countervailing points.[34] First, the British West Indies was far more valuable to Britain in the decade or so leading up to 1807 than it had been formerly. Second, the property value of the slave colonies had doubled between 1789 and 1814. Third, Britain's share of this increasingly profitable slave trade peaked just before abolition, as did the share of British capital that went into the trade. Fourth, Britain's slave system had reached nowhere near its "maximum economic potential." Fifth, in the years leading up to abolition, Britain's trade with Europe had been very badly hit by the attempts of France and Britain to destroy each other's commerce through legislation, while military disaster in Argentina had strangled hopes of opening alternative markets in South America. All this made the slave trade central to commercial prosperity. Drescher concludes that British slavery was "a dynamic system" that was "aborted in its prime." Indeed, "the trade pendulum was swinging slaveward" at the very time when Parliament decided to put a stop to it. "Given Europe's growing need for sugar, coffee, and cotton, given the African coast with its social machinery in place for dealing up human beings, and given Britain with its capital, its fleet, and its new lands, there existed as devastating an economic combination [in favor of the slave trade] at the end of the eighteenth century as at the beginning!" Nor is Drescher's argument based only on statistical hindsight, since he also shows that contemporaries were aware of the true position, hence the title of one of his books, *Econocide*, implying that the abolition was a case of attempted economic suicide.[35]

It would thus appear that slavery still represented (in Simon Schama's colorful phrase) "a Klondike of money," and that abolition was "an absolutely spectacular act of irrationality."[36] A common mistake, however, is to suppose that because British abolitionists behaved in defiance of market profitability they must therefore have been moved by altruism. It is obvious now that the Atlantic trade underpinned the prosperity of huge swaths of eighteenth-century British society as well as that of the slavers themselves, but there was no such awareness at the time. The concept of econocide presupposes the sense of a shared national interest, yet contemporaries were all too aware of competition between different domestic interests in a zero-sum economy and shared a Malthusian sense that one group's gain was likely to be another's loss. Supercynics might note that Wilberforce's family wealth was based not on cotton but on the Baltic wool trade passing through the nonslaving port of Hull, and might also reflect that up-and-coming "Manchester men" would do anything to puncture the disdain of "Liverpool gentlemen."[37] No doubt this argument should not be pushed too far, but it may not be very surprising that a Parliament of landowners was persuaded to curb the enormous profits of the West Indian trade. Quite apart from the politics of envy, there was a concern that those profits were dangerously speculative, especially so given the prospect of slave revolts, and might precipitate a financial crash.[38] Economic stability was more important to parliamentarians than profit, particularly at a time when Britain stood alone against Napoleon.

If it is almost certainly not the case that anti–slave trade campaigners acted out of economic self-interest, what about the motives of those politicians whose agency was paramount in 1807? A more convincingly cynical argument is that abolition was a cover for imperial control. The British Empire is famously said to have been acquired in a fit of absence of mind, but this was manifestly not the case with the first (mid-eighteenth-century) empire, which was gained in a series of upfront wars against the French, nor with the late-nineteenth-century Scramble for Africa. It does, however, apply to the second empire, accumulated between 1789 and 1850, though "state of denial" might be a better description than "absence of mind." Whereas foreigners saw brutal imperialism, the British saw only a liberating force and Protestant mission.[39] The main avenues of this second empire were not territorial but maritime, and it was the mighty Royal Navy that serviced and protected its shipping lanes and trading stations, entrepôts, and naval bases. Slave trade abolition gave the Navy a convenient excuse to stop and search other nations' vessels and to confiscate any that were guilty of what is now called extraordinary rendition. (The Americans got so fed up by the tactic that they declared war on Britain in 1812.) In this way antislavery undoubtedly became a prop of imperial ambition. Nevertheless, it is hard to see it as a *motivating* force behind the decision of 1807.[40]

Ultimately there is no escaping the fact that religion was the main impulse behind abolition, but that in itself says very little, given the varieties of belief that obtained. Clarkson worked closely with his fellow foot soldiers, the Quakers, whom he found "cold and prudent, . . . lukewarm, cautious, and worldly-wise," but undeniably virtuous. Having become "nine parts in ten of their way of thinking," he eventually abandoned his Anglican orders.[41] His religious beliefs could, like theirs, be described as humanitarian, or *this*-worldly. He saw slavery as a blot on a loving God's creation and as contradicting such Quaker imperatives as equality and nonviolence. He was instinctively unsympathetic therefore to Wilberforce's Anglican evangelical otherworldly emphasis on sin, salvation, judgment, heaven, and hell. Wilberforce's impulse, unlike Clarkson's, was missionary rather than humanitarian, and it had two foci. One was the need to redeem a British society that had become mired in luxury and corruption and religious indifference. Like Hannah More, he believed that the work of national redemption had to be attempted top down, starting with a reformation of the manners of the rich. Self-evidently the traffic in Negroes stood between the slave owners and their personal salvation, but since all Britons potentially benefited from the wealth generated by sugar and slaves, the whole of society was in spiritual danger. Wilberforce's second focus was on the souls of the slaves themselves. He and the other so-called "Saints" in Parliament were not initially motivated by concern for their material condition. This is not to deny that, like almost everyone who took the trouble to find out about the slave trade, he came away horrified by its cruelties, but the Saints were not fundamentally driven by humanitarian sensibilities. Life was a place of moral trial, a moral obstacle course standing between each soul and heaven, and slaves were no more born to be happy than anyone else. The fundamental problem with slavery was that its victims were not free to think, not free to choose Christ and reject Satan, and therefore not able to be saved. An important factor here was the rapid rejection of high Calvinist views in the 1770 and 1780s. For example, many members of the Countess of Huntingdon's Connexion, a Methodist sect with Calvinist views, openly supported slavery, but the tendency of most religious thought was increasingly Arminian, by which is meant the belief that everyone is given the offer of salvation and that no one's spiritual fate is preordained. Furthermore, many of those who clung to Calvinistic tenets in formal terms significantly modified their position. They now argued that, while God might have preordained individuals to salvation, still the choice was open to sanctification, in which case slaves must be free to make that great choice.[42]

Evangelicals were often criticized for what Dickens called their "telescopic philanthropy," meaning the contrast between their bleeding-heart compassion for slaves and their indifference to the relief of poverty and misery at home, including that of workers or wage slaves in the new mechanized industries. The extreme version of this charge is to say that evangelicals with business interests deliberately targeted an external abuse in order to divert attention away from British capitalism, that is, from a system of domestic exploitation that benefited them directly. It is always difficult for historians to know how to deal with such accusations of bad faith, but in regard to the less extreme version of the charge, which is that they were hypocrites, it is only fair to say that evangelicals genuinely believed that domestic wage slaves *were* free agents operating within a free capitalist market, a market they thought reflected the divine economy, tempting and testing human beings and putting them on their everyday moral mettle.[43] For them, instinctively, freedom and capitalism were compatible, whereas freedom and slavery were not.

It might be supposed that Clarkson's humanitarian religion, based on the light and love of God, was joyful and generous in tone, and that Wilberforce's sin-obsessed missionary approach was repressive, tremulous, and penitential. In fact the opposite was true. A seriously earnest man, Clarkson "seems to have had no sense of humour at all," though according to Hugh Brogan's entry in the *Oxford Dictionary of National Biography*, "he liked others to be merry," whereas Wilberforce *was* merry, jocund even. He was charismatic, outgoing, and altogether captivating, a loving and playful father to his six children. Doomy without being gloomy, he dwelt on the dangers of sin and the potential for damnation, but only in order to accentuate positives like faith, salvation, and redemption. Clarkson's labors were vital to the cause, but his nagging approach would never have persuaded cynical MPs, where Wilberforce was crucial in creating the necessary vitality and enthusiasm.

Another central ingredient of evangelical religion was the notion of retributive justice. Its importance can be gauged from the eagerness with which Pitt appropriated it, in contrast to Fox, whose speeches were marvelously humane and enlightened but not evangelical. According to Fox, the slave trade was an abominable traffic in human flesh, "a system of rapine, robbery, and murder," and a violation of "the principles of justice, humanity, truth, and honour," but he irritated even sympathetic MPs by his appeals to "public opinion" and to "the principles of real liberty, the happiness of mankind, the rights of nature." These tactless words were spoken just twenty-five days after revolutionary France had declared war on England in the name of liberty, equality, and fraternity. Pitt, by contrast, intoned that the slave trade had infused a poison into British commerce that corrupted every participant, subverted the order of nature, and aggravated every natural barbarity:

> Thus, Sir, has the perversion of British commerce carried misery instead of happiness to one quarter of the globe. . . . How shall we ever repair this mischief? How shall we hope to obtain, if it be possible, forgiveness from Heaven for these enormous evils we have committed, if we refuse to make use of those means which the mercy of Providence hath still reserved to us for wiping away the guilt and shame with which we are now covered? If we refuse even this degree of compensation, if, knowing the miseries we have caused, we refuse even now to put a stop to them, how greatly aggravated will be the guilt of Great Britain!

Fortunately, evangelicals believed that the greater one's spiritual danger, the more glorious was the deliverance therefrom. Thus Pitt proceeded to explain the mercy in the curse. Precisely because Britain had plunged more "deeply into this guilt" than any other nation, there was no other nation that was so likely to be "looked up to as an example, if she should have the manliness to be the first in decidedly renouncing it." "It is as an atonement for our long and cruel injustice towards Africa, that the measure . . . most forcibly recommends itself to my mind."[44] Of course, this was blatant humbug. Pitt was no more an evangelical than he was queen of the May. But he knew how to sound like one, and as a celibate and self-righteous workaholic he pulled it off. The unkempt, womanizing, and casinoholic Fox would never have got away with it even had he tried. And Pitt's rhetoric struck a chord with the parliamentary classes, who were the only people who could actually *do* abolition.

Chronology is significant here. A sense that the British nation had been divinely chastised for its sins was evident in the lamentations that followed the loss of the American colonies. As Lord Camden insisted in 1783, "this nation requires virtue as well as talents to save it," a sentiment that helps explain the hundreds of moral reform movements that proliferated during the years immediately following.[45] However, the outbreak of provincial and popular abolitionism in 1787, a point at which bullish optimism was beginning to return along with prosperity, seems to have had a quite different stimulus. The foreign and domestic crises of 1792–93 reintroduced an apocalyptic note, and that was subsequently intensified by the threat of invasion and by the symbolism of Nelson and Napoleon slogging it out in the Holy Land at the battle of the Nile (1798). These events stimulated many apocalypse watchers to anticipate the imminent return of Christ and the end of the world, at least in its current dispensation. They also gave rise to liberationist beliefs of a type espoused by the first prominent abolitionist, Granville Sharp, who was fascinated by scripture prophecies and who insisted that Napoleon was "the little horn on the head of the fourth beast," as foretold in the book of Daniel. However, like most late-eighteenth-century premillenarians, Sharp was too radical to be effective politically.[46] As for mainstream evangelicals, their retributive tones sometimes sounded apocalyptic, but most were not so much waiting for Armageddon as worrying about how God might punish them both in this world and the next. It was a constant puzzle to know why infidel France had been granted so much military success. Spencer Perceval (prime minister, 1809–12) comforted himself with the observation that, since French power and opinions had "made their greatest impression" in Catholic countries, Napoleon had evidently been "raised up by Providence for the overthrow of the Popish superstitions."[47] But given Britain's own military failings, this led to the frightening reflection that Napoleon might be, not a pointer to the end of the world, but the all too worldly instrument of divine chastisement.

Hence a strain of parliamentary rhetoric that historians have largely neglected, one that oscillated between an introspective craving for atonement and a crusading humanitarian optimism. The slave trade was a "foul iniquity" that would "completely justify the avenging angel, in entirely extirpating [this nation] from the face of the earth," said James Adair in 1796,[48] while, according to Bishop Barrington in 1807, "without abolition Britain would look in vain hereafter for the glories of the Nile or of Trafalgar."[49] "God has entered unto judgement with us," echoed James Stephen, "we must, I repeat, look to Africa, and to the West Indies, for the causes of his wrath."[50] During a debate on a proposed sale of crown lands in Trinidad in 1802, a sale he feared would lead to increased slave labor, George Canning pronounced, "Providence has determined to put to the trial our boasts of speculative benevolence and intended humanity. . . . This day is a day of tests. I trust we shall all abide the trial."[51] And at the very last Sir Thomas Turton begged the Commons to take "one great step towards averting the wrath of Heaven from us."[52] These and the scores of similar imprecations cannot all have been humbug, but even if they were it would still be the case that the speakers expected the humbug to resonate with MPs. Equally telling is the fact that many speakers on the other side considered such appeals to the dispensations of providence worthy of lengthy rebuttal.[53]

Atonement was just one of several routes into abolition, but a particular salient one at the start of 1807. With hindsight it can be seen that the battle of Trafalgar in October 1805 put an end to the threat of invasion, but in 1806–7 it was the country's continuing vulnerability that was most apparent. It was widely seen as portentous that victory had cost the life of the messianic figure Nelson, and since then both Pitt and Fox had died. Worse still, the king was intermittently mad, and a supposedly sea-green pillar of rectitude, Lord Melville, had been impeached for high-level corruption. Meanwhile on the Continent, Napoleon, described by Perceval in October 1806 as the woman in Revelation 17:3–6, "who rides upon the beast, who is drunk with the blood of the saints, the mother of harlots," was at the very height of his powers, having crushed Austria yet again in December, while England once again stood alone against him. In this context, abolition looks more like a spiritual insurance policy than "the most altruistic act since Christ's crucifixion," which is how one contemporary described it.[54] All this suggests that religion was indeed the driving force behind the final act of abolition, but not religion of the humanitarian type that is normally credited. What in particular stands out is the deep-seated ambivalence with which contemporaries regarded the issue. Perhaps the 2007 remembrances hit the mark after all.

Notes

This chapter, a truncated version of which appeared in the *Eagle* (2007): 63–79, is based on a talk given at a conference held to commemorate abolition and to honor Clarkson and Wilberforce at St. John's College, Cambridge, in February 2007. Since then the afterhistory of abolition has been interestingly described in John Oldfield, *Chords of Freedom: Commemoration, Ritual and British Transatlantic Slavery* (Manchester: Manchester University Press, 2007).

1. For an account of more than one hundred commemorative events in Whitehaven, Manchester, Wisbech, Bristol, and many other parts of Britain, see the guidebook produced by Anti-slavery International, Thomas Clarkson House, the Stubble Yard, Broomgrove Road, London SW9 9TL.

2. William Hague, *William Wilberforce: The Life of the Great Anti-Slave Trade Campaigner* (London: HarperPress, 2007); Stephen Tomkins, *William Wilberforce: A Biography* (Oxford: Lion Hudson, 2007); Kevin Belmonte, *William Wilberforce: A Hero for Humanity* (Grand Rapids, MI: Zondervan, 2007); Belmonte, *A Journey through the Life of William Wilberforce* (Green Forest, AR: New Leaf, 2007); Eric Metaxas, *Amazing Grace: William Wilberforce and the Heroic Campaign to End Slavery* (San Francisco: HarperSan Francisco, 2007); John Piper, *Amazing Grace in the Life of William Wilberforce* (Wheaton, IL: Crossway, 2006); Henry Wheeler, *The Slaves' Champion: The Life, Deeds, and Historical Days of William Wilberforce* (Green Forest, AR: New Leaf, 2007); Andrew Edwards and Fleur Thornton, *William Wilberforce: The Millionaire Child Who Worked So Hard to Win the Freedom of African Slaves* (Leominster: Day One, 2006). See also William Wilberforce, *Real Christianity: A Nation Was Blind until One Man Made Them See*, ed. Bob Beltz (Ventura, CA: Regal Books, 2007).

3. Unsurprisingly, Agbetu's protest was dealt with indulgently by the clerical bouncers on duty, notwithstanding their fears of danger to members of the royal family, the episcopate, and Parliament. According to a report in the *Times*, Westminster Abbey officials, while regretting that the outburst had interrupted the flow of "a deeply meaningful service," nevertheless claimed that "in such, fortunately rare, circumstances it is sensible to allow people to speak for a short time before inviting them to leave—if necessary with some assistance." *Times* (London), 28 March 2007, 23.

4. *Times,* 10 February 2007, 16.

5. Bro. K. Bangarah, "Will the Real William Wilberforce Please Stand Up?" *Pambazuka News,* February–March 2007.

6. Yasmin Alibhai Brown, "At Last, the National Conscience Is Awake," *Independent* (London), 27 November 2006.

7. Martin Kettle, "The Story of Empire Is Not One of Unalloyed Shame," *Guardian* (London), 31 March 2007, 35.

8. Gillian Reynolds, "Slavery—A Topic That Makes Everyone Angry," *Daily Telegraph* (London), 27 March 2007, B15.

9. Ken Livingstone, 21 March 2007, as reported in *Guardian,* 24 March 2007, 12.

10. *Observer* (London), 26 November 2006, 1, 10.

11. *Independent,* 7 February 2007.

12. *Times,* 23 October 1905, 10.

13. W. E. H. Lecky, *History of European Morals* (London: Longmans, Green, 1884), 153; Lecky, *A History of England in the Eighteenth Century* (London: Longmans, Green, 1892), 370–71.

14. J. L. Le B. Hammond, *Charles James Fox: A Political Study* (London: Methuen, 1903), 234.

15. Élie Halévy, *England in 1815*, trans. E. I. Watkin and D. A. Barker (London: T. Fisher Unwin, 1924), 459; Reginald Coupland. *Wilberforce: A Narrative* (Oxford: Clarendon Press, 1923); Coupland, *The British Anti-slavery Movement* (London: T. Butterworth, 1933).

16. *Times*, 13 July 1930, 8; 29 July 1933, 13.

17. For a sophisticated attempt based on parliamentary speeches, see Seymour Drescher, "People and Parliament: The Rhetoric of the British Slave Trade," *Journal of Interdisciplinary History* 20, no. 4 (1990): 561–80.

18. Firstly and most famously, C. L. R. James, *The Black Jacobins: Toussaint l'Ouverture and the San Domingo Revolution* (London: Secker and Warburg, 1938); more recently, Michael Duffy, "The French Revolution and British Attitudes to the British West Indian Colonies," in *A Turbulent Time: The French Revolution and the Greater Caribbean*, ed. David Gaspar and David Geggus (Bloomington: Indiana University Press, 1997), 78–101.

19. W. B. Hamilton, as quoted in Roger Anstey, *The Atlantic Slave Trade and British Abolition, 1760–1810* (London: Macmillan, 1975), 399n.

20. Stephen, an evangelical lawyer and member of the London Abolition Committee, liaised with the Pitt and Grenville governments in the months leading up to abolition.

21. St. John's College Library, Cambridge (hereafter cited as SJCL), Clarkson 2/21, Clarkson to John Wadkin, 7 April 1806.

22. Anstey, *Atlantic Slave Trade*, 407–8.

23. According to a contemporary survey, 172 members of the new parliament were "staunch friends" of abolition, 69 were "friendly," 100 "adverse," and the rest "doubtful." British Library, Holland House Papers, Add. MS 51917 (1806); Stephen Farrell, "Contrary to the Principles of Justice, Humanity and Sound Policy: The Slave Trade, Parliamentary Politics and the Abolition Act, 1807," in *The British Slave Trade: Abolition, Parliament and People*, ed. Farrell, Melanie Unwin, and James Walvin (Edinburgh: Edinburgh University Press, 2007), 141–202.

24. The film *Amazing Grace* was mocked in some quarters for allotting Fox a starring role in the crucial abolitionist debate of 23 February 1807, even though he had in reality died five months previously. On the other hand, if a filmmaker is ever to be allowed any poetic license, this piece of liberty taking seems justified. Clarkson assured a friend that "Fox, during his illness, never forgot the Abolition. He declared often in the midst of his pains, that the measure lay nearer to his heart than any other, even nearer to it than the Peace, which he was then endeavouring to make for Europe." SJCL, Clarkson, 2/25, Clarkson to John Wadkin, late 1806. The deathbed bit might of course be mythical, but Clarkson was no sentimentalist and the substance of his remarks seems justified. Indeed, a desire to do "what Charles would have wanted" may well have swelled abolitionist numbers in the division lobbies.

25. SJCL, Clarkson, 2/19 (7), Clarkson to Joseph Taylor, 26 January 1807.

26. SJCL, Clarkson, 1/1, Thomas Clarkson, MS diary.

27. Seymour Drescher, *Capitalism and Anti-Slavery: British Mobilization in Comparative Perspective* (Houndmills, Basingstoke: Macmillan, 1986), 70–84; J. R. Oldfield, *Popular Politics and British Anti-slavery: The Mobilisation of Public Opinion against the Slave Trade, 1787–1807* (Manchester: Manchester University Press, 1998), 96–124.

28. Adam Hochschild, *Bury the Chains: The British Struggle to Abolish Slavery* (London: Macmillan, 2005), 1–8.

29. Christopher Leslie Brown, "Evangelicals and the Origins of Anti-slavery in England," in *Oxford Dictionary of National Biography*, ed. Lawrence Goldman (Oxford: Oxford University Press, 2007), http://www.oxforddnb.com/view/theme/96075. See

also Brown, *Moral Capital: Foundations of British Abolitionism* (Chapel Hill: University of North Carolina Press, 2006).

30. Clare Midgley, *Women against Slavery: The British Campaigns, 1780–1870* (London: Routledge, 1992), 17–18, 51–56.

31. It has been calculated that as many as three hundred thousand British families boycotted West Indian produce. Such direct actions almost certainly had more to do with spontaneous religious impulses than with so-called civil society.

32. "It is conceivable that another advocate could have been found in Parliament.... But another Clarkson is unimaginable." Ellen Gibson Wilson, *Thomas Clarkson: A Biography* (Houndmills, Basingstoke: Macmillan, 1989), 1. For attempts by Wilberforce's sons to belittle Clarkson's contribution, see Hochschild, *Bury the Chains,* 349–52.

33. Robert Isaac Wilberforce and Samuel Wilberforce, *The Life of William Wilberforce,* 5 vols. (London: John Murray, 1838), 1:343.

34. A few recent historians have looked to revive Williams's main premise—that the slave trade had begun to be an "economic impediment" to the mother country. If proven, the thesis would damage Drescher's arguments, but they would not necessarily establish the case that British abolitionists acted out of material self-interest. See Selwyn H. H. Carrington, "*Capitalism and Slavery* and Caribbean Historiography: An Evaluation," *Journal of African American History* 88, no. 3 (2003): 304–12.

35. Seymour Drescher, *Econocide: British Slavery in the Era of Abolition* (Pittsburgh: University of Pittsburg Press, 1977). It is sometimes argued, in response to Drescher, that British merchants and manufacturers must have foreseen the long-term decline of the slave trade, what with native revolts in the Caribbean and the moral outcry against it at home. However, businessmen do not and probably cannot put long-term considerations above immediate ones. Such awareness might well have led them to diversify their interests, but not to foreclose on a flourishing branch of trade.

36. *Sunday Times* (London), 25 March 2007.

37. And not solely out of parochial rivalry, but in a sincere attempt to argue for the moral superiority of "organic" manufacturing industry to "speculative" and impersonal commerce. Rachel Martin, "The Manchester Business Community and Antislavery, 1787–1833" (PhD diss., University of Cambridge, 2002), 52–113.

38. It was suggested above that in themselves the slave revolts were more likely to have stiffened parliamentarians against abolition, but there is one rather subtle reason for thinking that they might have helped the cause. The British West Indian planters had had an ambiguous position in eighteenth-century society, being half landlords (with the additional kudos of a feudal hold over human bodies) and half merchants, profiting from trade in sugar and cotton. The slave revolts might well have undermined their claim to be legitimate landlords, and might therefore have made it easier for a parliament of landlords to turn against them.

39. In maintaining such a comforting self-image, it helped that the most brutal territorial expansion in the 1790s and 1800s was being conducted, not by the British state, but by the East India Company. This meant the *state* could play the goody-goody, as it did with the evangelicals' other great legislative achievement, the "pious clause" of 1813, whereby India was opened up to missionaries. Boyd Hilton, *A Mad, Bad, and Dangerous People? England 1783–1846* (Oxford: Clarendon Press, 2006), 223–51.

40. Especially given that Grenville was strongly opposed to imperial adventures.

41. Hannah More to Lady Middleton, 10 September 1787, quoted in Brown, *Moral Capital,* 445; Wilson, *Thomas Clarkson,* 145.

42. For discussions on this topic, I am grateful to Dr. Gareth Atkins of Magdalene College, Cambridge.

43. Boyd Hilton, *The Age of Atonement: The Influence of Evangelicalism on Social and Economic Thought, 1795–1865* (Oxford: Clarendon Press, 1988), 115–62.

44. William Pitt, *The Speeches of the Right Honourable William Pitt in the House of Commons,* ed. W. S. Hathaway, 2nd ed. (London: Longman, Hurst, Rees, and Orme, 1808), 1:385–88, 396 (2 April 1792); William Cobbett, ed., *The Parliamentary History of England, from the earliest period to the year 1803* (London: T. C. Hansard), 28:75 (12 May 1789), 29:344–45 (19 April 1791), 30:518 (26 February 1793).

45. Joanna Innes, "Politics and Morals: The Reformation of Manners Movement in Later Eighteenth-Century England," in *The Transformation of Political Culture: England and Germany in the Late Eighteenth Century,* ed. Eckhart Hellmuth (Oxford: Oxford University Press, 1990), 57–118.

46. Premillenarian religion did not begin to influence conservative circles until the later 1820s. It might have been a factor behind the abolition of colonial slavery in 1833, since such calamities as the return of cholera to these shores two years earlier was frequently blamed on national sins.

47. Denis Gray, *Spencer Perceval: The Evangelical Prime Minister, 1762–1812* (Manchester: Manchester University Press, 1963), 45–46.

48. Cobbett, *Parliamentary History,* 32:750–51 (18 February 1796).

49. William Cobbett, ed., *Cobbett's Parliamentary Debates,* (London: R. Bagshaw), 8:670–71 (5 February 1807).

50. [James Stephen], *The Dangers of the Country: By the Author of* War in Disguise (London: J. Butterworth and J. Hatchard, 1807), 115–16.

51. Cobbett, *Parliamentary History,* 35:868 (27 May 1802).

52. Cobbett, *Parliamentary Debates,* 9:61 (6 March 1807).

53. For example, by pointing out that "the era in which the slave trade was authorized and encouraged by the British legislature was one of distinguished prosperity." George Hibbert and Captain Herbert, in Cobbett, *Parliamentary Debates,* 9:115, 134 (16 March 1807).

54. David Brion Davis, *Slavery and Human Progress* (New York: Oxford University Press, 1984), 116–53.

THREE

Empire without America
British Plans for Africa in the Era of the American Revolution

CHRISTOPHER LESLIE BROWN

BRITISH ENTERPRISE in Africa still fares poorly in the new scholarship on the expanding empire of the late eighteenth century. The spirit
of integration that is meant to guide the new Atlantic history has yet
to inspire sustained engagement with British ambitions and activities
on the eastern side of the Atlantic. We have an increasing number of
works that try to link the histories of Britain, Ireland, North America,
and the Caribbean. But the British experience in Africa rarely claims
attention outside the traditional focus on the contours of the Atlantic
slave trade. That scholarship swells and deepens at an impressive rate
but progresses, typically, on a separate track from the renaissance in
British Atlantic and British imperial history, and concentrates usually
on questions restricted to its particular concerns. The cliometric staples
that preoccupy slave trade scholars—directions and flows, volumes
and prices, sex ratios and mortality rates—leave few opportunities for
comparative work with other areas of British enterprise, outside the
study of migration. To appreciate the range of British ambitions in the
eighteenth century, we have to go back more than forty years, to Philip
Curtin's *Image of Africa* or Vincent Harlow's *Founding of the Second British
Empire.* On the character of British outposts on the coast at midcentury,
the most comprehensive studies remain essays in the *Cambridge History of the British Empire,* now at least sixty years old, or the even more
venerable research by Eveline C. Martin on the Company of Merchants

Trading to Africa.[1] More recent overviews, the new *Oxford History of the British Empire* most notably, neglect these topics entirely.[2] There are exceptions, of course. David Hancock, for example, puts a Bance Island slaving fort at the center of a far broader story about merchants and trade in the eighteenth century.[3] Emma Christopher has described the experience of slave ship sailors during the months that they spent on the West African coast. And there is the work of Randy Sparks on the Robin Johns of Efik, in the Bight of Biafra, slave traders betrayed into slavery in Dominica who managed an escape to Bristol before returning to their home and to the slaving businesses they temporarily had lost. Certain Africanists have begun to place their subject in an Atlantic context—Michael Gomez, Robert Harms, Robin Law, Paul Lovejoy, Kristin Mann, and Joseph Miller in particular.[4] Nonetheless, most scholars of the eighteenth-century British Empire still tend to treat the British in Africa as a wholly separate subject.

To a point, this is how it should be. British enterprise in Africa was different from British enterprise in the Americas or, for that matter, British enterprise in India. There was little migration, very small settlements, few missionaries, limited power, minimal property, no colonial government. One business predominated—the trade in human bodies—which was sufficiently unique in organization and in its moral implications to demand a distinct historical scholarship. The story of the British in Africa is, first and foremost, the story of the Atlantic slave trade. Yet, the obvious and important differences between British trade in Africa and British enterprise elsewhere must not blind us to promising opportunities for comparison. At present, for example, we know almost nothing about the small garrisons sent to man the slave forts on what the British knew as the Gold Coast and Slave Coast during the eighteenth century. And too little attention has been given to early British ambitions to capture West African territory. Most scholars know of the challenges the British government faced in governing the territories captured from France, Spain, and the rulers of the Mughal Empire following the Seven Years' War. But even specialists sometimes forget that in 1765 Britain also established a colony in West Africa, more than two decades before the better-known settlement for black loyalists at Sierra Leone. Parliament assigned to this new province of Senegambia a governor, council, courts, and constitution in the same years that it also authorized rather different governments for the Floridas, Quebec, and the Ceded Islands in the West Indies. British appointees conspired to transform Senegambia into personal fiefdoms in the same years that British speculators schemed to seize the new lands and revenue available in the Caribbean, India, and North America.[5] There is an overlooked history here, distinct from the history of the slave trade, that resembles in striking ways activity elsewhere in the eighteenth-century empire.

The Senegambia colony garners little interest because, in part, it was an abysmal failure. The British exercised only nominal control over the region, and only for twenty-five years. Like other eighteenth-century attempts to exercise authority in Africa, it would seem a mere curiosity, of no more than antiquarian interest. It happens that such ambitions would matter a great deal, in time, though in an unforeseen and un-intended way. Yet subsequent influence is not the only measure of historical importance. The history of failure can be as instructive as the record of success, if only for what it reveals about the distance between ambitions and capacities, if only for reconstructing the mental world of "projectors" and entrepreneurs who wished to reorient the direction of British overseas enterprise. The hoped-for empire, what speculators en-visioned, depended only loosely on the "facts" of empire, what we know as the geography and chronology of imperial practice. Frequently, what some intended exceeded what any could achieve. Limited footholds for trade often inspired hopes of dominion. Fantasies of direct rule, at times, long preceded the actual command of territory. This was as true for the African coast throughout the eighteenth century as for Guiana and Providence Island in the seventeenth century, or the Floridas and the Ohio valley after the Seven Years' War.

For all the wealth the slave trade produced, some familiar with the coast thought the potential for commerce with Africa scarcely tapped. This view prevailed particularly among those unsuccessful in the com-petition to procure slaves for the American colonies. In sporadic fits of enthusiasm, the Royal African Company asked its agents to promote the export trades in cotton, indigo, pepper, and medicines. The company at times took the further step of sending out to the coast seeds, mills, and technicians to set up plantations of its own. The Royal African Com-pany cultivated indigo along the Sherbro River in the 1690s and again, with brief success, at Cape Coast Castle early in the eighteenth century. These modest achievements owed much to the initiative of Sir Dalby Thomas, the energetic and ambitious chief factor at Cape Coast Castle from 1703 and probably the first British official to espouse agricultural "improve-ment" in West Africa. Before his death, in 1711, he wrote officials in

London about supplementing the several acres of indigo at Cape Coast with corn, cotton, and sugar worked by slave labor, in the hope that, in time, the region could support a British colony. These ideas continued to circulate long after Thomas left the scene. In 1715 the Royal African Company funded a short-lived project to seek gold mines near the coast. In 1718 they considered manufacturing rum. Exploration of the African interior figured in the fiction of Daniel Defoe, who published two defenses of the Royal African Company in the 1710s and sent his fictional Captain Singleton on a transcontinental trek through southern Africa. James Brydges, the Duke of Chandos and a prominent voice in company affairs, renewed plantation schemes a decade later, convinced that Africa could "become as beneficial to England as America is to Spain." Under his leadership, in the early 1720s, the Royal African Company sent out to Cape Coast Castle both gins to foster an export trade in cotton and teams of Cornish miners to draw ores from Akan goldfields.[6]

These projects, both real and imagined, were doomed by the inability of the British to establish ascendancy anywhere in Africa. Like other Europeans, British visitors suffered from high mortality rates on the coast. Military and political authority, moreover, rested unambiguously with African elites. Until the capture of Senegal in 1758, the British possessed no territory in Africa. Factors, soldiers, traders, and artisans in the hundreds occupied the scattered forts during the eighteenth century. But these establishments were little more than trading posts held at the pleasure of local rulers, to whom the British paid tribute or annual rent. The British garrisons kept the commerce open to British ships. African political and commercial elites in the coastal towns, however, prevented the formation of sizable British settlements, an opposition that the slave traders were neither equipped nor inclined to overcome. The hundreds of independent British merchants who outfitted ships for Africa found returns in the slave trade far more enticing than uncertain long-term investments in commercial agriculture, where they lacked secure claims to land.[7]

The Royal African Company, in theory, was better suited to attempt projects unlikely to yield quick returns. But its weak political standing in England, its outsize debt, and unreliable agents hindered even its modest attempts to generate a trade in staple crops. Its successor, the Company of Merchants Trading to Africa, suffered as well from limited funds. Even more, though, it never established more than nominal control over its employees on the coast. The organizations responsible for overseeing the Africa trade struggled to maintain the forts, provision the garrisons, and instill a semblance of discipline. They stood no chance of setting up plantations in Africa on their own.[8] The Board of Trade added to these difficulties after 1750 by discouraging private efforts to plant British colonists anywhere in Africa. In 1752 the board forbade officials at the Gold Coast from reviving cotton and indigo plantations on the grounds of Cape Coast Castle, in part because cultivation in Africa could harm the profitability of colonial settlements in the Americas.

This restricted if judicious definition of national interest infuriated those enamored with grandiose fantasies of establishing British imperial power in Africa. Students of the eighteenth-century empire know Malachy Postlethwayt as the chief propagandist for the Royal African Company and, as such, a leading apologist for the Atlantic slave trade in the 1740s. Few, though, have noticed his more general commitment to extending the reach of the British state deep into the African hinterland, or the consequences of that commitment to his evolving view of the Atlantic slave trade, a shift evident in his later publications.[9] Postlethwayt believed that great wealth awaited the nation that secured for itself a commerce in the natural products of Africa. For this reason, he thought it was a serious mistake to allow the independent merchants to monopolize the Africa trade. If these individual traders succeeded well in securing profits for themselves and conveying Africans to the Americas, they had not done and would not do enough to advance the nation's strategic interests in Africa as a whole. The state, he argued, needed to promote what later generations would come to know as legitimate commerce, in particular by deepening official investment in the Royal African Company. Its declining fortunes he regarded as symptomatic of a more general failure among politicians to grasp the national importance of the Africa trade or its possibilities.

Postlethwayt had a personal interest in keeping the Royal African Company afloat. He served on its Court of Assistants for more than a dozen years before it was disbanded in 1750. In three increasingly alarmist pamphlets published in the 1740s, he warned that abandoning the company would mean throwing the slave trade into the arms of European competitors. As it was, he stated, the exclusive privileges enjoyed by the Compagne des Indes enabled France to supply its colonies with slaves at a cheaper price, permitting the cultivation of sugar at a lower cost, allowing French sugar to undersell British sugar in European markets and, in turn strengthening the French merchant marine. While France kept the purchase price of slaves low by restricting the number of French ships on the Africa coast, British merchants drove up their own costs through reckless bidding wars on each cargo. Only the Royal African Company, Postlethwayt insisted, could discourage such free-for-alls by negotiating for all British traders a set price from African suppliers. Furthermore, only sufficient funding for the company's forts in Africa could keep the French from encroaching on British trade along the Gambia River and prevent the Dutch from seizing control of traffic along the Gold Coast. Postlethwayt accepted that independent merchants would predominate in the carrying trade across the Atlantic. He proposed for the Royal African Company a sphere of activity better suited to its coastal establishment. In addition to warehousing captives for British merchants, he thought the forts should serve as stations from which to carry "*British* produce and Manufactures into the very heart of Africa, where they have not yet reached." This was a task that only a joint-stock company could perform. And the prospects, he added parenthetically, were limitless. "It is certainly our fault," he declared, "if we do not render the *African trade* as valuable to Great Britain as the *Mines of Peru, Mexico,* and the *Brazils* are to the *Spanish* and *Portuguese.*"[10]

Few before the American Revolution went further than Postlethwayt in imagining West Africa as a future seat of British power. The idea of a British empire in Africa figured prominently in his several publications on trade and commercial policy, even after the Royal African Company lost its charter. Increasingly, he looked with hope to the East India Company, which already had routine access to the textiles most valued by African consumers. Even more, Postlethwayt explained, the East India Company possessed the capital required to build forts and factories in the interior and, thereby, forge alliances with "negro princes." In time, he predicted, trade with Africa would surpass commerce with Asia and America. Postlethwayt described Africans as "savages." But he also thought their extensive trading networks evidence of great wealth and stable polities. Commerce, Postlethwayt insisted, would civilize Africans, as it had American Indians and, in turn, instill a dependence on British goods. Sending out British colonists to the coast in substantial numbers would inspire the peoples of Africa to embrace European tastes and manners. They would "become so civilized as to clothe, and live more and more according to the European mode." The desire for imported manufacturers, in turn, would move Africans to offer up precious commodities and clear the way, on their continent, for the cultivation of crops valued in European markets. Postlethwayt waxed rhapsodic contemplating the possibilities. "None except the Portuguese," he remarked, "have made any use of all the land, the fruitful soil lies waste, a very established country, pleasant vallies, banks of rivers, spacious plains capable of cultivation to unspeakable benefit, in all probability will remain fallow and unnoticed."[11] Postlethwayt considered the West African hinterland a vast unimproved common. His plans for commercial agriculture represented a grand scheme of enclosure.

Such ambitions seemed less far-fetched at the end of the Seven Years' War, after the British navy secured the Senegal River trade from the French. Among commentators on empire, the new province of Senegambia, like the new territories in North America and the Caribbean, generated great expectations. The new province seemed to allow for the founding of a permanent beachhead on the African coast. Within a year of his arrival, Governor Charles O'Hara had devised plans to establish white colonists several hundred miles up the Senegal River, near what he thought to be extensive gold mines and "prodigious quantities of Rice, Wax, Cotton, Indigo, & Tobacco." His successor, Matthias McNamara, would try to arrange for a colony of convicts along the Senegal in 1776. Among British commentators as well, the new colony of Senegambia, like the new territories in North America and the Caribbean, generated grand (even grandiose) fantasies of imperial greatness. Thomas Whateley thought it opened the way for an "Improvement in Power, in Commerce, and in Settlement, to a Degree, perhaps, of Colonization." Arthur Young predicted the introduction of "European customs and refinements" to create a demand for British manufactures in what most regarded as an immensely populous region. John Campbell emphasized the commodities that might be acquired from Africa and proposed encouraging "the natives" to settle near the forts and cultivate export corps. O'Hara predicted that in time Senegambia would become "one of the richest Colonies, belonging to his Majesty," that British colonists would "extend over every part of this Continent that was worth while to settle."[12]

A British empire in Africa, in the late eighteenth century, was more easily imagined than accomplished, however. The eighteen years of British "rule" in Senegambia turned out to be an unqualified failure for the British. Without colonists, Senegambia was a colony only in name. The elaborate constitution proved wholly inappropriate for a province that never boasted more than a few dozen British residents. Charles O'Hara, governor from 1765 to 1776, moreover, had little interest in and no skill for civil administration. He managed to increase the volume of the slave trade by instigating wars upriver. But because he terrorized the francophone African Creoles residing along the Senegal, Britain never reaped the full benefits of the trade in staple crops. Dissension, backbiting, and corruption plagued the first British "province" in Africa. Few in England mourned the loss when the French captured Fort Lewis in 1779, during the American Revolution.[13] The settlement did succeed, however, in producing a constituency in Britain for the colonization of Africa. Despite the obvious hazards, despite the undistinguished results of the first experiment, those who had resided in Senegambia for any length of time returned to Britain convinced that on the African coast, if given another chance, they could build a fortune for themselves, and perhaps for the nation too.

The British defeat in the American War of Independence gave the Senegambia veterans additional arguments for a second attempt at colonization. The familiar lures remained: the mysteries of the unexplored interior, the likely market in Africa for British goods, the potential for commodity production in a tropical climate. What made the proposals of the 1780s different, what accounts for their quantity and variety, were the still uncertain consequences of American independence. The loss of the thirteen North American colonies threatened to rob the empire of American consumers, a vast supply of staple crops, and the principal source of foodstuffs for Caribbean plantations. In the end, of course, American independence proved less detrimental to the imperial economy than feared at the time. After the America war, British Atlantic trade would enter a period of explosive growth. At its close, though, no one could know what the future held for British trade. It seemed possible that Britain would need to look elsewhere for markets, for commodities, for provisions to supply the West Indian colonies. If the American rebellion succeeded, Senegambia governor John Clarke predicted in 1777, "the remaining Provinces of the empire may rise in their Claims to public attention." The Gambia River district, declared the opposition gadfly Temple Luttrell in 1777, might provide "every valuable production we receive from America." "With proper care," he argued, "the advancement of the general trade to Africa" might "save the *debris* of this once mighty empire, when America shall be no longer ours." "The improvement of your marine nurseries and an extension of your commerce to Africa," he told the House of Commons, "might yet maintain the British realm in splendor and prosperity, when her colonies on the other side of the Atlantic are totally separated from her empire."[14]

Empire in Africa, several entrepreneurs agreed, could compensate for losses in America. Between 1783 and 1788, more than a dozen schemes materialized to transform or expand British enterprise on the African coast. Returned Senegambia administrators came forward with plans to colonize the Gambia River district, to which Britain retained exclusive trading rights at the peace. The British government struggled during and after the American war to find a place to dump felons sentenced to transportation. Charles O'Hara led a delegation to Whitehall that proposed a convict colony several hundred miles up the Gambia River. A rival, Edward Morse, bombarded the government in the same years with schemes to populate the region with British settlers and diversify the export trade. He stressed not only the likely take in staple crops. A colony on the Gambia, he argued, might also provision the Caribbean islands with "lumber, corn, and other Necessaries which heretofore they received from America." In a similar report, Daniel Houghton, a returned Senegambia soldier and future Gambia explorer, urged that Africa could supply crops no longer available within British territories. He recommended particularly the great quantity and high quality of Gambia cotton as a substitute for the plantations lost with the return of Tobago to France at the 1783 peace.[15]

Several scholars have discussed these proposals—Philip Curtin and Vincent Harlow, most notably—but the measure of their importance, wrongly, has been tied to their very limited impact on government priorities or imperial practice. The state, of course, made almost no attempt to establish sovereignty in West Africa during the 1780s, or many decades after. Holding European rivals at bay, keeping trade open to British merchants, minimizing costs—these were the primary concerns. Otherwise, the state delegated oversight to the slave traders, who cared not at all for the promotion of colonies or commercial agriculture. This hands-off policy resembled the stance government had taken toward the East India Company. But, because of its sizable revenues and, after 1757, large territorial possessions, politicians had come to take a persistent interest in the affairs of the East India Company by the 1780s. The African trade, by contrast, failed to win the sustained attention of a particular office or official. Always, ministers of state treated British posts in West Africa like a backwater. There was little in the way of policy or strategy, rarely evidence of vision or initiative. An ambitious few outside the halls of power formulated plans for a British empire in Africa. But where decisions were made, conveying slaves to the American colonies remained the leading concern.

Ironically, it took ethical concerns and moral aims, more than a desire for wealth or national power, to generate broad interest in schemes promoting commercial expansion in Africa. The prospect of reordering the African trade would prove most compelling to the early opponents of colonial slavery, to idealists looking for ways to strike down the plantation complex. Students of British abolitionism typically describe the movement as the result of religious beliefs, philosophical ideas, political agendas, and reform networks, sometimes, too, as a consequence of class interests and class conflict. But not enough has been said about the role of confidence, about the heightened faith in the possibility of reform, about the ways prospects for success enabled attempts to succeed. To act, individuals had to believe, beforehand, that acting might work. Overlooking this fact has helped scholars miss the critical, if almost entirely accidental, role of commercial speculators in the rise of abolitionism. The early abolitionists needed what entrepreneurs possessed in abundance: the capacity to imagine the future as radically different from the past, a vision for enterprise in Africa centered on agricultural exports, the ability to argue in the language of national interest. The speculators' ambitions helped the opponents of the slave trade see possibilities they otherwise might have missed. If "legitimate trade" with Africa held genuine promise, then emancipation or abolition would pose little threat to commerce and empire, indeed antislavery might even open the way to an even more lucrative branch of overseas trade.

One example must suffice to illustrate the crosscurrents at work. The "traffic" in "rational beings" will continue until the "pecuniary interests of Europeans can be diverted into another channel." So a frustrated John Fothergill decided in the late 1770s, after a dozen years of unsuccessful lobbying. Years before, the Quaker elder had written optimistically of instituting a settlement for liberated slaves in the Americas, perhaps at Tobago or St. Vincent's. But the loss of the thirteen colonies had discouraged state intervention in colonial affairs, forcing him, and others, to shelve schemes for a comprehensive emancipation. "It was not a time," he confessed to Granville Sharp in 1779, "to hope much good to liberty." Yet Fothergill was a scientist, as well as an abolitionist, and thus often in the company of cosmopolitan men preoccupied with experiments in social improvement and the promotion of useful knowledge. In collaboration with Joseph Banks and others, Fothergill sent a botanist, Henry Smeathman, out to the Grain Coast in 1771 to study the flora and fauna.[16] Like other Europeans in Africa not involved in the slave trade, Smeathman became entranced by the prospects for agricultural development and the opportunities for self-promotion. He returned to England in 1780 with elaborate plans to colonize Sierra Leone with black loyalists, redeemed slaves, and white craftsmen, who, he declared, in three or four decades would transform the entire continent, by teaching Africans better habits, by displaying to them "good government and education." Above all, Smeathman wanted to make a profit. To support the scheme, he lined up London investors, who cared not at all about slavery but a good deal about the potential returns in African cotton.[17] Fothergill, Sharp, and others, though, envisioned such a settlement as a beachhead for civilization, as a way to reconceive labor, commodity production, the British presence in Africa.[18]

We know now that colonization schemes worked poorly as antislavery initiatives. The Sierra Leone settlement, launched in 1787, nearly equaled the disaster of Senegambia.[19] At the time, though, no one knew which method of attacking slavery, if any, would succeed. Every imaginable way of ending the slave system, to some degree, looked unpromising. What had become clear to moralists was the wisdom of investing in the vision, if not the schemes, of entrepreneurs like Henry Smeathman. In the early 1780s an unusual alliance of interests took shape. Idealists began to describe slave trade abolition not only as morally just but also as the best way to foster legitimate commerce. Ending the slave trade need not result in the sacrifice of shipping, commerce, and revenue, they learned to argue. Instead, Britain should encourage agriculture in Africa, reduce dependence on slave labor in the Caribbean, and replace the Atlantic slave trade with a shuttle traffic from Africa to Britain in staple crops. "It will scarcely be believed," one commentator wrote in 1785, "that a commercial nation extended itself so strenuously to destroy and exterminate those people, who might have been excellent customers." James Ramsay, who had opposed American independence, now thought it offered Britain a chance to start anew. He hoped energies would shift to Africa, where the nation, he explained, could enjoy an extensive trade without the expense of overpriced Caribbean sugar and without the unpaid debts of West Indian planters. If the sun was setting on empire in the west, in the east there dawned opportunities for new enterprise, unburdened by rebellious British colonists and untainted by a dependence on slave labor.[20]

Within five years, by the late 1780s, the superiority of legitimate commerce had become fundamental to antislavery argument. A black abolitionist cataloged for Charles Jenkinson, the first minister of trade, the many reasons to exploit the natural bounty of the African soil. "A commercial intercourse with Africa," Olaudah Equiano explained, "opens an inexhaustible Source of Wealth to the manufacturing interest of Great Britain: and to all which the Slave trade is a physical obstruction." "The Population, Bowels, and surface of Africa abound in valuable and useful returns: the hidden treasures of Countries will be brought to light and Circulation." "Industry, Enterprise, and Mining will have proportionally their full Scope, as they civilize. In a Word, it lays open an endless Field of Commerce to the British Manufacturer and Merchant Adventurer."[21]

In retrospect, Equiano's enthusiasm for British expansion into Africa is deeply ironic, if not tragic. Later generations would have their doubts about extractive economies and commercial dependence. But few, in the 1780s, including Equiano, could anticipate the inequalities that would ensue from the ideas all abolitionists embraced. And if foreseen, no one in the eighteenth century had a language with which to critique the practice of informal empire.[22] The abolitionists did not intend to exchange one form of exploitation for another. They took up the ideas of profiteers to make slave trade abolition attractive, to win support from skeptical politicians and an uncertain public. In the process, though, they succeeded where men like Postlethwayt had consistently failed, in popularizing the idea of enhancing British power on the coast. Postlethwayt had been sure that opening new channels of commerce with Africa would aid merchants and the state. He could not have guessed that the opponents of the slave trade would make this case more effectively than those, like himself, concerned, above all, with the assertion of imperial authority. In the eighteenth century abolitionists would need the dreams of men like Postlethwayt to make the case for slave trade abolition. In the nineteenth century entrepreneurs would use the sanction provided by abolitionism to justify incursions on the African mainland, to propagate Christianity, Commerce, and Civilization.[23]

Historians long have understood that, in the words of one study, antislavery "contributed one major impulse leading to British imperialism in Africa."[24] We also, now, can stand the familiar argument on its head. The dream of exploiting the African soil—dreams that intensified at the end of the American war—contributed one major impulse leading to British abolitionism. Perhaps we can go further. The movement could not have begun in the absence of those ambitions, at least as it did and when it did—sufficient reason alone to revisit the eighteenth-century British encounter with Africa, and in much greater depth.

Notes

1. Philip Curtin, *The Image of Africa: British Ideas and Action, 1780–1850* (Madison: University of Wisconsin Press, 1964); Vincent Harlow, *New Continents and Changing Values*, vol. 2 of *The Founding of the Second British Empire, 1763–1793* (London: Longmans, Green, 1964), 280–93; Eveline C. Martin, "The English Slave Trade and the African Settlements," in *The Cambridge History of the British Empire*, vol. 1, *The Old Empire, from Beginnings to 1783*, ed. Holland Rose, A. P. Newton, and E. A. Benians (Cambridge: Cambridge University Press, 1929), 437–59; E. Martin, *The British West African Settlements, 1750–1821: A Study of Local Administration* (London: Longmans, Green, 1927). Also see the emerging work of Ty M. Reese, "Liberty, Insolence, and Rum: Cape Coast Castle and the American Revolution," *Itinerario* 28, no. 3 (2004): 18–37; Reese, "Sheep in the Jaws of So Many Ravenous Wolves: The Slave Trade and Anglican Missionary Activity at Cape Coast Castle, 1752–1816," *Journal of Religion in Africa* 34, no. 3 (2004): 348–72; Reese, "The Drudgery of the Slave Trade: Labor at Cape Coast Castle, 1750–1790," in *The Atlantic Economy during the Seventeenth and Eighteenth Centuries: Organization, Operation, Practice, and Personnel*, ed. Peter A. Coclanis (Columbia: University of South Carolina Press, 2005), 277–96.

2. This is a more general shortcoming of the otherwise wide-ranging work on the eighteenth-century empire by P. J. Marshall, the volume's editor. Note also, in this vein, the almost complete silence about enterprise in Africa in H. V. Bowen, *Elites, Enterprise, and the Making of the British Overseas Empire, 1688–1775* (London: St. Martin's, 1996).

3. David Hancock, *Citizens of the World: London Merchants and the Integration of the British Atlantic Community, 1735–1785* (Cambridge: Cambridge University Press, 1995), 1–2, 172–220; Emma Christopher, *Slave Ship Sailors and their Captive Cargoes, 1730–1807* (Cambridge: Cambridge University Press, 2006); Randy L. Sparks, *The Two Princes of Calabar: An Eighteenth-Century Atlantic Odyssey* (Cambridge, MA: Harvard University Press, 2004).

4. See, for example, Joseph C. Miller, *Way of Death: Merchant Capitalism and the Angolan Slave Trade, 1730–1830* (Madison: University of Wisconsin Press, 1988); John Thornton, *Africa and Africans in the Making of the Atlantic World* (Cambridge: Cambridge University Press, 1992); Michael A. Gomez, *Exchanging Our Country Marks: The Transformation of African Identities in the Colonial and Antebellum South* (Chapel Hill: University of North Carolina Press, 1999); Robin Law and Kristin Mann, "West Africa in the Atlantic Community: The Case of the Slave Coast," *William and Mary Quarterly* 56, no. 2 (1999): 307–34; David Richardson and Paul Lovejoy, "Trust, Pawnship, and Atlantic History: The Institutional Foundations of the Old Calabar Slave Trade," *American Historical Review* 104, no. 2 (April 1999): 333–55; Robin Law, *Ouidah: The Social History of a West African Slaving Port, 1727–1892* (Oxford: James Currey, 2004).

5. The political history of Senegambia is treated in E. Martin, *British West African Settlements*, 80–102; John M. Gray, *A History of the Gambia* (London: Frank Cass, 1940), 234–75; Frederick Madden and David Fieldhouse, eds., *Imperial Reconstruction, 1763–1840*, vol. 3 of *Select Documents on the Constitutional History of the British Empire and Commonwealth* (New York: Greenwood, 1987), 491–505.

6. David Eltis, *The Rise of African Slavery in the Americas* (Cambridge: Cambridge University Press, 2000), 241–44; Robin Law, "King Agaja of Dahomey, the Slave Trade and the Question of West African Plantations: The Embassy of Bulfinche Lambe

and Adomo Tomo in England, 1726–1732," *Journal of Imperial and Commonwealth History* 19, no. 2 (May 1991): 155–58; K. G. Davies, *The Royal African Company* (London: Longmans, 1975), 132–33, 220–21, 344–45; Walter Rodney, *A History of the Upper Guinea Coast, 1545–1800* (Oxford: Oxford University Press, 1970), 167–70; Nigel Tattersfield, *The Forgotten Trade: Comprising the Log of Daniel and Henry of 1700 and Accounts of the Slave Trade from the Minor Ports of England, 1698–1725* (London: J. Cape, 1991), 91–92; Kwame Daaku, *Trade and Politics on the Gold Coast, 1600–1720* (Oxford: Clarendon Press, 1970), 45–46; Colin Palmer, *Human Cargoes: The British Slave Trade to Spanish America, 1700–1739* (Urbana: University of Illinois Press, 1981), 36; Tim Keirn, "Daniel Defoe and the Royal African Company," *Bulletin of the Institute of Historical Research* 61 (1988), 243–47; Roxann Wheeler, *The Complexion of Race: Categories of Difference in Eighteenth-Century British Culture* (Philadelphia: University of Pennsylvania Press, 2000), 107–9; Larry Stewart, *The Rise of Public Science: Rhetoric, Technology, and Natural Philosophy in Newtonian Britain, 1660–1750* (Cambridge: Cambridge University Press, 1992), 320–24; J. E. Inikori, *The Chaining of a Continent: Export Demand for Captives and the History of Africa South of the Sahara, 1450–1870* (Mona, Jamaica: University of West Indies Press, 1992), 47–50 (Chandos, 48); Inikori, *Africans and the Industrial Revolution in England* (Cambridge: Cambridge University Press, 2002), 385–88. The account presented in this paragraph and the pages that follow touch on a vast subject that deserves a more extended discussion that it can receive here. Readers should be aware that comparable ambitions developed elsewhere in Europe during the eighteenth century, with comparably limited results. The international history of schemes for plantations, colonies, and legitimate commerce in Africa before the 1780s remains unwritten. For the Dutch, see Inikori, *Africans*, 385–88. For the French, see William B. Cohen, *The French Encounter with Africans: White Response to Blacks, 1530–1830* (Bloomington: Indiana University Press, 2003), 155–66.

7. For general statements on European vulnerability in Africa during the eighteenth century, see J. D. Fage, "African Societies and the Atlantic Slave Trade," *Past and Present* 125, no. 1 (1989): 97–115; Robin Law, "Here Is No Resisting the Country: The Realities of Power in Afro-European Relations on the West African 'Slave Coast,'" *Itinerario* 18, no. 2 (1994): 50–64. The isolated conditions endured by Britons at work on the coast are evoked in Hancock, *Citizens of the World*, 195–98, and even more recently, Emma Christopher, *Slave Ship Sailors*, 125–62. Mortality rates among Royal African Company employees are treated in K. G. Davies, "The Living and the Dead: White Mortality in Africa, 1684–1732," in *Race and Slavery in the Western Hemisphere: Quantitative Studies,* ed. Eugene D. Genovese and Stanley Engerman (Princeton: Princeton University Press, 1975), 83–98. The difficulty of competing with the American plantations is considered in Inikori, *Africans*, 388–89, 393.

8. On the weaknesses of Royal African Company oversight, see Law, "King Agaja," 157–58; Davies, *Royal African Company*, 344–49. For the Company of Merchants Trading to Africa, see E. Martin, *British West African Settlements*, 43–56.

9. Very little of Postlethwayt's correspondence appears to survive, but much can be gleaned about his life from his several publications (see bibliography). Also see Peter N. Miller, *Defining the Common Good: Empire, Religion, and Philosophy in Great Britain* (Cambridge: Cambridge University Press, 1994), 163–69; William Darity Jr., "British Industry and the West Indies Plantations," in *The Atlantic Slave Trade: Effects on Societies, Economies, and Peoples in Africa, the Americas, and Europe,* ed. Joseph E. Inikori and Stanley L. Engerman (Durham: Duke University Press, 1992), 270–73; Curtin, *Image of Africa*, 70; E. A. J. Johnson, *Predecessors of Adam Smith: The Growth of British Economic Thought* (New York: Prentice Hall, 1937), 185–205. Only a handful of studies have been

alert to the way Postlethwayt's published views shifted over time. See, for example, J. Robert Constantine, "The African Slave Trade: A Study of Eighteenth Century Propaganda and Public Controversy" (PhD diss., Indiana University, 1953), 45–51; David Brion Davis, *The Problem of Slavery in Western Culture* (Oxford: Oxford University Press, 1966), 160–61; Angelo Costanzo, ed., *The Interesting Narrative of the Life of Equiano* (Peterborough, ON: Broadview Press, 2001), 25–26, 300–303.

10. Malachy Postlethwayt, *The African Trade, the great pillar and support of British plantation America* (London: J. Robinson, 1745), 41. See also, [Postlethwayt], *The Importance of Effectually Supporting the Royal African Company of England* (London: M. Cooper, 1745); Postlethwayt, *The National and Private Advantages of the African Trade Considered: being an enquiry, how far it concerns the trading interest of Great Britain, effectually to support and maintain the forts and settlements in Africa; belonging to the Royal African Company of England . . . with a new and correct map* (London: J. and P. Knapton, 1746). The first of these tracts the English Short Title Catalog wrongly attributes to Charles Hayes, Director of the Royal African Company. Postlethwayt identifies himself as the author in his *In Honour to the Administration: The importance of the African expedition considered: with copies of the memorials . . . the whole as planned and designed by Malachy Postlethwayt . . . to which are added, observations, illustrations, the said memorials* (London: C. Say, 1758), 270–73.

11. Malachy Postlethwayt, *Honour to the Administration*, 59, 85, 93. Similar passages appear in the 1757 and 1766 editions of Postlethwayt's *Universal Dictionary of Trade and Commerce and Britain's Commercial Interest, Explained and Improved in a Series of Dissertations*, 2 vols. (London, 1757).

12. Martin, *British West African Settlements*, 80–102; John M. Gray, *A History of the Gambia* (London: Frank Cass, 1940; 1966 reprint), 234–75; H. A. Wyndham, *The Atlantic and Slavery* (Oxford: Oxford University Press, 1935), 51–58; Madden and Fieldhouse, *Imperial Reconstruction*, 491–505; PRO, CO 267/1, Charles O'Hara to the Earl of Dartmouth and the Board of Trade [26 July 1766]; Arthur Young, *Political Essays Concerning the Present State of the British Empire* (London: W. Strahan and T. Cadell, 1772), 527–28; John Campbell, *A Political Survey of Britain being a series of reflections on the situation, lands, inhabitants, revenues, colonies, and commerce of this island* (London: Richardson and Urquhart, 1774), 633; Thomas Whateley, *Considerations on Trade and Finances of this Kingdom, and on the means of Administration, with Respect to the Great National Objects since the Conclusion of the Peace*, 3rd ed. (London: J. Wilkie, 1766), 129–30.

13. The earlier history by Martin, Gray, and Wyndham carefully avoid mention of O'Hara's depredations. His military career is outlined in William D. Griffin, "General Charles O'Hara," *Irish Sword* 10, no. 4 (1972): 179–87. For his subsequent role fighting in North America and the Caribbean during the American Revolution, see George C. Rogers, "Letters of Charles O'Hara to the Duke of Grafton," *South Carolina Historical and Genealogical Magazine* 65, no. 3 (1964): 158–80; Andrew Jackson O'Shaughnessy, *An Empire Divided: The American Revolution and the British Caribbean* (Philadelphia: University of Pennsylvania Press, 2000), 232. Brief but more balanced assessments of O'Hara's administration appear in James Searing, *West African Slavery and Atlantic Commerce: The Senegal River Valley, 1700–1860* (Cambridge: Cambridge University Press, 2003), 114, 153; Boubacar Barry, *Senegambia and the Atlantic Slave Trade* (Cambridge: Cambridge University Press, 1998), 67–68, 87.

14. John Cannon, "The Loss of America," in *Britain and the American Revolution*, ed. H. T. Dickinson (London: Longman, 1998), 244–46; Governor John Clarke to Lord George Germain, 12 September 1777, in Madden and Fieldhouse, *Imperial*

Reconstruction, 504; *Parliamentary History of England, from the Earliest Period to the Year 1803* 19 (London: T. C. Hansard, 1814), 307, 314, 315.

15. PRO, HO 7/1, "Minutes of the Committee of the House of Commons Respecting a Plan for the Transporting Felons to the Island of Le Maine in the River Gambia"; Alan Frost, *Convicts and Empire: A Naval Question, 1776–1811* (Oxford: Oxford University Press, 1980), 8–9, 28–37; Frost, *Botany Bay Mirages: Illusions of Australia's Convict Beginnings* (Melbourne: Melbourne University Press, 1994), 101–9; Patrick Webb, "Guests of the Crown: Convicts and Liberated Slaves on McCarthy Island, the Gambia," *Geographical Journal*, 160, no. 2 (1994): 136–42; PRO, CO 267/7, Edward Morse to Lord Sydney, 6 March 1783; PRO, CO 267/8, Morse, "A Comparative Statement of the Advantages and Disadvantages to be expected from the Territory of the River Gambia in the Hands of the African Company or erected in a Colony"; PRO, CO 267/20, Daniel Francis Houghton to Thomas Townshend, 24 February 1783; Robin Hallett, *The Penetration of Africa: European Exploration in North and West Africa to 1815* (New York: Routledge and Kegan Paul, 1965), 219–24. The reader should keep in mind that the West African coast was just one of several regions considered for British colonization after the American war. This was a moment when entrepreneurs pushed, as well, expeditions against Panama, Peru, and Chili, expeditions conceived as voyages of conquest that might yield a British empire in South America. See Frost, "Shaking off the Spanish Yoke: British Schemes to Revolutionize Spanish America, 1739–1807," in *Science and Exploration in the Pacific: European Voyages to the Southern Oceans in the Eighteenth Century*, ed. Margarette Lincoln (Woodbridge, Suffolk: Boydell Press, 1998), 27–32.

16. John Coakley Lettsom, "Some Account of the Late John Fothergill," in *The Works of John Fothergill*, ed. Lettsom (London: Charles Tilley, 1783), xlvi–xlvii; John Fothergill to Granville Sharp, 11 March 1779, in Granville Sharp, *Memoirs of Granville Sharp*, ed. Prince Hoare (London: Henry Colburn, 1820), 188.

17. Stephen Braidwood, *Black Poor and White Philanthropists: London's Blacks and the Foundation of the Sierra Leone Settlement, 1786–1791* (Liverpool: Liverpool University Press, 1994), 7–12; PRO, T1/631, "The Memorial of Henry Smeathman to the Lords Commissioners of his Majesty's Treasury," 17 May 1786; "Substance of Two Letters addressed to Dr. Knowles of London, on the Productions and Colonization of Africa by Dr. Henry Smeathman," in C. B. Wadström, *An Essay on Colonization, particularly applied to the Western Coast of Africa* (London: Darton and Harvey, 1794), 197–207.

18. Braidwood, *Black Poor,* 5–8; Granville Sharp, "Memorandum on a Late Proposal to be Made on the Coast of Africa," in Sharp, *An Account of the Constitutional English Polity of Congregational Courts* (London: B. White and C. Dilly, 1783), 263–81; Sharp, *A Short Sketch of Temporary Regulations (Until Better Shall Be Proposed) for the Intended Settlement on the Grain Coast of Africa, Near Sierra Leone* (London: H. Baldwin, 1786); Henry Thornton, "General Outlines of a Settlement on the Tooth or Ivory Coast of Africa," in *The Papers of William Thornton*, ed. C. M. Harris (Charlottesville: University Press of Virginia, 1995), 38–41.

19. A thorough discussion appears in James W. St. G. Walker, *The Black Loyalists: The Search for a Promised Land in Nova Scotia and Sierra Leone, 1783–1870* (Toronto: University of Toronto Press, 1976), 94–114, 145–240.

20. George Gregory, *Essays, Historical and Moral* (London: J. Johnson, 1785), 328; James Ramsay, *An Enquiry into the Effects of Putting a Stop to the African Slave Trade, and of granting Liberty to the Slaves in the British Sugar Colonies* (London: James Phillips, 1784).

21. Gustavus Vassa, Late Commissary for the African Settlement, to the Right Honourable Lord Hawkesbury, 13 March 1788, in Olaudah Equiano, *Olaudah Equiano:*

The Interesting Narrative and Other Writings, ed. Vincent Caretta (New York: Penguin Books, 1995), 333–34.

22. As Anthony Pagden reminds us, most theorists of empire, by the end of the eighteenth century, had come to regard commerce as a civilizing agent, far preferable to attempts at dominion or universal monarchy. Pagden, *Lords of All the World: Ideologies of Empire in Spain, Britain, and France, c. 1500–1800* (New Haven: Yale University Press, 1995).

23. Curtin, *Image of Africa,* pts. 1, 2; Howard Temperley, *White Dreams, Black Africa: The Antislavery Expedition to the River Niger, 1841–1842* (New Haven: Yale University Press, 1991); T. C. McCaskie, "Cultural Encounters: Britain and Africa in the Nineteenth Century," in *The Oxford History of the British Empire,* vol. 3, *The Nineteenth Century,* ed. Andrew Porter (Oxford: Oxford University Press, 1999), 664–89.

24. Ralph Austen and Woodruff D. Smith, "Images of Africa and British Slave-Trade Abolition: The Transition to an Imperialist Ideology, 1787–1807," *African Historical Studies* 2, no. 1 (1969): 69–83.

FOUR

Ending the Slave Trade

A Caribbean and Atlantic Context

PHILIP D. MORGAN

THE ABOLITION of the slave trade was an improbable event. Before the late eighteenth century some Europeans felt unease about the thought of shipping enslaved Africans, but most viewed the practice as morally indistinguishable from shipping any other commodity. In the 1783 trial concerning the *Zong,* a slave ship in which sailors threw overboard 133 enslaved Africans to claim the insurance, Lord Chief Justice Mansfield stated that "the case of slaves was the same as if horses had been thrown overboard." When the first Quaker petition for abolition arrived in Parliament in the same year, the Commons categorically dismissed it. Yet, within a decade, the same body voted overwhelmingly for it, even though full success had to wait another fifteen years. The African slave trade, long considered the foundation of Britain's colonial economy, suddenly became superfluous.[1]

Unexpectedly, too, abolition occurred as the slave trade was booming. At the end of the eighteenth century and the beginning of the nineteenth, the transatlantic slave trade, the largest forced transoceanic migration in history, was at its height. From 1780 to 1810 an annual average of eighty thousand shackled Africans traversed the Atlantic. In those three decades, just over a half the Africans came in ships flying the flags of Britain, the United States, or Denmark. Yet by the second decade of the nineteenth century almost no Africans crossed the Atlantic in such ships—for each of these three nations had abolished the trade. The Atlantic slave trade died an unnatural and quick death. A massive withdrawal from transatlantic slaving occurred with astonishing rapidity.[2]

The mention of the three nations that abolished the trade in the first decade of the nineteenth century merits a brief recapitulation. The first slave-trading state in Europe to abolish the trade was Denmark. In March 1792 the royal Danish government issued a decree banning the import of slaves into the Danish West Indies and their export from the Danish establishments on the Gold Coast. The law was not to take effect for ten years—not till 1 January 1803—reflecting the gradualist tendencies in eighteenth-century antislavery. The prime mover behind this decision, the minister of finance, Ernst Schimmelmann, was a reformer, but he was also the largest slave owner in the Danish West Indies and a prominent shareholder in the Danish slave-trading company. The slave trade was insignificant to Denmark's overall economy; the maintenance of the forts and factories on the African coast was costly; and, perhaps most important, the Danish authorities were convinced that the British and French would soon abolish the slave trade and anticipated that they would then exert pressure on the smaller slave-trading nations to do the same. Anxious to avoid a maritime clash with the major powers, the Danish action was a preemptive strike.[3]

The campaign against the Atlantic slave trade began, however, not in Denmark or Britain but in North America. After the Seven Years' War, settler elites from Massachusetts to Virginia took steps to restrict or halt the importation of slaves. Their actions can be traced to the emergence of antislavery opinion but owed even more to the long-standing desire in North America to exercise control over who came to colonial shores. In all these colonies, too, the slave population grew naturally and the import of Africans had become largely unnecessary. Still, attempts to block the Atlantic slave trade before the American Revolution largely represented a demand for colonial self-determination. Without the prior anxiety about the impact of slave imports on colonial society, and the lack of necessity for African newcomers in most places, the moral case against the Atlantic slave trade would have carried far less weight. After the revolution, each state, some quickly, others laggardly, passed prohibitory or restrictive legislation against the slave trade. Moreover, when the delegates to the Constitutional Convention met in 1787, they included a compromise slave-trade clause, "weighted with circumlocution and ambiguity," that confirmed Congress's power to regulate

foreign commerce, permitted importation of Africans, yet set a prob-
able target date for the slave trade's prohibition—twenty years hence, in
1808—an even more gradualist measure than the Danish decree. When
Congress passed the slave trade act (on 2 March 1807), three weeks
before the British House of Commons, the United States was a minor
player in the transatlantic slave trade; most Southern planters were not
threatened by, indeed favored, the halting of slave imports; antislavery
activists mounted no tumultuous battle against the inhuman traffic; and
the nation was more preoccupied with ex-vice president Aaron Burr's
plans to stir the Southwest to fight for independence and Napoleon's
continental blockade than by the ending of the slave trade. This was the
Quiet Abolition, as one historian terms it.[4]

The last nation of these three to act—but by far the most important—
was Britain. Its abolition was anything but quiet: rather, it was national,
broad based, and aggressive, compared to its localized, elite, and timid
European and American counterparts. Indeed, British abolitionists
mobilized one of "the greatest of all human rights movements." Within
the first year of the campaign, tens of thousands of men and women
signed petitions against the traffic. At the bar of public opinion, abolitionists seemed to vanquish the slave traders almost overnight. If the
question could have been put to referendum, perhaps the British slave
trade would have been abolished in 1788. Despite the initial flush of
enthusiasm, however, Parliament was only slowly persuaded that slave
trade abolition would serve the national interest. In 1792, MPs voted by
a large majority in favor of abolition, but it was gradual; they postponed the
date of commencement for four years; and the House of Lords failed to
ratify that decision. When in 1796 Parliament again took up the issue,
France's abolition of slavery, its Reign of Terror, and the conflagration
in St. Domingue rendered abolitionism suspect. Set back for a decade,
British abolition did not reemerge powerfully until 1804, when another
three years of maneuvering climaxed with the favorable vote on 25
March 1807.[5]

This brief account of these three nations' abolitions aims in part to
show that ending the slave trade was international in scope, but also to
demonstrate that it always involved political machinations, a mix of
moral and material motives. Abolition is too often depicted as the selfless overcoming the selfish. Abolitionists conceived of their program
this way. As a Rhode Island abolitionist put it in 1789, promoting abolition requires making "a much stronger impression upon the mind" of

public officials than any other topic, for there was no natural "abolition-ist" constituency, "no private interest" behind abolitionism. This way of telling the story—the disinterested versus the interested—is gripping. It is David versus Goliath, the weak overcoming the strong. The achieve-ment of abolition is seemingly an unusual example of morals triumphing over power, principles over pragmatism, ideals over economics. All the more so since historians have now demonstrated that slave trade abolition ran directly counter to Britain's economic interests. But in fact effective opposition to the British slave trade, just like its defense, depended on the influence of powerful interests. Why otherwise would the antislav-ery writer William Dickson, before commencing his tour of Scotland in 1792, receive instructions from the London Abolition Committee to contact key people and work on their "interest"?[6] So what were some of the key interests that facilitated abolition? One has already been mentioned—colonial aspirations for self-determination after the Seven Years' War—but others deserving of consideration are (1) the improv-ing tendencies of Caribbean planters, (2) entrepreneurial schemes for imperial expansion after the American Revolution, (3) slave resistance, most dramatically represented in the revolt in St. Domingue, and (4) strategic attempts by the British state during the Napoleonic Wars to achieve competitive advantage. These four interests will be the focus of this chapter.[7]

In suggesting that there were powerful forces opposed to the Atlan-tic slave trade, my aim is emphatically not to devalue the abolitionist achievement or to reduce moral principles to crass material interests. The extent of the moral revolution is captured in David Brion Davis's words that, for thousands of years, "people thought of sin as a form of slavery," but then, in the late eighteenth century, they began "to think of slavery as sin." Furthermore, abolitionists unquestionably emphasized moral, as opposed to economic or political, reasons for action. While accepting that a profound moral transformation had occurred, I seek to expand the frame of reference beyond the narrative of abolitionist initiatives and to suggest that moralism and interests converged in complicated ways. Al-though abolition was ultimately a political decision at the center, broader forces far from metropolitan capitals shaped those legislative decisions.[8]

THE CARIBBEAN context most commonly linked to abolition is the so-called decline thesis, associated with historians Lowell Ragatz and

Eric Williams. They have argued that British abolition was preceded by a sharp diminution in the value of slavery, and hence of the slave trade, to the imperial economy. The planters suffered from limited and marginal resources for expansion, soil exhaustion, rising costs for their provisions and labor, falling prices for their sugar. Some of these characterizations were true: the Caribbean islands experienced lower returns during and after the American Revolution; a series of severe hurricanes devastated parts of the Caribbean in the 1780s, and planters in the older islands, with rather limited natural resources, faced acute problems, most especially from fierce international competition. Nevertheless, over the whole period from 1783 to 1807, the British slave system rebounded. It enlarged its frontier, its relative proportion of British trade, its imports and exports, its share of world sugar and coffee production, and its overall size, both absolutely and relative to other colonial systems. In the first decade of the nineteenth century, the British Caribbean produced about 60 percent of the world's sugar and 50 percent of all coffee. The value of the slave trade and the slave colonies to Britain had never been greater; neither had their prospects for future growth been brighter when the British Parliament severed the umbilical link with Africa. British slavery declined, but only after the abolition of the British slave trade.[9]

If economic decline is not the relevant theme for linking the Caribbean to abolition, then arguably the alternative—improvement—is. This claim may seem fanciful, for was not the West Indian Creole, much like the East Indian nabob, a pariah? Each was stigmatized as profit obsessed, morally degraded, schooled in tyranny, not fully British. Countering this stereotype, however, are the extensive relief campaigns mounted by thousands of ordinary donors across Britain to aid British West Indian victims of perhaps the deadliest hurricanes they ever experienced. The increasing integration of the Atlantic world, an expanded sense of British nationalism that viewed far-off colonists as fellow subjects, wartime politics that suggested the importance of rewarding loyal colonists already suffering hardships, and the emergence of humanitarian sensibility (one symptom of which, of course, was the movement for abolition) help explain "the largest and most significant relief effort of the eighteenth century." In 1781 one British official described the relief funds as "a striking proof of the warm affection borne by the People of England to their fellow subjects in the West Indies." Perhaps trying to respond in kind, many planters increasingly styled themselves as enlightened paternalists, committed to the amelioration of slavery. In

1774 a Jamaican debating society had declared the slave trade contrary to morality. In part the planters' strategy was defensive, trying to stave off abolitionist attack and deflect their weakened political leverage that followed the American Revolution, but in other ways it owed more to economic concerns that predated the war and the abolitionist movement. Ironically, many West Indian planters came to share an interest in some of the same outcomes as abolitionists, even though they wanted to reform and buttress slavery, not end it.[10]

Amelioration took many forms. One aspect was diversification of the economy. Planters promoted alternatives to sugar, such as coffee and cotton. By the end of the eighteenth century the British West Indies produced almost 40 percent of the raw cotton imported into Britain; and by 1805 the old Dutch Guiana colonies supplied more cotton to Britain than all the British West Indies combined. Jamaican exports went from being 90 percent sugar in 1770 to less than 70 percent fifty years later. On some late-eighteenth-century plantations slaves spent only a third of their time on cash crops. Planters paid far more attention to livestock husbandry than ever before, and they introduced new pasture grasses to improve cattle fodder. With better-fed livestock, the plow could supplement the customary hoe, and more manure improved crop yields. Planters also encouraged locally grown food; many allowed their slaves more time to work their provision grounds, the average size of which roughly doubled from about 1750 to 1810. Native-born slaves made nutritional gains: they were on average three to four centimeters taller than their African counterparts. Many consequences flowed from diversification.[11]

Changes in labor organization formed another part of the reforms. Planters hired jobbing gangs to work at the most arduous tasks, thereby conserving their own workforces. They tried to calibrate their gangs so that they were well adapted to the capacities of their slaves. In daily labor assignments, planters often divided slaves into smaller work groups, or squads. They sometimes overlooked typical European gender norms in order to choose the best and most experienced work leaders for the task at hand. Some planters tried to set production quotas, offering the gang the incentive of free time once benchmarks were met. One planter even suggested a semantic shift: slaves should be renamed assistant planters. By the end of the eighteenth century slaveholders worked their laborers harder than ever before, demanding that they learn the skills necessary to perform a variety of tasks, eliminating the highs and lows in annual labor demand by growing cash and provision crops and raising more stock. While planters espoused humanitarian reform and searched for methods and tools to reduce burdensome work, the labor saved was always invested elsewhere. A growing attention to efficiency spelled an intensification of work for slaves.[12]

Agricultural reform contributed to a general culture of improvement, manifest in the introduction of new commercial and food crops, the rise of botanic gardens, the formation of agricultural societies, a burgeoning literature on plantation management, and the emergence of a class of professional estate attorneys and managers. Absenteeism was growing on some islands, but rather than just sapping the fiber of society—as many have assumed—the practice helped create a trusteeship that inducted merchants and lawyers into the plantocracy. It resulted in the introduction of improved accounting methods. Many absentees led the way in technological and investment innovation. In 1775 absentees owned 30 percent of Jamaica's sugar estates but produced 40 percent of the island's sugar and rum; this above-average performance was partly a function of scale, but it also owed something to managerial acumen. Planters read the ever-expanding literature devoted to management practices and scientific husbandry. Described by one traveler as "the best treatise on planting" and by Dr. James Grainger, author of *The Sugar Cane* (1764), as "an excellent performance," Samuel Martin's *Essay upon Plantership* appeared in at least seven editions between 1750 and 1802. Martin urged planters to treat their slaves with "tenderness and generosity"; the aim was to induce "love" by setting an example of "benevolence, justice, temperance, and chastity." When Janet Schaw, a Scot, visited Martin's Greencastle estate in Antigua in 1774, she described the eighty-year-old planter in rosy terms, as "a kind and beneficent Master," who was "daily employed" to render the island "more improved."[13]

By the late eighteenth century, in part because of planters' pronatalist policies—providing relief immediately before and after childbirth, offering financial and other incentives for childrearing, buttressing family structures, reducing physical punishments, supplying better medical care—slave populations in some parts of the British West Indies began to grow naturally. Progressive planters now thought that slave births could exceed deaths. In 1786 a Barbadian plantation manual argued that slaves "fed plentifully, worked moderately, and treated kindly . . . will increase in most places" and "decrease in no place." The following year, Rev. Robert Nickolls, describing himself as "a native of the West-Indies," claimed that, "with tolerable treatment," island blacks were "prolific and long-lived." Just over a decade later, the planter-dominated assemblies in islands as different developmentally as Grenada and St. Kitts claimed that slave reproduction could be improved so as to remove the need for African importation. A growing number of British Caribbean planters, much like their North American counterparts, then, saw no threat from the abolition of the slave trade and indeed had an interest in its cessation. West Indian planters were far from monolithic in their attitudes to abolition. In 1801 a Barbadian attorney, in discussion with an absentee proprietor, said he would as soon advise throwing money into the sea as recommending the purchase of Africans. Three years later a Barbadian resident reported that abolition would not harm his island but would halt the expansion of newer territories such as Demerara. For planters in the older islands, the desire to increase slave prices by limiting supply was a reason to favor abolition. By removing the least defensible aspect of the slave system, it was also possible to argue that the institution would be strengthened rather than weakened.[14]

Schemes to improve the lot of slaves became bones of contention between antislavery and proslavery forces. In 1775 Samuel Martin's hope that he might be "a loved and revered father" to his slaves was tempered by the fear that metropolitan defenders of slaves could "instill such enthusiastic notions of liberty, as may occasion revolutions in our colonies." Tortola slaveholder Samuel Nottingham's decision to enfranchise twenty-five slaves in 1776, endow them their own land, and provide a cash inheritance resulted in either a model, self-sustaining community or a stark economic failure, depending on who was telling the story. Similarly, Joshua Steele's experiments on his own estate in Barbados in the 1780s, which involved banning the use of the whip, offering premiums for task work, paying his enslaved workers, and establishing a system of copyhold tenancy, became in the opposing forces' narratives either a noble experiment or an unrealistic pipe dream. Prominent abolitionists praised Steele; local planters portrayed him as eccentric, ignorant, and then, the harshest cut of all, of being tyrannical. A war of representation occurred over such figures. Even an ostensibly proslavery tract, such as the former overseer who signed himself SK and wrote about his experiences on the island of Antigua in 1789, provided "a rich fund of emotive material for anti-slavery writers," indicating that he was "already affected by the dominant discourse of anti-slavery."[15]

The Danish commission established in 1791 to consider the abolition of the transatlantic slave trade linked Caribbean amelioration to abolition.

While it was not prepared to make any statutory inroads into the masters' discretion in matters relating to food, clothing, housing, or medical care, since that would have been interfering in the individual's right of property, the commission recommended a royal order aimed at better propagation of the Gospel, enforcement of marriage among the slaves, and improved education of slave children. Individual planters in the Danish West Indies, like their British counterparts, proclaimed that slaves worked effectively when humanely treated and that natural reproduction was feasible. Count Schimmelmann, a key member of the commission and a concerned absentee proprietor, claimed that he rarely had to buy new Africans and that slaves on his estates were close to reproducing their own numbers.[16]

It is easy to dismiss these planter improvements as mere window dressing. The slave system at bottom depended on force and violence. Slavery was a vicious system of labor exploitation and the aim was to extract the greatest possible product from the enslaved people. Yet without the evidence that slaves were capable of freedom—which enlightened planters in fact promoted—the abolitionists would have had a much harder uphill battle. Moreover, Caribbean planters were the first to suggest that the empire as a whole, not merely slaveholders, should take responsibility for the slave system, a claim that ironically proved of great value to abolitionists hoping to make antislavery a public concern. The abolitionists viewed eradication of the slave trade as a vital building block in the creation of a new order. No longer able to recruit from Africa, planters would have to attend more carefully to their slaves as a means of encouraging natural increase. But planters had anticipated the abolitionists and were busily creating the new order—subject to the constraints imposed by their slaves. Thus, for example, by encouraging the so-called provision-ground system, in which areas of land were allocated to the enslaved on which they were required to produce most of their own food, those slaves able to take advantage of it developed an autonomous domestic economy and an internal marketing system that effectively provisioned all sectors of the population. By the early nineteenth century many Caribbean slaves effectively constituted a protopeasantry.[17]

In short, farsighted planters and industrious slaves provided important grist for the abolitionist mill. Abolitionists had an unshakeable faith that individuals worked more productively if moved by incentive rather than by force. The planters' schemes to make their slaves work more industriously—whether by task rather than by gang labor, or by greater use of hired labor that might involve a form of wages, or by extending the opportunity for self-purchase—coincided with the abolitionists' optimistic assumption. Abolitionists also held sacred the right to self-possession, so planter plans to develop the slaves' provision grounds, encourage marriage, and promote fertility were more than compatible with abolitionist commitments. Finally, abolitionists had an unquestionable confidence in the human capacity for moral development, so again attempts to reform the worst features of slave laws and to encourage missionary activity met with approval. Planters and abolitionists had more in common than is commonly assumed; and planter interests were not as opposed to the ending of the slave trade as is often imagined. There was, of course, a "West India interest," but it did not always speak with one voice. Moreover, even as early as 1792, according to one influential report, the Society of West India Planters and Merchants "would have acquiesced" in the parliamentary vote to abolish the slave trade, if 1800, not 1796, had been the date set for its ending. Fifteen years before abolition occurred, apparently influential West Indians were sufficiently resigned to their fate to accept an eight-year delay in implementation.[18]

JUST AS the Caribbean became important in providing evidence of compelling alternatives, so Africa, from the abolitionist perspective, served a similar role. Schemes to colonize Africa or to promote legitimate commerce, while long present, proliferated in the 1780s and 1790s. They now appear whimsical, but at the time an almost delirious, speculative fervor gripped their promoters. Situated in the center of the globe, Africa allegedly would support the produce of both east and west; optimists thought that the cultivation of both tea and sugar would flourish there. Not just its central location, but its supposed rich soil and unbounded population, promising cheap labor for hire, made Africa the ideal commercial partner. Partnership is not quite the right term, for the abolitionist project was inherently imperialist. It involved a projected alternative course for the economic development of Africa and an assertion of the responsibility and right of Europeans to decide the future of that continent. Redemption was a key concept. Just as British antislavery as a whole became a means to redeem the nation, so West African locales became the target for separate schemes to rebirth both slaves and convicts as free people. But whatever the ultimate import of these metropolitan fantasies about vast plantations, profitable trade, penetration of the interior, and redemptive utopias, their significance for abolition's prospects is evident. Without the long-standing hopes for a commercial empire in Africa, the abolitionists would have faced a much tougher struggle.[19]

The connection between abolitionism and African colonization is well evident among the Danes. From the time the Danish government began to negotiate the ban on the slave trade, it investigated in earnest the agricultural potential of the territory around the Danish forts. What helped make the ban feasible were glowing reports that new plantations in Africa could in time supply Denmark with sugar, as well as with cotton, coffee, and other tropical products. To be sure, the Danish plantations on the Gold Coast never amounted to much, but to dismiss them is to ignore the whole history of colonialism, which is full of uncertain beginnings and failures. Their promise undoubtedly bolstered Danish resolve to abolish the slave trade. In 1787, Paul Isert returned from a three-year tour of duty as fort surgeon in the Danish establishments on the coast, believing that if the cultivation of luxury tropical crops could be introduced on the West African coast, "the shameful exportation of Blacks from their happy fatherland could gradually be stopped." Isert returned to Africa the following year and began establishing a colony named in honor of the crown prince. Isert soon died but others followed. They experimented with sugarcane, coffee, indigo, and cotton, and they employed slave labor. Throughout the period of considering abolition of the slave trade, the Danish government actively pursued the planting of an agricultural colony on the Guinea coast. Essentially, Danish authorities hoped to transfer the basic structure of West Indian economies to the African littoral.[20]

In England, schemes for exploiting Africa's agricultural potential had an even longer history. In the first decade of the eighteenth century Sir Dalby Thomas, the chief factor at Cape Coast, was, as Christopher Brown notes, "probably the first British official to espouse agricultural 'improvement' in West Africa." At midcentury Malachy Postlethwayt thought a British empire in Africa could liberate the continent from the Atlantic slave trade. A vast interior trade remained to be tapped, he thought, and the slave trade hindered the development of these more lucrative branches of commerce. He was not alone in imagining African colonization, particularly through contact with interior peoples, as the route to slave trade abolition. The American Revolution gave a major impetus to such visionary plans. As early as 1777 one British parliamentarian juxtaposed the anticipated loss of an American empire with the prospective addition of an African empire in which the trade in goods would involve "quantities beyond arithmetical calculation." In 1783, Henry Trafford thought all the staples of the Americas could be resituated in Africa and grown far more cheaply because of an African free-labor market. Six years later, a resident of Manchester argued for the practicability of substituting a trade in products for the slave trade, declaring it would "make us amends, ten thousand fold" for the lost colonies. An African empire could compensate for losses in America.[21]

Indeed, the 1780s saw, as Deidre Coleman has noted, "a torrent of utopian ideas and fantasies about the sorts of traffic and exchanges that might be conducted on the west coast of Africa." Some schemes were fantastic. In 1781 Henry Smeathman's quixotic modeling of labor on a West African termitarium (coincidentally the termite, a superant, just happened to be white) involved a disturbing, futuristic vision of the needs and values of Britain's emerging capitalist order, regulating and disciplining the local Africans through the division of labor, and allied to notions of interracial propagation. While Smeathman in many ways looked to the future, Carl Wadström and his collaborators offered a plan that looked backward. They admired Africa for its feudal features and offered a labor model of "gentle Servitude" in which "every Native redeemed from Slavery shall be free after a Service or Apprenticeship of a few Years." Far-fetched as many of these schemes undoubtedly were, they served a larger purpose. Abolitionists gained a hearing in part because they could refer to the existence of a seemingly powerful alternative to the Atlantic slave trade. Seduced by visions of what Philip Curtin called "tropical exuberance," scores of ecstatic projectors thought West Africa a place of untapped wealth. If a commercial empire in Africa was not only "practicable" but "prudent," to use Wadström's words, then abolition was not such a risky proposition.[22]

The Sierra Leone settlement established in 1786 as an asylum for black loyalists represented the most concrete result of this intensified interest in West Africa. The Sierra Leone Company thought of its black settler population as subordinate agents in a commercial enterprise. Most of the items in Thomas Clarkson's famous chest, with its many compartments and trays, which he touted all across Britain, were devoted to the goods that could come from Sierra Leone and other parts of Africa: a score of hardwood varieties, ivory, musk, peppers, gums, cinnamon, rice, tobacco, indigo, cotton, and African manufactures. As Marcus

Wood notes, his chest was "both a moveable lecture kit and a beautifully choreographed travelling salesman's sample case." Similarly, Zachary Macauley, governor of Sierra Leone in the 1790s (and ex-overseer of a West Indian slave plantation), promoted the possibilities of coffee production. He thought the flavor of the African coffee bean equal to its West Indian counterpart.[23]

The black loyalists, like so many freedpeople throughout the Americas, sought independence through the ownership of small farms. Frustrated with the small allotments of land, outraged at the imposition of annual quitrents, concerned with protecting their dissenting churches, suspicious of the emphasis the company placed on plantation development, and contemptuous of being treated as less than "free British subjects," black settlers engaged in constant, running battles with the authorities. In part their actions seem a revival of republican principles, the transmission of American political ideology to the shores of West Africa, a "contentious little *America* in West Africa," as Simon Schama puts it. Black loyalists rediscovered in Africa their true American selves, it would seem, but they also appealed for nothing more than what been promised them before departing for Africa. Above all, they wanted land, security, and autonomy. By contrast, the company had plantation-scale aspirations and emphasized sugar production—"Saccharomania," as Wadström termed it. The settlers preferred small-scale agriculture, although they built ships, raised livestock, and expanded trade with native villages. After the rebellion of 1800 some moved to slaving forts to engage in commerce and many seemingly forgot their antislavery commitments, purchasing native children under the thinly veiled guise of apprenticeship. Their turn to commerce and embrace of slavery reflected values and behaviors that were as deeply rooted in the American societies from which they had escaped as were the communitarian visions that had earlier inspired them.[24]

BLACKS PROVED powerful agents not just in Sierra Leone. The ten thousand or so blacks living in Britain in the era of abolition had a singularly important part to play, since they were so close to the seat of metropolitan power. Their resistance helped put the legality of slaveholding on trial in English and Scottish courts in the 1760s and 1770s. Fugitive slaves such as James Somerset and Joseph Knight effectively ended slaveholding in Britain one decade after the Seven Years' War.

Notable individual cases of black activism occurred: Olaudah Equiano's bringing the infamous case of the *Zong* to the attention of Granville Sharp; Ottobah Cugoano's role as probably the first "to recommend that the Royal Navy patrol the Atlantic Ocean and intercept merchants trafficking in slaves"; or the anonymous black sailor's report that the British navy in the Caribbean routinely violated international law by selling as slaves free blacks and coloured sailors taken off French ships instead of treating them as prisoners of war. By their actions and their complaints, black slaves kept constant pressure on white abolitionists.[25]

Similarly, resistance to the slave trade in Africa and on the high seas had an impact in Britain. Some Britons became aware that particular African kingdoms, usually for limited periods, prohibited enslavement and refused to sell slaves. That Africans distinguished between legal and illegal forms of enslavement also became evident. The growing practice of pawning was open to abuse, and where Europeans seized free persons as slaves, their African relatives went to great lengths to have them returned. Aggrieved Africans sometimes retaliated against European ship captains who they felt acted illegally. Reports of slave revolts on the Middle Passage, now known to have occurred on about one in ten slave-trading voyages, were commonplace. Of the six hundred or so reported shipboard rebellions or attacks from onshore, the vast majority occurred in the eighteenth century. Their frequency and success rate rose over the course of the century. That slave traders had to invest significant sums in preventive measures must have been widely known in slave-trading ports, and some people surely became aware that slavers avoided the African regions generating the most shipboard revolts.[26]

Once in the Americas, the slaves, by their defiance, their attempts to escape, their Maroon communities, and their revolts, challenged the fictions of domination and submission around which slavery was constructed. In 1788, West Indian planter and MP Sir James Johnstone argued in favor of prompt abolition to reduce expectations among the slaves that emancipation was imminent. He had heard that Grenadian slaves proclaimed, "Mr Wilberforce for negro! Mr Fox for negro! Parliament for negro! God Almighty for negro!" Slaves also gave essential ammunition to abolitionists, who made much of the tales of planter persecution and savage repression. Since abolitionists, like most planters, took it for granted that Africans, rather than Creoles, were especially prone to rebel, a pragmatic reason existed for abolishing the slave trade.[27]

On the other hand, activist slaves wreaking vengeance could be counter-productive to the antislavery cause. For this reason, antislavery iconography foregrounded the kneeling supplicant, a far more palatable figure than the armed slave. Furthermore, as a constant, slave resistance can hardly explain why the abolition of the slave trade came to the fore of public debate in the late eighteenth century, unless it was simply by cumulative weight of example. The American War of Independence, it is true, marked a decisive upturn in slave restiveness, with plots uncovered everywhere from Pennsylvania to Georgia, from Jamaica to Antigua; thousands of slaves escaped North American slavery, leading one historian to term it "the greatest slave rebellion in North American history." But the last four years of the war saw no actual slave rebellions, and there were none during the 1780s, when abolitionism as a movement took hold. This twelve-year period of seeming quiescence in the British West Indies has been described as "probably the longest interval of apparent peace between masters and slaves in the entire slave period."[28]

That intense slave resistance might have been counterproductive is also suggested by the Dutch example. Colonists from the Netherlands probably confronted the most vigorous slave resistance of any imperial power. For more than a century, they faced the largest Maroon community per capita in the Americas; their Guiana colonies were a "theater of perpetual war"; and in 1763 a slave uprising in Berbice was probably the largest, longest and most successful slave revolt in Caribbean before St. Domingue. Despite—or perhaps in part because of—widespread and long-lived slave rebelliousness, Dutch abolitionism never took hold.[29]

Arguably, far more important than the simple incidence of slave resistance was its changing character. The revolutionary era's ideals of liberty and equality created a radically new climate. Seemingly, slave resistance assumed a new, ideological dimension. It was evident in Jamaica's great slave rebellion of 1776, the first on that island to be led by skilled native-born or Creole slaves, who, according to one resident, had been much influenced by "disaffected" whites who openly expressed their sympathy for the mainland patriots. As one merchant put it, "Can you be surprised that the Negroes in Jamaica should endeavour to Recover their Freedom, when they dayly hear at the Tables of their Masters, how much the Americans are applauded for the stand they are making for theirs." In 1791 a worried Jamaica resident reported that "a body of Negroes . . . had assembled drinking King Wilberforce's health out of a cat's skull." In Dominica in the same year, a slave revolt supposedly occurred in pursuit of "what [the slaves] term their 'rights.'" "These doctrines, which are novel among the negroes," the account continued, "have originated from the new language and proceedings in this country [England] respecting the Slave Trade." Reflecting on the impact of their own Revolution, one Virginian put it well when he said, before the event, slaves "fought [for] freedom merely as a good, now they also claim it as a right." In past slave societies, slaves had attempted to overthrow slavery, but never before had slaves challenged slavery, speaking the language of natural rights.[30]

More common than slaves emphasizing their rights, however, was their claim that they merely sought to gain a freedom already granted them by the king, but which the colonists were withholding. The myth of a benign monarch betrayed by others is of course a commonplace, but it may have had special resonance for slaves because of their homeland traditions of chiefdom and monarchy. Thus slaves often tended to present themselves as defenders of church and king rather than as seekers of the rights of man. Claiming a freedom bestowed by royal writ is not the same as asserting a universal right to individual liberty, although Laurent Dubois has a point when he notes that "evocations of the king did not necessarily imply a rejection of the language of republicanism." He has found evidence of ideological syncretism, but still the slaves' discourse can often seem extremely traditional. Perhaps the best that can be said is that slaves spoke with several voices and had multiple aims. Most fundamentally, of course, they simply sought freedom. The ideals of the democratic revolutions resonated most clearly with the free blacks and free coloureds of the Caribbean, and with some of the most creolized of slave leaders. Slaves wanted freedom; the free people of color wanted equality with whites and were the ones demanding equal rights.[31]

If slave resistance within the British Empire cannot really help explain abolition too readily, perhaps the greatest slave revolt of all time—that of St. Domingue, beginning in 1791, which in turn inspired a great wave of slave revolts lasting throughout the decade—was pivotal. It was undoubtedly a turning point in the history of New World slavery and marked the first major blow to Atlantic slave systems. Its impact has been likened to the Hiroshima bomb, a never-to-be forgotten event. Its import was magnified because it occurred in the wealthiest Caribbean colony, the true powerhouse of the Atlantic economy. What, for slave owners, was their worst nightmare, was, for blacks, the inspiration that self-liberation was possible. News of the revolt spread widely and rapidly. Within a month of the 1791 uprising, Jamaican slaves had composed songs about it. Slave owners soon began complaining of a new "insolence" on the part of their slaves.[32]

But its impact on the antislavery movement in Britain was mixed. In the beginning, the massive revolt seemed to favor abolitionist arguments: they could point to slaves vindicating their humanity, they could stress that the revolt was a direct result of the huge influx of Africans that immediately preceded it. Precisely those arguments held some sway in Parliament and help explain the favorable 1792 vote against the slave trade. But abolitionists were soon on the defensive because, as news circulated from St. Domingue, freedom for blacks seemed to bring only economic ruin and indiscriminate slaughter. Despite the later romanticization of Toussaint-Louverture, the overriding image of the Haitian Revolution was negative: the atrocities committed by the slaves, their continuing poverty, and constant political upheavals lost them sympathizers. Moreover, the outbreak of war between Britain and France in 1793 inevitably pushed reform off center stage; abolitionists had to be wary of seeming to be associated with Jacobinism. Furthermore, by the spring of 1794 British troops in the Caribbean had great initial successes, taking French Martinique, Guadeloupe, St. Lucia, and roughly one third of St. Domingue, with prospects of taking the whole in short order. Grandiose visions floated of restoring the British Empire to the commercial heights of before 1776. Imperial patriotism squelched abolitionism.[33]

The French National Convention's outlawing of slavery in all its colonies in February 1794, however, changed everything, particularly the nature of the war. By 1795, French armies that included large numbers of emancipated slaves seriously threatened British Caribbean colonies. In that year impressive struggles erupted in two nominally British West Indian islands—Grenada and St. Vincent—that Britain had acquired from France in the 1760s. There, extraordinary alliances between white and colored proprietors and the mass of slaves destroyed more lives and property than any other slave uprisings in the history of British slavery. At the same time, the largest Maroon community at Trelawney Town in Jamaica also rose in revolt. These rebellions could be explained away as involving those groups least integrated into the British plantation system: the francophone free blacks and slaves in the Ceded Islands, the black Caribs, and the Maroons. In imperial consciousness, these rebellions were largely French invasions, and policymakers dispatched them out of mind much as they did the black Caribs by deporting them to Roatan and the Maroons by shipping them off to Nova Scotia. Nevertheless, when the 1792 resolution calling for an end to the slave trade in four years came up for discussion in the mid-1790s, the times were unpropitious for abolitionism.[34]

Furthermore, in 1795–96 the British government responded to the dangers in the Caribbean by sending the biggest expedition yet to sail from British shores. They managed to save the British islands but suffered defeat in St. Domingue at a staggering cost. Major rebellions and devastating white mortality were the predominant features of the Caribbean in the 1790s; neither helped the abolitionists.[35]

BUT OTHER aspects of the long war in the Caribbean were more helpful to the abolitionist cause, especially if they could be presented as being in the national interest. At least five such developments fit the bill.

First, in the mid-1790s, in response to the heavy mortality of white troops, the British began recruiting their own slave troops—by war's end twelve regiments—who provided up to a third of the colonial garrisons. They proved their worth and helped save the British regime of slavery in the Caribbean. Ironically, the British government was, for the most part, buying these slaves from transatlantic slavers—making it the largest single purchaser of African arrivals and giving the British government a direct stake in the perpetuation of the trade. But, at war's end, abolitionists not only made the case that the British owed a debt to these slave soldiers, but that their courage and fidelity undercut all the stereotypes of slaves in general. There was a nice symmetry when, in the same year that the British government abolished the slave trade, it also emancipated the entire ten thousand men of the West India Regiments.[36]

Second, by the early nineteenth century British national security interests had shifted away from the Caribbean. The British withdrawal from St. Domingue in 1798 was part of that decision. Another occurred in 1802, when by the terms of the Treaty of Amiens, Britain returned all her West Indian conquests, except Trinidad. When war resumed the following year, the Caribbean assumed a lower priority, because of its reputation as a graveyard for soldiers and a realization that overseas adventures could undermine European strategy. Moreover, after so much blood and money had been spent on the Caribbean, too, the post–American independence argument that Parliament should not interfere in matters strictly colonial lost some of its force. The swing of formal empire to the east occurred not after the American Revolution but after the Anglo-French War in the Caribbean.[37]

Third, the Haitian Revolution's role in weakening French commercial competition was an important prerequisite for British politicians' responding to abolitionist pressure. The defeat of Napoleon's expeditionary force meant that the French were no longer a significant threat in the Caribbean. Patriotic hostility to France also ennobled antislavery, since Napoleon had restored slavery and the slave trade in what remained of the French Caribbean; Toussaint's betrayal by the French and his death in a French prison (1803) also evoked sympathy. In addition, the war helped destroy the French navy. Surely, as Michael Duffy notes, it was no mere "coincidence that the slave trade was finally abolished by Britain in the very year that the size of the French navy fell to its lowest point?"[38]

Fourth, the declaration of Haiti's independence in 1804 undoubtedly led to a resurgence in British abolitionism, making the cause seem both "more necessary" (because of the example of violent self-liberation) and "less problematical" (lessening fears that the French would or could step into the breach if the British withdrew from the trade). Pro-slavery and anti-Haiti up to that point, the London *Times* suddenly switched in favor of abolition.[39]

Finally, while ending the supply of slaves to foreigners had emerged as a proposal as early as 1792, abolitionists were able to extend the argument to newly conquered territories (on the grounds that they were often returned at peace and that the British had merely strengthened competitors) and thereby promote both aims in terms of national and military self-interest. Thus in 1802, Parliament limited the future supply of slaves to Trinidad, which, as Roger Anstey notes, was "the first major attempt by the abolitionists to achieve significant lessening of the slave trade specifically to British possessions on grounds other than the general principle." Three years later, they were able to do the same by gaining an order-in-council limiting supplies to the newly conquered Dutch Guiana. And finally, in 1806, Parliament ended the British slave trade to foreign colonies and conquered islands, which at that time amounted to about three-quarters of all British slaving. A year before final abolition, then, the abolitionists had succeeding in ending the bulk of the British slave trade by emphasizing the strategic interests of the British state in wartime.[40]

In short, the Haitian Revolution had contradictory effects. For British abolitionism, it was at first encouraging, then set back the movement for a decade, before finally Haiti's emergence as a weak state in 1804 created a more favorable antislavery moment. In general, St. Domingue's destruction was an immense boost to plantation slavery. It created a huge economic opportunity for planters throughout the hemisphere to take advantage of the resulting high prices; planters, with access to undeveloped land everywhere from Cuba to Brazil to Jamaica, clamored for more African slaves. Such certainly explains South Carolina's decision in December 1803 to reopen its slave trade. South Carolinians anticipated a bonanza with large planter demand for slaves from the west, a direct consequence of the Louisiana Purchase, which was of course predicated on the defeat of Napoleon's army in St. Domingue, and thus a direct example of the stimulus the Haitian Revolution gave to the demand for more African slaves. At the same time, however, the rest of the United States was shocked and angered by South Carolina's action. The Haitian Revolution thus strengthened the political argument for pressing Congress to outlaw the American slave trade in 1807. The Haitian Revolution's economic impact was primarily to augment plantation slavery, but its political impact went in the other direction—facilitating attempts in both Britain and the United States to curtail that same expansion. After the reverses in the Caribbean campaigns of the 1790s, imperial policymakers began to think defensively. There was no strong political impulse to open new plantation frontiers. They took Trinidad as a base for contraband trade with the Spanish Main.[41]

THIS QUICK sketch of some larger contexts and three abolitions—four, if you count the Haitian—has suggested some of the cosmopolitan, international flavor of the movement to end the slave trade at the end of the eighteenth and beginning of the nineteenth centuries. Abolition was hardly a parochial British affair. Danes, Americans, Haitians, and Britons knew and responded to what the others were doing. Planters and slaves in the Caribbean, black settlers and white adventurers in Africa, black rebels throughout the Atlantic, the St. Domingue slave revolt, and strategic national interests shaped abolitionist discourse and metropolitan actions. The coincidence of four countries abolishing the slave trade in the first decade of the nineteenth century also suggests that the British antislavery movement was no mere "historical accident," "a contingent event that just as easily might never have occurred." Such a claim is surely an exaggeration. To say that the abolitionist campaign "had its roots in a distinct and distinctive moment in British imperial history" is true, but that the same decision occurred in other countries at roughly the same time indicates broader forces were at work.[42]

Furthermore, to explicate the domestic and international forces in play when the first decisions to end the transatlantic slave trade were made means attending as closely to interests as to abolitionists. British abolition took its first inspiration from colonial interests aimed at achieving political autonomy; by their commitment to improvement, Caribbean planters paradoxically found some compatibility with abolitionist aims, even as those commitments arose out of defensiveness and political weakness; slaves were natural allies of abolitionists, although ironically they seem to have impeded as much as furthered abolitionist goals; and abolition's final realization in 1807 depended heavily on the enactment of earlier legislation that prohibited the British slave trade to foreign colonies in the West Indies, a decision that made sense to Parliament when Britain dominated the sea lanes and when supplying rivals with slaves was construed as strengthening competitors. By looking at slave trade abolition in this way, as a coalescence of interests and ideology rather than as a triumph of ideology over interests, it may no longer be possible to consider it an example of "the most altruistic act since Christ's crucifixion," as some contemporaries viewed it, or alternatively, using historian W. E. H. Lecky's often-quoted words, as probably one of "the three or four perfectly virtuous acts recorded in the history of nations," but perhaps an entangled world of pragmatism and principle is preferable to an ethereal realm of pure moral consciousness.[43]

Notes

1. Documents Relating to the Case of the Ship *Zong*, 1783, 3, 21, REC/19, National Maritime Museum, Greenwich. During the 1807 deliberations in the U.S. Congress over the slave trade, Virginian John Randolph argued that "the transportation of slaves must be considered like the transportation of indigo, coffee, or tobacco." *U.S. Gazette*, 16 February 1807. For the course of British abolition, see David Brion Davis, *Inhuman Bondage: The Rise and Fall of Slavery in the New World* (New York: Oxford University Press, 2006), 231–49; Adam Hochschild, *Bury the Chains: The British Struggle to Abolish Slavery* (London: Macmillan, 2005). "An African Merchant" argued that the African trade was "the foundation of our commerce, the support of our colonies, the life of our navigation, and first cause of our national industry and riches." African Merchant, *A Treatise upon the Trade from Great-Britain to Africa, humbly recommended to the Attention of Government* (London: R. Baldwin, 1772), 7.

2. For the most current figures, see David Eltis and David Richardson, "A New Assessment of the Transatlantic Slave Trade," in *Extending the Frontiers: Essays on the New Transatlantic Slave Trade Database*, ed. Eltis and Richardson (New Haven: Yale

University Press, 2008), 1–60. Of course, 1807 did not end the slave trade, only parts of it—essentially its Northern Atlantic component. After 1807 the South Atlantic system strengthened, with about three million Africans—a quarter of all those carried across the Atlantic—reaching the New World, primarily Brazil.

3. Joshua Evans Loftin, "The Abolition of the Danish Slave Trade" (PhD diss., Louisiana State University, 1977); Svend E. Green-Pedersen, "The Economic Considerations behind the Danish Abolition of the Negro Slave Trade," in *The Uncommon Market: Essays in the Economic History of the Atlantic Slave Trade,* ed. Henry A. Gemery and Jan S. Hogendorn (New York: Academic Press, 1979), 399–418; Green-Pedersen, "Slave Demography in the Danish West Indies and the Abolition of the Danish Slave Trade," in *The Abolition of the Atlantic Slave Trade: Origins and Effects in Europe, Africa, and the Americas,* ed. David Eltis and James Walvin (Madison: University of Wisconsin Press, 1981), 231–58; Hans Christian Johansen, "The Reality behind the Demographic Arguments to Abolish the Danish Slave Trade," in Eltis and Walvin, *Abolition,* 221–30; Erik Gøbel, "The Danish Edict of 16th March 1792 to Abolish the Slave Trade" in *Orbis in Orbem: Liber amicorum Jan Everaert,* ed. Jan Parmentier and Sander Spanoghe (Ghent: Academia Press, 2001), 251–63; Gøbel, "The Danish Edict of 1792 to Abolish the Slave Trade" (unpublished conference paper, 2007, in possession of author).

4. Christopher Leslie Brown, *Moral Capital: Foundations of British Abolitionism* (Chapel Hill: University of North Carolina Press, 2006), 107, 135–39, 142–44, 151; Don E. Fehrenbacher, *The Slaveholding Republic: An Account of the United States Government's Relations to Slavery* (New York: Oxford University Press, 2001), 16, 41–43 (quotation on 41), 135–49; Donald Robinson, *Slavery in the Structure of American Politics* (New York: Norton, 1979), 295–346; Matthew E. Mason, "Slavery Overshadowed: Congress Debates Prohibiting the Atlantic Slave Trade to the United States, 1806–1807," *Journal of the Early Republic* 20 (Spring 2000): 59–81; Mason, *Slavery and Politics in the Early American Republic* (Chapel Hill: University of North Carolina Press, 2006), 9–41; Robin Blackburn, *The Overthrow of Colonial Slavery, 1776–1848* (London: Verso, 1988), 286 (quotation).

5. Roger Anstey, *The Atlantic Slave Trade and British Abolition, 1760–1810* (London: Macmillan, 1975); James Walvin, *England, Slaves, and Freedom, 1776–1838* (Jackson: University of Mississippi Press, 1986), 97–123; Seymour Drescher, *Capitalism and Antislavery: British Mobilization in Comparative Perspective* (Houndmills, Basingstoke: Macmillan, 1986); J. R. Oldfield, *Popular Politics and British Anti-slavery: The Mobilisation of Public Opinion against the Slave Trade, 1787–1807* (Manchester: Manchester University Press, 1998); Judith Jennings, *The Business of Abolishing the British Slave Trade, 1783–1807* (London: Frank Cass, 1997); Hochschild, *Bury the Chains,* 112 (quotation); Drescher, "Public Opinion and Parliament in the Abolition of the British Slave Trade," in *The British Slave Trade: Abolition, Parliament and People,* ed. Stephen Farrell, Melanie Unwin, and James Walvin (Edinburgh: Edinburgh University Press, 2007), 42–65.

6. Thomas Arnold to Pennsylvania Abolition Society, 12 May 1789, in Richard S. Newman, *The Transformation of American Abolitionism: Fighting Slavery in the Early Republic* (Chapel Hill: University of North Carolina Press, 2002), 25–26; William Dickson, "Diary," 1792, inside cover, in Iain Whyte, *Scotland and the Abolition of Black Slavery, 1756–1838* (Edinburgh: Edinburgh University Press, 2006), 75. For the economic cost of British abolition, see Chaim D. Kaufmann and Robert A. Pape, "Explaining Costly International Moral Action: Britain's Sixty-Year Campaign against the Atlantic Slave Trade," *International Organization* 53, no. 4 (1999): 631–68.

7. These interests are by no means comprehensive. Against the proslavery argument that the slave trade was the nursery of seamen, abolitionists argued it was their graveyard. The "maritime interest" could be enlisted on behalf of abolition. See Christopher

Lloyd, *The Navy and the Slave Trade: The Suppression of the African Slave Trade in the Nineteenth Century* (London: Frank Cass, 1968); Whyte, *Scotland and Abolition*, 96.

8. David Brion Davis, *The Problem of Slavery in Western Culture* (Ithaca: Cornell University Press, 1966), 90; Seymour Drescher, "People and Parliament: The Rhetoric of the British Slave Trade," *Journal of Interdisciplinary History* 20, no. 4 (1990): 561–80.

9. Lowell J. Ragatz, *The Decline of the Planter Class in the British Caribbean, 1763–1833: A Study in Social and Economic History* (New York: Century, 1928); Eric Williams, *Capitalism and Slavery* (Chapel Hill: University of North Carolina Press, 1944). The most effective rebuttal is Seymour Drescher, *Econocide: British Slavery in the Era of Abolition* (Pittsburgh: University of Pittsburgh Press, 1977). See also J. R. Ward, *British West Indian Slavery, 1750–1834: The Process of Amelioration* (Oxford: Clarendon Press, 1988); John J. McCusker, "The Economy of the British West Indies, 1763–1790: Growth, Stagnation, or Decline?" in *Essays in the Economic History of the Atlantic World*, ed. McCusker (London: Routledge, 1997), 310–31. The best effort at resuscitation of the Williams thesis is David Beck Ryden, "Does Decline Make Sense? The West Indian Economy and the Abolition of the British Slave Trade," *Journal of Interdisciplinary History* 31, no. 3 (2001): 347–74, and *West Indian Slavery and British Abolition, 1783–1807* (Cambridge: Cambridge University Press, 2009). For a judicious summary, see David Richardson, "The Ending of the British Slave Trade in 1807: The Economic Context," in Farrell, Unwin, and Walvin, *British Slave Trade*, 127–40.

10. David Lambert, *White Creole Culture, Politics and Identity during the Age of Abolition* (Cambridge: Cambridge University Press, 2005), 11–20; Matthew Mulcahy, *Hurricanes and Society in the British Greater Caribbean, 1624–1783* (Baltimore: Johns Hopkins University Press, 2006), 147, 173 (quotations); Ragatz, *Planter Class*, 242; Andrew Jackson O'Shaughnessy, *An Empire Divided: The American Revolution and the British Caribbean* (Philadelphia: University of Pennsylvania Press, 2000), 239–48.

11. David Eltis, *Economic Growth and the Ending of the Transatlantic Slave Trade* (New York: Oxford University Press, 1987), 5–6; Michael Duffy, "World-Wide War and British Expansion, 1793–1815," in *The Oxford History of the British Empire*, vol. 2, *The Eighteenth Century*, ed. P. J. Marshall (Oxford: Oxford University Press, 1998), 192; J. R. Ward, "The British West Indies in the Age of Abolition, 1748–1815," in Marshall, *Eighteenth Century*, 422; Ward, *British West Indian Slavery*, 62–95, 113, 195–98; Justin Roberts, "Working between the Lines: Labor and Agriculture on Two Barbadian Slave Plantations, 1796–1797," *William and Mary Quarterly* 63, no. 3 (2006): 551–86; Edward Long, *The History of Jamaica*, 3 vols. (London: T. Lowndes, 1774), 1:435–64; Heather Cateau, "Conservatism and Change Implementation in the British West Indian Sugar Industry, 1750–1810," *Journal of Caribbean History* 29, no. 1 (1995): 1–36. If diversification seems an unlikely ally of abolitionism, consider that Tench Coxe, who played a major role in formulating U.S. economic policy during the Washington and Jefferson administrations and who became secretary of the newly re-formed Pennsylvania Abolition Society in 1787, made diversification of Southern agriculture the key to his hopes of ending slavery. See Jacob E. Cooke, *Tench Coxe and the Early Republic* (Chapel Hill: University of North Carolina Press, 1978), 92–94, 106, 149.

12. Heather Cateau, "The New 'Negro' Business: Hiring in the British West Indies 1750–1810" in *In the Shadow of the Plantation: Caribbean History and Legacy*, ed. Alvin O. Thompson and Woodville K. Marshall (Kingston: Ian Randle, 2002), 100–120; *Gentleman's Magazine* 59 (1789): 334; Roberts, "Working between the Lines," 551–86; B. W. Higman, *Slave Population and Economy in Jamaica, 1807–1834* (Cambridge: Cambridge University Press, 1976), 187–211; Higman, *Slave Populations of the British Caribbean, 1807–1834* (Baltimore: Johns Hopkins University Press, 1984), 179–204; Philip D. Morgan,

"Task and Gang Systems: The Organization of Labor on New World Plantations," in *Work and Labor in Early America*, ed. Stephen Innes (Chapel Hill: University of North Carolina Press, 1988), 189–220.

13. David Watts, *The West Indies: Patterns of Development, Culture, and Environmental Change since 1492* (Cambridge: Cambridge University Press, 1987), 382–447; Richard H. Grove, *Green Imperialism: Colonial Expansion, Tropical Island Edens and the Origins of Environmentalism, 1600–1800* (Cambridge: Cambridge University Press, 1995), 264–308; B. W. Higman, *Plantation Jamaica, 1750–1850: Capital and Control in a Colonial Economy* (Kingston: University of the West Indies Press, 2005), 18, 22–29, 41–112, 137–293; Douglas Hall, "Absentee Proprietorship in the British West Indies, to about 1750," *Jamaican Historical Review* 4 (1964): 15–35; Trevor Burnard, "Passengers Only: The Extent and Significance of Absenteeism in Eighteenth-Century Jamaica," *Atlantic Studies* 1, no. 2 (2004): 178–95; Samuel Martin, *Essay upon Plantership, Humbly inscrib'd to all the Planters of the British Sugar-Colonies in America.* (Antigua: T. Smith, 1750); John Carter Brown Library, Providence, RI, Codex Eng. 74, Thomas Hulton, "Account of Travels," 54; Thomas W. Krise, ed., *Caribbeana: An Anthology of English Literature of the West Indies, 1657–1777* (Chicago: University of Chicago Press, 1999), 168; Richard B. Sheridan, "Samuel Martin, Innovating Sugar Planter of Antigua, 1750–1776," *Agricultural History* 34, no. 3 (1960): 126–39; Natalie Zacek, "Cultivating Virtue: Samuel Martin and the Paternal Ideal in the Eighteenth-Century English West Indies," *Wadabagei: A Journal of the Caribbean and Its Diaspora* 10, no. 3 (Autumn 2007): 8–31; Janet Schaw, *Journal of a Lady of Quality: Being the Narrative of a Journey from Scotland to the West Indies, North Carolina, and Portugal, in the Years 1774 to 1776*, ed. Evangeline W. Andrews and Charles M. Andrews (New Haven: Yale University Press, 1921), 103–6. For insights into late-eighteenth-century agricultural improvement, see John Dovaston, "Agricultura Americana, or Improvements in West-India Husbandry Considered," John Carter Brown Library, Codex Eng. 60; Nicholas Robson, *Hints for a General View of the Agricultural State of the Parish of Saint James, in the Island of Jamaica* (London: John Stockdale, 1796).

14. Edwin Lascelles et al., *Instructions for the Management of a Plantation in Barbados. And for the treatment of Negroes* (London, 1786), 2; Rev. Robert Boucher Nickolls, *Observations, Occasioned by the Attempts made in England to Effect the Abolition of the Slave Trade* (Kingston: G. Francklyn, 1789), 17 (and see 33–34 for a letter to Nickolls from a long-time resident of the West Indies that names ten estates that "kept up their stock of Negroes by the natural increase"); Sheila Lambert, ed., *House of Commons Sessional Papers of the Eighteenth Century*, 132 vols. (Wilmington, DE: Scholarly Resources, 1975), 87:439; 122:70, 96; John Cobham to John W. Nelson, 31 October 1801, cited in S. D. Smith, *Slavery, Family and Gentry Capitalism in the British Atlantic: The World of the Lascelles, 1648–1834* (Cambridge: Cambridge University Press, 2006), 265; Samuel Watt to James Watt, 30 September 1804, cited in Nini Rodgers, *Ireland, Slavery and Anti-slavery: 1612–1865* (Houndmills, Basingstoke: Palgrave Macmillan, 2007), 86. See also B. W. Higman, "Slavery and the Development of Demographic Theory in the Age of the Industrial Revolution," in *Slavery and British Society, 1776–1846*, ed. James Walvin (Baton Rouge: Louisiana State University Press, 1982), 164–94.

15. Samuel Martin, *A Short Treatise on the slavery of Negroes in the British Colonies* (Antigua: Robert Mearns, 1775), 11–12; Seymour Drescher, *The Mighty Experiment: Free Labor versus Slavery in British Emancipation* (New York: Oxford University Press, 2002), 110–13; D. Lambert, *White Creole Culture*, 41–72; S. K., *A Short and Impartial Account of the Treatment of Slaves in the Island of Antigua . . .* (Cork: John Cronin, 1789); and Rodgers, *Ireland*, 180–81.

16. Neville A. T. Hall, *Slave Society in the Danish West Indies: St. Thomas, St. John, and St. Croix*, ed. B. W. Higman (Mona, Jamaica: University of the West Indies Press, 1992), 192–93; Green-Pedersen, "Slave Demography," 231–58; Gøbel, "Danish Edict," 251–63.

17. Christopher L. Brown, "The Politics of Slavery," in *The British Atlantic World, 1500–1800*, ed. David Armitage and Michael J. Braddick (New York: Palgrave Macmillan, 2002), 220; Sidney W. Mintz, *Caribbean Transformations* (Baltimore: Johns Hopkins University Press, 1974), 151–52, 180–213.

18. Karl Watson, "Capital Sentences against Slaves in Barbados in the Eighteenth Century: An Analysis," in Thompson and Marshall, *Shadow of the Plantation*, 196–221; Stephen Fuller, *The New Act of Assembly of the Island of Jamaica* (London: B. White, 1789); Anstey, *Atlantic Slave Trade*, 319. For the lobby, see Alexandra Franklin, "Enterprise and Advantage: The West India Interest in Britain, 1774–1840" (PhD diss., University of Pennsylvania, 1992); Andrew O'Shaughnessy, "The Formation of a Commercial Lobby: The West India Interest, British Colonial Policy and the American Revolution," *Historical Journal* 40, no. 1 (1997): 71–95.

19. Deirdre Coleman, *Romantic Colonization and British Anti-slavery* (Cambridge: Cambridge University Press, 2005), 1–133; Brown, *Moral Capital*, 259–330. See also John Hippisley, *Essays: I, On the Populousness of Africa . . .* (London: T. Lownds, 1764); Hippisley, "On the Populousness of Africa: An Eighteenth-Century Text," *Population and Development Review* 24, no. 2 (1998): 601–8; R. Mansell Prothero, "John Hippisley on the Populousness of Africa: A Comment," ibid., 609–12. Hippisley, who served as an officer of the Company of Merchants Trading to Africa and briefly as governor of Cape Coast Castle, argued that Africa "could spare thousands, nay, millions more, and go on doing the same to the end of time." He also hinted that traders should "soften the misery" of slaves "by every safe and reasonable indulgence that their humanity can suggest."

20. Daniel Hopkins, "Peter Thonning's Map of Danish Guinea and Its Use in Colonial Administration and Atlantic Diplomacy, 1801–1890," *Cartographica* 35, nos. 3–4 (1998): 99–122; Hopkins, "Danish Natural History and African Colonialism at the Close of the Eighteenth Century: Peter Thonning's 'Scientific Journey' to the Guinea Coast, 1799–1803," *Archives of Natural History* 26 (1999): 369–418; Hopkins, "The Danish Ban on the Atlantic Slave Trade and Denmark's African Colonial Ambitions, 1787–1807," *Itinerario* 25, nos. 3–4 (2001): 154–84; Hopkins, "Denmark's Prohibition of the Slave Trade and African Colonial Policy, 1787–1850" (unpublished conference paper, 2007, in possession of author).

21. Brown, *Moral Capital*, 266 (Thomas), 269–75 (Postlethwayt), 277–78, 279 (Trafford); Temple Luttrell, 28 May 1777, "Proceedings in the Commons on the State of the African Company, and of the Trade to Africa," in William Cobbett, ed., *Parliamentary History of England from the earliest period to the year 1803*, 36 vols. (London: T. C. Hansard, 1806–20), 19, col. 306; British Library, London, Add MSS 38345, Henry Trafford, "Plan of an Universal Revolution of Commerce"; John Lowe Jr., *Liberty or Death: A Tract, by Which is Vindicated the Obvious Practicability of Trading to the Coasts of Guinea, for Its Natural Products, in Lieu of the Slave-Trade* (Manchester: : J. Harrop, 1789), 32, cited in Coleman, *Romantic Colonization*, 2, 13–17. For an early American position, see James Swan, *A Dissuasion to Great-Britain and the Colonies, from the Slave Trade to Africa . . .* (Boston: E. Russell, 1772). For suggestions that Ireland concentrate on valuable African commodities, see [Frederick Jebb], *Thoughts on the Discontents of the People last Year respecting the Sugar Duties . . .* (Dublin: W. Wilson, 1781); *Observations on the Advantages which would arise to this country from opening a trade with the Coast of Africa, with a plan for the same by which the Slave-Trade may be Ultimately Abolished* (Dublin, 1785).

22. Coleman, *Romantic Colonization,* 28 (quotation); Carl B. Wadström, *Observations on the Slave Trade, and a Description of some Part of the Coast of Guinea* . . . (London: J. Phillips, 1789); Wadström, *An Essay on Colonization, particularly applied to the Western Coast of Africa* . . . , 2 vols. (London: Darton and Harvey, 1794–95), 1:iii (quotation); August Nordenskiöld, *Plan for a Free Community upon the Coast of Africa* . . . (London: R. Hindmarsh, 1789), 50 (quotation); Philip D. Curtin, *The Image of Africa: British Ideas and Action, 1780–1850,* 2 vols. (Madison: University of Wisconsin Press, 1964), 1:60 (quotation).

23. Thomas Clarkson, *The History of the Rise, Progress, and Accomplishment of the Abolition of the African Slave-Trade* . . . , 2 vols. (London: Longman, Hurst, Rees, and Orme, 1808), 2:14–16, see also 1:302–4, 373, 383, 474; Marcus Wood, "Packaging Liberty and Marketing the Gift of Freedom: 1807 and the Legacy of Clarkson's Chest," in Farrell, Unwin, and Walvin, *British Slave Trade,* 203–23 (quotation, 218), 308–13 (the chest itself); Huntington Library, San Marino, CA, Macauley MSS, Zachary Macauley Journal, folder 16, 24 November 1796, folder 18, 5 January 1797.

24. Simon Schama, *Rough Crossings: Britain, the Slaves, and the American Revolution* (New York: HarperCollins, 2006), 389 (quotation); Wadström, *Colonization,* 2:249–59. See also Christopher Fyfe, *A History of Sierra Leone* (London: Oxford University Press, 1962), 1–126; Fyfe and Charles Jones, eds., *Our Children Free and Happy: Letters from Black Settlers in Africa in the 1790s* (Edinburgh: Edinburgh University Press, 1991); Stephen Braidwood, *Black Poor and White Philanthropists: London's Blacks and the Foundation of the Sierra Leone Settlement, 1786–1791* (Liverpool: Liverpool University Press, 1994); Coleman, *Romantic Colonization,* 106–33; Cassandra Pybus, *Epic Journeys of Freedom: Runaway Slaves of the American Revolution and Their Global Quest for Liberty* (Boston: Beacon Press, 2006), 139–55; James Sidbury, *Becoming African in America: Race and Nation in the Early Black Atlantic* (New York: Oxford University Press, 2007).

25. Douglas A. Lorimer, "Black Slaves and English Liberty: A Re-examination of Racial Slavery in England," *Immigrants and Minorities* 3, no. 2 (1984): 121–50; Lorimer, "Black Resistance to Slavery and Racism in Eighteenth-Century England," in *Essays on the History of Blacks in Britain: From Roman Times to the Mid-twentieth Century,* ed. Jagdish S. Gundara and Ian Duffield (Brookfield, VT: Avebury, 1992), 59–70; Brown, *Moral Capital,* 283–84, 297; Duke University, William Wilberforce Papers, Granville Sharp to William Wilberforce, 4 June 1795, cited in Julius S. Scott, "Afro-American Sailors and the International Communication Network: The Case of Newport Bowers," in *Jack Tar in History: Essays in the History of Maritime Life and Labour,* ed. Colin D. Howell and Richard J. Twomey (Fredericton, New Brunswick: Acadiensis Press, 1991), 50–51. For more on Somerset and Knight, see Ruth Paley, "After Somerset: Mansfield, Slavery and the Law in England, 1772–1830," in *Law, Crime and English Society, 1660–1830,* ed. Norma Landau (Cambridge: Cambridge University Press, 2002), 165–84; "Somerset's Case Revisited," Forum, *Law and History Review* 24, no. 3 (2006): 601–71; Whyte, *Scotland and Abolition,* 16–20, 22–30, 32–36.

26. Richard Rathbone, "Some Thoughts on Resistance to Enslavement in West Africa," *Slavery and Abolition* 6, no. 3 (1985): 173–84; Winston McGowan, "African Resistance to the Atlantic Slave Trade in West Africa," *Slavery and Abolition* 11, no. 1 (1990): 1–29; Ismail Rashid, "Escape, Revolt, and Marronage in Eighteenth and Nineteenth Century Sierra Leone Hinterland," *Canadian Journal of African Studies* 34, no. 4 (2000): 656–83; Walter Hawthorne, "Nourishing a Stateless Society during the Slave Trade: The Rise of Balanta Paddy-Rice Production in Guinea-Bissau," *Journal of African History* 42, no. 1 (2001): 1–24; Martin A. Klein, "The Slave Trade and Decentralized Societies,"

ibid., 49–65; David Richardson, "Shipboard Revolts, African Authority, and the Atlantic Slave Trade," *William and Mary Quarterly* 58, no. 1 (2001): 69–92; James F. Searing, "No Kings, No Lords, No Slaves: Ethnicity and Religion among the Sereer-Safèn of Western Bawol, 1700–1914," *Journal of African History* 43, no. 3 (2002): 407–29; Robin Law, "Legal and Illegal Enslavement in West Africa, in the Context of the Trans-Atlantic Slave Trade," in *Ghana in Africa and the World: Essays in Honor of Adu Boahen*, ed. Toyin Falola (Trenton, NJ: Africa World Press, 2003), 513–33; Sylviane A. Diouf, ed., *Fighting the Slave Trade: West African Strategies* (Athens: Ohio University Press, 2003); Randy L. Sparks, *The Two Princes of Calabar: An Eighteenth-Century Atlantic Odyssey* (Cambridge, MA: Harvard University Press, 2004). For slave resistance on the Middle Passage, see David Eltis and Martin Halbert, eds., *The Trans-Atlantic Slave Trade Database: Voyages* found at http://www.slavevoyages.org/tast/index.faces. For African resistance, search under Voyage Outcome in Basic Variables in the Voyages Database tab. See also Eric Robert Taylor, *If We Must Die: Shipboard Insurrections in the Era of the Atlantic Slave Trade* (Baton Rouge: Louisiana State University Press, 2006).

27. Cobbett, *Parliamentary History*, 27: col. 504; Sir Lewis Namier and John Brooke, *The House of Commons, 1754–1790*, 3 vols. (London: Oxford University Press, 1964), 2:686, cited in James W. LoGerfo, "Sir William Dolben and the Cause of Humanity: The Passage of the Slave Trade Regulation Act of 1788," *Eighteenth-Century Studies* 6, no. 4 (Summer 1973): 431–51, esp. 439. For a work that argues for the positive relationship between slave revolts and the abolitionist cause, but from a post-1816 viewpoint, see Gelien Matthews, *Caribbean Slave Revolts and the British Abolition Movement* (Baton Rouge: Louisiana State University Press, 2006).

28. Marcus Wood, *Blind Memory: Visual Representations of Slavery in England and America, 1780–1865* (New York: Routledge, 2000), 22–23; Gary B. Nash, *The Forgotten Fifth: African Americans in the Age of Revolution* (Cambridge, MA: Harvard University Press., 2006), 23 (quotation); Nash, *Race and Revolution* (Madison: University of Wisconsin Press, 1990), 57; Michael Craton, *Testing the Chains: Resistance to Slavery in the British West Indies* (Ithaca: Cornell University Press, 1982), 180.

29. Seymour Drescher, *From Slavery to Freedom: Comparative Studies in the Rise and Fall of Atlantic Slavery* (New York: New York University Press, 1999), 218; Gert Oostindie, ed., *Fifty Years Later: Antislavery, Capitalism, and Modernity in the Dutch Orbit* (Pittsburgh: University of Pittsburgh Press, 1996), 17; Marjoleine Kars, who has shared some of her unpublished papers, is writing a book on the Berbice slave revolt of 1763.

30. Craton, *Testing the Chains*, 172 (Jamaica), 225 (Dominica); O'Shaughnessy, *Empire Divided*, 153 (Jamaica); National Library of Wales, Aberystwyth, Thomas Barritt to Nathaniel Phillips, 8 December 1791, quoted in Clare Taylor, "Planter Attitudes to the American and French Revolutions," *National Library of Wales Journal* 21, no. 2 (1979): 113–30 (quotation, 124); Philip D. Morgan, *Slave Counterpoint: Black Culture in the Eighteenth-Century Chesapeake and Lowcountry* (Chapel Hill: University of North Carolina Press, 1998), 667; Davis, *Inhuman Bondage*, 144–47, 149.

31. David Patrick Geggus, "Slavery, War, and Revolution in the Greater Caribbean, 1789–1815," in *A Turbulent Time: The French Revolution and the Greater Caribbean*, ed. David Barry Gaspar and Geggus (Bloomington: Indiana University Press, 1997), 1–50; Geggus, *Haitian Revolutionary Studies* (Bloomington: Indiana University Press, 2002), 12, 36–37, 123, 127–29, 142–43, 266n33; Brendan McConville, *The King's Three Faces: The Rise and Fall of Royal America, 1688–1776* (Chapel Hill: University of North Carolina Press, 2006), 175–82; John Thornton, "I Am the Subject of the King of Kongo: African Political Ideology and the Haitian Revolution," *Journal of World History* 4 (Fall 1993): 181–214; Laurent Dubois, *Avengers of the New World: The Story of the Haitian*

Revolution (Cambridge, MA: Harvard University Press, 2004), 106–9 (quotation, 107), 158–60, 182–83.

32. Davis, *Inhuman Bondage*, 157–74; David Patrick Geggus, ed., *The Impact of the Haitian Revolution in the Atlantic World* (Columbia: University of South Carolina Press, 2001), x; Laurent Dubois and John D. Garrigus, *Slave Revolution in the Caribbean, 1789–1804: A Brief History with Documents* (New York: Palgrave Macmillan, 2006); Robin Blackburn, "Haiti, Slavery, and the Age of the Democratic Revolution," *William and Mary Quarterly*, 3d ser., 63, no. 4 (2006): 643–74.

33. David Patrick Geggus, "British Opinion and the Emergence of Haiti, 1791–1805," in Walvin, *Slavery and British Society*, ed. Walvin, 123–49.

34. Laurent Dubois, *A Colony of Citizens: Revolution and Slave Emancipation in the French Caribbean, 1787–1804* (Chapel Hill: University of North Carolina Press, 2004), esp. 222–48; Craton, *Testing the Chains*, 180–94, 211–23; Drescher, *Capitalism and Antislavery*, 104–6.

35. Michael Duffy, *Soldiers, Sugar, and Seapower: The British Expeditions to the West Indies and the War against Revolutionary France* (Oxford: Clarendon Press, 1987); David Patrick Geggus, *Slavery, War, and Revolution: The British Occupation of Saint Domingue, 1793–1798* (Oxford; Clarendon Press, 1982).

36. Roger Norman Buckley, *Slaves in Red Coats: The British West India Regiments, 1795–1815* (New Haven: Yale University Press, 1979); Philip D. Morgan and Andrew Jackson O'Shaughnessy, "Arming Slaves in the American Revolution," in *Arming Slaves from Classical Times to the Modern Age*, ed. Christopher Leslie Brown and Morgan (New Haven: Yale University Press, 2006), 180–208.

37. Duffy, "World-Wide War," and Ward, "The British West Indies in the Age of Abolition," in Marshall, *Eighteenth Century*, esp. 195–96, 420–21; Michael Duffy, "The French Revolution and British Attitudes to the West Indian Colonies" in Gaspar and Geggus, *Turbulent Time*, 78–101, esp. 96.

38. Duffy, "French Revolution," 95 (quotation).

39. Geggus, "British Opinion," 123–49; Geggus, "Haiti and the Abolitionists: Opinion, Propaganda and International Politics in Britain and France, 1804–1838," in *Abolition and Its Aftermath: The Historical Context, 1790–1916*, ed. David Richardson (London: Frank Cass, 1985), 113–40, esp. 116–17.

40. Anstey, *Atlantic Slave Trade*, 279, 334 (quotation), 346–49, 356, 367–82.

41. Geggus, ed., *Impact of the Haitian Revolution*, 10–13; Jed Handelsman Shugerman, "The Louisiana Purchase and South Carolina's Reopening of the Slave Trade in 1803," *Journal of the Early Republic* 22, no. 2 (2002): 263–90.

42. Brown, *Moral Capital*, 30, 462.

43. David Brion Davis, "Capitalism, Abolitionism, and Hegemony," in *British Capitalism and Caribbean Slavery: The Legacy of Eric Williams*, ed. Barbara A. Solow and Stanley L. Engerman (Cambridge: Cambridge University Press, 1987), 215; William E. H. Lecky, *A History of European Morals from Augustus to Charlemagne*, 2 vols. (London: Longmans, Green, 1869), 1:161.

FIVE

Emperors of the World

British Abolitionism and Imperialism

SEYMOUR DRESCHER

IN 1799, midway into the twenty-year debate on British slave trade abolition, the Earl of Westmoreland rose in the House of Lords to mock the
Sierra Leone Company's directors as quixotic visionaries, attempting to
ban a vast international trade along a broad swath of the coast of Africa:
"Can a miserable settlement on the coast of Africa alter the manners of
Kingdoms larger than Europe?" Who, he asked, were "this great company, these emperors of the world, who measure their empire by degrees
and lines of the globe . . . ? Will you decree *your* colonies to decline?"[1]

Less than two decades later an abolitionist delegation arrived in Paris
with the aim of persuading the restored French monarchy to renounce
the slave trade. The French colonial minister was appalled: "Do you
English mean to bind the world?" Nearly two centuries later historian
Howard Temperley concluded that one could easily understand why
Southern slaveholders and Indian sepoys should have responded violently to what they saw as an attempt to impose an alien and destructive
way of life upon them.[2]

Reviewing British slave trade abolition from the perspective of two
centuries, how may we assess its impact in relation to the phenomenon
we began to call imperialism a little over a century ago? The context of a
commemoration is not fixed once for all in human memory or historical
discourse. It shifts over time, sometimes churning up long-forgotten or
barely noticed debris from far upstream.

For almost a century and a half after 1807, the historiographical context of British slave trade abolition seemed clear. Abolition was part of Britain's unchallenged status at the center of the movement to eliminate slavery from the world. Symptomatic was the centenary of British colonial slave emancipation, in 1933. It was celebrated in Hull, Wilberforce's birthplace, as a national and imperial triumph. The London *Times* accurately headlined the event as the Centenary of Wilberforce. G. M. Trevelyan and Reginald Coupland agreed that abolition had elevated all mankind to a higher plane. The national memory was refreshed by a roll call of the gallant band of Saints led by their English hero.[3]

The beneficiaries were also appropriately noted: West Indians assembling in devotion to await the sunrise of freedom, and the natives of Africa, still unaware that future British rule would entail the end of slavery in the "heart of darkness." The story was dramatic, the motivation clear, the ending happy. Abolitionism had made Britain safe for reform, the West Indies safe for freedom, and Africa safe for domination. Embedded in the celebration was an explicit justification of British imperialism. Coupland concluded, almost in passing, that the abolitionist crusade had guaranteed that the empire would do right by its African subjects.

Fifty years later, during the last great commemoration of abolitionism before this year's bicentenary, the context had changed utterly. In 1983, I attended an academic conference at the University of Hull entitled "Abolition and Its Aftermath." I noted that the Saints had virtually vanished from the program. There were no papers devoted specifically to British abolitionism, nor to its saints, not even a paper on William Wilberforce himself. I was reminded of William Cobbett's quip when he was forced to leave England in 1816. He consoled himself with the thought, "No Wilberforces! Think of *that!* No Wilberforces!"[4]

WHAT HAD happened in the half century between 1933 and 1983 was a dramatic demolition of the whole structure of European overseas empire that had dominated so much of the earth in 1933. In the wake of the Second World War the collapse of imperialism proceeded even more rapidly than its fluctuations and extensions during previous centuries. One aspect of the demolition was a historiographic revaluation of the great campaign against the slave trade and slavery by the world's paramount empire. The emblematic work in this process was, of course, Eric Williams's *Capitalism and Slavery* (1944). Williams's study was, among other things, an explicit devaluation of the significance of morality in the destruction of British slavery and an implicit devaluation of Britain's use of abolitionism as a justification for imperial rule in the whole of its Afro-American orbit. In Williams's perspective slavery provided the basis for British economic expansion up to the Industrial Revolution, and Britain's antislavery in turn provided the basis for its imperialism: "The defense or attack," he concluded, "is always on the high moral or political plane. The thing defended or attacked is always something that you can touch or see, to be measured in pounds sterling or pounds avoirdupois, in dollars and cents, yards, feet and inches. This is not a crime. It is a fact."[5]

Within this frame of reference moral and political motivations and outcomes were so conflated with economic motivations that they could be treated as functions of economic forces. Thirty years ago it was unusual to argue that in 1807 slavery was not a wasted enterprise that could easily be terminated in exchange for accumulating moral capital.[6]

So where do we stand at the bicentennial of British slave trade abolition? Perhaps it is significant that a book entitled *Moral Capital* appeared on the eve of this commemoration. It is a deeply researched study of the foundations of British abolitionism. The Wilberforce Centre for the Study of Slavery and Emancipation was launched at Hull.

The point is not that British abolition was again to be treated as one of the "three or four perfectly virtuous pages" in the history of nations. Eric Williams saw to that. It does mean, however, that the moral and political dimensions of both abolitionism and its consequences are being reenvisioned as complex human activities with origins in specific political contexts and diverse effects. Some were clearly contrary to the logic of economics or political economy. To put it succinctly, the current mood reopened the historiographical landscape to the study of abolitionism and its political outcomes as autonomous processes in the dismantling of the transoceanic slave trade.[7]

I'd like to consider one such process, the relation of abolitionism to British imperialism. For the sake of analysis I distinguish imperialism from another phenomenon, *colonialism*. The latter term was initially used to describe European settlement in non-European areas of the earth. Colonialism applied to European settlements in large portions of North America, South America, Australia, New Zealand, and Eurasia that were dominated by populations of permanent European residents. Nineteenth-century British expansion after abolition had little to do with its policies toward the slave trade or slavery. I will define imperialism by the features developed at the apogee of European domination over overwhelmingly non-European societies during the nineteenth and twentieth centuries and by its distinguishing difference from other forms of expansion—trade, exchange, and migration. Classic imperialism is a form of political incursion, or a policy aiming at incursion, into the sovereignty of another state or community. Its agents usually believed that they represented a superior civilization in situations of unequal power, culture, morality, or religion.[8]

I will emphasize the relation of British abolitionism to imperialism from about the 1780s to the 1870s, when the most salient objective of British abolitionism beyond its own empire was the ending of the transoceanic slave trade. Let's begin with two observations. During the decades before slave trade abolition, in 1807, British traders were the single most important carriers of Africans to the New World. Even more significantly, during those decades Britain aimed to use its position as the world's premier naval power to expand both its slave system and its dominance over rival European producers of tropical staples.

The first site of imperialism to be examined is therefore the British Caribbean. When both popular and parliamentary abolitionism emerged in the 1780s, the British West Indies was still Britain's premier imperial possession. Its relative place in the empire had only been enhanced by the loss of the continental colonies. For the previous century and a half, conquests of foreign slave colonies and slave trade factories had been causes for national celebration. The retention of the threatened British possessions during the American War of Independence was hailed in the metropolis as one of the few consoling outcomes of the conflict. In imperial calculations the British sugar colonies had become, in Michael Duffy's words, not just a jewel in the imperial crown "but now virtually the crown itself."[9]

Despite the emergence of popular abolitionism in 1788–92 the British government viewed the outbreak of war with France in 1793 as yet another opportunity to expand its slave empire in the Caribbean in order to add to Britain's commercial and naval supremacy. Only the outcome of the great slave revolution in the Caribbean and the fortunes of war in Europe prevented the permanent acquisition of a vast new slave empire from the French. Nevertheless, fifteen years of warfare at enormous human cost allowed the British to open two new potential frontiers for slavery (Spanish Trinidad, Dutch Demerara and Berbice) before they shut down their transatlantic slave labor supply in 1807. These two underdeveloped colonies, first captured in the late 1790s, contained far more arable land than Britain had acquired in two centuries of previous conflicts in the Caribbean. Trinidad alone, definitively acquired in 1802, could have kept British slavers occupied for another century. By 1814 the British also retained possession over the island of Mauritius, in the Indian Ocean, and the Cape Colony, in South Africa. The first was seized from the French (1810) and the second from the Dutch (1806). Thus, by the end of the Napoleonic Wars the British had more than doubled the size of their imperial slave populations at the end of the War of American Independence. They had doubled the capital invested in slave production. They dominated the Western world's sugar market more thoroughly than at any point in the history of the transatlantic slave system. And the British Empire had increased its potential for further expansion tenfold.[10]

Even before the passage of abolition, in 1807, however, the British government, under abolitionist pressure, had begun to constrict the development of these new slave frontiers. After the fall of Napoleon however, the fate of Britain's slave empire without fresh labor supplies became increasingly clear. From 1815 the British share of slave-produced staples in the world market declined steadily. Those of slave-importing Cuba and Brazil correspondingly expanded. This was most graphically demonstrated in the staple-export statistics of Trinidad and Cuba, which was retained by Spain during the French Wars. During the first half of the nineteenth century Trinidad's sugar exports reached only twenty thousand tons per year. Cuba's exports, fed by the African slave trade, soared to over three hundred fifty thousand tons per year. The contrast between Cuba and Trinidad was emblematic of the trajectories of the two Caribbean slave empires. On the eve of British abolition its Caribbean colonies produced well over half the sugar reaching the North Atlantic market. The Spanish Caribbean accounted for only 12 percent. In 1850 the British West Indian share had dropped to 13 percent. Its Spanish counterpart had risen to 27 percent. By the end of the era of Cuba's slave trade, in 1870, that island alone delivered 42 percent of the world's tropical sugar to the market. No wonder the *Times* lamented that Trinidad would have developed far more rapidly under the corrupt and authoritarian domination of Spain than it had under British colonial rule.[11]

Decade after decade the British government hobbled the imperial growth of its slave empire, in full awareness of the consequences of abolitionist policies. From the outset parliamentarians knew the consequences of allowing the resumption of the slave trade by other colonial powers. As early as 1814, James Stephen, Britain's most knowledgeable abolitionist and a member of Parliament, warned the prime minister, Lord Liverpool, that allowing other Europeans to reopen the slave trade would help them to raise sugar at lower cost. In 1814 a profound contradiction was opening up between Britain's imperial economic interest and its unilateral prohibition of the slave trade. That contradiction continued for more than half a century after abolition of the British slave trade. The same situation prevailed in the slave trade itself. On the eve of abolition in 1807 about 40 percent of captive Africans crossing the Atlantic were being landed in British ports.

By the end of the Napoleonic Wars the British government's theoretical alternatives were clear: they could employ a variety of diplomatic, economic, and military pressures trying to choke off the trade in Africans while maintaining abolition in the British colonies, or they could conditionally restore the African trade to the British system until an effective international agreement outlawed the traffic.[12]

The first option was employed for the next two generations, despite considerable expense, endless diplomatic complications, and enormous opportunities for evasion by foreign merchants and their rulers. The British slowly developed an elaborate treaty network and a large naval patrol to curtail the transatlantic slave trade. Despite this effort more than three million Africans were delivered to the Americas in defiance of that policy for six decades after 1807.[13]

The second option needed to rely only on effective multinational reciprocity. It protected both British imperial and colonial interests. It would have minimized diplomatic complications, maximized the competitive position of British slavery, and prevented or slowed any decline in Britain's world position in tropical production. It would have eliminated the policing costs of the British navy and would certainly have benefited the British consumer. The human costs would have been borne chiefly by Africans, who had neither capital nor votes in metropolitan policy. Yet the second option was never even considered. Forced to fight the battle of world sugar production on untenable terms, Britain did not so much as hint at employing its most effective precautionary weapon—the reopening of the British slave trade.

If revival remained an unthinkable alternative at the return of peace in Europe, it was because the aversion to British slaving relied on something independent of economic arguments. The source of silence, inexplicable within contemporary economic parameters, lay in the thunderous British popular petition against the Anglo-French treaty that allowed the temporary revival of the French slave trade. The most numerous petitions in British history covered the tables of both houses of Parliament in June and July 1814. So, when all the economic and demographic indicators pointed in one direction, the empire took the other.[14]

In this case the relation of abolitionism, and particularly the abolition of the slave trade, to imperial interests seems fairly straightforward. Britons abruptly ceased to be the major economic players in the slaving system. Thereafter Britons could play only clandestine and indirect roles in its continuation, often as investors, consumers, and slaveholders outside the empire. In that capacity they helped expand the wealth and power of foreign states and empires more than their own.

Abolitionists thus clearly helped reduce the value and relative imperial significance of the British slave complex after 1807. They played a similar, if less intentional, role on the coast of Africa. In terms of imperialism, abolitionists undertook their most important West African venture before 1807. It was managed by the government-chartered Sierra Leone Company. The principal directors of the company were leading philanthropists, including Wilberforce himself. Some of them had sponsored relief for the black poor in London and a failed settlement in Sierra Leone in 1787.

The second colony was constituted along lines that were closer to contemporary mercantilist models. The rationale for the enterprise was that an efficient and economically competitive colony would have greater chances for success than the earlier failed attempt at freeholders' democracy. The directors of the Sierra Leone Company envisioned their colony as an experiment in head-to-head competition between cultivation by free labor in Africa and slavery in the West Indies. The new company's mercantile profits and success would also hopefully undermine slavery in an ever-widening arc beyond the core zone with a protected "legitimate" trade.[15]

British parliamentary approval for the new company was obtained in partial compensation for Parliament's defeat of a slave trade bill in April 1791. Although the directors did not look forward to spectacular profits, their employers were explicitly informed that their main and immediate priority was commercial viability. The Sierra Leone Company was so quickly and heavily subscribed that abolitionists boasted of having to take precautions to see that the West Indians did not attempt to obtain a substantial share of the capital. Company directors and the first governor felt that the St. Domingue slave uprising opened up an ideal—perhaps divinely ordained—opportunity. In European markets, sugar was selling at prices that had not been offered for almost a century.[16]

Their colony, however, could not rely on capital and providence alone. It also depended on the voluntary recruitment of free workers. Many African Americans who had gained freedom at the end of the American War of Independence were struggling in very difficult conditions in Nova Scotia. Thomas Clarkson's brother John traveled to Canada to recruit settlers for the new African colony. The response was overwhelming. Thinking that there was ample acreage available to ensure an independent existence, nearly thirteen hundred free blacks volunteered to move to Sierra Leone. Unfortunately, they were deceived in the amount of land they had been assured. They were equally disappointed by the political rights they were denied in the governance of the colony.[17]

Whatever their role in the new colony, the Nova Scotians' demands for full political participation in a self-governing colony did not add to the attractiveness of the experiment for the investors. The Sierra Leone experiment managed to endure through enormous initial difficulties, including internal strife, overgovernance, heavy mortality, and a devastating French raid in 1794. The chief complaint of the governors and directors turned out to be the difficulty of obtaining steady farm labor from either white or black overseas settlers or from native Africans. Successive waves of migrants failed to meet the directors' expectations and hopes. A decade after its launching, the company's entire capital had diminished by more than 90 percent from its heady subscription days.

In 1807, on the verge of bankruptcy, the Sierra Leone Company petitioned the government for the colony's transfer to the crown. Its directors acknowledged their inability to compete with the slave traders. Among their arguments for British retention of the colony, its economic value and potential were not even mentioned. The directors' only hope was that the imminent closing of the slave trade might remove "the want of a regular supply of labourers," at that point "far below the demand." A year before the company's petition, the government had already contemplated breaking up the colony to reinforce its black West India regiments. Sierra Leone's performance as a colony was regarded as so poor that negotiations between the company and the government had to be conducted in secret until after the passage of the Abolition

Act, in 1807. Wilberforce feared that any news of the impending transfer would be used as antiabolitionist propaganda.[18]

Within months of the passage of the Abolition Act, the British government took over full responsibility for the colony and its expenses. Members of Parliament who opposed the transfer noted that the project had already cost the government more than £900,000 in subsidies, in addition to the vanished private capital. No MP argued for Crown Colony status on the grounds that the settlement could somehow match the Caribbean as a producer of sugar. Supporters of colonization had already argued that most of the expended funds were justifiable as a rescue operation. The British were morally obliged to sustain both the voluntary black refugees from Nova Scotia and the contingent of Jamaican Maroons who had been forcibly deported to Africa. Maintenance of the colony was also defended on humanitarian terms, as a potential asylum for slaves rescued by British warships from the African slave trade.

When the British government undertook control of the already heavily subsidized colony, its status as a humanitarian haven for freed slaves was confirmed. Despite the high costs of maintenance, it was arguably cheaper for the state to pay for its continuance as a refuge than to create a new asylum somewhere else on the African coast. The very existence of the colony proved that an orderly society could be maintained in Africa without reliance on either slavery or the slave trade. The subsidy, however, meant that Sierra Leone also stood as a failed "experiment" in quasi-forced migration.[19]

Sierra Leone's controversial status as a failed economic venture did not end with its change of legal status. During the following decades some of the colony's employees were accused of participating in the slave trade, of sanctioning coerced labor, and of constraining the free movement of labor and trade. Opponents even insisted that Sierra Leone remained as much a clandestine nest of the slave trade as under the company's rule. A high volume of slaving took place just beyond the jurisdiction of the colony.

In other respects there was also a good deal of continuity in attitudes toward the African colony. The African Institution, founded in 1808, combined the roles of advocates for abolition and a Sierra Leone lobby. For antiabolitionists and those hostile to budgetary waste, the African colony was a grave of Europeans and a drain on the imperial treasury. Most ministers retreated to minimalism, wearily noting that "whatever might be thought of the propriety of an establishment like

Sierra Leone," it was, at least, an indispensable port of debarkation for captured victims of the slave trade and at best a potential "nucleus of African civilization."[20]

Defenders of Sierra Leone were eager to keep it out of all discussions of slavery or abolition, but the most sustained parliamentary attack on the colony was undertaken soon after the first popular mobilization for gradual emancipation, in 1823. Following years of parliamentary sniping and threatening motions to reconsider the expediency of British withdrawal from Sierra Leone, a prominent Radical, Joseph Hume, launched a major attack in 1830. For Hume, Sierra Leone was an empirically rich experiment. More than four decades' worth of economic and demographic data had accumulated. In both the colony's "foundings" (1788, 1792) a large proportion of the colonists, black and white, had died. Considering the cumulative expenditure of "nearly three millions of money" and "evils so dreadful that he would not shock the House by reading them," Joseph Hume threw the mortality figures into the balance against the whole settlement. With its annual death rate of 160 per thousand, Sierra Leone ranked below that of every contemporary Caribbean slave colony. Thomas Fowell Buxton, the parliamentary leader of the abolitionists, responded. He agreed "that the experiment of Sierra Leone had failed." He objected only to Hume's recommendation of withdrawal. Uprooting seventeen thousand liberated Africans, who were also British subjects, would be enormously expensive and utterly inhumane. The British had assumed responsibility for and were bound, in good faith, to keep it.[21]

It was not only critics of Sierra Leone who were wary about intrusions of Europeans as managers of the "civilization" of Africans. Abolitionists had already learned one lesson well. As early as the passage of the slave trade abolition act and Sierra Leone's absorption into the empire, Wilberforce's own evangelical branch of the Established Church directly opposed any further territorial ambitions in Africa. The *Christian Observer,* an Anglican periodical, was aroused against suggestions that Britain use the worldwide conflict against Napoleon as an opportunity to seize African coastal territory in order to prevent a postwar Franco-Dutch revival of the slave trade. The *Christian Observer* noted that any further occupations could be misconstrued. The British could be accused of "inducing African princes to give up liberty." "[Nor] would a satisfactory reply be easily found, should it hereafter be said that the princes of Africa had been robbed of their independence, and the people of their liberty, while too ignorant to understand the value of the privileges they surrendered."

What was most to be feared, however, was that dominion held out "a lure to injustice too strong, we fear, for the political virtue of any nation; and when we see the vast strides which our ambition has so lately made in the east [India], under the plausible pretexts of consulting . . . the happiness of the native principalities and the safety of our own estab-lishments, we dread lest the existence of similar temptations in another continent should lead to the perpetration of similar enormities." In such an event Britain would rightly be held to account for having passed off "a solemn mockery on mankind, by professing to abandon injustice in one form to while determined to pursue it in another."[22]

As for Sierra Leone itself, the periodical reluctantly assented to governmental control only as a lesser evil to a private colony charter, because "the country is now so wakeful to all her interest, the number of our political citizens so large and the general opinion so powerful, that neither public nor private rapacity are likely to escape correction." Even so, it concluded, strict limits should be prescribed against expansion.

The theme of strict limitations became the leitmotif of British policy in West Africa during the British leadership against the slave trade for more than sixty years. Even at the peak of abolitionist political power and global ambitions, in 1840, Secretary for War and the Colonies Lord John Russell authorized renewal of a campaign to expand Anglo-African anti–slave trade treaties with the strict proviso that they would call for no annexation of territory. Ministers far less sympathetic to the abolitionists were inclined to suggest the abandonment of West Africa altogether.[23] Even James Stephen, the Colonial Office's most influential abolitionist undersecretary, was opposed to any further British penetration of Africa: "[If] we could acquire the dominion of the whole of that continent, it would be but a worthless possession."[24] Nothing could more decisively demonstrate the distance between the utopian ambitions of the first decade of the abolitionists at the end of the eighteenth century and the deep skepticism of abolitionists, politicians, and the Colonial Office during the first three-quarters of the nineteenth century.

That pessimism was deepened by the most ambitious British intru-sion of all into Africa during the age of the transatlantic slave trade. It was undertaken at the peak of British abolitionism's political strength, at the end of the 1830s. The movement had just demonstrated its po-litical popularity in two mass petition campaigns. A weakening Whig government desperately needed abolitionist support to maintain its dwindling parliamentary majority. Buxton seized the opportunity to request the government's sponsorship of an expedition into the interior of Africa. Thirty years of British naval and diplomatic activity, he argued, had failed to halt or even substantially diminish the volume of the trade. The solution was to plant the seeds of agriculture and legitimate commerce within the heart of the continent.

Although Buxton quickly obtained Russell's support, most abolitionists were totally opposed to the project. It entailed dispatching naval vessels up the Niger River. Force might have to be used, if only in self-defense. The important Quaker and pacific element in the movement would not support even that potential use of force. The national Anti-slavery Society refused to approve of the Niger expedition. Its leaders felt that the entire attempt to strike at the African supply side of the trade was misplaced. The whole project was also ignored by the first World Anti-slavery Conference, which met in London in June 1840.[25]

Nonabolitionists were equally unimpressed by the proposal. Britain's intellectual elite had no qualms about predicting the experiment's imminent failure on scientific grounds. For the Radical *Westminster Review,* the African experiment had already been tried at Sierra Leone for two generations. The same venture, under the same patronage, would lead to the same failure. Of Sierra Leone, it concluded, "We do not believe that any colony of Great Britain presents such a lamentable result." The *Spectator* suggested that, as far as the government was concerned, "the wiser plan" would be to "take the money and throw it into the sea, for thereby no lives will be lost."[26]

Both political economy and epidemiology forecast the failure of the venture, and so it turned out. Fevers killed or disabled the bulk of those who sailed up the Niger. Some of the survivors, who briefly established an experimental farm along the river, were accused of using whips to extract work from their "idle and promiscuous" remnant of laborers. Buxton could do no better than to bow before the facts and before God. To the second World Anti-slavery Convention, in 1843, he confessed that "it is essential that I show the complete failure of that remedy." Fifty years' experience at Sierra Leone were sufficient. They had proven beyond measure the deadliness of West Africa. Providence itself had "erected a wall of malaria around it which we cannot break through." For the world beyond the abolitionists, the Niger expedition was a grim reenactment of the age-old tale of the white man's grave, now embroidered with a cautionary narrative about the folly of the antislavery imagination.[27]

Thus ended the last major project of British expansion in West and Central Africa for the duration of the Atlantic slave trade. It is noteworthy in this context that both the British Anti-Slavery Society and the British Aborigines Protection Society not only opposed further annexation but echoed the *Christian Observer*. Toward the end of the slave trade both organizations urged that the West African colonies be abandoned on the grounds that "British rule had brought chiefly injustice and misgovernment." The three successive colonial undersecretaries between the 1830s and 1860s also welcomed a loosening of ties with Britain.[28]

Imperialism, in the sense of extending domination in Africa, was thus the last thing on the minds of British policymakers or the public press throughout the period of the suppression of the transatlantic slave trade. On the contrary, as the trade registering its last major shipments in 1863 the (hardly abolitionist) *Times* asked and answered its own rhetorical question in relation to a conflict in Gambia:

> Who ever heard of a War in Gambia? What do we know of the King of Bedaboo, and why should we rejoice at having taught him a "severe lesson!" What harm has he done us and why should we be anxious to pay an additional income tax for the pleasure of killing . . . his sable subjects? As it stands it looks as much like a piratical inroad as any exploit we ever read about. . . . Who ordered it? And who will pay for it? . . . Can it be possible after all the lessons we have received of the inflammatory character of little wars we can find ourselves in the thick of a "war upon Gambia" without notice, and so far as we know, without reason?[29]

Well after the end of the Atlantic trade the *Times* was still asking, even of Sierra Leone, "Does it really need an Englishman [even as governor]? Is it really so indispensable?" And on the very eve of Britain's first serious expansion into the interior of the Gold Coast, in 1873, the *Times* continued its rhetorical sneering: "Why do we retain or even extend what we call a Protectorate over this pestiferous coast?"[30]

The definitive ending of transoceanic slave migrations, in the mid-1860s, coincided with a major discussion of British imperialism Africa. A costly war with the Ashanti on the Gold Coast revived calls on both sides of the aisle in Parliament for an end to British civil establishments.

In 1865 a select committee on West Africa rehearsed the familiar theme that Sierra Leone had failed. It added that the slave trade was now winding down and that the most flourishing legitimate African trade was occurring in areas outside British jurisdiction. The committee's final report recommended that no more territory was to be annexed except in the interests of efficiency or reducing expenditures. The committee advised that the ultimate object of the government should be withdrawal from all of West Africa, with the possible exception of the main settlement of Sierra Leone. The naval patrol itself was terminated in 1870.[31]

The most decisive military intrusions entailing slave trade abolition occurred in naval actions outside sub-Saharan Africa. The first took place during the formative period of Britain's post-Napoleonic abolitionist policy. The second occurred near the end. Britain's single most important naval operation against the slave trade was undertaken in the absence of metropolitan abolitionist agitation and had nothing to do with transatlantic slaving. When the British foreign minister began his diplomatic campaign at the Congress of Vienna in 1815 to internationalize the condemnation of the slave trade, the political and material costs of accumulating "moral capital" were quickly apparent. The British were accused of hypocrisy by cynical or hostile European diplomats. Why were the British concerned with the plight of black Africans to the exclusion of enslaved Europeans in North Africa? The ultimate response was the British fleet's bombardment of Algiers in 1816. The battle of Algiers was the largest armed humanitarian intervention in British military history. It was also the largest cannonade against an onshore target by a naval force during the age of sailing ships. British seamen suffered a higher rate of casualties than they endured at the battle of Trafalgar, in 1805.[32]

The incursion resulted neither in British territorial expansion nor the liberation of any Britons. Every one of the more than three thousand liberated slaves were continental Europeans. This imperialist venture was not registered in many, if any, commemorations of abolition. The abolitionists themselves showed no particular interest either in promoting or thereafter celebrating the original expedition. The British were certainly not accused of having favored Africans. There were none among the liberated Algerian slaves.

Britain's most decisive imperial military action against the African slave trade actually occurred in 1850 on the coast of Brazil. Brazil was then, as it had been for most of the three and a half centuries of the transatlantic slave trade, the largest recipient of Africans bound for the Americas. It had also reaped the greatest benefit from the Anglo-American abolitions of 1807. The naval action against slaving on the coast of Brazil ironically occurred just as British public support for naval activity was reaching a low ebb. Fortunately for abolitionists, the British naval action coincided with a Brazilian determination to end the importation of slaves. The transoceanic slave trade was momentarily reduced by 90 percent, but Britain gained no further influence over Brazilian trade or policy than it had achieved before the action.[33]

British intrusions on foreign sovereignty in favor of abolition were more diplomatic and fiscal than military. For two generations after 1807 the British attempted to build a naval inspection network that would close off the possibility of slaving vessels sailing with impunity under foreign flags. The network was never completed. The French never conceded a full right of search. America, as the major slaveholding republic in the New World, remained determined to avoid British imperial intrusion. For six decades the United States refused to enter into any agreement that would have compromised its sovereignty. Only in the dark days of its own military crisis, in 1862, did the Union agree to a mutual "right of search" of suspected slavers. Within five years the transatlantic Atlantic slave trade had been brought to an end.[34]

In short, the six-decade British campaign for the suppression of the slave trade entailed "imperialist" methods by mixtures of coercion and intimidation, stretching and breaching international law. It also inspired British governments to occasional blockades and armed interventions in Ouidah, Dahomey, and Lagos. These actions were always examined in Parliament, where the underlying defense of the actions was that a moral imperative to put down the slave trade overrode legal constraints of international law. Coastal blockades of Lisbon or West African ports certainly constituted violations of the sovereignty of Portuguese and West African polities. In this respect they were actions of little consequence to British economic, political, or strategic domination.[35]

The self-imposed limitations of British governments in relation to the Afro-Atlantic world should not be taken to imply any limitations on British imperial expansion in general. In the two generations between Waterloo and the ending of the transatlantic slave trade, the British Empire accounted for nine-tenths of the non-Europeans under European domination. In 1870 Britain could and did claim an empire unequaled in the history of the world. But the empire's expansion to western regions of North America, Southeast Asia, and the Pacific entailed neither an expansion of slavery nor an invocation of antislavery principals as an ideological justification for such expansion.

In attempting to abolish the slave trade while extending the growth of tropical and semitropical trade, British policy did breed deep counterproductive as well as counterimperialist tendencies. The result was a penumbra of alternative coerced labor migrations. The disposition of recaptives landed in Sierra Leone for forty years after 1807 was only the beginning of an ever-widening stream of unfree labor migration. Britain's self-limitation on territorial expansion meant that a vast slaving zone remained open in the interior, beyond British sovereignty. Europeans at best only whittled away at the networks of African enslavement and distribution. Not until the end of the nineteenth century did serious enforcement take place.

In Sierra Leone recaptive children were "apprenticed" to settlers, allowing for unregulated coerced labor and sexual exploitation. Only after decades of denunciation was the system ended in 1847.[36] The British diplomatic mode of slave trade abolition unintentionally created another stream of unfree labor into the Americas. Recaptives were placed by Anglo-European judicial commissions into the hands of residents of Cuba and Brazil as *emancipados*. For many this turned out to be a form of "apprenticeship for life." No effective mechanisms were put in place to supervise and enforce liberation of former recaptives from masters at the end of their terms of service.[37] Not until the 1860s, at the close of the transatlantic slave trade, did the British again move forcefully (with another blockade and seizure of Brazilian vessels) to recoup the liberty of emancipados.

The largest legacy of bonded labor migration, however, occurred within the confines of the empire. Faced by pressures of competition with slave-importing Caribbean islands and Brazil, the British government allowed its West Indian colonies to turn to India for the recruitment of indentured servants. For a very brief period British abolitionists were able to brand this system a "new slave trade." By the late 1840s, however, the government definitively redesignated this contracted workforce as a system of voluntary labor. The result was that far more indentured laborers were recruited for long-distance migration within both hemispheres in the century after British abolition than had been transported to the Americas in the century before it. International abolition of the slave trade thus left a long stream of unfree labor in its wake.[38]

Abolitionism cast an even longer shadow across Africa. In the 1880s and 1890s, during the Scramble for Africa, antislavery became a major rationalization for the legitimizing and creation of European spheres of dominion. The abolition of slavery and the slave trade may ironically have removed one of the most glaring impediments to imperial expansion. Abolitionists and radicals could no longer point to tolerance of slavery as characteristic of European imperial injustice over non-Europeans. But the possibilities and practicality of a large-scale imperial project were probably even more reflective of the economic and military gap that opened between Europeans and non-Europeans during the course of the nineteenth century.[39]

Abolitionism could and did rationalize, but clearly did not cause, that imperial expansion. This effect can be most readily seen in the two major European imperialist conferences on Africa held in Europe (Berlin in 1884, Brussels in 1889). At Berlin, European powers were concerned primarily with the rules for carving up territory. Slave trade abolition was no more than a symbolic afterthought. Britain sought "to carry off all the honours of the meeting by being the first to propose (on so fitting an occasion) an international declaration in relation to the *traffic in slaves.*"[40] The aim, among almost all conferees, was to minimalize any obligations entailed in a general declaration against the trade. In the end the Berlin conference restricted its resolution to support for Britain's priority— the interdiction of the seaborne trade. Only a vague phrase committed the European signatories to suppress slavery itself. Five years later, at the Brussels conference, the slave trade was more clearly the center of diplomatic attention. Here too, however, control over the slavery itself remained within the sovereign domain of individual imperial powers.

After Brussels, European attempts to quickly convert their new dominions into profitable colonies led them to create state-sponsored coerced labor systems in place of the institution of slavery. The Berlin and Brussels treaties transformed antislavery from an incentive for ending the enterprise of coerced African migration into a rationalization for political domination. A movement that had ended an era of individual bondage functioned as a rationalization for the indefinite dependency of peoples.[41]

After two hundred years it is appropriate to reconsider the abolitionists' process in a more bicentennial and global perspective. For a thousand years before 1800 a deadly slave trade had thrived across the Sahara and the Indian Ocean. Between the fifteenth and nineteenth centuries another transatlantic coerced migration ruthlessly fed one of the most coercive systems in human history.

Until the last third of the eighteenth century a policy of eliminating these intercontinental trades and the institutions they sustained had never been seriously undertaken by any sovereign ruler or parliamentary body. By the end of the Napoleonic Wars, Britain's national legislature had shut down a principal transoceanic trade in human captives. Outside Parliament one great national mobilization after another had launched the world's leading commercial and naval power into a sustained campaign to end that entire trade. For yet another century every major British abolitionist initiative would be advertised to foreign powers and to the world as a major objective of the government and the nation. By 1815, British abolitionism had also elicited the first international treaty declaration against the slave trade. A century after its political emergence abolitionism was routinely invoked by European powers as a major justification for imperial expansion and political domination.

Abolitionism did not halt imperialism, but it shaped even that procession of pride and power more profoundly than we realize. By the end of the nineteenth century antislavery had become the gold standard of "civilization." Without abolitionism late-nineteenth-century imperial expansion would have incorporated both slavery and the slave trade into the toolbox of European and Muslim imperialisms. Not just millions, but tens of millions of Africans might have continued to be captured and deported. Millions more would have died en route from the African interior, in transcontinental journeys and in "seasonings."[42]

Whether or when the ending of this pervasive institution would have been provoked by other political and economic developments remains unclear. We know that in the early twentieth century new ideologies and new institutions came to power within Europe itself. They assembled deadly combinations of racial or ethnic victimization, coerced migrations, deadly degradation, and slave labor. During the second third of that century such massive institutions extended halfway around the globe. This suggests that slavery's nineteenth-century chances of survival beyond Europe and its twentieth-century successors within Europe might have been mutually sustaining in the absence of abolitionism's prior success. All around us remains overwhelming evidence that abolition eliminated only one major network of human brutality and death. Yet it is hard to imagine a world that would not have been far worse off without its elimination.

Notes

This chapter benefited from discussions at the Centre of African Studies, University of Cambridge; the Association for the Study of World African Diaspora, in Barbados; and a conference at Fordham University School of Law. I also express my appreciation for an early reading by Stanley L. Engerman.

1. Westmoreland's speech may be found in John Debrett, *The Parliamentary Register,* ser. 3, vol. 8 (London, 1799), 586, emphasis added. On the whole debate, see Roger Anstey, *The Atlantic Slave Trade and British Abolition, 1760–1810* (London: Macmillan, 1975), 331.

2. For the quotations, see Robin Blackburn, *The Overthrow of Colonial Slavery, 1776–1848* (London: Verso, 1987), 320; Howard Temperley, "Anti-slavery as a Form of Cultural Imperialism," in *Anti-slavery, Religion and Reform,* ed. Christine Bolt and Seymour Drescher (Folkestone: Dawson, 1980), 335–50 (quotation, 349).

3. For an extended analysis of the construction of British public memory concerning the abolition of the slave trade and slavery, see J. R. Oldfield, *Chords of Freedom: Commemoration, Ritual and British Transatlantic Slavery* (Manchester: Manchester University Press, 2007), esp. chap. 4.

4. Seymour Drescher, "The Historical Context of British Abolition," in *Abolition and Its Aftermath: The Historical Context, 1790–1916,* ed. David Richardson (London: Frank Cass, 1985), 4. Other events in the 1983 commemorations of slave emancipation at Hull did include considerations of both abolitionism and Wilberforce. When a descendant of Wilberforce was invited to speak at the academic conference, his primary role was, significantly, to introduce the conference's honored speaker. The honoree himself was the Trinidadian intellectual C. L. R. James, author of *The Black Jacobins: Toussaint L'Ouverture and the San Domingo Revolution* (London: Secker and Warburg, 1938), a classic account of the St. Domingue slave revolution.

5. Eric Williams, *Capitalism and Slavery,* (Chapel Hill: University of North Carolina Press, 1944), 211. See also David Brion Davis, *The Problem of Slavery in the Age of Revolution, 1770–1823* (Ithaca: Cornell University Press, 1975); Thomas Bender, ed., *The Antislavery Debate: Capitalism and Abolitionism as a Problem in Historical Interpretation* (Berkeley: University of California Press, 1992); Seymour Drescher, "The Antislavery Debate," *History and Theory* 32, no. 3 (October 1993): 311–29, review essay of *The Antislavery Debate: Capitalism and Abolitionism as a Problem in Historical Interpretation*, ed. Thomas Bender (Berkeley: University of California Press, 1992). For a recent discussion of the role of moral considerations in British abolition see David Brion Davis, *Inhuman Bondage: The Rise and Fall of Slavery in the New World* (New York: Oxford University Press, 2006), chap. 12.

6. See Seymour Drescher, *Econocide: British Slavery in the Era of Abolition* (Pittsburgh: University of Pittsburgh Press, 1977), 165. For a recent summary of the literature, consult Christopher Leslie Brown, *Moral Capital: Foundations of British Abolitionism* (Chapel Hill: University of North Carolina Press, 2006), 14–16.

7. Brown, *Moral Capital,* esp. introd., epilogue. See also Robert William Fogel, *The Fourth Great Awakening and the Future of Egalitarianism* (Chicago: University of Chicago Press, 2000); Fogel, *The Slavery Debates, 1952–1990: A Retrospective* (Baton Rouge: Louisiana State University Press, 2003), where the Nobel laureate in economics argues for the power of morality in changing the course of history.

8. See P. J. Cain and A. G. Hopkins, *Innovation and Expansion,* vol. 1 of *British Imperialism* (London: Longman, 1993), 42–43.

9. Michael Duffy, "The French Revolution and British Attitudes to the West Indian Colonies," in *A Turbulent Time: The French Revolution and the Greater Caribbean,* ed. David Barry Gaspar and David Patrick Geggus (Bloomington: Indiana University Press, 1977), 79.

10. On British fortunes in the Caribbean, see David Patrick Geggus, *Slavery, War, and Revolution: The British Occupation of Saint Domingue, 1793–1798* (New York: Oxford University Press, 1982); Michael Duffy, *Soldiers, Sugar, and Seapower: The British*

Expeditions to the West Indies and the War against Revolutionary France (Oxford: Clarendon Press, 1987). On British slavery's economic status in both the empire and the world market from 1800 to 1815, see, for example, Drescher, *Econocide,* chaps. 5, 9; David Eltis; *Economic Growth and the Ending of the Transatlantic Slave Trade* (New York: Oxford University Press, 1987), chap. 1; David Eltis, Frank D. Lewis, and David Richardson, "Slave Prices, the African Slave Trade, and Productivity in the Caribbean, 1674–1807," *Economic History Review* 58, no. 4 (2005): 673–700; Ralph Davis, *The Industrial Revolution and British Overseas Trade* (Leicester: Leicester University Press, 1979), tables 38–64; Joseph E. Inikori, *Africans and the Industrial Revolution in England: A Study in International Trade and Economic Development* (New York: Cambridge University Press, 2002), table 4.2. For a contemporary estimate of the British slave empire in 1814, see P. Colquhoun, *A Treatise on the Wealth, Power and Resources of the British Empire* (London: J. Mawman, 1815), chaps. 1, 3, 10, 11, 12.

11. See Drescher, *Econocide,* chap. 6; Eltis, *Economic Growth,* chaps. 1, 13; David Eltis, "The Traffic in Slaves between the British West India Colonies," *Economic History Review* 25, no. 1 (1972): 55–64.

12. Drescher, *Econocide,* 156–60; Eltis, *Economic Growth,* chap. 1.

13. See David Eltis, Stephen D. Behrendt, David Richardson, and Herbert S. Klein, eds., *The Trans-Atlantic Slave Trade Database* (Atlanta: Emory University, 1999–), http://www.slavevoyages.org/tast/index.faces.

14. Seymour Drescher, "Public Opinion and Parliament in the Abolition of the British Slave Trade," in *The British Slave Trade: Abolition, Parliament and People,* ed. Stephen Farrell, Melanie Unwin, and James Walvin (Edinburgh: Edinburgh University Press, 2007), 42–65.

15. Seymour Drescher, *The Mighty Experiment: Free Labor versus Slavery in British Emancipation* (New York: Oxford University Press, 2002), chap. 6.

16. Drescher, *Econocide,* 114–19.

17. Cassandra Pybus, *Epic Journeys of Freedom: Runaway Slaves of the American Revolution and Their Global Quest for Liberty* (Boston: Beacon Press, 2006); Simon Schama, *Rough Crossings: Britain, the Slaves, and the American Revolution* (New York: HarperCollins, 2006). For a concise exploration of the vision and difficulties of the Sierra Leone Company, see Suzanne Schwarz, "Commerce, Civilization and Christianity: The Development of the Sierra Leone Company," in *Liverpool and Transatlantic Slavery,* ed. David Richardson, Schwarz, and Anthony Tibbles (Liverpool: Liverpool University Press, 2007), 252–76.

18. See British Library, Add Mss 58978, fol. 119, Grenville Papers, Correspondence with Wilberforce, Wilberforce to Grenville, September 20, 1806; fol. 157, Correspondence with Auckland, Grenville to Lord Auckland, William Eden 1st Baron Auckland, August 10, 1806.

19. Drescher, *Mighty Experiment,* 93–96.

20. Ibid., 97.

21. Ibid., 99–100.

22. *Christian Observer,* April 1807, 256.

23. Christopher Fyfe, *A History of Sierra Leone* (Oxford: Oxford University Press 1962), 165, 217.

24. Philip D. Curtin, *The Image of Africa: British Ideas and Action, 1780–1850,* 2 vols. (Madison: University of Wisconsin Press, 1964), chaps. 5–7.

25. Howard Temperley, *White Dreams, Black Africa: The Antislavery Expedition to the River Niger, 1841–1842* (New Haven: Yale University Press, 1991), chaps. 6, 7.

26. Drescher, *Mighty Experiment,* 166–67.

27. Ibid., 168.

28. Fyfe, *Sierra Leone*, 335.

29. *Times* (London), 12 April 1861, 8, col. f.

30. Ibid., 8 August 1873.

31. Fyfe, *Sierra Leone*, 336–39.

32. W. I. Clowes, *The Royal Navy, a History From the Earliest Times to the Present* (London: Sampson, Low 1901), 228.

33. See Leslie Bethell, *The Abolition of the Brazilian Slave Trade: Britain, Brazil and the Slave Trade Question, 1807–1869* (Cambridge: Cambridge University Press, 1970), 228–50; Jeffrey D. Needell, *The Party of Order: The Conservatives, the State, and Slavery in the Brazilian Monarchy, 1831–1871* (Stanford: Stanford University Press, 2006), 138–55.

34. See Don E. Fehrenbacher, *The Slaveholding Republic: An Account of the United States Government's Relations to Slavery,* completed by Ward M. McAfee (New York: Oxford University Press, 2001), chaps. 5, 6.

35. See Robin Law, "Abolition and Imperialism: International Law and the British Suppression of the Atlantic Slave Trade," paper presented at "Domestic and International Consequences of the First Governmental Efforts to Abolish the Atlantic Slave Trade," conference, Accra and Elmina, Ghana, 8–12 August 2007. My thanks to the author for allowing me to consult his manuscript. On the larger issues of law raised by British suppression, see Eltis, *Economic Growth*, 119–22.

36. Allen M. Howard, "Nineteenth-Century Coastal Slave Trading and the British Abolition Campaign in Sierra Leone," *Slavery and Abolition* 27, no. 1 (2006): 23–49.

37. See David R. Murray, *Odious Commerce: Britain, Spain, and the Abolition of the Cuban Slave Trade* (New York: Cambridge University Press, 1988), chap. 13; Bethell, *Brazilian Slave Trade*, 380–83. I omit detailing the long list of practices by which Britain attempted to bring pressure to bear on civil society in foreign countries to accelerate the abolition of the slave trade or slavery. On the example of Brazil, see Richard Graham, *Great Britain and the Onset of Modernization in Brazil, 1850–1914* (London: Cambridge University Press, 1968), 169–70; Eltis, *Economic Growth,* 107–19, chap. 12; Robert L. Paquette, *Sugar Is Made with Blood: The Conspiracy of La Escalera and the Conflict between Empires over Slavery in Cuba* (Middletown, CT: Wesleyan University Press, 1988).

38. Drescher, *Mighty Experiment,* chaps. 10–11.

39. Jennifer Pitts, *A Turn to Empire: The Rise of Imperial Liberalism in Britain and France* (Princeton: Princeton University Press, 2005), 17–18.

40. Suzanne Miers, *Britain and the Ending of the Slave Trade* (New York: Longman, 1975), 171.

41. Seymour Drescher, *Dilemmas of Democracy: Tocqueville and Modernization* (Pittsburgh: University of Pittsburgh Press, 1968), 191–95.

42. In this respect, whatever the cost of life, wealth, and trauma to slave traders and slaveholders arising from British slave trade interdiction must be offset by the more precious benefits accruing to potential victims. "Seasoning" was the initial period after the Middle Passage, during which slaves were acclimated to the disease environment and the disciplinary regimen of the New World plantations. See also Eltis, "Abolition of the U.S. and British Slave Trade" (see note 35, above). My thanks to the author for permission to consult his manuscript. For sustained British attempts, after the Scramble, to defend coerced Africans beyond the boundaries of British jurisdiction, see Kevin Grant, *A Civilised Savagery: Britain and the New Slaveries in Africa, 1884–1926* (New York: Routledge, 2005), chaps. 2, 5.

SIX

Abolition and Imperialism

*International Law and the British Suppression
of the Atlantic Slave Trade*

ROBIN LAW

THE CONNECTION between abolition and imperialism has various aspects. Most obviously, the cause of abolition of the slave trade
was subsequently co-opted in justification of the European partition
of Africa, notably at the Congress of Brussels in 1890.[1] At a more fundamental level, it can be argued that the abolitionist project was in an
important sense inherently imperialist, since it involved a proposed
alternative course for the development of Africa, and thus implicitly
asserted a supposed responsibility and right of Europeans to decide the
future of that continent.[2] And finally, the British suppression of the
slave trade was in practice carried out, in part, by "imperialist" methods,
that is, by coercion and intimidation of other states—albeit normally by
techniques of "informal imperialism," rather than actual annexation.[3]
This chapter focuses on a particular dimension of this last aspect: the
tendency of the British campaign for the suppression of the slave trade
to adopt methods that were in breach of international law (or, in the
more usual contemporary parlance, the law of nations). The best-known
instances of this propensity to illegality related to other European and
American nations, in particular the unilateral British decisions to arrest
suspected slave ships belonging to Portugal (1839) and to make such
seizures within Brazilian national waters (1850).[4] But the abolitionist

campaign also came to involve a systematic encroachment on the sovereignty of states in Africa.

This issue has attracted little scholarly attention hitherto, apart from a brief but valuable treatment by David Eltis (1987).[5] The issue is discussed in this chapter with primary reference to two interrelated episodes in the British campaign to suppress the slave trade, on the section of the West African coast known as the Bight of Benin: the naval blockade of Ouidah, the port of the kingdom of Dahomey (in the modern Republic of Benin), and the military intervention in the coastal state of Lagos (in Nigeria), both in 1851–52. Earlier discussions of these incidents have not generally given any prominence to the issues of international law which they raised,[6] but this aspect seems critical to their long-term significance.

Principles and Precedents

The issue of African sovereignty became critical for British policy when the campaign to suppress the slave trade moved from a focus on action on the demand side (closing down the demand for slaves in the Americas) to the supply side (shutting off the supply of slaves from Africa), a development that of course reflected frustration at the failure of earlier measures to end the trade. The shift in policy owed much to the leading abolitionist, Thomas Fowell Buxton, who from 1838 lobbied the government for the adoption of a more positive African policy, submitting the detailed proposal subsequently published as *The African Slave Trade and Its Remedy*. Buxton's main emphasis was on the promotion of exports of agricultural produce from Africa as a substitute for the slave trade, but he also proposed, as "preparatory measures," the negotiation of treaties for the abolition of the slave trade with African states and more effective naval action to prevent ships embarking slaves.[7] The idea of such treaties was not altogether new: there were precedents in British policy in the Indian Ocean, where treaties abolishing or restricting the slave trade had been made with the king of Imerina, in Madagascar, in 1817 and the sultan of Muscat in 1822, and already in February 1838 a memorandum drawn up in the Slave Trade Department of the Foreign Office had suggested extending the treaty system to cover "the whole line of the coast of Africa."[8]

The proposed strengthening of naval patrols also raised questions of relations with African states, since the means envisaged included the pursuit and arrest of suspected slave ships close to the shore or within navigable rivers rather than cruising out at sea, and this implied the entry of British warships into their national waters—conventionally defined as extending three miles offshore (the range of cannons). In August 1838 the foreign secretary, Lord Palmerston, sought advice from the queen's advocate, the government's senior legal adviser, as to whether British warships could take such action "without regard to any supposed rights of the native states in whose rivers or ports [slave ships] are found"; the latter opined that it was "not very likely" that African rulers would object but suggested that resolution of the legal issue could be put off until such a case should arise—which noncommittal formulation the Foreign Office took as authorizing such action.[9] It was clearly preferable, however, if possible to obtain the consent of the local authorities, and the proposed treaties with African rulers were intended to secure not only the prohibition of slave exports but also authority for the British navy to enter their national waters to suppress the trade. A draft treaty circulated in 1840 by the colonial secretary, Lord John Russell, thus included the provision that "the officers of the Queen of England may seize . . . every vessel or other boat of other nations found carrying on the trade in slaves in the waters belonging to the Chief of ___."[10]

In Africa, the first test of the new policy came at the Gallinas River (in modern Sierra Leone), a center of illegal slave trading by Spanish merchants.[11] In 1840, Capt. Joseph Denman was blockading the river, to prevent slave exports. This was itself an action of dubious legality, since blockade, in the strict sense of the term—the interdiction of all trade—was legal only in time of war: on an earlier occasion, when the governor of the British colony of Sierra Leone instituted a blockade of the coast to the east (including the Gallinas), the Colonial Office wrote to warn him: "I must remind you on no account to place under blockade any part of the Coast which does not belong to a Country with which His Majesty may not [sic] be in a state of actual hostility. A blockade is strictly a belligerent measure, and authorized only by a state of War. It is not one to which you can have recourse solely for the purpose of putting down the Slave Trade."[12] Moreover, the British action on this occasion allegedly included encroachments into local territorial waters, against which the local ruler sent a letter of protest, explicitly invoking international law: "If it is on account of the Spanish vessels resorting to this port that this blockade is put on our port, we beg to inform your honourable Court to let that matter take its course, as the law of all nations, natural in a cause, that is, for the enemy to be taken in three leagues [sic: = miles] of the land, and no nearer. . . . We therefore, think it ought to be allowed the same lenity as other nations have, although we are Africans, viz. for your ships of war to take up their anchor out of our port, and to take these law-breakers three leagues from the land, and no nearer." Denman himself claimed that this reference to national waters had been "inserted by the influence of the white slave-traders" and was of no real concern to the local rulers;[13] but even if the precise wording of the protest was very likely suggested to them by foreign advisers, there seems no reason to doubt the concern of African rulers to defend their territorial waters.[14]

In November 1840 the dispute escalated when the governor of Sierra Leone informed Denman that British subjects (Africans from the colony) were being held as slaves in the Gallinas country and requested him to liberate them, if necessary by force. Denman grasped the excuse to take a naval force into the river, where he seized canoes belonging to Spanish slave traders and liberated the slaves they were carrying (all of them, not only those found to be British subjects). He then negotiated with the local rulers for a treaty to abolish the slave trade; but the latter refused to accept this, on the grounds that the slave trade "was expressly permitted by their laws, and they could not abolish that which the law sanctioned," promising only to refer the matter to "their council by which their laws are established."[15] However, they did accept a treaty, on 21 November 1840, whereby they agreed to destroy the factories (or "barracoons") belonging to foreign slave traders and deliver the slaves held in them, and to expel the slave traders themselves from the country. Denman accordingly burned down the factories, and the goods in them were plundered by the local people. The destruction of the barracoons at the Gallinas was soon followed by similar action elsewhere: Denman himself burned barracoons at New Cestos, further southeast along the coast (in modern Liberia), in March 1841, and another officer did likewise at Shebar, northwest of the Gallinas, later in the same year.

In destroying the barracoons, Denman had acted on his own initiative, without instructions from his superiors, but his action was approved by the government retrospectively. Foreign Secretary Palmerston recommended to the Admiralty that "similar operations should be executed against all the piratical slave trade establishments which may be met with on parts of the Coast not belonging to any civilised power." Initially, he stipulated that officers "should endeavour to obtain the formal permission of the native chiefs for the destruction of the slave factories within their territories," as had indeed been done at the Gallinas (though not at

New Cestos or Shebar); but in a subsequent communication he relaxed this proviso, instructing that "if such an agreement should in any case be found impossible, the commander of Her Majesty's cruizers would be perfectly justified in considering European slave dealers established in the territory of a native chief as persons engaged in a piratical undertaking, and the British commander would be warranted in landing and destroying the barracoons, and the goods contained in them, and in liberating and carrying off to Sierra Leone the slaves whom they might find therein."[16] (The significance of these allusions to piracy will be discussed later.)

Despite the initial euphoria that it evoked on the British side, the impact of Denman's action at the Gallinas was short-lived. By 1845 foreign slave traders were again settled there, contrary to the treaty he had obtained from the local authorities. When the British protested, the Gallinas rulers explicitly repudiated the treaty, as having been signed under duress: "What [Denman] states concerning that Treaty, is not fact; the reason of our signing the Treaty was through forcibility. . . . [He said] if you don't sign the Treaty, I will shoot you." "They had been surprised and forced unwillingly by Captain Denman to sign a treaty, which could not be binding on them in those circumstances." And again in 1847: "In regard to the treaty between them and Captain Denman, he [the local ruler] said he did not consider it binding, as he and all were forced into the signing of it at the point of a bayonet."[17]

Moreover, the legality of Denman's actions was also queried in Britain, following a change of government (from Whig to Conservative) in 1841. In 1842 the new foreign secretary, Lord Aberdeen, consulted the queen's advocate, the same who had been noncommittal over intrusions into African national waters in 1838 but who now ruled unequivocally against the actions that had been taken onshore: "He cannot take upon himself to advise that all the proceedings described as having taken place at Gallinas, New Cestos and Sea Bar [Shebar] are strictly justifiable, or that the instructions to Her Majesty's naval officers, as referred to in these papers, are such as can with perfect legality be carried into execution . . . blockading the rivers, landing and destroying buildings, and carrying off persons held in slavery in countries with which Great Britain is not at war, cannot be considered as sanctioned by the law of nations, or by the provisions of any existing treaties." Consequently, Aberdeen directed that naval officers should henceforth refrain from destroying factories and liberating slaves from them, "unless the power upon whose territory or within whose jurisdiction the factories or the slaves are found, should, by treaty with Great Britain, or by formal written agreement with British officers, have empowered Her Majesty's naval forces to take these steps for the suppression of the slave trade." Instructions issued by the Admiralty to naval officers in 1844 (drawn up by a committee that included Captain Denman) stipulated that they should not take any "coercive measures" to put down the slave trade upon the territory of an African ruler, without either his "signed consent" or a prior "engagement" authorizing such action. They also specified (ironically, in view of Denman's own actions at the Gallinas), "Threats or intimidation are never to be used, to induce Native Chiefs to conclude the Engagement."[18]

Denman was also sued for damages by one of the Spanish slave traders, Juan Tomás Burón, for the destruction of his property at the Gallinas: the case was not heard until 1848, when the court found in Denman's favor.[19] The judgment did not (as some modern accounts suggest) uphold the legality of Denman's actions, but ruled only that he could not be held personally liable, since he had been acting as an agent of the British state. But the practical effect was the same, in that it served to remove the threat of legal action against naval officers, who were thereby encouraged to return their attention to suppressing the slave trade at the Gallinas. The queen's advocate this time supplied a supportive legal opinion, that war against the local rulers would be justified by their breach of the treaty of 1840 (requiring the expulsion of foreign slave traders), and in 1849 a naval force again entered the Gallinas River, destroyed the onshore factories, and instituted a blockade. Under this pressure, the Gallinas rulers did now accept a treaty for the abolition of the slave trade, on 2 February 1850.[20] This successful coercion of the Gallinas was regularly cited as a precedent for subsequent action elsewhere, including against Dahomey and Lagos.

The Blockade of Dahomey

The case of Dahomey is of especial interest, because in this case at least the idea of territorial waters, which Europeans were expected to respect, was incontestably well established locally. In 1703 the king of Hueda (which preceded Dahomey in control of the port of Ouidah) had required representatives of the European companies trading there to sign a treaty prohibiting hostilities in the Ouidah roadstead or within sight of the town, and stipulating that in time of war ships leaving Ouidah must be allowed twenty-four hours' grace before they might be pursued. The policy was maintained by the kings of Dahomey, after their conquest of Ouidah in 1727, with recurrent warnings to Europeans there to keep the peace.[21] By the end of the eighteenth century, however, although the Dahomean authorities were still seeking to uphold the principle, there were signs of increasing reluctance on the part of Europeans to continue to respect it. The French revolutionary government, during its antislavery phase (1794–1802), decided that, since it no longer had any interest in the slave trade at Ouidah, it could breach the neutrality of the port with impunity, to raid British and Portuguese shipping there.[22] The British in turn captured a French ship at Ouidah in 1803, provoking the Dahomeans to arrest a British factor who was trading onshore, on suspicion of collusion in the attack. This was perhaps mainly a symptom of the growing arrogance of British maritime power, which engendered a disregard for the rights of neutrals in wartime, evident in Europe (e.g., the attack on the Danish fleet at Copenhagen in 1801) as well as in Africa. But it is noteworthy that the arrested factor defended himself by denying Dahomean territorial rights in local waters, claiming that the incident had occurred "without the limits of the Dahomian dominions, which extended no farther than the beach; and on that domain which is everywhere ours—the sea."[23]

The British navy's operations against the slave trade from 1808 onward also sometimes involved the seizure of ships at Ouidah, in violation of Dahomean national waters and the neutrality of the roadstead. The records of judicial proceedings arising from such captures, however, do not register any concern for, or even any awareness of, this as an issue.[24] The rulers of Dahomey did continue to insist on the inviolability of Dahomean national waters. In 1845, King Gezo asked a visiting British explorer to "make intercession with Her Majesty of England to send an order to our men-of-war not to take any ships till they had entirely left the coast"; the latter, however, evidently did not understand the king's point, replying irrelevantly that it was to his advantage for ships to be captured after embarking slaves, as that would increase effective demand. Again in 1849, when Britain and Dahomey were engaged in discussions on the abolition of the slave trade, Gezo requested that pending the conclusion of these negotiations, "in the meantime . . . the Commander-in-Chief [of the British navy's West African squadron] will not allow slave-vessels to be taken in the roads of Whydah [Ouidah], as being under his protection"; but on that occasion no response at all was made by the British. As late as 1864, Gezo's successor, Glele, was still demanding that the British should cease to capture slave ships "near his beach"; the British envoy's response on this occasion, that "even in war a three-mile offing annuls the protection of a neutral territory," suggests that he too had failed to grasp that the complaint was precisely against the arrest of ships within Dahomean national waters.[25]

The British government had initiated negotiations with Gezo for the abolition of the slave trade from 1847, and in 1849 Palmerston (now again foreign secretary) appointed John Beecroft as British consul for the Bights of Benin and Biafra, and specified the conclusion of an anti-slave trade treaty with Dahomey as one of his priorities. However, a mission to Dahomey in May–July 1850 was a failure. From this experience, Beecroft concluded that only coercion would induce Dahomey to give up the slave trade and recommended that its port of Ouidah should be blockaded, although adding the proviso "if international law will admit of it."[26] The qualification was, indeed, a pertinent one, since, as noted earlier, a blockade was legally permissible only in war.

The negotiations of 1850 had, however, also raised other issues, which might potentially be used to justify the proposed action. Beecroft learned that a British subject from Sierra Leone was held captive in Dahomey; but this man was liberated on his demand. Gezo had also declared his intention to attack the town of Abeokuta, to the east, where a number of British subjects (European missionaries and Sierra Leoneans) were settled. When Beecroft raised this, Gezo insisted that he would attack Abeokuta, and that the British subjects there should be removed, for their own safety. The British naval commander in chief in West Africa, Commodore Arthur Fanshawe, wrote to Gezo warning him not to attack Abeokuta, because of the British subjects resident there: "if they receive any [injury] from your hands, it will be considered an act of hostility against the Queen of England and the English people, and will cause the coast of your Majesty's dominions to be immediately invested and blockaded by Her Majesty's ships under my command, and all trade stopped." Dahomey did proceed to attack Abeokuta, in March 1851, but its forces were repulsed. In consequence, Fanshawe agreed with Beecroft that "unless actual outrage or injury to a British subject should occur," the projected blockade of Dahomey should not be implemented, but referred the matter back to the British government.[27]

However, the missionaries at Abeokuta had reported, on the testimony of prisoners taken in the attack, that no instructions had been given to the Dahomean forces to respect the lives of British subjects there. Palmerston seized on this to infer that, if Abeokuta had been taken by the Dahomeans, the British subjects there "would probably have been reduced to slavery, or have perished by the sword," and accordingly in September 1851 instructed the Admiralty that, in retaliation for Gezo's disregard of the representations made on this matter, Dahomey should after all be blockaded. On the face of it, therefore, the blockade was instituted, not for any harm done to British subjects, but for harm they might hypothetically have suffered, if events had turned out differently. However, Palmerston's real intention was clearly to coerce Gezo into accepting abolition of the slave trade: his instructions continued that the blockade should not be raised until the king accepted a treaty to ban the slave trade (and, for good measure, to abolish human sacrifices and guarantee protection for Christian missionaries) and that if he had meanwhile made such a treaty, it should not be proceeded with. In December 1851 the commander in chief, now Commodore Henry William Bruce, duly ordered a blockade, to begin on 1 January 1852. In a letter to Gezo announcing this, he did not mention the supposed issue of the security of British subjects but represented the blockade as intended to secure the suppression of the slave trade, and also peace with Abeokuta.[28]

Under this pressure, Gezo now agreed to accept a treaty, on 13 January 1852. However, he refused to sign the standard treaty, but only a single-clause text banning the export of slaves from his dominions; the clauses he declined to accept included provision for the abolition of human sacrifices, the expulsion of foreign slave traders and destruction of barracoons and, perhaps most importantly, authorizing British military intervention to put down any recurrence of the slave trade. He also rejected attempts to insert clauses requiring protection for Christian missionaries and peace with Abeokuta.[29] The British negotiators were sent back in February to urge the signing of the full treaty, but Gezo refused to make any further concessions, asserting that this would constitute a surrender of sovereignty.[30] He also demanded that British warships should be withdrawn from the roadstead at Ouidah, arguing (quite correctly, under international law) that to send warships into the national waters of another state was an act of war.[31] In the face of this intransigence, the blockade was raised in June 1852. The attempt to coerce Dahomey thus failed; the British did not obtain an enforceable treaty, and slave exports from Dahomey continued into the 1860s. This was, of course, an illustration of the limitations of British sea power, in relation to an inland state such as Dahomey, a fact Gezo was well aware of: as he told the British negotiators, "we could attack Whydah, if we liked, and might land and take a few men, but we could not come to Abomey [the Dahomean capital, sixty miles from the coast], because there was no water."[32]

A further legal anomaly relating to the blockade may be noted. Palmerston's instructions had been for the blockade of "the Dahomian coast," but the notification of the blockade applied to "all the ports and places . . . situated in the Bight of Benin," excepting only Badagry, to the east, where it was believed that the slave trade was already stopped.[33] This, in fact, included several places outside Dahomean territory, to both east and west. Under pressure of the blockade, the king of Porto-Novo, to the east, also signed a treaty to abolish the slave trade on 17 January 1852; and several places along the coast west of Ouidah—such as Grand Popo, Agoué, Little Popo—signed treaties between 23 January and 2 February. Consequently, the blockade of these places was lifted on 11 February, while that on Dahomean ports continued. Commodore Bruce initially justified the extension of the blockade to the whole of the Bight by uncertainty as to the "exact limits" of Dahomean authority; but this is contradicted by the negotiation of separate treaties with these other communities. In his official notification of the blockade, he also cited the king of Porto-Novo, as well as those of Dahomey and Lagos, as having refused to give up the slave trade "in defiance of repeated warnings"; but in fact no proposals had been addressed to Porto-Novo on this matter, before the negotiation of the treaty in January 1852. The inclusion of Porto-Novo in the blockade seems to have owed more to the success of Abeokuta, in its representations to the British, in conflating its separate differences with Dahomey, Lagos, and Porto-Novo into a supposedly active alliance against Britain's interests and abolitionist policy. The extension of the blockade to ports west of Ouidah lacked even this fig leaf of justification. In a later statement, Bruce claimed to have been "acting upon the spirit" of his instructions in extending the blockade from Dahomey to its neighbors, which, if that spirit is understood to include a readiness to go beyond the letter of international law, may be reckoned accurate enough.[34]

Regime Change at Lagos

The British had, meanwhile, also taken action to put down the slave trade at Lagos, which was, from its geographical situation—close to the coast and accessible by water through an inlet from the sea—more vulnerable to naval coercion. This reorientation of interest toward Lagos was partly a response to the failure of the mission to Dahomey in 1850; but it was reinforced by pressure from the British missionaries at Abeokuta, who wished to improve the security of their adoptive homeland, against the threat from Dahomey, by opening trade (for the supply of arms) with Lagos. The situation at Lagos was complicated by the fact that the incumbent king, Akitoye, had been deposed in favor of his nephew Kosoko in 1845 and had settled at Badagry, to the west, with the support of Abeokuta, from where he hoped to recover possession of Lagos. The missionaries therefore proposed that Britain should support Akitoye in regaining his throne.

Already in April 1850, on receipt of the news of the imposition of the treaty abolishing the slave trade on the Gallinas kingdom, Palmerston suggested to the Admiralty that an attempt should be made to "induce" the king of Lagos to conclude a similar treaty by "a rigid watch upon his port" (a wording that implied something short of a full blockade). Independently of this, following his failure in Dahomey in July, Consul Beecroft also suggested that action should be taken at Lagos, by negotiating a treaty for the suppression of the slave trade with the exiled Akitoye and reinstating him as king. Palmerston enthusiastically took up the suggestion, writing to the Admiralty in October, again urging that an agreement should be made with the king of Lagos, and in case of a refusal, explicitly suggesting the use of force against him: "that measures similar to those which were enforced against Gallinas, should be brought to bear upon Lagos, or that steps should be taken to replace in authority at Lagos the former chief." In February 1851 he wrote to Beecroft urging him to follow this up, and suggesting that, if the king proved unwilling to sign a treaty, he should be threatened with coercion: "you should beg him to remember that Lagos is near to the sea, and that on the sea are the ships and the cannon of England; and also to bear in mind that he does not hold his authority without a competitor, and that the chiefs of the African tribes do not always retain their authority to the end of their lives."[35] The 1844 instructions prohibiting "threats or intimidation" were evidently now a dead letter.

In urging intervention at Lagos, in contrast to his uncertainty in relation to Dahomey earlier, Beecroft insisted, "We are not prevented by any international law that I am aware of."[36] This confidence that the proposed intervention at Lagos was consistent with international law requires some comment. The central tradition of interpretation of the "law of nations," as expounded in the classic work of the Swiss jurist Emmerich de Vattel (1758), condemned interference in the internal government of another sovereign state but made a qualification in cases of civil war, when it was permissible to assist the party judged "to have right on its side," if requested to do so.[37] The assumption that intervention in support of Akitoye would be legal evidently depended on the understanding of his status as the "legitimate" king and the incumbent Kosoko as a "usurper," which was of course how Akitoye presented the issue. Whether matters were quite so simple may be questioned, however. Kosoko in fact belonged to the senior branch of the royal family, which by local rules had a prior claim on the succession to the throne; and versions of local traditional history recorded later generally present Kosoko himself as the "rightful heir" and claim that he had been passed over in favor of Akitoye only because he was physically unavailable, being then in exile.[38] The British themselves, indeed, endorsed this view retrospectively: in 1862, when Kosoko was permitted to return to Lagos, now a British colony, the governor explained the decision as a matter not only of policy, but of "sheer justice," since "Kosoko by the law of the country is the rightful heir to the throne."[39]

It is interesting, also, to contrast the attitude taken by British naval officers when a civil war broke out in Badagry in June 1851, between the partisans of Akitoye and a faction allied to Kosoko at Lagos. Although the former were victorious, further attacks from Lagos were feared, and the British missionaries and traders resident in the town requested the landing of an armed force for their protection, but Commodore Bruce took the view that "the quarrel between Badagry and Lagos is purely of a domestic nature, and not one which warrants a neutral Power to interfere in a hostile manner." It was likewise explained to Abeokuta, which also requested intervention, that "we do not interfere with the internal arrangements of other people, but leave them to settle their own affairs, so long as British subjects are protected and unmolested by the Government of the country in which they reside." Although in this case a British subject, a merchant, had actually been killed, it was judged that there was no clear evidence that this was done by the Lagos people. All it was felt appropriate to do, therefore, was to send a letter to Kosoko urging that, in the event of further hostilities, his forces should refrain from attacking houses that flew the British flag. Moreover, Palmerston approved this decision as "perfectly right in not landing a force to interfere in this quarrel between the native tribes."[40]

In the case of Lagos, however, Palmerston decided on intervention. In September 1851, in the same letter that authorized the blockade of Dahomey, he instructed the Admiralty to "consider the practicability" of an operation against Lagos to restore Akitoye. Meanwhile, Commodore Bruce had himself independently recommended a blockade of Lagos. This was ostensibly on the grounds of threats to British subjects: Kosoko not only had failed to give guarantees of the security of those at Badagry but also was reported to have "forcibly detained" a British trader onshore at Lagos while a cargo of slaves was being embarked (though it does not appear that this man ever complained about his treatment). But he also justified the proposed action, explicitly, as a means of suppressing the slave trade. Consul Beecroft, in advance of receiving any instructions from London, proceeded to put his plan into execution. He first visited Lagos, on 20 November 1851, to urge Kosoko to sign a treaty against the slave trade, and on a refusal, applied to the locally available naval officers (Commodore Bruce being absent) for assistance to "compel him to make a treaty, or dethrone him and replace the rightful heir." This was done under the authority of Palmerston's dispatch of 21 February, although that, as was later pointed out, authorized Beecroft only to threaten, not to carry out, military intervention.[41] The action also breached the 1844 standing instructions to naval officers, in resorting to force without the authority of the commander in chief.[42]

A first attack on Lagos, on 25 November, was beaten off. Bruce was critical of the action; but by now he had received instructions from the Admiralty to dethrone Kosoko, and he adopted the convenient fiction that Kosoko had initiated the hostilities by firing on the British party—although resistance to an armed incursion into his national waters was manifestly, under international law, a justified act of self-defense.[43] The British again attacked Lagos on 26 December, and this time Kosoko was driven out. Akitoye was restored and duly signed a treaty to abolish the slave trade, on 1 January 1852.

Within the British government, Palmerston's determination to intervene at Lagos had been resisted by the first lord of the Admiralty, Sir Francis Baring. Although this was due in part to a general reluctance to commit the navy to difficult and costly enterprises, it also reflected doubts about the legality of this particular action. Palmerston's invocation of the precedent of the Gallinas was brushed aside as irrelevant: "In the Gallinas, we had a treaty which had been broken—and we blockaded the coast because we had a right of war from their having neglected to carry out their treaty agreements." But in the case of Lagos, since there was no such treaty, "I doubt we had a right to make war against him or depose him if he carries on the slave trade."[44] The prime minister, Lord John Russell, also had doubts but eventually agreed to "wink at any violation of Vattel's rules with regard to a slave trading chief."[45]

By the time news of the attack on Lagos reached England, Palmerston had been replaced as foreign secretary by Lord Granville, whose own attitude was less aggressive but who found himself trapped by developments on the ground in Africa. On learning of the first, unsuccessful, attack, he condemned Beecroft for exceeding his instructions but accepted that in the circumstances a second attack on Lagos was now necessary, "to do away with the bad moral effect which has been produced on the natives."[46] Privately, stronger views were expressed; an official minuted, "It is clear we had no right to do this."[47] But the subsequent success of British arms cleared away all scruples: on receipt of the news, Granville wrote to "entirely approve" of the action, as having effected the suppression of the slave trade at Lagos.[48] In the final analysis, the result evidently justified the means.

There remained critics, however. In Parliament, Lord Canning, formerly Aberdeen's undersecretary at the Foreign Office, questioned the propriety of intervention in the internal affairs of an African state ("to depose one Negro king and to set up another"), although he did not frame his objection in terms of international law.[49] There was more explicit challenge to the legality of the action in the press.[50] This provoked a response in an anonymous pamphlet defending the intervention, which, in part, sought to refute the suggestion that it had been contrary to international law. The pamphlet argued that, over and above the imperative of suppressing the slave trade, "the conduct of Lagos towards English subjects created in itself an unquestionable cause of war." The reference here was not to the spurious suggestion that the Lagosians had started the war but to the destruction of British lives and property at Badagry in 1851, and also to an earlier incident, the mistreatment of Sierra Leonean British subjects who had landed at Lagos in 1839.[51] But the former, as noted earlier, had been rejected as justifying British intervention at the time it happened, while the latter (which occurred before Kosoko's accession) had never been raised in the negotiations which preceded the attack.

The dubious legality of their original intervention at Lagos was compounded when the British went on to annex it, obliging Akitoye's successor, Dosunmu, to accept a treaty of cession in 1861. In Parliament, when Sir Francis Baring, now out of office, protested that there was no justification for this in international law, the government's response was contemptuously dismissive: "He had really made a great deal of a very small matter. He spoke as if the King of Lagos were the head of a great independent State, instead of a petty chief exercising doubtful authority over a few people."[52] By clear implication, "petty" rulers in Africa were not entitled to the protection of international law.

The Issue of Piracy

As to the grounds on which African states were denied rights under international law, there were two different rationalizations, one of which related to the issue of piracy. Palmerston's letters to the Admiralty in 1841, quoted earlier, referred to slaving barracoons in Africa as "piratical establishments" and the slave trade as a "piratical enterprise." This language of piracy was again invoked by him in 1851, when urging action against Dahomey and Lagos: "Her Majesty's Government cannot any longer permit that the accomplishment of a great purpose . . . shall be marred and defeated by the criminal and piratical exertions of two barbarous African chiefs."[53] He had likewise earlier responded to Admiralty doubts about the legality of the proposed intervention at Lagos: "We have just as good a right to say to the chief of Lagos . . . you shall not capture and sell your fellow creatures, as we have to say the same thing to the Malays and Dyaks of the Indian seas"—alluding to recent naval actions against pirates in Borneo.[54] The same line was taken in the anonymous pamphlet quoted earlier, which argued, "It may be questioned whether, on the general principles of the law of nations, such places as Lagos can be deemed to possess rights as States, or be entitled to the observances of international law," since they were "criminal communities," which themselves habitually violated that law. The argument is supported by a citation from Vattel, justifying collective action against the piracy sponsored by the Barbary states of northwest Africa, and concludes, "As a nest of piracy and plunder, the destruction of Lagos was a duty owing by civilised nations to themselves, in vindication of the law of nations."[55]

These characterizations of the slave trade as piracy were more than mere rhetoric but were intended to carry practical implications. The point about piracy was that, under international law, since pirates were considered the common "enemies of [all] mankind [*hostes humani generis*]," they were subject to universal jurisdiction: that is, they could legitimately be arrested, tried, and punished by the authorities of any nation, irrespective of their own nationality—this was, in fact, the prototype of the modern concept of crimes against humanity. It was a commonplace of abolitionist argument that the practical difficulties of enforcing the banning of the slave trade might be resolved by deeming it to be piracy, since this would enable the British navy to arrest suspected slave ships of other nationalities. This had indeed initially been the official policy of the British government, proposed at the congress of the European powers at Verona in 1822, but it was not acceptable to other European nations, notably France, precisely because it would have authorized the British to arrest non-British ships.[56] A projected treaty between Britain and the United States in 1824 likewise bound each party to "use its influence with all other civilized nations, to procure from them the acknowledgement that the slave-trade is piracy under the law of nations," but it was not ratified by the Americans.[57] By 1838, however, the British government had concluded that a declaration of the slave trade as piracy under international law was undesirable, as well as impracticable, since the universal jurisdiction that it implied might be used by foreign governments to harass British citizens, on spurious charges of slave trading.[58]

The slave trade had been declared to be piracy (thereby making it a capital offence) by several individual European and American nations, first by the United States in 1820, and including Britain itself in 1824. The principle had also been incorporated into some of the anti–slave trade treaties made by Britain with other powers, notably those with Brazil in 1826 and Portugal in 1842;[59] and a declaration to this effect was also included in the Quintuple Treaty of 1841, made with France, Austria, Prussia, and Russia—though France insisted on its own exclusion from this clause, and in any case did not ratify the treaty.[60] But these acts were of course binding only on those nations that subscribed to them. A change in international law, however, could be effected only by the agreement of all concerned; and among major maritime nations, Spain, as well as France, resisted British pressure on this issue.[61] In fact, Palmerston himself had conceded the point in 1848, when consulted by the chair of the Parliamentary Select Committee on the Slave Trade: "The slave trade, though a greater moral crime than piracy, is not, like sea piracy, a crime which by the general and established law of nations any and every nation may punish, whatever may be the country to which the offenders belong."[62]

Strictly speaking, the charge of piracy against African rulers, as distinct from European slave traders, was in any case a nonsense, since piracy was, by definition, an offense committed on the high seas, outside national waters. It was also questionable whether even a collective decision by European and American powers, had it been attainable, could be binding on African states: as a British naval officer pertinently observed in 1849, whatever Europeans and Americans might do, "no native Government will declare the Slave Trade piracy."[63] But by the mid-nineteenth century, it was already widely assumed in Britain that the determination of international law was a matter for "civilized" nations exclusively.

African States and International Law

The second, and more important, rationalization related to the status of African states in international law. The mainstream tradition of interpretation of the latter asserted the equality of status of all sovereign states, including those in Africa. By the 1840s, however, opinion in Britain was moving toward regarding African states as not entitled to the protection of international law.[64] While this was in part a rationalization of the imperatives of imperialism, on an intellectual level it involved a shift from regarding international law as based on "natural law," hence equally applicable to everyone, to seeing it as based on consent and reciprocity, hence supposedly restricted to "civilized" nations. The explicit public debate on these issues related mainly to European dealings with Asian societies,[65] but, since African societies were generally regarded as even less civilized than those in Asia, the argument applied a fortiori to Africa.

This changing attitude toward the legal status of African states was already evident in 1841, when Palmerston directed that the proposed agreements to be made with African rulers for the abolition of the slave trade should be termed "arrangements" or "agreements," rather than "treaties." Although the reasons for this were partly practical (treaties required approval by the Privy Council, while agreements could be made on the authority of the Foreign Office alone), this terminology was also explicitly intended "to mark the distinction between Agreements with barbarous Chiefs and the international Compacts of Civilized States."[66]

The transitional state of opinion on this issue is also reflected in testimony presented to parliamentary select committees on the slave trade in the 1840s, for which one of the prominent expert witnesses was none other than Capt. Joseph Denman. In 1842, in defense of his action at the

Gallinas, Denman adopted a bewildering range of different positions. His primary justification was that he had intervened to rescue British subjects from slavery, but he also cited instances of the refusal of Spanish slave dealers there to assist the crews of British boats in difficulty, which he claimed to be "a fair subject of war," and asserted that action on this account was warranted against the local African rulers, as well as the foreign slave traders, on the grounds that "according to the law of nations" they could be held responsible for what happened within their national waters. For the destruction of the barracoons, he stressed that he had acted with the consent of the local authorities, but he also argued that the action would have been justifiable even without such permission, because "the law of nations can afford no sort of recognition of the dealing in slaves by Spaniards in a foreign country," even though he acknowledged that slave trading was not illegal under local African law. But, alongside these claims to conformity with international law, he also argued, contradictorily, that international law did not in fact apply to African states: "the native chiefs are not recognised amongst the nations of the world: they are in a barbarous state, and the law of nations, in my opinion, cannot apply to them further than for their own good and their own protection"—that is, the British were obliged to consider the interests of Africans, but not their wishes. In 1849 he added the argument that slave trading was equivalent to piracy and hence placed African states, like the Barbary states earlier, "out of the pale of nations." But he also elaborated the paternalistic stance that suppression of the slave trade was "for the advantage of Africa, and even of the chiefs themselves ultimately," and that "the position England should assume towards them is that of a grown-up person towards a child"—that is, it was for Europeans to determine what was good for Africa and impose it on Africans. But whether African rulers were to be treated as criminals or as legal minors, the practical implication was the same: "It seems to me utterly absurd to invest these petty barbarians with all the rights of civilized states, and to observe the forms of diplomacy in dealing with them."[67]

Another witness to the 1849 committee was the legal expert Stephen Lushington, who had participated with Denman in the drafting of the 1844 naval instructions. While he acknowledged that these had been framed "in conformity with the strict law of nations," he also argued that there was a case that the latter did not apply to African states: "these are barbarian powers, who never have acknowledged the law of nations at all; they are not bound by that law, and will not treat you according to that law"—that is, there was no basis of reciprocity. Consequently, although Britain was bound to observe "the principles of justice and equity" in its dealings with Africans, Lushington considered it questionable whether it was also bound by "the technical rules and regulations of the law of nations." As regards the destruction of onshore barracoons, without the permission of the local authorities, he concluded, equivocally, that it was "a question of great doubt . . . I am not prepared to say that Great Britain is not at liberty to exercise the right."[68]

In truth, this argument was in danger of proving too much, since if African states were not subject to international law, that implicitly negated the validity of treaties concluded with them. Such treaties, however, continued to be regarded as essential for the suppression of the slave trade, as has been seen, less because they were expected to be effective than because they provided a legal basis for British military intervention. Indeed, even in the later partition of Africa, European claims to African territory continued to be based mainly on bilateral treaties negotiated with local rulers, rather than unilateral annexation or right of conquest.[69] But this contradiction does not seem to have exercised British policymakers overmuch.

Palmerston himself also on occasion invoked the idea that international law did not apply in dealings with African states. In a parliamentary debate in 1844, seeking to defend himself against the implication of Aberdeen's ruling two years before, that his own African policy violated international law, he recalled that earlier in the same year the government had defended the launching of an unprovoked war against Sind, in India, on the grounds that the law of nations, which governed relations among "civilized" nations, was not applicable in encounters with "barbarism." But, he argued, if this was true of Indian states, which were in only "a semi-barbarous state of society," the law of nations could not then logically apply to "the half naked and uncivilized chiefs of Africa." However, this ad hominem argument was perhaps merely opportunistic. In the following year he argued rather that if African rulers refused to cooperate in the suppression of the slave trade, "such conduct . . . would be a case of war within the law of nations. . . . I cannot see anything in the law of nations to prevent you having recourse to hostile measures to compel such a chief to concur in a legitimate purpose."[70] This anticipated the justification he would later advance for making war on Lagos. But the claim that persistence in slave trading could be a casus belli was in manifest contradiction to established understandings of international law, which held that, although one nation had an obligation to promote the improvement ("perfection") of others, it was not permissible to use force to this end.[71] The argument depended, in fact, on the conflation of slave trading with piracy, which Palmerston himself repudiated in 1848, as quoted earlier. The real underlying argument, it may be suggested, was rather that the moral imperative to put down the slave trade overrode such legal constraints.

A RECENT study of Palmerston's policy in Africa, by Roderick Braithwaite, emphasizes his "unwavering pursuit of the principle that states should observe 'international law.'"[72] But Palmerston's commitment to international law was, in reality, evidently situational and opportunistic, or at least selective. His central concern was of course to uphold the rights of British subjects in foreign jurisdictions, most notoriously in the Don Pacifico case of 1850; and it is this issue to which Braithwaite refers, his study relating specifically to an incident at the Rio Nuñes (in modern Guinée) in 1849, when a Franco-Belgian naval force destroyed property belonging to British merchants. Respect for African sovereignties, on the other hand, evidently did not figure largely in Palmerston's conception of the law of nations. By the 1850s, however, public concern over these issues of legality was waning. It seems symptomatic that when Parliament debated (and rejected) a motion for the withdrawal of the British navy's antislaving squadron in 1850, only one of the speakers in favor cited its violation of international law.[73] By the time of the actions against Dahomey and Lagos in 1851–52, those who disputed that the suppression of the slave trade afforded legal grounds for military intervention were evidently marginalized.

Lord Aberdeen in 1842 had ruled that "however desirable it may be to put an end to the slave trade, a good, however eminent, should not be attained other than by lawful means."[74] But, in the event, that is precisely what happened. Whether this disregard for African sovereignty was effective in bringing the slave trade to an end is debatable; on the face of it, the more decisive factor was the closing down of the remaining American markets for slaves, in Brazil and Cuba. The longer-term implications for Afro-European relations, however, seem clear. Eltis suggested that the attacks on onshore slaving establishments in 1840–41 represented "a watershed in official relations between European and

African powers." This perhaps gives insufficient weight to the subsequent doubts and disputes over the legality of these operations; arguably, the real watershed came with the coercion of Dahomey and Lagos, in 1851–52. But the end result is not in doubt: "in the official mind the legal and moral barriers to the European partition of Africa were cleared away."[75] This too has to be acknowledged as part of the legacy of the British campaign against the slave trade.

Notes
Abbreviations

NA   National Archives, London
PP   Parliamentary Papers (UK)

An abbreviated version of this paper in Hebrew translation was published in *Zmanim: A Historical Quarterly* (published in Tel Aviv) no. 107 (2009): 40–49.

1. See Suzanne Miers, *Britain and the Ending of the Slave Trade* (London: Longman, 1975).

2. See Ralph A. Austen and Woodruff D. Smith, "Images of Africa and British Slave-Trade Abolition: The Transition to an Imperialist Ideology, 1787–1807," *African Historical Studies* 2, no. 1 (1969): 69–83; A. G. Hopkins, "The 'New International Economic Order' in the Nineteenth Century: Britain's First Development Plan for Africa," in *From Slave Trade to "Legitimate" Commerce: The Commercial Transition in Nineteenth-Century West Africa*, ed. Robin Law (Cambridge: Cambridge University Press, 1995), 240–64. In a wider perspective, see Howard Temperley, "Anti-slavery as a Form of Cultural Imperialism," in *Anti-slavery, Religion and Reform: Essays in Memory of Roger Anstey*, ed. Christine Bolt and Seymour Drescher (Folkestone: Dawson, 1980), 338–50.

3. The view that British policy toward Africa in the mid-nineteenth century was not imperialist rests on a narrow (and old-fashioned) understanding of imperialism as territorial annexation. See R. J. Gavin, "Palmerston and Africa," *Journal of the Historical Society of Nigeria* 6, no. 1 (1971): 93–99.

4. Leslie Bethell, *The Abolition of the Brazilian Slave Trade: Britain, Brazil, and the Slave Trade Question, 1807–1869* (Cambridge: Cambridge University Press, 1970), 155–63, 325–26.

5. David Eltis, *Economic Growth and the Ending of the Transatlantic Slave Trade* (New York: Oxford University Press, 1987), 119–22. The matter is touched on only superficially (basically as a practical obstacle to be overcome) in earlier studies: W. L. Mathieson, *Great Britain and the Slave Trade, 1839–1865* (London: Longmans, Green, 1929), 62–63, 92–93; Christopher Lloyd, *The Navy and the Slave Trade* (1949; repr., London: Frank Cass, 1968), 97–8; W. E. F. Ward, *The Royal Navy and the Slavers: The Suppression of the Atlantic Slave Trade* (London: Allen and Unwin, 1969), 176–79.

6. An exception, for Lagos, is the brief study by Robert Gavin, "Nigeria and Lord Palmerston," *Ibadan: A Journal Published at the University College* 12 (1961): 24–27 (extracted from a PhD thesis that remained unpublished). Only passing mention of the issue is made, for example, by Robert S. Smith, *The Lagos Consulate, 1851–1861* (London: Macmillan, 1978); Martin Lynn, "Consul and Kings: British Policy, the Man on the Spot, and the Seizure of Lagos, 1851," *Journal of Imperial and Commonwealth History* 10, no. 2 (1982): 150–67. For Dahomey, see Robin Law, "An African Response to Abolition:

Anglo-Dahomian Negotiations on Ending the Slave Trade, 1838–77," *Slavery and Abolition* 16, no. 3 (1995): 281–310.

7. Thomas Fowell Buxton, *The African Slave Trade and Its Remedy*, 2nd ed. (1840; repr., London: Frank Cass, 1967), 283–300.

8. NA, FO84/262, memorandum [by James Bandinel, 12 February 1838], enclosed (in part) in J. Backhouse to Admiralty, 14 April 1838.

9. NA, FO83/2347, Sir John Dodson to Palmerston, 3 August 1838.

10. "Draft Agreement with African Chiefs," July 1840, in *British Policy towards West Africa: Select Documents, 1786–1874*, ed. C. W. Newbury (Oxford: Clarendon Press, 1965), 151.

11. PP, Report from the Select Committee on the West Coast of Africa 1842, app. 22, Correspondence Relative to the Slave Trade at the Gallinas.

12. Lord Bathust to Sir Neil Campbell, 25 October 1826, in Newbury, *British Policy*, 143. Denman later claimed that he had not instituted a "blockade" in a full sense, but was intercepting only slave ships. Denman to Lord Aberdeen, 18 March 1848, in PP, Reports from the Select Committee on the Slave Trade, 1848–49, 2nd Report, Minutes of Evidence, sec. 1245.

13. PP, 1842 Select Committee, app. 22, encl. 1 in no. 1, King Siaka to Governor of Sierra Leone, [September 1840]; encl. 5 in no. 1, Denman to Governor of Sierra Leone, 28 November 1840.

14. Cf. the response to the Gallinas action by the rulers of nearby Shebar: ibid., Minutes of Evidence, sec. 6812, Henry, Johnny, and Jack Tucker to Denman, 2 December 1840, "It don't concern with us as [slave ships] comes to us, if you meet them outside to sea, but coming in the rivers and destroying places." Likewise, King Pepple of Bonny (in southeastern Nigeria) in 1824 complained of the entry of a British warship (engaged in a maritime survey, rather than suppression of the slave trade) into his waters "without his permission." K. Onwuka Dike, *Trade and Politics in the Niger Delta, 1830–1885* (Oxford: Clarendon Press, 1956), 16–17.

15. PP, 1842 Select Committee, app. 22, encl. 5 in no. 1, Denman to Governor of Sierra Leone, 28 November 1840.

16. NA, FO84/383–84, Backhouse to Admiralty, 6 April 1841; Lord Leveson to Admiralty, 28 July 1841.

17. PP, Correspondence Relating to the Slave Trade 1845, class A, encls. 68, 108 in no. 9, Chiefs of Gallinas to Commodore Jones, 26 January 1845; Jones to Lieutenant-Governor of Sierra Leone, 24 February 1845; 1847–48, class A, encl. 1 in no. 292, Commander Dixon to Commander Manning, 19 December 1847.

18. Aberdeen to Admiralty, 20 May 1842; Admiralty Instructions to Senior Officers for negotiating with Chiefs of Africa, 12 June 1844, both in Newbury, *British Policy*, 162–63, 166.

19. *Buron v. Denman*, 2 Exchequer 167, 14–16 February 1848.

20. PP, 1848–49 Select Committee, 1st Report, app. 7, Sir Charles Hotham to Admiralty, 13 February 1849, with enclosures; Correspondence Relating to the Slave Trade 1850–51, class A, no. 161, Commodore Fanshawe to Admiralty, 4 February 1850, with enclosures.

21. Robin Law, *Ouidah: The Social History of a West African Slaving "Port," 1727–1892* (Oxford: James Currey, 2004), 36–37, 123; text of treaty in R. Père [Jean-Baptiste] Labat, *Voyage du chevalier des Marchais en Guinée, isles voisines, et à Cayenne fait en 1725, 1726 & 1727*, 2nd ed., 4 vols. (Amsterdam: Aux dépens de la Compagnie, 1731), 2:88–91.

22. Memorandum of Capt. Eyriès, 1795, in Simone Berbain, *Le comptoir français de Juda (Ouidah) au XVIIIe siècle* (Paris: Institut Français d'Afrique Noire, 1942), 95.

23. John M'Leod, *A Voyage to Africa* (1820; repr. London: Frank Cass, 1971), 113–14.

24. On two occasions, in 1827 and 1839, the masters of ships taken at Ouidah challenged the legality of their capture on the grounds that, because of the existence of a Portuguese fort there, these were *Portuguese* national waters, within which the British had no legal right of arrest, but the British brushed the argument aside, on the grounds that the fort was no longer officially occupied. Law, *Ouidah*, 187. In 1840 a British warship even fired on a flagstaff on the beach at Ouidah (which was thought to be signaling a warning to slave ships of its presence), a flagrantly illegal act that seems to have raised no qualms on the British side. Ibid., 190–91.

25. John Duncan, *Travels in Western Africa in 1845 and 1846*, 2 vols. (1847; repr., London: Frank Cass, 1968), 2:263; PP, Slave Trade, class B, encl. 8 in no. 9, King of Dahomey to Commodore Fanshawe, 18 October 1849; Slave Trade 1864, class B, no. 19, Consul Burton to Earl Russell, 23 March 1864.

26. PP, Slave Trade 1850–51, class B, no. 9, Consul Beecroft to Viscount Palmerston, 22 July 1850. Documents relating to Dahomey are cited here from the Slave Trade series; many of them are also included in Papers Relative to the Reduction of Lagos by Her Majesty's Forces (1852).

27. PP, Slave Trade 1850–51, class A, encl. in no. 225, Fanshawe to King of Dahomey, 23 July 1850; 1851–52, class A, no. 142, Fanshawe to Admiralty, 30 March 1851.

28. PP, Reduction of Lagos, no. 43, Palmerston to Admiralty, 27 September 1851; Slave Trade 1851–2, class A, encl. in no. 194, Commodore Bruce to King of Dahomey, 17 December 1851.

29. PP, Slave Trade 1852–53, class A, encls. 1, 5 in no. 71, Commander T. G. Forbes to Bruce, 18 January 1852; class B, encl. 21 in no. 4, Vice-Consul Fraser to Beecroft, 17 January 1852.

30. It would be "selling his country." NA, FO84/886, Journal of Vice-Consul Fraser, 1–2 March 1852.

31. "If a man-of-war anchors off a town—it means war!" Ibid., 1 March 1852.

32. Ibid., 27 February 1852.

33. Badagry was under the control of a pro-British faction, following a civil war in June 1851 (as noted below).

34. PP, Slave Trade 1851–2, class A, no.186, Bruce to Admiralty, 6 December 1851; encl. 1 in no. 188, Bruce to Governor of Sierra Leone, 6 December 1851; 1852–3, class A, no. 71, Bruce to Admiralty, 11 February 1852.

35. PP, Reduction of Lagos, no. 6, Lord Eddisbury to Admiralty, 22 April 1850; no. 9, Beecroft to Palmerston, 22 July 1850; encl. 2 in no. 10, Addington to Admiralty, 11 October 1850; no. 25, Palmerston to Beecroft, 21 February 1851.

36. PP, Reduction of Lagos, no. 32, Beecroft to Palmerston, 21 February 1851. Leading Brazilian merchant José Domingos Martins, based at Porto-Novo, who also supported the restoration of Akitoye at Lagos, likewise urged that "international law could not be brought in consideration at all." Ibid., encl. 2 in no. 39, Rev. C. A. Gollmer to Beecroft, 18 March 1851.

37. Emmerich de Vattel, *The Law of Nations*, rev. ed. (London: G. G. and J. Robinson, 1797), book 2, chap. 4, sec. 54–57, book 3, chap. 18, sec. 296.

38. See, for example, John B. Losi, *History of Lagos* (Lagos: African Education Press, 1967), 24, 29. Kosoko's father, Osinlokun (r. 1821–29), was Akitoye's elder brother. However, although the principle of primogeniture was asserted at Lagos, royal successions frequently deviated from it in practice.

39. PP, Slave Trade 1862, encl. in no. 18, Governor Freeman to Duke of Newcastle, 7 June 1862.

40. PP, Reduction of Lagos, encl. 1 in no. 41, Bruce to Admiralty, 31 July 1851; encl. 19, Captain Jones to Basorun of Abeokuta, 18 July 1851; no. 46, Addington to Admiralty, 18 October 1851.

41. PP, Reduction of Lagos, no. 43, Palmerston to Admiralty, 27 September 1851; encl. 1 in no. 60, Bruce to Admiralty, 1 November 1851; encl. 1 in no. 56, Commander Heath to Admiralty, 17 December 1851.

42. It also breached an Anglo-French convention of 1845 that prohibited resort to force to suppress the slave trade by either party, without the consent of the local commanders of both navies. This objection was raised in advance of the action, but not subsequently alluded to. PP, Reduction of Lagos, encl. in no. 61, Bruce to Admiralty, 1 November 1851.

43. PP, Reduction of Lagos, encl. 1 in no. 70, Bruce to Admiralty, 2 January 1852. The British party had carried a flag of truce, but this was a transparent deceit. Bruce himself had condemned "that a flag of truce should have been displayed under circumstances which could scarcely warrant a hope of its being respected." Ibid., encl. 1 in no. 65, Bruce to Admiralty, 19 December 1851.

44. Broadlands Papers, University of Southampton, Baring to Palmerston, 20 October 1850, quoted in Eltis, *Economic Growth,* 121.

45. Quoted in Gavin, "Nigeria," 25.

46. PP, Reduction of Lagos, no. 64, Earl Granville to Beecroft, 24 January 1852.

47. NA, FO84/858, minute, 11 January 1852, re: Beecroft to Palmerston, 26 November 1851. The signature to this note is not clear, but likely it is "W. H. W[ylde]," a clerk in the Foreign Office.

48. PP, Reduction of Lagos, no. 75, Granville to Beecroft, 23 February 1852.

49. *Hansard Parliamentary Debates,* 3rd ser., vol. 119, 638–39 (17 February 1852).

50. For example, the *Daily News* (London), 10 January 1852, condemned it as "not . . . lawful or moral."

51. *The Destruction of Lagos* (London: James Ridgway, 1852), 21.

52. *Hansard,* 3rd ser., vol. 167, 502–10 (12 June 1862), Austen H. Layard, Foreign Under-Secretary.

53. PP, Reduction of Lagos, no. 43, Palmerston to Admiralty, 27 September 1851.

54. Broadlands Papers, Palmerston to Baring, 31 July 1851, quoted in Eltis, *Economic Growth,* 122.

55. *Destruction of Lagos,* 19–21.

56. Paul Michael Kielstra, *The Politics of Slave Trade Suppression in Britain and France, 1814–48: Diplomacy, Morality and Economics* (Basingstoke: Macmillan, 2000), 121–22.

57. W. E. B. DuBois, *The Suppression of the African Slave-Trade to the United States of America, 1638–1870* (1896; repr., Mineola, NY: Dover, 1970), 139–40, 258.

58. NA, FO84/262, Bandinel, memorandum, cited in Eltis, *Economic Growth,* 85.

59. Bethell, *Abolition,* 60, 187.

60. Kielstra, *Politics,* 176–77, 203, 215.

61. David Murray, *Odious Commerce: Britain, Spain and the Abolition of the Cuban Slave Trade* (Cambridge: Cambridge University Press, 1980), 82, 93,182–83, 255–56, 261, 319–20. It was only in 1885, at the Congress of Berlin, that a collective declaration was made by the major European powers, including France and Spain (plus the United States and the Ottoman Empire), that the slave trade was forbidden under international law, and even this fell short of declaring it to be piracy. Miers, *Britain,* 171–73.

62. PP, Reports from the Select Committee of the House of Lords on the Slave Trade, 1849–50, 3rd report, app. 6, Eddisbury to William Hutt, 20 July 1848.

63. Lieutenant [Frederick E.] Forbes, *Six Months' Service in the African Blockade, from April to October, 1848* (1849; repr., London: Dawsons of Pall Mall, 1969), vii. Likewise, no

African state subscribed to the Berlin Act of 1885, apart from Zanzibar, which was not represented at the conference but adhered to the act subsequently (1886).

64. Philip D. Curtin, *The Image of Africa: British Ideas and Action, 1780–1850,* 2 vols. (Madison: University of Wisconsin Press, 1964), 1:279–80, 2:465–66.

65. Jennifer Pitts, "Boundaries of Victorian International Law," in *Victorian Visions of Global Order: Empires and International Relations in Nineteenth-Century Political Thought,* ed. Duncan Bell (Cambridge: Cambridge University Press, 2007), 67–88.

66. James Stephen, minute on Treaty with Kataba, 6 September 1841, in Newbury, *British Policy,* 225. In this, however, British official usage was not consistent: the agreement made in 1852 with Dahomey was still regularly termed a treaty, although the actual document signed employed the term "engagement."

67. PP, 1842 Select Committee, minutes of evidence, 24 June 1842, sec. 6743, 6747, 6785–86; Select Committee of the House of Lords, 1st report, minutes of evidence, 6 July 1849, sec. 4514, 4516.

68. PP, Select Committee of the House of Lords, 1st report, minutes of evidence, 9 May 1849, sec. 1145.

69. Charles Henry Alexandrowicz, *The European-African Confrontation: A Study in Treaty Making* (Leiden: A.W. Sijthoff, 1973).

70. *Hansard,* 3rd ser., vol. 76, 940–41 (16 July 1844), vol. 80, 213 (5 May 1845).

71. Vattel, *Law of Nations,* book 2, chap. 1, sec. 6–7.

72. Roderick Braithwaite, *Palmerston and Africa: The Rio Nuñez Affair—Competition, Diplomacy and Justice* (London: British Academic Press, 1996), 206–8, 287–93.

73. *Hansard,* 3rd ser., vol. 109, 1132–38 (19 March 1850), Thomas Chisholm Anstey, an Irish radical.

74. Aberdeen to Admiralty, 20 May 1842, in Newbury, *British Policy,* 162–63.

75. Eltis, *Economic Growth,* 121–22.

SEVEN

Racial Violence, Universal History, and Echoes of Abolition in Twentieth-Century Zanzibar

JONATHON GLASSMAN

THE IDEAS and discourses of abolitionism continued to exert an impact on Africa long after the end of slavery. Their most obvious legacy lay in the colonial project that dominated the continent's political life throughout the first half of the twentieth century. Colonial rulers imagined the suppression of slavery as but the first of a series of steps undertaken in the name of a moral obligation to free Africans from barbarism and bring them into the age of civilization and modernity.[1] This civilizing mission, and the historicist vision in which it was embedded, continued to shape governing policies right into the postwar years, which Frederick Cooper has characterized as the era of "developmental" colonialism.[2] Developmentalism, of course, remains a dominant discourse today. So one might argue that in a general sense the legacy of abolitionism continues to shape how Western governments and aid agencies deal with Africa (and, not infrequently, how the African governments with which they partner deal with their citizens), insofar as they act from a perceived obligation to impose modernity and progress on a backward part of the world.

Yet although such connections to the historicist discourses of latter-day rulers are relatively easy to trace, the same cannot be said for the tangled threads that tie abolitionism to twentieth-century popular political thought. But the connections are plainly there, and reconstructing them provides an opportunity for confronting the complex nature of intellectual discourse in the colonial world, in particular for examining how historical memories of slavery were constructed and the role those constructed memories played in shaping popular subjectivities, sometimes in profound ways.

A Monument to Abolition

There is perhaps no better place to listen for the echoes of abolitionism than Zanzibar, a pair of islands just off the East African coast, which since the 1870s has been emblematic of the African slave trade and Britain's civilizing mission to end it. Early in the nineteenth century Arab princes from Oman established a sultanate in Zanzibar, which subsequently became a hub of international trade linking the Swahili coast to markets and ideas from deep in the continental interior and across the western Indian Ocean, Islamic Middle East, and North Atlantic. Zanzibar Town soon became a bustling metropolis, hosting merchants and visitors from throughout the world. Among them were American and European merchants and a steady stream of Western visitors, many of the latter passing on their way to or from India or (after the opening of the Suez Canal) southern Africa. Westerners found the sultanate an exotic anachronism, an oriental despotism that managed to linger even while engaged directly with the forces of Western-influenced commercial progress.

For many, those backward qualities were best represented by the ruling elite's continuing addiction to slavery, after even the retrograde plantocrats of the U.S. South had been wrenched from it.[3] The most famous Western visitors were missionaries and abolitionist travelers like David Livingstone who used Zanzibar as a staging post for expeditions to the mainland and for campaigns against the so-called Arab slave trade that gripped the region long after the transatlantic trade had been suppressed. Although in the middle decades of the century British diplomats and naval officers had persuaded the sultans to ban the export of slaves out of East Africa, savvy entrepreneurs at the coast purchased slaves that were still brought from the interior, putting them to work on their own plantations of clove and coconut. (That this expansion of plantation slavery was largely driven by demands for the commodities of "legitimate commerce" was an irony fully understood by British consuls, though rarely mentioned openly.)[4] Zanzibar Town's slave market, one of the last places on earth where slaves were openly bought and sold, became a favored destination for Western visitors, who were titillated by coming face to face with what they liked to think of as the barbarism they themselves had left behind. Lurid descriptions of the market by journalists and missionaries made Zanzibar a byword for Arab slavery. In 1873, Britain finally pressured the sultan to close the market, and a quarter century later, after his successors had come under full British "protection," slavery itself was abolished.

Today, Zanzibar is known in the West largely for its pristine beaches. Yet the associations between Zanzibar, slavery, and abolition remain strong, and the slave market remains a tourist destination. On any day during the tourist season, groups of Europeans can be seen wending their way through the alleys of Stone Town, led by local guides toward the Mkunazini quarter, on the old town's eastern edge. Their destination is the Anglican Cathedral Church of Christ, better known as the Slave Market Church. In 1873, the year the market was closed, the

The Cathedral Church of Christ, or "Slave Market Church," in a photo taken sometime between 1879 and 1897. Courtesy of the Winterton Collection of East African Photographs, Melville J. Herskovits Library of African Studies, Northwestern University, Evanston, Illinois.

Universities' Mission to Central Africa secured possession of the site and on Christmas day laid the foundation stone for its mother church. Although the UMCA struggled to find converts in the overwhelmingly Muslim islands, the cathedral, with its towering stone roof, made a vivid local impression. Its builders filled it with symbolic details amplifying its power as a monument to Britain's moral crusade against slavery, including illustrative windows and a crucifix carved from the tree under which Livingstone died. The high altar, the missionaries claimed, was erected on the very spot where the market's whipping post once stood, thus drawing an eloquent analogy between the sufferings of the slaves and those of "He . . . 'by Whose stripes we are healed.'"[5]

No tour of the slave market is complete without a visit to the notorious "slave chambers," a pair of low-ceilinged rooms in the basement of St. Monica's Hostel, a large building next to the church. This is the place that usually elicits the guides' most impassioned stories. A hundred slaves or more, they say, were packed into these chambers at night and made to sleep atop concrete platforms that run along the walls. (The platforms are ornamented with manacles and chains.) Most suffocated from overcrowding, visitors are told, but the fraction who survived, like those who survived the routine whippings meted out where the altar now stands, proved their strength to prospective buyers.

These and other unlikely stories about the Zanzibar slave market have been repeated uncritically to the world at large, including by scholars who ought to know better, and they played a prominent part in the Anglican Church's official celebrations commemorating the bicentennial of the Abolition Act.[6] The narratives all emphasize the brutality of the slave market; the more colorful examples tell of slave children being randomly killed, their throats slit where the church's baptismal font now stands.[7] They also emphasize the market's antiquity. Slaves are said to have been sold on the site for centuries or even a millennium.[8] Above all, the stories emphasize the racial aspects of the suffering, with those who bought and sold slaves simply referred to as the Arabs and their victims as blacks or Africans.

Yet virtually none of the stories are true. The most gruesome are obviously absurd: it flies in the face of logic to imagine businessmen routinely destroying most of their merchandise in this way. (Why Western visitors are so willing to believe such fantasies is a question best taken up elsewhere.) The structure that houses the slave chambers was built as a hospital by the missionaries themselves, twenty years *after* the slave market was closed. The concrete platforms in the basement are plainly recognizable as dry storage, meant no doubt for medical supplies.[9] But even the narratives' more plausible themes cannot be substantiated. The market's antiquity is vastly exaggerated: large-scale slave trading had been part of Zanzibar's economy for only two or three generations, not centuries,[10] and in fact the Mkunazini market had existed for only a few decades at the time it was shut down.[11]

The stories' most misleading aspects are what they imply about the nature of slavery in Zanzibar, especially, as we will see below, its racial aspect: it is a serious distortion to suggest that all masters and slave traders were Arabs. It is equally misleading to suggest that racial animus prompted masters to treat their slaves worse than chattel. Here one must walk a fine line between accepting the sensationalist fictions told in Mkunazini and seeming to apologize for slavery. The horrors of the long-distance trade that brought slaves from the interior are well documented,[12] and the degradations they suffered in the Zanzibar market are described in numerous eyewitness accounts left by Western observers. But although nearly all those accounts were animated by abolitionist zeal and as such might reasonably be suspected of exaggeration, none so much as hint at the kind of details contained in the slave chamber narratives (I haven't even found mention of a whipping post). Even the missionaries, despite their self-righteous contempt for slave traffickers, nevertheless admitted that once in the islands most slaves were subjected to a form of slavery that was relatively mild.[13]

So, where did the slave market myths originate? It would be simplistic to attribute them solely to the influence of abolitionist rhetoric. Some may have originated as elaborations of stories told about notoriously cruel masters, perhaps exaggerated for narrative color. But it is significant that they share key motifs with legends once used to describe powerful men who were neither Arabs nor even slave masters.[14] The slave chamber stories can be recognized as a variant of such a motif, common not only in this region but elsewhere in the world, which tells of dead bodies immured in the walls and foundations of large buildings. Such myths link massive structures with the power of those who built and used them, and that power with their inhumanity.[15] Michel-Rolph Trouillot notes that investing a building with such tales bestows the tales with added weight and the ability to mute alternative narratives. "The bigger the material mass," he writes, "the more easily it entraps us."[16]

This dynamic has been observed of the better known slave trade monuments at Cape Coast and Gorée, where the close, massive walls (in spaces where, as in St. Monica's, captives are said to have suffocated to death) contribute to inducing in visitors a visceral, emotional response.[17]

The parallels with stories at the West African sites are probably not entirely coincidental.[18] The transatlantic trade, of course, figures prominently in the diasporic imagination of pan-Africanism, and pan-Africanism occupied a central place in the thinking of those who are most immediately responsible for having preserved and propagated Zanzibar's slave market myths: racial nationalists who in 1964, a few weeks after the withdrawal of the British, overthrew the sultanate and the domination of the islands' Arab elite. These activists and ideologues claimed to be acting to redress the wrongs that Arabs had inflicted on their ancestors; stories of slavery were couched as memories of historical experience. Yet few were actually descended from the slaves who suffered in the Mkunazini market. Many identified themselves ethnically as the descendants of the islands' original inhabitants, people who had never been enslaved. Others were recent immigrants, or their children, who had crossed from the mainland voluntarily during the twentieth century to work on the islands' clove and coconut estates. And although a handful of the racial nationalists were indeed descended from slaves, for the most part their ancestors had been *mateka* (recaptives, as their West African counterparts were called): that is, slaves liberated by British antislavery cruisers as they were being smuggled into the islands, who never experienced being sold in the Mkunazini market or being exploited by a Zanzibari planter.[19] In the 1950s and 1960s intellectuals drawn from these groups, affiliated with the African Association and its offshoot, the Afro-Shirazi Party (ASP), crafted historical narratives in an effort to persuade all islanders not of obvious Middle Eastern ancestry to imagine themselves as part of a racial community who shared a history of oppression at the hands of Arabs. Their efforts contributed to an acute degree of racial polarization, culminating in the early 1960s in pogroms in which people who identified themselves as Africans or blacks (the latter my imprecise rendering of the Swahili term *magozi*)[20] attacked those whom they vilified as Arab settlers and slave drivers.

Today, the myths of the slave chambers are kept alive mostly by a handful of committed ideologues of Zanzibar's ruling Revolutionary Party, the successor to the ASP.[21] But in the years leading up to the 1964 revolution these and other memories of slavery were central to how significant numbers of islanders thought about their subject positions, resulting in the transgressive racial violence that I will touch on below. Focusing on how such narratives were generated reminds us that historical memories are usually not memories at all—not something actually remembered—but forms of historical consciousness that have been crafted by intellectuals, usually with the aim of fostering particular ways of imagining a collective self. In Zanzibar, the intellectuals who were responsible for crafting the prevailing memories of "Arab slavery" engaged with many streams of discourse, both locally inherited and borrowed from overseas, the latter including abolitionist historical discourses introduced by colonial educators. To that extent, then, the racial violence of the early 1960s, which some Zanzibaris still invoke in debates over current politics, can be said to have constituted an echo of abolitionism.

This suggestion raises two puzzles. First is the question of how abolitionist historicism, which one must assume was a fairly recondite set of notions to most Zanzibaris, became prominent, if not hegemonic, by the end of the colonial era. The answer to this question is not as simple as it may seem. And second, how did something as remote from lived experience as a historical narrative come to impel significant numbers of ordinary people (including people who could not be described as intellectuals) to transgress previously normative standards of behavior toward their neighbors? How did historical narratives of slavery shape the violence of a pogrom?

Abolitionism and Universal History

Abolitionism's role in the creation of the racial thought that divided Zanzibar would seem, at first glance, relatively straightforward. That is the position taken by many East African intellectuals, particularly from Zanzibar or other parts of the Swahili coast. Abolitionist texts were commonly used in colonial schools, especially schools run by missionaries. So a common explanation points to the stories of "Arab slavery" as evidence that Zanzibar's racial polarization was a direct product of colonial indoctrination, which purposely introduced forms of racial resentment that undermined older, more flexible notions of ethnic identity. Such an interpretation is derived directly from the polemics of the 1950s and 1960s, when the racial nationalists affiliated with the African Association and its successor, the ASP, were derided by their political rivals as *wamisheni,* or people of the missions, implying not only that they were colonial lickspittles but also Christians, and, as such, not true

Zanzibaris.[22] Abolitionism in this view, like racial thought more generally, was a key component of the colonization of consciousness.[23]

But relying on assumptions of colonial indoctrination can result in
only a caricature of colonial intellectual history that neglects the creative
work done by a variety of local thinkers. If instead we examine the precise conversations and debates in which historical memories of slavery
were constructed, we find a different and more complex story. Missionaries in fact played only a limited role in education in Zanzibar, where,
unusually for a British colony, schools were run by the government.[24]
(It is indeed true that a handful of mission-educated Christian literati,
the descendants of mateka, were among those who founded the African
Association in the 1930s. But by the time that racial invective became
pronounced, in the 1950s, they had long since passed from the scene,
pushed aside by racial nationalists who for the most part were poorly
educated and, like virtually all islanders, Muslim.)[25] And most of the
teachers in those schools were not Europeans but Zanzibaris, including
many of the polemicists who would later excoriate the racial nationalists
for having been indoctrinated by colonial ideology.

These government schoolteachers in fact were the ones most responsible for introducing islanders to historicist lessons about civilization,
barbarism, and slavery. By the early 1930s they formed the core of a
self-aware intelligentsia whose mission, as they saw it, was to promote
the values of modernity and nation building. Virtually all were young
men drawn from elite landowning families who identified themselves
as Arabs. This was in accord with overall government policy. Colonial
Zanzibar was technically a protected Arab state (the sultan remained
the head of state), and the leading Arab families were regarded as a
racial elite. Students were selected to attend the Teachers' Training
College—for many years Zanzibar's sole postprimary institution—with
an eye toward training them to become enlightened rulers in a modern,
paternalist state. After serving as classroom teachers, many went on to
careers in the civil service, journalism, and other professions. In all these
capacities, they were to be Zanzibar's leading intellectuals throughout
the final three decades of the colonial era, exerting an impact on political discourse far greater than any European educators. And a key
component of that impact lay in the historical narratives they crafted
and propagated as part of their nation-building project.[26]

In stressing this intelligentsia's role in shaping islanders' modern historical consciousness, I do not intend to deny the influence of colonial

discourse: after all, the intelligentsia, of all Zanzibaris, had experienced the most sustained exposure to colonial education, an influence they openly acknowledged. Indeed, some of their earliest statements on history and nation building appeared in a journal published by the Department of Education, written when they were student teachers. But rather than simply parrot the historicist concepts learned from their British mentors, they made use of them in creative ways, selectively combining them with an array of other discursive elements—some borrowed from other parts of the world, some inherited locally. Eventually their historical narratives were picked up by some of their own nonelite students and protégés who developed them in yet new directions, resulting in the bitter intellectual ferment of the 1950s.

It has become something of a commonplace in the literature on nationalism that nationalist intellectuals could not simply invent compelling historical narratives however they pleased. Rather, they were limited by the need to make use of "what was there"—limited, that is, by the need to incorporate some of the fundamental motifs already current in the popular imagination.[27] In the case of Zanzibar, those motifs included a long-established tradition of Arabcentric thinking, by which people on the Swahili coast liked to distinguish themselves from their non-Muslim neighbors by tracing their ancestry to mythical immigrants from the Islamic heartlands of the Middle East. The leading families of the coast had long thought of themselves as Arabs or Persians, inventing genealogies if necessary. These were not the hard racial boundaries that contemporary Westerners usually think divide Arabs from Africans. Rather, they were much more flexible markers, of status, wealth, and power. In short, to stake a claim to status involved claiming Arab or Persian ancestry. Such Arabcentrism must have been agreeable to the immigrants associated with the sultanate's ruling dynasty and no doubt helped them become accepted as patrons and overlords in the first place. In any case, the newcomers had always married locally, and by the time of British conquest their descendants had long been naturalized, their mother tongue Swahili rather than Arabic. Still, the concept of Arab domination persisted, not simply because of British encouragement, but also because of how well it fit with long-established traditions.

Between the wars the new intelligentsia devoted much effort to elaborating these traditions in historical terms. One of their favorite themes was the history of "civilization" and its necessary foil, barbarism. This was also a favorite of their British mentors, who, throughout the empire, set students to write compositions on the benefits derived from civilized rule. The standard theme of such compositions, of course, concerned how Africans would advance in civilization by adapting the Western values introduced by Britain.[28] But Zanzibar's young intelligentsia argued that islanders, unlike the subjects of the mainland colonies, had alternative models from which to draw. In essays and journal articles, some of which involved erudite philological reconstructions, they observed that the Swahili word for civilization, *ustaarabu*, connoted the process of becoming like an Arab. Historical narratives described how the peoples of the coast had benefited from centuries of exposure to the civilizing influences of Arab immigrants and conquerors and hence had become more advanced than the benighted barbarians of the continental interior (the source, not coincidentally, of the islands' slaves).

Such narratives fit well with the kind of history this intelligentsia had learned in government schools. Pedagogues at the Teachers' Training College stressed the civic importance of studying and indeed writing history. The main texts used in government schools, including a set of Swahili-language primers coauthored by Zanzibari staff, were shaped by an explicit paradigm of diffusionist universal history.[29] Taking up themes that can be traced to Schiller, Hegel, and Ranke, they presented the proper units of history as races or nations, and the proper subject matter the advance of "civilization." The latter was a task always accomplished by small nations that had attained levels of enlightenment higher than the global standard of their particular epoch.[30] The key lessons concerned Greeks, Romans, Hebrews, and the British themselves. But the few lessons on African history also stressed the role of Arabs. Indeed, the texts taught that the East African coast was one of the few parts of the continent that even had a proper history, precisely because of its long involvement with Arabs.

On the face of it, such accounts seem a far cry from the abolitionist narratives crafted by nineteenth-century evangelicals, in which Arabs and their religion were demonized as baneful influences. However, it must be borne in mind that abolitionism was not simply a doctrine but was rather part of a broader ideology or discourse—about progress, capitalism, and free labor—that was capable of sustaining several variants.[31] In the first half of the nineteenth century Christian and secular variants vied for predominance in Britain and the United States. But by the time Britain was establishing colonial administrations early in the twentieth century, the evangelical version had become marginalized and the missionaries' concerns for spreading the gospel merely tolerated, at best; in a place like Zanzibar, where administrators relied on the goodwill of the islands' ruling Arab families (to say nothing of the overwhelmingly Muslim population), the evangelical version would have been highly impractical. At any rate, the two variants had much in common. Both were resolutely historicist, holding that abolition was a necessary step in the direction of moral and economic progress, and although the evangelicals had sometimes inserted eschatological overtones, by the close of the century the prevailing ideas of historical movement were the secular ones that had originated with the moral philosophers of the Scottish Enlightenment.[32] The secular ideas were what shaped the classic colonial-era texts on East African history. These were written by Sir Reginald Coupland, Beit Professor of Colonial History at Oxford, who had begun his career with a biography of Wilberforce and had subsequently turned to East Africa via an interest in another abolitionist icon, John Kirk, who as British consul general at Zanzibar was chiefly responsible for the 1873 anti–slave trade treaties. For Coupland, stopping the slave trade was "an essential prerequisite of orderly evolution in the twentieth century."[33] In his analysis of the *longue durée,* the slave trade figured as a tragedy not because it advanced Arab influence in East Africa, but, quite the contrary, because it impeded what otherwise might have been the Arabs' fuller civilizing influence on the "more backward, more passive" peoples of Africa. Coupland's abolitionism, like abolitionism generally, was an integral part of an overall vision of diffusionist universal history, a vision made explicit on the opening pages of a book tellingly entitled *East Africa and Its Invaders.*[34]

Coupland's two volumes of East African history, like the more accessible school texts studied and taught in Zanzibar's classrooms, had a palpable impact on the ideas and even the language of the new intelligentsia, whose own historical narratives focused on how civilization was spread by advanced "nations" and "races" that remained more or less discrete units over time. However, colonial schooling was not the only vector for the introduction of universal history. Many of the young intellectuals, and their parents, had kept abreast of pan-Arab nationalism, reading journals published in Cairo and Damascus. And pan-Arabism, too, owed much to the concepts of universal history, including *volkisch* German historiography and the Semitic wave theory, associated with the American Egyptologist James Henry Breasted.[35] It was not uncommon for nationalist thinkers elsewhere to craft critiques of colonialism from the same historicist concepts that had been used to justify European rule.[36] In this case, the intelligentsia used historicism to advance the argument that Zanzibar had no need of British rule, because islanders had long had their own local agents of the civilizing process: the Arab settlers from whom the intelligentsia themselves were descended.

Although such teachings were intended to foster a sense of national pride, they inevitably did so in ways that emphasized the distance between elites and subalterns—a distance that the discourses of universal history encouraged thinking of in racial terms. So, for example, whenever a foil was needed to highlight islanders' comparatively superior level of civilization, it was found in the backward customs of mainland Africans, many of whom, or their children, worked on the islands' estates. The intelligentsia also engaged in projects of cultural and religious reform that aimed to rid Zanzibar of customs that the elite deemed unfortunate survivals from the islanders' own uncivilized past. All these lessons implied that indigenous islanders (that is, islanders who were not members of elite Arab families) had played only secondary roles in Zanzibar's history of civilization. The implication would later encourage anti-Arab sentiments among many of them.

But these lessons' bitterest legacy would be what they taught about slavery. Universal history had treated slavery not only as a key element of barbarism but also as part of the universal human experience, one that Europeans had learned to leave behind.[37] The intelligentsia stressed this universality. The practice of slavery did not mark Arabs as more brutal or inhuman than other nations, they argued; after all, the West had abandoned it only a few generations before they had. In fact, the history of slavery in East Africa demonstrated the opposite. Taking their cue from pan-Arab rhetoric that was widespread at the time, the intelligentsia contrasted the supposedly benign practices of Arab slavery (as they called it) with the crueler regimes of racial slavery practiced in the New World. Thus they used lessons from universal history to score points about the elevated morality of Arab and Islamic civilization. In 1937 a Zanzibari undergraduate at Makerere University published a widely circulated polemic in which he claimed that Zanzibar slaves had been so happy with their bondage "that they loathed freedom." The author was Ali Muhsin al-Barwani, scion of a prominent landowning family, who in the 1950s would become one of Zanzibar's leading nationalists, the founder of the monarchist Zanzibar National Party (ZNP).[38] Ali Muhsin never abandoned these apologies for Zanzibar slavery. For him

and for other members of the Arab elite, the apologies were necessi-
tated by abolitionist canards against Arab honor. They also constituted
a nationalist attempt to paper over the divisions in Zanzibar society that
the intelligentsia themselves defined in racial terms. So, for example,
their accounts of slavery stressed the propensity of "Arab" masters to
marry their "African" slaves—a practice that resulted, they argued, in
Zanzibar's typical racial "intermingling" and interracial harmony.[39] To
anticipate my argument a bit: such narratives of intermarriage would
later backfire, when racial nationalists reinterpreted them as tales of rape.

Whether or not the intelligentsia's apologies were accepted by non-
elites, they reproduced two significant historical misunderstandings
about slavery. First is the mistaken assumption that, despite its long
and varied history, an institution like slavery can be characterized and
labeled in fixed terms. In fact, although slavery in the Arab Middle
East (and Islamic Africa) was indeed often "benign" compared to New
World forms, the East African experience alone demonstrates that such
relaxed forms of bondage could become transformed, according to time
and circumstance, into gang slavery.[40] So the label Arab slavery in fact
corresponded to no single set of practices. It is ironic that in responding to the challenge posed by abolitionism, the pan-Arab nationalists
should have contributed to the further reification of a concept that abolitionism itself had done so much to propagate.[41] But labels like Arab
slavery were also central to the broader discourses of universal history
from which abolitionism had emerged, in which institutions were believed to reflect discrete national spirits. In this case, the intelligentsia
argued that Zanzibari slavery reflected the humane paternalism of Arab
civilization. Later, some of the intelligentsia's students would argue that
it reflected quite different qualities.

Further, whatever slavery in Zanzibar may have looked like at any
given moment, there was nothing particularly Arab about it. This
second misunderstanding stemmed not so much from imported phi-
losophies as from local usages: in particular, from the well-established
Arabcentric traditions mentioned earlier. Within those traditions a
claim of Arab status had connoted an absence of slave ancestry and
possession of the wealth and power that had come, at least in part, from
the possession of slaves. Conversely, slave status connoted an ancestral
background of barbarism, which is to say ancestral origins in the African interior, outside the world of Islam. In a sense, then, the distinction
between slave and free had been marked ethnically, but that distinction

had been perceived chiefly as one between barbarism and civilization rather than between racial categories as the latter are conventionally understood today. In other words, contrary to the racialized histories of "Arab slavery" that were so central to abolitionism, many slave masters lacked Middle Eastern ancestry altogether.

Yet despite all this, and despite the obstacles it placed in the way of their project to build a unified nationalist consciousness, the intelligentsia spoke and wrote of Arab slavery. In part the choice had been forced on them by past practices in the construction of ethnic difference—an example of the limits on historical invention. But the term also accorded with their overall narratives of universal history. Careful readers of their historical essays would have noticed that enslavement had been a key mechanism by which Arabs had civilized the coast. To be sure, most of the essays dealt with slavery only obliquely, if at all. But a constant theme was religion: the central benefit brought by Arab contact and conquest, in those narratives, had been the introduction of monotheism, the key quality that elevated the people of the coast over the barbarians of the interior. Bringing the barbarian to the faith had once been the classic justification of slavery in Islamic doctrine. In the middle decades of the twentieth century, that doctrine could be seen lingering in the intelligentsia's historical essays, which seemed to apologize for slavery by suggesting that it was one of the mechanisms by which Arabs had civilized the region's African inhabitants.[42]

Slavery Narratives and Postwar Racial Polarization

The acute racialization of Zanzibari political discourse was a product of the nationalist mobilization that began during and after World War II. The leading figures in this racialization were drawn not from the elite intelligentsia, but were rather activists and journalists from more humble backgrounds: urban workers, squatters and laborers on the clove estates, and villagers from the fringes of the colonial economy. Most had had only a few years of schooling, at best. Their teachers—both in the classroom and, in several instances, as their early political mentors—included members of the elite intelligentsia.

Yet by the early 1950s these subaltern intellectuals were elaborating a nationalist rhetoric that differed decidedly from the intelligentsia's. Whereas the latter argued that divisions of race and status be set aside in common devotion to the values of civilization and Islam, the subalterns countered with a nationalist vision based on the solidarities of race. Still, when crafting the historical narratives on which they based their vision of racial nationalism, the subalterns could not but think within frameworks that had been provided in large part by the intelligentsia themselves. Those were the frameworks of universal history, in which the only active subjects in East Africa were Arabs and Europeans.[43] So they took up the intelligentsia's narratives of Arab colonization and civilization, inflecting them, however, as counternarratives of Arab conquest and enslavement. In these revisionist tasks, the subaltern intellectuals were assisted especially by the intelligentsia's frequent emphasis on the martial exploits of the Arab heroes who figured prominently in their East African histories.[44] They were also assisted by the intelligentsia's teachings on "Arab slavery." But rather than a stage through which all nations pass on their climb toward enlightenment, in the subalterns' writings Arab slavery became an indelible mark of racial sin. Indeed, many of the subaltern journalists preferred the metonym (Arab) *filth* (*uchafu*).[45]

In thus revising these historical narratives, the subaltern intellectuals drew on a world of influences as wide as the elite intelligentsia's. Abolitionism, of course, was among them. But a more immediate influence was pan-Africanism—although many of pan-Africanism's roots, too, could be traced to abolitionism and the attendant concepts of universal history.[46] Pan-Africanism had been introduced to the islands by immigrant workers from Tanganyika and Kenya. Unlike islanders, the immigrants felt little attraction to the civilizational ideals contained in the intelligentsia's narratives of coastal exceptionalism, which excluded them as irredeemable barbarians. The mainlanders' tribal associations, on the other hand, expressed a nativist rhetoric that disdained Arabs as non-Africans. By the late 1940s urban trade unions embracing both mainlanders and islanders were speaking in unambiguously pan-Africanist terms. Subalterns espousing such views revived the moribund African Association, which in 1948 began publishing the first of what would be many crude weekly papers propagating pan-Africanist rhetoric.[47]

In these papers, the African Association journalists argued that all people of African ancestry shared a common national identity fixed in nature and the blood, and that by these criteria Zanzibar's Arabs were aliens. Yet it would be as misleading to imply that racial thinking in East Africa originated solely with pan-Africanism as it would be to argue that it originated solely with abolitionism. The intelligentsia's rhetoric of universal history, after all, had also relied on racial categories. And much of that rhetoric, in turn, was derived from locally inherited concepts. Significantly, even the most militant of the pan-Africanist journalists accepted the intelligentsia's teachings that the nation must be built on values of civilization and modernity, that those values had been introduced from overseas, and that Africans in the interior had received them later than Africans at the coast. The pan-Africanists, however, denied that Africans had received those values from Arabs, arguing instead that they had received them from Europeans. The African Association and the ASP, in fact, were notoriously conservative. At a time when Kwame Nkrumah and Julius Nyerere were using pan-Africanist appeals to challenge colonial rule, Zanzibar's pan-Africanists were lauding the British for having civilized the continent and suppressed the slave trade.[48]

It is in these pronouncements that we can finally hear straightforward echoes of classic abolitionist rhetoric. The African Association and ASP journalists published numerous essays recounting the selfless heroism of Livingstone, Kirk, and other Britons who worked to suppress the East African slave trade. These essays occasionally referred to the Slave Market Church: a memorial, read one, "to the good done by Queen Victoria in eradicating slavery."[49] But the main thrust of such narratives was not so much to praise the Europeans as to contrast them with the other "light-skinned" people[50] who had been the region's main agents of historical change. Indians brought us modern business practices, the journalists wrote, but otherwise did us little good. Arabs, they admitted, had taught us "true religion," but they also came to enslave us. Significantly, however, when the journalists turned to describe the actual practice of slavery, they did not draw on abolitionist sources. Ancient tales of slaves buried in the foundations of buildings, for instance, were revived in variants that specified Arab oppressors.[51] More tellingly, inflammatory descriptions of Arabs' sexual abuse of their slaves were crafted in direct response to the intelligentsia's own writings and radio speeches lauding intermarriage between "Arab" masters and slave or "African" women (both sides made these elisions), a practice that the subaltern intellectuals depicted as concubinage and rape.[52] My point, then, is that despite all their encomiums to British abolitionists, the racial nationalists' historical myths were not simply the products of colonial indoctrination. (Indeed, when debating the nature of plantation slavery, it was the intelligentsia, not the subalterns, who were able to back up their position by quoting Livingstone and Coupland chapter and verse.) Rather, they were the products of their own creative labor, reimagined from a variety of sources.

Between 1957 and 1963 the British administration prepared Zanzibar for self-rule by staging a succession of four bitterly fought elections. During those years, virtually every aspect of civil society became rent by conflicts between the two main electoral blocs, one led by the subaltern pan-Africanists of the ASP, the other by elite pan-Arabists of Muhsin's ZNP.[53] Both sides made use of historical narrative in ways that cranked up racial tensions. The elite nationalists asserted that the ASP's supporters were all mainlanders whose barbarism threatened the islands' unique civilization. Such rhetoric drew on older discourses that linked mainland ancestry, barbarism, and slave status; in fact, the elite politicians went out of their way to malign their rivals as slave descendants. The subalterns, in contrast, harped on the inherited blood guilt of Arab slavery, arguing that no self-respecting African could make common cause with those whom they vilified as settlers and slavers. This mutual dehumanization soon produced sporadic acts of violence. By mid-1961, on the eve of the third election, the invective had become apocalyptic, the racial nationalists urging that the time had come to end millennia of Arab domination. (The improbable figure was derived from the intelligentsia's own historical narratives, which in turn probably got it from Coupland.) The alternative, they warned, was grim. The visiting Tanganyikan nationalist Bibi Titi Mohamed gave a series of speeches on behalf of the ASP in which she alleged that the Arabs were planning to kill the Africans after independence or reenslave them. She bolstered her case by reminding audiences of the history of slavery, describing how Arab masters had castrated male slaves, forced females to sweep the floors with their breasts, and committed other atrocities. The texts of her speeches were circulated in the political press of both sides.[54] On election day, June 1, riots broke out that eventually claimed sixty-eight lives, virtually all the victims of anti-Arab pogroms. Those pogroms proved a dress rehearsal for the much worse racial violence that would accompany the revolution of January 1964.

Historical Memory, Remembered Memory, and Racial Violence

On the preceding pages I've tried to demonstrate how abolitionist understandings of slavery echoed down through the colonial era not as fixed doctrine but as a set of discursive themes, embedded in universal history, that were creatively adapted, recombined, and reproduced by local thinkers. The net result of this creative work was the emergence, on both sides of the political divide, of a historical consciousness that interpreted Zanzibar's past in racial terms. My approach thus far has been fully compatible with the so-called constructivist literature on ethnic and national identity, insofar as I have focused on the role played by intellectuals—elite and subaltern—in imagining racial and national communities.[55]

But the culmination of these processes in widespread popular violence raises questions that challenge any attempt to deal with historical memory simply as a metaphor for the historical consciousness elaborated by intellectuals. In Zanzibar that violence transgressed all established norms of moral behavior and expressed a deeply (if momentarily) held conviction that certain racial others needed to be purged from the moral communities in which until recently they had been accepted as members. So long as we restrict our analysis to the level of intellectual work, it is difficult to comprehend how historical narratives could have so profoundly reshaped personal subjectivities. In other words, to understand how a historically imagined sense of the collective self could have led ordinary people to countenance killing their neighbors, one must understand how historical narratives had become perceived as internal, as part of one's psychology, or inner consciousness.[56] Close observers of communal violence in South Asia and elsewhere have noted that collective identities can achieve such power only when they become the stuff of *violent subjectivities:* that is, when they come to shape a sense of self based on *personal* experiences of violence, real or imagined, that in turn can seem to justify counterviolence as revenge or preemption.[57] So, keeping in mind the centrality of historical narratives to any sense of the collective self, the puzzle becomes this: How did those narratives become reproduced in people's minds at the level of lived experience? How did historical "memory"—in this case, "memories" of slavery— become *remembered* memory?

These literatures suggest that we can address this question by looking at the acts of violence themselves.[58] At first glance this strategy may seem counterintuitive, for our natural assumption is that violent acts are *preceded* by violent communal loyalties and in fact grow out of them. Yet as several scholars have observed, the motivations that initially bring people to join a communal riot are heterogeneous and often, in the first instance, have little to do with murderous racial hatred.[59] Perhaps the most common factor is intimidation: the threat that many members of the crowd feel is posed to their own safety should they fail to demonstrate sufficient loyalty to the project of ethnic cleansing. Such threats are conveyed by what Paul Brass has called "riot specialists": in the Zanzibar case, low-level political cadres, often local thugs, who played informal coordinating roles by targeting Arab victims.[60] People caught up in the crowd, or even bystanders, were often forced to join the community of killers—as, for example, when a spear or machete was passed from hand to hand and each member of the crowd intimidated into stabbing or slashing an already fallen body.[61]

But the very act of participation, even if compelled, can have the effect of reproducing discourses about the dehumanization of the racial other at an intensely personal level. In part this is a function of the stylized nature of the violence typically inflicted by racial mobs: what Primo Levi described (in another context) as "nonutilitarian violence."[62] Such violence is deeply rhetorical; it makes the victim seem personally culpable of the historical outrages for which she is being punished. It is also deeply transgressive. Gratuitously maiming a neighbor, repeatedly mutilating her already dead body and throwing it in a latrine, and other acts such as I will describe in a moment: all these, even if committed reluctantly, can spark a psychological crisis on the part of the perpetrator that is most readily resolved by accepting the logic of racial histories. Racial violence, then, was a site where violent historical narratives, in this case including narratives that had been shaped by abolitionist discourse, were reproduced among perpetrators, victims, and witnesses; where they were reenacted, as it were, in the here and now.

Space will allow for only a few examples, from the 1961 election riots. The most common victims of the pogroms were so-called Manga Arabs: not members of the creolized landowning elite, but mostly poor immigrants from the Arabian peninsula, who earned their livings as peddlers, small shopkeepers, and (by reputation) petty criminals. Their victimization had much to do with their vulnerability: many lived isolated in rural districts, including the squatter districts where most of the killing was done, and as newcomers enjoyed few well-developed ties to others in the community. But the patterns of killing, and the rhetoric that accompanied and at times prompted it, bespoke specific historical narratives in which Manga figured as exemplars of violent Arab oppression, especially in their storied roles as slave raiders, kidnappers, and enforcers for the planter elite. During the political crisis leading up to the June pogroms, rumors swirled that the Manga were sharpening their weapons to attack and reenslave Africans on behalf of the ruling Arabs. Riot specialists urged the pogroms as acts of preemption.[63]

Sexual assault is a common component of communal violence. Given a discursive context in which combatants and political actors are generally assumed to be male, the practice is often interpreted as signaling an assault on the enemy's manhood, that is, on his ability to fulfill the masculine function of protecting and controlling his women.[64] In this case, the rapes that accompanied the pogroms also had a prehistory specific to the above-mentioned historical debates about slavery and intermarriage. Those debates had culminated in veiled threats from the pan-Africanists of a program of racial leveling that would involve taking the daughters of Arabs. They made good on those threats during the pogroms of 1961 and 1964, and more formally and explicitly in 1970, when senior members of the revolutionary government forced families of Middle Eastern descent to give them their teenage daughters in marriage.[65]

The disembowelment of women was a wound that attained a particularly high profile, becoming the stuff of much rumor, propaganda, and fantasy. It, too, frequently appears in the global annals of racial and ethnic violence. Like the killing of children, it can be understood as an attack on the enemy's ability to reproduce; that is, it is a discursive act shaped by the idiom of descent that underlies all racial thought.[66] Yet once more in Zanzibar it also echoed specific historical narratives about the cruelties of "Arab slavery."[67] In her speeches of May 1961, Titi Mohamed repeated the story of an Arab mistress who wondered what a human fetus looked like; to gratify her curiosity, her husband disemboweled a pregnant slave. (As with the slaves-in-the-foundations motifs, this story most likely originated as a myth about power in general that had no necessary connection to Zanzibar, Arabs, or even slavery.)[68] During the riots such wounds were probably less common than the rumors about them, which were amplified by the political press. But the discrepancy only emphasizes the peculiar power of rhetoricized violence.[69] A pointed demonstration comes in a case in which no disembowelment in fact occurred. It happened on the third day of the riots, when a mob killed a pregnant Manga Arab while ransacking her family's shop. The main witnesses were the victim's husband and teenage son. But the court was forced to reject their testimony when, contrary to the coroner's evidence, they insisted that she had been disemboweled. (The husband was particularly adamant.) We can only speculate why they so undermined their own credibility, but a likely explanation is that, having undergone the trauma of seeing her murdered, they sincerely imagined her disembowelment. If so, this would be a remarkable instance of how historical discourse (perhaps compounded by the husband's anxieties concerning his wife's reproductive powers) can shape the personal memories of people caught up in racial violence.[70]

This incident represents a compressed example of a complex process that was common during and after the riots. On the one hand, the circulation of abolitionist historical narratives had shaped some of the violence directed against Arabs. But at the same time, the threats conveyed by those narratives (and there is little doubt that they were intended as threats),[71] coupled with reports that the threats had been carried out, confirmed the images of mainlander barbarism that had circulated in pan-Arabist circles. Thus discourse about historical violence, and violence shaped by that discourse, contributed to a spiral of reciprocal dehumanization.[72] The incident also suggests how rumor played a role in widening the ranks of witnesses, to the point that they included people who had not actually been present. Scholars have observed that the power of a rumor—the power that makes people want to believe the rumor and gives them the urge to pass it on—comes from its mythic quality, that is, from its ability to dramatize epistemological categories.[73] The same can be said for the stylized violence of the racial mob. Rhetoricized violence, then, is a rich subject for rumor. Scholars have also observed that the circulation of rumors helps cement bonds of community among those who hear and retell them. So rumor, a medium that practically compels belief, can be a powerful factor in creating violent group subjectivities. In this case, rumors that African mobs were disemboweling pregnant Arabs apparently convinced this woman's husband and son that they had witnessed a similar act. Their fantasies in this regard constituted a secondary or tertiary reverberation of historical narratives about Arab slavery.

Through both direct eyewitness and the witness of rumor, the June 1961 riots were themselves transformed into a core historical memory: what Sudhir Kakar calls a "chosen trauma,"[74] expressive of a community's sense of victimization and deferred revenge. Memories of this trauma, conjured by the simple word *June,* haunted both sides throughout the sultanate's remaining two and a half years. During that time, the pan-Arabists became ever more shrill in their dehumanization of those they identified as mainlanders and slave descendants, exaggerating stories of June in ways calculated to demonstrate their innate barbarism. The pan-Africanists, for their part, rumored that scimitar-wielding Manga Arabs were mobilizing to exact revenge for the June killings, and that the pan-Arabist parties had plans to reenslave Africans after independence, kill their male children, and force their daughters into sexual service.[75] As is commonly the case, intellectuals from the racial category that provided most of the killers nevertheless told tales of the pogroms from the perspective of victims: the event that sparked the riots was allegations that the ZNP had stolen the June election, and in the months that followed ASP rumormongers threatened a repeat should such theft be tried again.

The extent to which the 1961 riots had themselves become mythologized can be seen in how they eventually colored the slavery narratives that had done so much to shape them in the first place. A school text published three years after the revolution told of an Arab who, having raped one of his slaves, killed her and threw the body in a latrine.[76] My readers will remember that this was exactly the fate that had befallen many victims of the anti-Arab pogroms. The history lesson, then, can be seen as a version of what right-wing Hutu propagandists in Rwanda called "accusations in the mirror," by which they accused Tutsis of the outrages they themselves were plotting in the 1990s.[77] But in Zanzibar the accusations were projected back in time into the historical era. Historical narratives about slavery and living memories of more recent racial violence thus became intertwined and in fact indistinguishable, in a process that continued well after the sultanate was overthrown. The process in fact continues today, as rivals in Zanzibar's ongoing political stalemate, heirs of the pan-African and pan-Arab political traditions, invoke memories, historical and remembered, of Arab slavery and mainlander barbarism. In allowing the slave chambers to determine which of these tendentious narratives they will repeat, visitors to the Slave Market Church thus choose sides in an acrimonious political debate.

This case demonstrates how abolitionist narratives about slavery long ago slipped the control of the abolitionists and their direct intellectual heirs and were instead transformed in a variety of ways by local thinkers, combined with local myths and incorporated into latter-day political agendas. I am aware that few readers will be pleased by this story. Those who wish to celebrate the abolitionists and their intellectual legacy may find it a rude intrusion. And those who regard abolitionism as an element of the colonization of consciousness will also be displeased, insofar as I may seem to have absolved the abolitionists and their colonial descendants of direct responsibility for the racialism of mid-twentieth-century Zanzibari politics. To both charges, I can simply plead that the historian's job is neither to place laurels nor to heap blame, but to try to understand, with as much empathy as possible, what historical actors have made of the variety of inheritances left them.

Notes

1. For a useful statement see Martin A. Klein, "Modern European Expansion and Traditional Servitude in Africa and Asia," introduction to *Breaking the Chains: Slavery, Bondage and Emancipation in Modern Africa and Asia*, ed. Klein (Madison: University of Wisconsin Press, 1993), esp. 18–19.

2. Frederick Cooper, *Africa since 1940: The Past of the Present* (Cambridge: Cambridge University Press, 2002). Cooper himself showed how aspirations of modernity shaped colonial policies regarding slavery in the part of the continent discussed in this chapter. Cooper, *From Slaves to Squatters: Plantation Labor and Agriculture in Zanzibar and Coastal Kenya, 1890–1925* (New Haven: Yale University Press, 1980).

3. For British and American views of how the practice of slavery marked the U.S. South as backward and "retrogressive," see the final chapters of David Brion Davis, *Slavery and Human Progress* (New York: Oxford University Press, 1984).

4. Steven Feierman, "A Century of Ironies in East Africa," in *African History*, ed. Philip D. Curtin, Feierman, Leonard Thompson, and Jan Vansina (London: Longman, 1995), 352–76. For the British consul's awareness of the ironies in the 1870s, see Jonathon Glassman, *Feasts and Riot: Revelry, Rebellion, and Popular Consciousness on the Swahili Coast, 1856–1888* (London: Heinemann, 1995), 82–83.

5. Anne E. M. Anderson-Morshead, *The History of the Universities' Mission to Central Africa, 1859–1898*, 3rd ed. (London: UMCA, 1902), 94. Other details about the building of the cathedral are taken from Reginald Coupland, *The Exploitation of East Africa, 1856–1890*, reprint ed. (Evanston: Northwestern University Press, 1967), 205–6, 362.

6. Probably the most widely known account is in Henry Louis Gates's television series. Gates, *Wonders of the African World*, 3 videocassettes (Alexandria, VA: PBS Home Video, 1999). In February 2007 the world's attention was drawn to the slave market narratives when the Primates of the Anglican Communion, meeting in Dar es Salaam to debate the crisis over gay clergy, crossed the Zanzibar Channel to take Eucharist in the Slave Market Church, and the following month in London they showed a related video during the bicentennial commemoration of the Abolition Act; the video is available on YouTube: Lambeth Press, "Archbishops' Reflections on the Slave Pits in Zanzibar," http://www.youtube.com/watch?v=NBTErUDIcz8, posted 8 March 2007. See also "Anglican Primates Visit Former Slave Market in Zanzibar," *Anglican Journal* (Toronto), 19 February 2007. Other recent examples of uncritical repetition of the slave market stories include Ben Webster, "Legacy of Oppression," *Ottawa Sun*, 7 January 2007; Gertrude Majyambere, "Slavery Marks Linger On in Zanzibar," *New Times* (Kigali), 23 March 2006; Leanne Larmondin, "A Place Where Good Followed Evil," *Ministry Matters*, http://www.generalsynod.anglican.ca/ministries/departments/mm/2003/winter/mm11.html; Susi O'Neill, "The Blood of a Nation of Slaves in Stone Town," *Pilot Destination Guide*, http://www.pilotguides.com/destination_guide/africa/tanzania-zanzibar/slave_trade.php (accessed 23 May 2009). The latter is an especially colorful account taken from a guidebook series connected to the popular Globe Trekker television series.

7. In a version of the latter tale that I heard in August 2007, the Christian guide emphasized that "the Arabs" took care to drain all the blood from the bodies, in what he clearly intended as an echo of Islamic halal slaughtering practice.

8. "This [St. Monica's] is a terrible place . . . , the site of one of the greatest human atrocities ever, lasting a staggering one thousand years throughout modern history" (O'Neill, "Blood of a Nation"). "How long it [the Mkunazini slave market] had been there as a curse upon earth no one knows, but for generations men and women had been sold there" (Anderson-Morshead, *Universities' Mission*, 86).

9. My guess is that these platforms, and the hospital's basement in general, captured the local imagination simply because most Zanzibari buildings don't have basements. For St. Monica's and the rest of the Mkunazini mission complex, see Anderson-Morshead, *Universities' Mission;* "The New Hospital at Zanzibar," *Central Africa* 9 (1891): 133–36; letters from J. S. Wimbush and C. A. Smythies, *Central Africa* 11 (1893): 65, 70; Universities' Mission to Central Africa, *East Africa in Picture* (London: UMCA, 1900), 15–16. Prita Meier has kindly pointed my attention to a source from 1902 that suggests a connection in the popular imagination between cellars and slaves: Sorabji Manekji Darookhanawala, "Africa in Darkness," in *Two Indian Travellers: East Africa 1902–1905,* ed. Cynthia Salvadori (Mombasa: Friends of Fort Jesus, 1997), 180.

10. Zanzibar became an entrepôt for large-scale slave trading only in the late eighteenth century. Abdul Sheriff, *Slaves, Spices and Ivory in Zanzibar, 1770–1873: The Integration of an East African Commercial Empire into the World Economy, 1770–1873* (London: James Currey, 1987). Thomas Vernet has recently reassessed the volume of the Swahili slave trade before that time. But the trade he reconstructs bypassed Zanzibar and the central part of the Swahili coast altogether and in any case never reached the inflated numbers implied by the myths. Vernet, "Le commerce des esclaves sur la côte swahili, 1500–1750," *Azania* 38 (2003): 69–97.

11. This statement is inferred from a discussion by Richard Burton, who without naming the neighborhood indicates that the market was on the eastern edge of Stone Town, near the tidal inlet. This was probably Mkunazini. Sometime between 1835 and Burton's visit in 1857, the market was moved at least three times: first to Shangani, at the western end of Stone Town, then to Kiungani, outside town, and finally to Mkunazini. Burton, *Zanzibar: City, Island, and Coast,* 2 vols. (London: Tinsley Brothers, 1872), 1:351. In fact, months before the June 1873 decree abolishing the open marketing of slaves, the Mkunazini site had already been closed and the market moved yet again. Coupland, *Exploitation,* 205–6.

12. See Edward Alpers, "Indian Ocean Middle Passages: The Slave Trade from Eastern Africa and Madagascar," paper presented at "Monsoons and Migrations: Unleashing Dhow Synergies," Zanzibar International Film Festival, 5–7 July 2005; Alpers, "The Story of Swema," in *Women and Slavery in Africa,* ed. Claire Robertson and Martin Klein (Madison: University of Wisconsin Press, 1983), 185–99; Marcia Wright, *Strategies of Slaves and Women: Life Stories from East Central Africa* (New York: L. Barber, 1993); W. Gervase Clarence-Smith, ed., *The Economics of the Indian Ocean Slave Trade in the Nineteenth Century* (London: Frank Cass, 1989).

13. Paul Lovejoy and others have observed that after colonial conquest, in 1890, colonial officials had powerful rationales to moderate their abolitionism, and accordingly they apologized for continuing institutions of slavery on which they needed to rely to maintain social order and economic production. While this argument is undoubtedly correct, it does not apply to the missionary abolitionists who wrote before the 1880s. I have written in depth on slaves' resistance to the shifting burdens of their oppression: see especially *Feasts and Riot.* Lovejoy's argument is stated most succinctly in

Transformations in Slavery: A History of Slavery in Africa (Cambridge: Cambridge University Press, 2000); for Zanzibar he relies on the research of Fred Morton, which was later published as *Children of Ham: Freed Slaves and Fugitive Slaves on the Kenya Coast, 1873 to 1907* (Boulder: Westview, 1990). See my critical review of the latter in *Journal of African History* 33, no. 1 (1992): 146–49. A highly ideological depiction of the missionaries' views can be found in Anderson-Morshead, *Universities' Mission.* Representative examples of other descriptions include Captain Smee's 1811 account, which is quoted extensively by John Gray, *History of Zanzibar, From the Middle Ages to 1856* (London: Oxford University Press, 1962), 104–6; Richard Burton's account from 1857, *Zanzibar,* 1:351–55, 453ff.; eyewitness accounts from the 1870s quoted at length in Robert Nunez Lyne, *Zanzibar in Contemporary Times* (London: Hurst and Blackett, 1905), 83; "The Slave Market at Zanzibar," *Illustrated London News,* 8 June 1872.

14. The links with less specific legends about power are most evident in the colorful stories about Arab masters circulated by Bibi Titi Mohamed and other racial nationalists in the early 1960s, discussed below. For example, stories told early in the century in Pemba about Mkame Mdume, who was said to have ruled long before the Portuguese arrived, around 1500, resemble not only the stories later told about Omani slave masters but also stories about Zigua potentates on the mainland. William Harold Ingrams, *Zanzibar, Its History and Its People* (London: Witherby, 1931), 140–44.

15. So these motifs appeared to me when I was told them in the mid-1980s about massive structures not only in Zanzibar but also on the mainland coast; many of these stories had nothing to do with "Arabs" or slavery. Similar pre-Omani tales were recorded by visitors and colonial officials in the late nineteenth and early twentieth centuries, for example, F. B. Pearce, *Zanzibar: The Island Metropolis of Eastern Africa* (London: Unwin, 1920), 173–77, 207. For examples of such motifs from other parts of the world, see Michel-Rolph Trouillot, *Silencing the Past: Power and the Production of History* (Boston: Beacon, 1995); Peter J. Carroll, *Between Heaven and Modernity: Reconstructing Suzhou, 1895–1937* (Stanford: Stanford University Press, 2006). The first mention I have found of the myths of the Zanzibar slave chambers is an isolated comment from 1894 that refers not to St. Monica's (then a recently opened mission hospital) but to the main mission house, which was torn down one year later. The author, writing in a missionary monthly, was told that the mission storerooms had been where "the slaves used to be herded at night." That is all that appears in this account and is the only explicit written reference to the slave chambers that I have found from before 1964. G. Mervyn Lawson, "A Description of Zanzibar City," *African Tidings* 55 (May 1894), 38. Thanks to Andreana Prichard for bringing this source to my attention.

16. Trouillot, *Silencing the Past,* 29–30.

17. When the veteran BBC announcer Moira Stuart, filming a segment for the special series *In Search of Wilberforce,* was shown the Door of No Return at Cape Coast Castle, "she is heard to exclaim, 'Oh My God,' before breaking down into tears, unable to speak." She afterward admitted that she regretted her display of emotion. "'I was very cross with myself for having the self-indulgent reaction of tears,' she tells this week's *Radio Times.*" David Smith, "Abolition's Forgotten Heroes," *Observer* (London), 4 March 2007. Smith also recounts that Stuart was shown "cells where prisoners starved or suffocated to death." Stuart's responses were hardly unique: see Edward M. Bruner, "Tourism in Ghana: The Representation of Slavery and the Return of the Black Diaspora," *American Anthropologist,* n.s., 98, no. 2 (1996): 290–304.

18. See Majyambere, "Slavery Marks," for rhetoric about a supposed "point of no return" at Mkunazini, rhetoric I also heard in August 2007. This rhetoric, well known from the West African sites, is one of the more obvious borrowings.

19. Of course, the islands' population also contained many who identified themselves as descendants of plantation slaves, most of whom probably supported the racial nationalists of the African Association and Afro-Shirazi Party. But few of the leaders or propagandists of those organizations identified themselves as such. Inconsistently for a party that claimed to speak for slave descendants, ASP leaders regarded imputations of slave ancestry as slander. In the early twentieth century it was common for the descendants of all but the last generation of slaves imported into the islands to mask their slave ancestry by identifying themselves as indigenous islanders (e.g., as Shirazi).

20. For discussion of the term *magozi*, see Glassman, "Sorting Out the Tribes: The Creation of Racial Identities in Colonial Zanzibar's Newspaper Wars," *Journal of African History* 41, no. 3 (2000): 395–428.

21. Such historical interpretations were official doctrine after 1964 and could be found as such in school texts. See, for example, Rungwe Kasanda Mwanjisi, *Abeid Amani Karume* (Nairobi: East African Publishing House, 1967), 50. However, in recent years the rising pressures of Islamist politics have muted public discussions of slavery, enmeshed as they are in Christian abolitionist discourse. I surmise that the specific myths of the Mkunazini slave chambers are mostly a post-1964 phenomenon (despite the laconic 1894 source cited above, Lawson, "Description"), largely because of their absence from prerevolutionary accounts where one would most expect to find them. The official *Guide to Zanzibar,* for example, did not shy away from recounting the tales of slaves buried in the foundations of buildings such as the Mambo Msiige, yet its description of the Mkunazini complex omitted any mention of the slave chambers. Zanzibar, Tourist Information Bureau, *A Guide to Zanzibar* (Zanzibar: Government Printer, 1952), 29, 34, 41–42.

22. The most prominent scholarly example of such analyses is Alamin Mazrui and Ibrahim Noor Shariff, *The Swahili: Idiom and Identity of an African People* (Trenton, NJ: Africa World Press, 1994); see esp. 35–36, 105–8, 131–35. Both the midcentury polemicists and the latter-day commentators (including Mazrui and Shariff) go one step further and argue that the racial nationalists were entirely foreigners from Tanganyika, Kenya, and Uganda. I have been told this repeatedly over the past decade, usually by Zanzibaris who are hostile to the government that has been in power since the 1964 revolution. One telling instance was at a scholarly conference in Zanzibar in July 2005, when a respected Zanzibari intellectual stated, to general approbation, that racial politics were entirely the work of foreigners and hence external to Zanzibar history. The historical evidence against such a view is overwhelming: although mainland immigrants did play a significant role, the main players had for the most part been born in the islands or had lived there since childhood. Another prominent interpretation—sympathetic more to the revolutionary regime than to its opponents—identifies as the prime vectors of colonial racial thought not the subaltern racial nationalists but the elite Arabs whose rule was propped up by British policy. In both cases the divide et impera motive attributed to the British is the same. The second interpretation is more prevalent in published works by guild historians, including Laura Fair, *Pastimes and Politics: Culture, Community, and Identity in Post-abolition Urban Zanzibar, 1890–1945* (Athens: Ohio University Press, 2001); Abdul Sheriff, "Race and Class in the Politics of Zanzibar," *Afrika Spectrum* 36, no. 3 (2001): 301–18; B. D. Bowles, "The struggle for independence," in *Zanzibar Under Colonial Rule,* ed. Abdul Sheriff and E. Ferguson (London: James Currey, 1991), 79–106; B. F. Mrina and W. T. Mattoke, *Mapambano ya ukombozi Zanzibar* (Dar es Salaam: Tanzania Publishing House, 1980).

23. Viewing abolitionism in this way is not unusual: literary scholars have engaged in debates over the extent to which the classic abolitionist text by Olaudah Equiano

might reflect an act of "mental colonization." For descriptions of this literature, see Ide Corley, "The Subject of Abolitionist Rhetoric: Freedom and Trauma in *The Life of Olaudah Equiano,*" *Modern Language Studies* 32, no. 2 (2002): 139–56; Joseph Fichtelberg, "Word between Worlds: The Economy of Equiano's *Narrative,*" *American Literary History* 5, no. 3 (1993): 459–80. By invoking the concept of colonization of consciousness in such broad terms, I oversimplify an enormously complex literature on Africa and South Asia. For a critique of some of the more simplistic readings of these literatures, see Ryan Dunch, "Beyond Cultural Imperialism: Cultural Theory, Christian Missions, and Global Modernity," *History and Theory* 41, no. 3 (2002): 301–25.

24. For a similar situation in colonial Sudan, see Heather Sharkey, *Living with Colonialism: Nationalism and Culture in the Anglo-Egyptian Sudan* (Berkeley: University of California Press, 2003).

25. The Christian literati were pushed aside in the mid- to late 1940s. I recount this history of the African Association in a book in progress tentatively entitled "War of Words, War of Stones: The Multiple Sources of Racial Thought in Colonial Zanzibar," chap. 4.

26. This and the next several paragraphs draw on my article "Slower than a Massacre: The Multiple Sources of Racial Thought in Colonial Africa," *American Historical Review* 109, no. 3 (2004): 720–54.

27. Tom Nairn, *The Break-up of Britain: Crisis and Neo-nationalism* (London: New Left Books, 1977), 340, as quoted in Shula Marks, "Patriotism, Patriarchy, and Purity: Natal and the Politics of Zulu Ethnic Consciousness," in *The Creation of Tribalism in Southern Africa,* ed. Leroy Vail (Berkeley: University of California Press, 1991), 215–40. The creation of historical narratives by Zulu ethnic nationalists has been especially well treated by historians and historical anthropologists, especially Carolyn Hamilton, *Terrific Majesty: The Powers of Shaka Zulu and the Limits of Historical Invention* (Cambridge: Harvard University Press, 1998). For an overview of similar literature, see Thomas Spear, "Neo-traditionalism and the Limits of Invention in British Colonial Africa," *Journal of African History* 44, no. 1 (2003): 3–27.

28. See the prizewinning 1947 essay by the Tanganyikan Salum M. Kombo, *Ustaarabu na maendeleo ya Mwafrika* (Nairobi: East African Literature Bureau, 1950), and the discussion in James R. Brennan, "Nation, Race and Urbanization in Dar es Salaam, Tanzania, 1916–1976" (PhD diss., Northwestern University, 2002). Kombo's essay reproduced lessons long taught in Zanzibar and Tanganyikan schools. See, for example, G. W. Broomfield and D. V. Perrott, *Habari za Walimwengu, Kitabu cha tatu, masimulizi ya Juma juu ya Waingereza* (London: Macmillan, 1954), a geography primer that had been in use in Zanzibar since at least 1927.

29. L. W. Hollingsworth, *Milango ya historia,* 3 vols. (London: Macmillan, 1925–31). Students in higher standards were also assigned Hollingsworth, *Short History of the East Coast of Africa* (London: Macmillan, 1929). These and other texts are discussed in Glassman, "Slower than a Massacre."

30. That such ideas can be found in Leopold von Ranke, who is usually associated with a more positivist notion of history, only accentuates their pervasiveness. See Ranke, "The Ideal of Universal History," in *The Varieties of History: From Voltaire to the Present,* ed. Fritz Stern, 2nd ed. (New York: Vintage, 1973), 54–62. For a subtle exploration of the implications of such thought, see Dipesh Chakrabarty, *Provincializing Europe* (Princeton: Princeton University Press, 2000).

31. The classic statement is David Brion Davis, *The Problem of Slavery in the Age of Revolution, 1770–1823* (Ithaca: Cornell University Press, 1975). See also Howard Temperley, "The Ideology of Antislavery," in *The Abolition of the Atlantic Slave Trade,* ed.

David Eltis and James Walvin (Madison: University of Wisconsin Press, 1981), 21–35; James Walvin, introduction to *Slavery and British Society,* ed. J. Walvin (Baton Rouge: Louisiana State University Press, 1982), 1–21. As Thomas Holt explains, this core part of Davis's argument has not been weakened by critiques of his analysis of the politics of the antislavery movement and how antislavery became government policy. Thomas C. Holt, "Explaining Abolition," *Journal of Social History* 24, no. 2 (1990): 371–78.

32. For an extended discussion, see Davis, *Slavery and Human Progress.* Refuting the influential analysis of J. B. Bury, Nathan Rotenstreich has demonstrated that secular ideas of progress and religious ideas of Providence have in fact frequently been compatible. Rotenstreich, "The Idea of Historical Progress and Its Assumptions," *History and Theory* 10, no. 2 (1971): 197–221.

33. Jack Simmons, introduction to Coupland, *Exploitation,* vii. Coupland's book was originally published in 1939.

34. Reginald Coupland, *East Africa and Its Invaders: From the Earliest Times to the Death of Seyyid Said in 1856* (Oxford: Oxford University Press, 1938) (quotation, 1).

35. Reeva Simon, "The Teaching of History in Iraq before the Rashid Ali Coup of 1941," *Middle Eastern Studies* 22, no. 1 (1986): 37–51; Simon, "The Imposition of Nationalism on a Non-nation State: The Case of Iraq during the Interwar Period, 1921–41," in *Rethinking Nationalism in the Arab Middle East,* ed. James Jankowski and Israel Gershoni (New York: Columbia University Press, 1997), 3–25; C. Ernest Dawn, "The Formation of Pan-Arab Ideology in the Interwar Years," *International Journal of Middle East Studies* 20, no. 1 (1988): 67–91; Nimrod Hurvitz, "Muhibb ad-Din al-Khatib's Semitic Wave Theory and Pan-Arabism," *Middle Eastern Studies* 29, no. 1 (1993): 118–34.

36. Gyan Prakash, "Writing Post-Orientalist Histories of the Third World: Perspectives from Indian Historiography," *Comparative Studies in Society and History* 32, no. 2 (1990): 383–408; Partha Chatterjee, *The Nation and Its Fragments* (Princeton: Princeton University Press, 1993). See also the incisive reading of Jomo Kenyatta's intellectual debt to Malinowski in Bruce Berman and John Lonsdale, "The labors of *Muigwithania:* Jomo Kenyatta as author, 1928–45," *Research in African Literatures* 29, no. 1 (1998): 16–42.

37. Such teachings about slavery abound in the writings both of the interwar (and postwar) intelligentsia as well as in the history texts they taught and learned from in government schools. For their appearance in a classic of Western historicist thought, see Friedrich von Schiller, "The Nature and Value of Universal History: An Inaugural Lecture (1789)," *History and Theory* 11, no. 3 (1972): 321–34. Although Schiller's use of the slave trade as an emblem of African barbarism (325–26) was used both in proslavery and antislavery rhetoric, by the mid-nineteenth century it was especially useful as an element of abolitionist vituperation. For example, it was part of the inflammatory 1856 speech that got Charles Sumner of Massachusetts clubbed senseless on the senate floor by Preston Brooks of South Carolina: Sumner asserted that Southern plantocrats had regressed to the barbarism of Africans who feed the slave trade. Davis, *Slavery and Human Progress,* 264.

38. A. Muhsin [Ali Muhsin al-Barwani], "Slavery as It Used to be Practised in Zanzibar," *Makerere College Magazine* 1, no. 4 (August 1937): 111; Muhsin, "An Undoubted Infamy and the Retort," *Al-Falaq,* 23 April 1938. Muhsin urged his readers to remember that in the past slavery had been considered "one of the inexorable laws of nature," a lesson he undoubtedly had drawn from Hollingsworth, whose influence he acknowledged to the end of his life. See Muhsin's memoirs, *Conflicts and Harmony in Zanzibar* (Dubai: Verf, 1997), where he expresses this acknowledgment—and repeats similar apologies for slavery.

39. E.g., Muhsin, "Slavery."

40. The classic example is Frederick Cooper's analysis of plantation slavery at Malindi and his comparisons with other parts of the Swahili coast. Cooper, *Plantation*

Slavery on the East Coast of Africa (New Haven: Yale University Press, 1977). Also see my own account of the rise of sugar plantations at Pangani, in *Feasts and Riot.*

41. For an exploration of the links between abolitionism and the concepts of "Islamic" and "Arab" slavery, see E. Ann McDougall, "Discourse and Distortion: Critical Reflections on Studying the Saharan Slave Trade," *Outre-mers: Revue d'histoire* 89, nos. 336–37 (2002): 195–227.

42. The intelligentsia's interwar writings on slavery are discussed more explicitly in Glassman, "Slower than a Massacre."

43. The subaltern intellectuals did not omit the role of Indians. In the intelligentsia's version, Indians were parasitic money lenders (this was especially the case in the virulent anti-Indian screeds of the Arab Association press in the 1930s) who battened on the flesh of Arab gentry and indigenous peasant alike. In the subaltern version, Indians were usually praised for having played the historical role of introducing modern business practices, though also, sometimes, castigated for it.

44. Such narratives were by no means produced exclusively under the influence of Western historical discourses. See the depiction of Arab conquest that Bushiri bin Salim al-Harthi recounted to Oscar Baumann and Hans Meyer in 1888. Baumann, *In Deutsch-Ostafrika während des Aufstandes* (Vienna, 1890), discussed in Glassman, *Feasts and Riot,* 235. To be sure, the intelligentsia usually emphasized that the Arab newcomers forged friendly alliances with indigenous elites, especially in throwing off Portuguese domination in the seventeenth and eighteenth centuries. But the subaltern journalists vigorously rejected the intelligentsia's contention that the Arab invaders had been invited by local rulers. See, for example, "Kale Hata Leo," *Afrika Kwetu,* 30 December 1954.

45. Among numerous examples of such rhetoric from the African Association's weekly paper, *Afrika Kwetu,* are "Maisha ya Waafrika katika Afrika," 16 October 1952; "Jimbo la Afrika, XI," 30 May 1957. The latter also refers to the building of the Slave Market Church as a memorial to the slave trade. This and the discussion in the next several paragraphs of the rhetoric of the subaltern journalists draws on Glassman, "War of Words," chap. 4 (see note 25, above); also see Glassman, "Sorting Out the Tribes."

46. See the discussions of Alexander Crummell, Edward Blyden, and Martin Delany in Kwame Anthony Appiah, *In My Father's House* (New York: Oxford University Press, 1992), 20ff.; J. Ayodele Langley, *Pan-Africanism and Nationalism in West Africa* (Oxford: Oxford University Press, 1973), chap. 1. For early pan-Africanism in East Africa, see Kenneth James King, *Pan-Africanism and African Education in East Africa* (Oxford: Oxford University Press, 1971).

47. The African Association had been in disarray until the late 1940s. I recount the early history of the African Association in Glassman, "War of Words." Published sources include Anthony Clayton, *The Zanzibar Revolution and Its Aftermath* (London: Hurst, 1981); John Iliffe, *A Modern History of Tanganyika* (Cambridge: Cambridge University Press, 1979), 406–22.

48. These positions constituted a reversion to ideas propounded a century earlier by some of the earliest figures in the history of pan-Africanist thought. Appiah, *My Father's House.* For Martin Delany, see also James T. Campbell, *Middle Passages: African American Journeys to Africa* (New York: Penguin, 2006), esp. 86–90.

49. "Afrika na visiwa vyake," *Afrika Kwetu,* 24 December 1954. (These details are not reproduced in the English version of this article.) Other references to the church include "Zanzibari," *Afrika Kwetu,* 16 June 1955; "Kuwa raia sio utumwa," *Afrika Kwetu,* 25 April 1957. I have found no explicit mention of the slave chambers, although I have found some ambiguous references to the church's "foundations" and (quite separately) to "godowns," where slaves were crowded in squalid conditions.

50. *Watu weupe*, lit., white people.

51. Bureau of African Affairs, *Historical Facts about the Zanzibar (Unguja) National Struggle* (Accra: Bureau of African Affairs, 1963), 8; Mwanjisi, *Abeid Amani Karume*, 50. Mwanjisi's account of how slaves were killed in the construction of the Mambo Msiige mansion in Zanzibar Town—to prevent another such building ever being built (Mambo Msiige means Things you will not imitate)—echoes older tales about ancient ruins from before the Omani period. See Ingrams, *Zanzibar*, 134–35, 143–44.

52. Glassman, "Sorting Out the Tribes." It is possible that these descriptions included a distant echo of an oblique, passing reference in an 1811 description of the slave market quoted at length by Coupland, *Invaders*, 184.

53. The best account of the politicization of civil society during these years is in Michael Lofchie, *Zanzibar, Background to Revolution* (Stanford: Stanford University Press, 1965). Also see Glassman, "War of Words," chap. 5, summarized in Glassman, "The Politicization of Civil Society during Zanzibar's Newspaper Wars," Northwestern-Wisconsin African History Workshop, Madison, 19 May 2007.

54. For accounts of this rhetoric, see Rhodes House Library, Oxford, Clarence Buxton papers, box 3/2, Mss. Brit. Emp., s. 390, evidence presented to the Foster-Sutton Commission; *Sauti ya Afro-Shirazi*, 5 May 1961; "Hatutakuwa watumwa/Never Shall Be Slaves," *Mwongozi*, 21 April 1961. Also see Mrina and Mattoke, *Mapambano ya ukombozi*, 80. These stories were widely circulated at the time and afterward; they contained several motifs—pregnant women disemboweled (discussed below), toothless old men forced to crack betel nuts with their gums, etc.—that appeared elsewhere in the region about powerful men generally, not necessarily Arab slave masters.

55. Among historians of Africa, the volume edited by Leroy Vail, *Creation of Tribalism*, is often taken as the model for the constructivist approach; see also Paris Yeros, ed., *Ethnicity and Nationalism in Africa* (Houndmills, Basingstoke: Macmillan, 1999), esp. Yeros's introduction. The interpretations of Yeros, Vail, and their colleagues all reflect the influence of Iliffe's chapter "The Creation of Tribes," in *Modern History of Tanganyika*. Across fields, probably the best-known constructivist approach is Benedict Anderson, *Imagined Communities: Reflections on the Origin and Spread of Nationalism* (London: Verso, 1983).

56. That is, how a sense of the collective self had become "beyond reason." Walker Connor, "Beyond Reason: The Nature of the Ethnonational Bond," *Ethnic and Racial Studies* 16, no. 3 (1993): 373–88. Such themes are common in a literature on ethnicity and nation that is sometimes described by its critics as neoprimordialist. See Donald Horowitz, *Ethnic Groups in Conflict* (Berkeley: University of California Press, 1985).

57. See Veena Das and Arthur Kleinman, introduction to *Violence and Subjectivity*, ed. Das, Kleinman, M. Ramphele, and P. Reynolds (Berkeley: University of California Press, 2000), 1–18.

58. The literature includes Claudine Vidal, "Le génocide des Rwandais tutsi et l'usage public de l'histoire," *Cahiers d'études africaines* 38, nos. 150–52 (1998): 653–65; Gyanendra Pandey, "In Defense of the Fragment: Writing about Hindu-Muslim Riots in India Today," *Representations* 37 (Winter 1992): 27–55; Sudhir Kakar, *The Colors of Violence: Cultural Identities, Religion, and Conflict* (Chicago: University of Chicago Press, 1996); Kakar, "Some Unconscious Aspects of Ethnic Violence in India," in *Mirrors of Violence: Communities, Riots, and Survivors in South Asia*, ed. Veena Das (Delhi, 1990), 135–45; Veena Das, "Communities, Riots, Survivors—The South Asian Experience," introduction to Das, *Mirrors of Violence*, 1–36; Allen Feldman, *Formations of Violence: The Narrative of the Body and Political Terror in Northern Ireland* (Chicago: University of Chicago Press, 1991).

59. Among the best-known studies in this regard are Gyanendra Pandey, *The Construction of Communalism in Colonial North India* (Delhi: Oxford University Press, 1990); also, Pandey, "Defense of the Fragment." Exemplary studies include Scott Straus, *The Order of Genocide: Race, Power, and War in Rwanda* (Ithaca: Cornell University Press, 2006); Robert Weinberg, "Anti-Jewish Violence and Revolution in Late Imperial Odessa, 1905," in *Riots and Pogroms,* ed. Paul Brass (New York: New York University Press, 1996), 56–88.

60. Paul Brass, "Discourses of Ethnicity, Communalism, and Violence," introduction to Brass, *Riots and Pogroms,* 12–16. Such figures are common in the literature on racial violence. Among the most compelling published accounts is Kakar, *Colors of Violence.*

61. This and much of what follows is based on Glassman, "Violence as Racial Discourse: The Zanzibar 'War of Stones' of June 1961," paper presented at the Seminar in African History, Culture, and Society, Emory University, 11 April 2007. The descriptions of racial violence are based in part on a critical reading of court records from murder and assault trials following the 1961 riots.

62. Levi's translator rendered his original phrase as "useless violence." This is inadequate to render the meanings conveyed by Levi's discussion of what he called, in the original, *violenza inutile.* Primo Levi, *The Drowned and the Saved,* trans. Raymond Rosenthal (New York: Summit Books, 1988), 105–26. For Levi's original *I sommersi e i salvati* (Turin: Einaudi, 1986).

63. A history of popular images of Manga Arabs can be found in Glassman, "War of Words," chap. 6. For a précis, see Glassman, "Crime and the Discourses of Ethnic Difference in Colonial Zanzibar," paper presented at "Monsoons and Migrations: Unleashing Dhow Synergies," Zanzibar International Film Festival, 5–7 July 2005.

64. For a suggestive discussion of similar issues, see Veena Das, *Life and Words: Violence and the Descent into the Ordinary* (Berkeley: University of California, 2007).

65. These debates are described in Glassman, "Sorting Out the Tribes," 421–25.

66. The discursive meanings attached to the killing of children are tantalizingly suggested by debates among the pogromists that are documented in the court records. Glassman, "Violence as Racial Discourse." Castration is another form of stylized violence that seems to signal meanings about reproduction and that in Zanzibar, incidentally, was also foreshadowed in the historical myths regarding slavery. Don Petterson records it taking place during the 1964 pogroms, although I have found only one reference to such wounds in the court cases ensuing from the 1961 riots. Petterson, *Revolution in Zanzibar: An American's Cold War Tale* (Boulder: Westview, 2002).

67. Similarly, at Pangani, a site on the mainland that witnessed the growth of a brutal form of sugar slavery in the 1860s and 1870s, tales were told of planters' assaults on slaves' powers of reproduction. Glassman, *Feasts and Riot,* 105–6.

68. In the legends about Mkame Mdume told in Pemba in the 1920s, disembowelment appears in a narrative apparently meant to highlight the tension within marriage between masculine authority and the need to respect the wife's reproductive powers. Ingrams, *Zanzibar,* 141–42. Or the disembowelment story may have had its origins in India. Chatterjee recounts a similar myth from an 1808 text concerning an oppressive nawab. Chatterjee, *Nation and Fragments,* 84.

69. For an example of such journalistic amplification, see "Time for Action," *Mwongozi,* 28 July 1961. But such wounds did occur. An example was the murder of Jokha binti Hamed at Jang'ombe on 3 June; when the police found her she was still alive. Zanzibar High Court Archives, High Court Session 18, 1961.

70. Zanzibar High Court Archives, High Court Session 12, 1961. For further discussion of this case, see Glassman, "Violence as Racial Discourse."

71. There is ample evidence that the historical narratives had been taken as threats. For the specific example of the disembowelment motifs, see "Kwa nini hamuikabili kweli?" *Mwongozi,* 15 September 1961.

72. This phrase is adapted from John Comaroff, "Of Totemism and Ethnicity," in *Ethnography and the Historical Imagination,* ed. Comaroff and Jean Comaroff (Boulder: Westview, 1992), 49–68.

73. I derive the phrase *epistemological categories* from Luise White, *Speaking with Vampires: Rumor and History in Colonial Africa* (Berkeley: University of California Press, 2000). Other sources for my thinking on rumor, and my language, include Veena Das, "Specificities: Official Narratives, Rumour, and the Social Production of Hate," *Social Identities* 4, no. 1 (February 1998): 109–30; Gyanendra Pandey, "The Long Life of Rumor," *Alternatives: Global, Local, Political* 27, no. 2 (2002): 165–190; Kakar, *Colors of Violence.*

74. Kakar adopts the term from Vamik Volkan. Kakar, *Colors of Violence,* 50. For a discussion of similar matters in the context of European history, see Mark Levene, introduction to *The Massacre in History,* ed. Levene and Penny Roberts (New York: Berghahn, 1999), 1–38.

75. For a condensed version of these rumors by someone who believed them, see John Okello, *Revolution in Zanzibar* (Nairobi: East African Publishing House, 1967), 94–95, 119–21.

76. Mwanjisi, *Abeid Amani Karume,* 50.

77. Alison Des Forges, *Leave None to Tell the Story: Genocide in Rwanda* (New York: Human Rights Watch, 1999).

Bibliography

Adams, John. *Remarks on the Country Extending from Cape Palmas to the River Congo.* 1822. Reprint, London: Frank Cass, 1966.

African Merchant. *A Treatise upon the Trade from Great-Britain to Africa, humbly recommended to the Attention of Government.* London: R. Baldwin, 1772.

Akveld, L. M. "Journaal van de reis van Piet Heyn naar Brazilië en West-Afrika 1624–25." *Bijdragen en medelingen van het historisch genootschap* 76 (1962): 85–174.

Alexandrowicz, Charles Henry. *The European-African Confrontation: A Study in Treaty Making.* Leiden: A. W. Sijthoff, 1973.

Alpers, Edward. "Indian Ocean Middle Passages: The Slave Trade from Eastern Africa and Madagascar." Paper presented at "Monsoons and Migrations: Unleashing Dhow Synergies," Zanzibar International Film Festival, 5–7 July 2005.

———. *Ivory and Slaves in East Central Africa: Changing Patterns of International Trade to the Later Nineteenth Century.* London: Heinemann, 1975.

———. "The Story of Swema." In *Women and Slavery in Africa,* edited by Claire Robertson and Martin Klein, 185–99. Madison: University of Wisconsin Press, 1983.

Anderson, Benedict. *Imagined Communities: Reflections on the Origin and Spread of Nationalism.* London: Verso, 1983.

Anderson-Morshead, Anne E. M. *The History of the Universities' Mission to Central Africa, 1859–1898.* 3rd ed. London: UMCA, 1902.

Annesley, George. *David Livingstone: Light-Bearer to Africa.* London: Macmillan, 1956.

Anstey, Roger. *The Atlantic Slave Trade and British Abolition, 1760–1810.* London: Macmillan, 1975.

———. "The Pattern of British Abolitionism in the Eighteenth and Nineteenth Centuries." In *Anti-slavery, Religion and Reform: Essays in Memory of Roger Anstey,* edited by Christine Bolt and Seymour Drescher, 19–42. Folkestone: Dawson, 1980.

Appiah, Kwame Anthony. *In My Father's House.* New York: Oxford University Press, 1992.

Apter, David. *The Political Kingdom in Uganda.* Princeton: Princeton University Press, 1961.

Austen, Ralph A., and Woodruff D. Smith. "Images of Africa and British Slave-Trade Abolition: The Transition to an Imperialist Ideology, 1787–1807." *African Historical Studies* 2, no. 1 (1969): 69–83.

Balandier, Georges. *Daily Life in the Kingdom of the Kongo from the Sixteenth to the Eighteenth Century.* Translated from the French by Helen Weaver. 1965. Translation, New York: Pantheon, 1968.

Barry, Boubacar. *Senegambia and the Atlantic Slave Trade.* Cambridge: Cambridge University Press, 1998.

Barwani, Ali Muhsin al-. *Conflicts and Harmony in Zanzibar.* Dubai: Verf, 1997.

Batsîkama ba Mampuya ma Ndwâla, Raphael. *L'ancien royaume de Congo et les Bakongo: Séquences d'histoire populaire.* Paris: L'Harmattan, 1999.

Beckles, H. McD. "Emancipation by Law or War? Wilberforce and the 1816 Barbados Slave Rebellion." In *Abolition and Its Aftermath: The Historical Context, 1790–1816,* edited by David Richardson, 80–104. London: Frank Cass, 1985.

Bell, Duncan. *The Idea of Greater Britain: Empire and the Future of World Order, 1860–1900.* Princeton: Princeton University Press, 2007.

Belmonte, Kevin. *William Wilberforce: A Hero for Humanity.* Grand Rapids, MI: Zondervan, 2007.

———. *A Journey through the Life of William Wilberforce.* Green Forest, AR: New Leaf, 2007.

Bender, Thomas. *The Antislavery Debate: Capitalism and Abolitionism as a Problem in Historical Interpretation.* Berkeley: University of California Press, 1992.

Berbain, Simone. *Le comptoir français de Juda (Ouidah) au XVIIIe siècle.* Paris: Institut français de l'Afrique noire, 1942.

Berman, Bruce, and John Lonsdale. "The Labors of *Muigwithania:* Jomo Kenyatta as Author, 1928–45." *Research in African Literatures* 29, no. 1 (1998): 16–42.

Bethell, Leslie. *The Abolition of the Brazilian Slave Trade: Britain, Brazil, and the Slave Trade Question, 1807–1869.* Cambridge: Cambridge University Press, 1970.

Blackburn, Robin. "Haiti, Slavery, and the Age of the Democratic Revolution." *William and Mary Quarterly,* 3d ser., 63 (2006): 643–74.

———. *The Making of New World Slavery: From the Baroque to the Modern, 1492–1800.* London: Verso, 1997.

———. *The Overthrow of Colonial Slavery, 1776–1848.* London: Verso, 1988.

Bowen, H. V. *Elites, Enterprise, and the Making of the British Overseas Empire, 1688–1775.* London: St. Martin's, 1996.

Bowles, B. D. "The Struggle for Independence." In *Zanzibar under Colonial Rule,* edited by Abdul Sheriff and E. Ferguson, 79–106. London: James Currey, 1991.

Braidwood, Stephen. *Black Poor and White Philanthropists: London's Blacks and the Foundation of the Sierra Leone Settlement, 1786–1791.* Liverpool: Liverpool University Press, 1994.

Braithwaite, Roderick. *Palmerston and Africa: The Rio Nuñez Affair: Competition, Diplomacy and Justice.* London: British Academic Press, 1996.

Brennan, James R. "Nation, Race, and Urbanization in Dar es Salaam, Tanzania, 1916–1976." PhD diss., Northwestern University, 2002.

Brown, Christopher L. *Moral Capital: Foundations of British Abolitionism.* Chapel Hill: University of North Carolina Press, 2006.

———. "The Politics of Slavery." In *The British Atlantic World, 1500–1800,* edited by David Armitage and Michael J. Braddick, 214–31. New York: Palgrave Macmillan, 2002.

Buckley, Roger Norman. *Slaves in Red Coats: The British West India Regiments, 1795–1815.* New Haven: Yale University Press, 1979.

Burnard, Trevor. "Passengers Only: The Extent and Significance of Absenteeism in Eighteenth-Century Jamaica." *Atlantic Studies* 1, no. 2 (2004): 178–95.

Buxton, Thomas Fowell. *The African Slave Trade and Its Remedy.* 1840. Reprint, London: Frank Cass, 1967.

Cadornega, António de. *História geral das guerras angolanas (1680–81),* edited by José Matias Delgado and Manuel Alves da Cunha. 1940–42. Reprint, Lisbon: Agência-Geral do Ultramar, 1972.

Cain, P. J., and A. G. Hopkins. *Innovation and Expansion.* Vol. 1 of *British Imperialism.* London: Longman, 1993.

Campbell, James T. *Middle Passages: African American Journeys to Africa.* New York: Penguin, 2006.

Campbell, John. *A Political Survey of Britain being a series of reflections on the situation, lands, inhabitants, revenues, colonies, and commerce of this island.* London: Richardson and Urquhart, 1774.

Cannon, John. "The Loss of America." In *Britain and the American Revolution*, edited by H. T. Dickinson, 233–57. London: Longman, 1998.

Carrington, Selwyn H. H. "*Capitalism and Slavery* and Caribbean Historiography: An Evaluation." *Journal of African American History* 88, no. 3 (2003): 304–12.

Carroll, Peter J. *Between Heaven and Modernity: Reconstructing Suzhou, 1895–1937*. Stanford: Stanford University Press, 2006.

Cateau, Heather. "Conservatism and Change Implementation in the British West Indian Sugar Industry, 1750–1810." *Journal of Caribbean History* 29, no. 1 (1995): 1–36.

———. "The New 'Negro' Business: Hiring in the British West Indies 1750–1810." In *In the Shadow of the Plantation: Caribbean History and Legacy*, edited by Alvin O. Thompson and Woodville K. Marshall, 100–120. Kingston: Ian Randle, 2002.

Chakrabarty, Dipesh. *Provincializing Europe*. Princeton: Princeton University Press, 2000.

Chanock, Martin. *Law, Custom, and Social Order: The Colonial Experience in Malawi and Zambia*. Cambridge: Cambridge University Press, 1985.

Charles, Elizabeth Rundle. *Three Martyrs of the Nineteenth Century: Livingstone, Gordon, Patteson*. London: Society for Promoting Christian Knowledge, 1927.

Chatterjee, Partha. *The Nation and Its Fragments*. Princeton: Princeton University Press, 1993.

Christopher, Emma. *Slave Ship Sailors and Their Captive Cargoes, 1730–1807*. Cambridge: Cambridge University Press, 2006.

Clarence-Smith, W. Gervase, ed. *The Economics of the Indian Ocean Slave Trade in the Nineteenth Century*. London: Frank Cass, 1989.

Clarkson, Thomas. *The History of the Rise, Progress, and Accomplishment of the Abolition of the African Slave-Trade*. 2 vols. London: Longman, Hurst, Rees, and Orme, 1808.

Clayton, Anthony. *The Zanzibar Revolution and Its Aftermath*. London: Hurst, 1981.

Clowes, W. I. *The Royal Navy, a History from the Earliest Times to the Present*. London: Sampson, Low, 1901.

Cobbett, William, ed. *The Parliamentary History of England, from the earliest period to the year 1803*. 36 vols. London: T. C. Hansard, 1806–20.

———, ed. *Cobbett's Parliamentary Debates*. 22 vols. London: R. Bagshaw, 1804–12.

Cohen, William B. *The French Encounter with Africans: White Response to Blacks, 1530–1830*. Bloomington: Indiana University Press, 2003.

Coleman, Deirdre. *Romantic Colonization and British Anti-slavery*. Cambridge: Cambridge University Press, 2005.

Colquhoun, P. *A Treatise on the Wealth, Power, and Resources of the British Empire*. London: J. Mawman, 1815.

Comaroff, John. "Of Totemism and Ethnicity." In *Ethnography and the Historical Imagination*, edited by John Comaroff and Jean Comaroff, 49–68. Boulder: Westview, 1992.

Comaroff, John, and Jean Comaroff. *Of Revelation and Revolution*. 2 vols. Chicago: University of Chicago Press, 1991 and 1997.

Connor, Walker. "Beyond Reason: The Nature of the Ethnonational Bond." *Ethnic and Racial Studies* 16, no. 3 (1993): 373–88.

Constantine, J. Robert. "The African Slave Trade: A Study of Eighteenth Century Propaganda and Public Controversy." PhD diss., Indiana University, 1953.

Cooke, Jacob E. *Tench Coxe and the Early Republic*. Chapel Hill: University of North Carolina Press, 1978.

Cooper, Frederick. *Africa since 1940: The Past of the Present*. Cambridge: Cambridge University Press, 2002.

————. *Colonialism in Question: Theory, Knowledge, History.* Berkeley: University of California Press, 2005.

————. *Decolonization and African Society: The Labor Question in French and British Africa.* Cambridge: Cambridge University Press, 1996.

————. *From Slaves to Squatters: Plantation Labor and Agriculture in Zanzibar and Coastal Kenya, 1890–1925.* New Haven: Yale University Press, 1980.

Cooper, Frederick, and Ann Laura Stoler. *Tensions of Empire: Colonial Cultures in a Bourgeois World.* Berkeley: University of California Press, 1997.

Corley, Ide. "The Subject of Abolitionist Rhetoric: Freedom and Trauma in *The Life of Olaudah Equiano.*" *Modern Language Studies* 32, no. 2 (2002): 139–56.

Cortesão, Armando, and Avelino Teixeira da Mota, eds. *Portugaliae monumenta cartographica.* Lisbon: Imprensa Nacional, 1960.

Costanzo, Angelo, ed. *The Interesting Narrative of the Life of Equiano.* Peterborough, ON: Broadview Press, 2001.

Coupland, Reginald. *The British Anti-slavery Movement.* London: T. Butterworth, 1933.

————. *The Empire in These Days: An Interpretation.* London: Macmillan, 1935.

————. *The Exploitation of East Africa, 1856–1890.* Evanston: Northwestern University Press, 1967.

————. *Kirk on the Zambezi: A Chapter of African History.* Oxford: Clarendon Press, 1928.

————. *Livingstone's Last Journey.* London: Macmillan, 1947.

————. *Wilberforce: A Narrative.* Oxford: Clarendon Press, 1923.

Craton, Michael. *Testing the Chains: Resistance to Slavery in the British West Indies.* Ithaca: Cornell University Press, 1982.

Curtin, Philip D. *The Image of Africa: British Ideas and Action, 1780–1850.* 2 vols. Madison: University of Wisconsin Press, 1964.

Daaku, Kwame. *Trade and Politics on the Gold Coast, 1600–1720.* Oxford: Clarendon Press, 1970.

Dalzel, Archibald. *The History of Dahomy, an Inland Kingdom of Africa, Compiled from Authentic Memoirs.* London: Spilsbury and Son, 1793.

Darity, William, Jr. "British Industry and the West Indies Plantations." In *The Atlantic Slave Trade: Effects on Societies, Economies, and Peoples in Africa, the Americas, and Europe,* edited by Joseph E. Inikori and Stanley L. Engerman, 247–79. Durham, NC: Duke University Press, 1992.

Darookhanawala, Sorabji Manekji. "Africa in Darkness." In *Two Indian Travelers: East Africa 1902–1905,* edited by Cynthia Salvadori. Mombasa: Friends of Fort Jesus, 1997.

Das, Veena. *Life and Words: Violence and the Descent into the Ordinary.* Berkeley: University of California Press, 2007.

————. "Specificities: Official Narratives, Rumour, and the Social Production of Hate." *Social Identities* 4, no. 1 (February 1998): 109–30.

Das, Veena, and Arthur Kleinman. Introduction to *Violence and Subjectivity,* edited by Das, Kleinman, Mamphela Ramphele, and Pamela Reynolds, 1–18. Berkeley: University of California Press, 2000.

Davidson, Basil. *Black Mother: The Years of the African Slave Trade.* Boston: Little, Brown, 1961.

Davies, K. G. "The Living and the Dead: White Mortality in Africa, 1684–1732." In *Race and Slavery in the Western Hemisphere: Quantitative Studies,* edited by Eugene D. Genovese and Stanley Engerman, 83–98. Princeton: Princeton University Press, 1975.

———. *The Royal African Company*. London: Longmans, 1975.

Davis, David Brion. "Capitalism, Abolitionism, and Hegemony." In *British Capitalism and Caribbean Slavery: The Legacy of Eric Williams,* edited by Barbara L. Solow and Stanley L. Engerman, 283–302. Cambridge: Cambridge University Press, 1987.

———. *Inhuman Bondage: The Rise and Fall of Slavery in the New World.* New York: Oxford University Press, 2006.

———. *The Problem of Slavery in the Age of Revolution, 1770–1823.* Ithaca: Cornell University Press, 1975.

———. *The Problem of Slavery in Western Culture.* Oxford: Oxford University Press, 1966.

———. *Slavery and Human Progress.* New York: Oxford University Press, 1984.

Davis, Ralph. *The Industrial Revolution and British Overseas Trade.* Leicester: Leicester University Press, 1979.

Dawn, C. Ernest. "The Formation of Pan-Arab Ideology in the Interwar Years." *International Journal of Middle East Studies* 20, no. 1 (1988): 67–91.

Deutsch, Jan-Georg. *Emancipation without Abolition in German East Africa, c. 1884–1914.* Oxford: James Currey, 2006.

Des Forges, Alison. *Leave None to Tell the Story: Genocide in Rwanda.* New York: Human Rights Watch, 1999.

Dike, K. Onwuka. *Trade and Politics in the Niger Delta, 1830–1885.* Oxford: Clarendon Press, 1956.

Diouf, Sylviane A., ed. *Fighting the Slave Trade: West African Strategies.* Athens: Ohio University Press, 2003.

Dirks, Nicholas. *Castes of Mind: Colonialism and the Making of Modern India.* Princeton: Princeton University Press, 2001.

Doyle, Shane. *Crisis and Decline in Bunyoro: Population and Environment in Western Uganda, 1860–1955.* Oxford: James Currey, 2006.

Drescher, Seymour. "The Antislavery Debate." *History and Theory* 32, no. 3 (October 1993): 311–29.

———. *Capitalism and Antislavery: British Mobilization in Comparative Perspective.* Houndmills, Basingstoke: Macmillan, 1986.

———. "*Capitalism and Slavery* after Fifty Years." *Slavery and Abolition* 18, no. 3 (1997): 212–27.

———. "The Decline Thesis of British Slavery since *Econocide*." *Slavery and Abolition* 7, no. 1 (1986): 3–24.

———. *Dilemmas of Democracy: Tocqueville and Modernization.* Pittsburgh: University of Pittsburgh Press, 1968.

———. *Econocide: British Slavery in the Era of Abolition.* Pittsburgh: University of Pittsburgh Press, 1977.

———. "Free Labor versus Slave Labor: The British and Caribbean Cases." In *The Terms of Labor,* edited by Stanley L. Engerman, 50–86. Stanford: Stanford University Press, 1999.

———. *From Slavery to Freedom: Comparative Studies in the Rise and Fall of Atlantic Slavery.* New York: New York University Press, 1999.

———. "The Historical Context of British Abolition." In *Abolition and Its Aftermath: The Historical Context, 1790–1916,* edited by David Richardson, 3–24. London: Frank Cass, 1985.

———. *The Mighty Experiment: Free Labor versus Slavery in British Emancipation.* New York: Oxford University Press, 2002.

————. "People and Parliament: The Rhetoric of the British Slave Trade." *Journal of Interdisciplinary History* 20, no. 4 (1990): 561–80.

————. "Public Opinion and Parliament in the Abolition of the British Slave Trade." In *The British Slave Trade: Abolition, Parliament and People,* edited by Stephen Farrell, Melanie Unwin, and James Walvin, 42–65. Edinburgh: Edinburgh University Press, 2007.

Dubois, Laurent. *Avengers of the New World: The Story of the Haitian Revolution.* Cambridge, MA: Harvard University Press, 2004.

————. *A Colony of Citizens: Revolution and Slave Emancipation in the French Caribbean, 1787–1804.* Chapel Hill: University of North Carolina Press, 2004.

Dubois, Laurent, and John D. Garrigus, eds. *Slave Revolution in the Caribbean, 1789–1804: A Brief History with Documents.* New York: Palgrave Macmillan, 2006.

DuBois, W. E. B. *The Suppression of the African Slave-Trade to the United States of America, 1638–1870.* 1896. Reprint, Mineola, NY: Dover, 1970.

Duffy, Michael. "The French Revolution and British Attitudes to the West Indian Colonies." In *A Turbulent Time: The French Revolution and the Greater Caribbean,* edited by David Gaspar and David Geggus, 78–101. Bloomington: Indiana University Press, 1997.

————. *Soldiers, Sugar, and Seapower: The British Expeditions to the West Indies and the War against Revolutionary France.* Oxford: Clarendon Press, 1987.

————. "World-Wide War and British Expansion, 1793–1815." In *The Oxford History of the British Empire.* Vol. 2, *The Eighteenth Century,* edited by P. J. Marshall, 184–95. Oxford: Oxford University Press, 1998.

Duncan, John. *Travels in Western Africa in 1845 and 1846.* 2 vols. 1847. Reprint, London: Frank Cass, 1968.

Dunch, Ryan. "Beyond Cultural Imperialism: Cultural Theory, Christian Missions, and Global Modernity." *History and Theory* 41, no. 3 (2002): 301–25.

Edwards, Andrew, and Fleur Thornton. *William Wilberforce: The Millionaire Child Who Worked So Hard to Win the Freedom of African Slaves.* Leominster: Day One, 2006.

Eltis, David. *Economic Growth and the Ending of the Transatlantic Slave Trade.* New York: Oxford University Press, 1987.

————. *The Rise of African Slavery in the Americas.* Cambridge: Cambridge University Press, 2000.

————. "The Traffic in Slaves between the British West India Colonies." *Economic History Review* 25, no. 1 (1972): 55–64.

————. "Was Abolition of the U.S. and British Slave Trade Significant in the Broader Atlantic Context?" Paper presented at "Domestic and International Consequences of the First Governmental Efforts to Abolish the Atlantic Slave Trade," conference, Accra and Elmina, Ghana, 8–12 August 2007.

Eltis, David, and Stanley Engerman. "The Importance of Slavery and the Slave Trade to Industrializing Britain." *Journal of Economic History* 60, no. 1 (2000): 123–44.

Eltis, David, Frank D. Lewis, and David Richardson. "Slave Prices, the African Slave Trade, and Productivity in the Caribbean, 1674–1807." *Economic History Review* 58, no. 4 (2005): 673–700.

Eltis, David, and David Richardson. "A New Assessment of the Transatlantic Slave Trade." In *Extending the Frontiers: Essays on the New Transatlantic Slave Trade Database,* edited by Eltis and Richardson, 1–60. New Haven: Yale University Press, 2008.

Engerman, Stanley. "The Slave Trade and British Capital Formation in the Eighteenth Century: A Comment on the Williams Thesis." *Business History Review* 46, no. 4 (1972): 430–43.

Equiano, Olaudah. *Olaudah Equiano: The Interesting Narrative and Other Writings.* Edited by Vincent Caretta. New York: Penguin, 1995.

Esteves, Maria Luísa Oliveira, ed. *Portugaliae monumenta africana.* 2 vols. Lisbon: Comissão Nacional para as Comemorações dos Descobrimentos Portugueses, 1995.

Fage, J. D. "African Societies and the Atlantic Slave Trade." *Past and Present* 125, no. 1 (1989): 97–115.

Fair, Laura. *Pastimes and Politics: Culture, Community, and Identity in Post-abolition Urban Zanzibar, 1890–1945.* Athens: Ohio University Press, 2001.

Farrell, Stephen. "Contrary to the Principles of Justice, Humanity and Sound Policy: The Slave Trade, Parliamentary Politics and the Abolition Act, 1807." In *The British Slave Trade: Abolition, Parliament and People,* edited by Farrell, Melanie Unwin, and James Walvin, 141–202. Edinburgh: Edinburgh University Press, 2007.

Fehrenbacher, Don E. *The Slaveholding Republic: An Account of the United States Government's Relations to Slavery.* Completed by Ward M. McAfee. New York: Oxford University Press, 2001.

Feierman, Steven. "A Century of Ironies in East Africa." In *African History,* edited by Philip D. Curtin, Feierman, Leonard Thompson, and Jan Vansina, 352–76. London: Longman, 1995.

———. *Peasant Intellectuals: Anthropology and History in Tanzania.* Madison: University of Wisconsin Press, 1990.

Feldman, Allen. *Formations of Violence: The Narrative of the Body and Political Terror in Northern Ireland.* Chicago: University of Chicago Press, 1991.

Fichtelberg, Joseph. "Word between Worlds: The Economy of Equiano's *Narrative.*" *American Literary History* 5, no. 3 (1993): 459–80.

Fogel, Robert William. *The Fourth Great Awakening and the Future of Egalitarianism.* Chicago: University of Chicago Press, 2000.

———. *The Slavery Debates, 1952–1990: A Retrospective.* Baton Rouge: Louisiana State University Press, 2003.

Forbes, Lieutenant [Frederick E.]. *Six Months' Service in the African Blockade, from April to October, 1848, in Command of HMS* Bonetta. 1849. Reprint, London: Dawsons of Pall Mall, 1969.

Franklin, Alexandra. "Enterprise and Advantage: The West India Interest in Britain, 1774–1840." PhD diss., University of Pennsylvania, 1992.

Frost, Alan. *Botany Bay Mirages: Illusions of Australia's Convict Beginnings.* Melbourne: Melbourne University Press, 1994.

———. *Convicts and Empire: A Naval Question, 1776–1811.* Oxford: Oxford University Press, 1980.

———. "Shaking Off the Spanish Yoke: British Schemes to Revolutionise Spanish America, 1739–1807." In *Science and Exploration in the Pacific: European Voyages to the Southern Oceans in the Eighteenth Century,* edited by Margarette Lincoln, 19–37. Woodbridge, Suffolk: Boydell Press, 1998.

Fuller, Stephen. *The New Act of Assembly of the Island of Jamaica.* London: B. White, 1789.

Fyfe, Christopher. *A History of Sierra Leone.* London: Oxford University Press, 1962.

Fyfe, Christopher, and Charles Jones, eds. *Our Children Free and Happy: Letters from Black Settlers in Africa in the 1790s.* Edinburgh: Edinburgh University Press, 1991.

Gavin, Robert. "Nigeria and Lord Palmerston." *Ibadan: A Journal Published at the University College* 12 (1961): 24–27.

———. "Palmerston and Africa." *Journal of the Historical Society of Nigeria* 6, no. 1 (1971): 93–99.

Geggus, David Patrick. "British Opinion and the Emergence of Haiti, 1791–1805." In *Slavery and British Society, 1776–1846,* edited by James Walvin, 123–49. Baton Rouge: Louisiana State University Press, 1982.

———. "Haiti and the Abolitionists: Opinion, Propaganda and International Politics in Britain and France, 1804–1838." In *Abolition and Its Aftermath: The Historical Context, 1790–1916,* edited by David Richardson, 113–40. London: Frank Cass, 1985.

———. *Haitian Revolutionary Studies.* Bloomington: Indiana University Press, 2002.

———, ed. *The Impact of the Haitian Revolution in the Atlantic World.* Columbia: University of South Carolina Press, 2001.

———. *Slavery, War, and Revolution: The British Occupation of Saint Domingue, 1793–1798.* Oxford: Clarendon Press, 1982.

———. "Slavery, War, and Revolution in the Greater Caribbean, 1789–1815." In *A Turbulent Time: The French Revolution and the Greater Caribbean,* edited by David Barry Gaspar and Geggus, 1–50. Bloomington: Indiana University Press, 1997.

Glassman, Jonathon. *Feasts and Riot: Revelry, Rebellion, and Popular Consciousness on the Swahili Coast, 1856–1888.* London: Heinemann, 1995.

———. "Slower Than a Massacre: The Multiple Sources of Racial Thought in Colonial Africa." *American Historical Review* 109, no. 3 (2004): 720–54.

———. "Sorting Out the Tribes: The Creation of Racial Identities in Colonial Zanzibar's Newspaper Wars." *Journal of African History* 41, no. 3 (2000): 395–428.

Gomez, Michael A. *Exchanging Our Country Marks: The Transformation of African Identities in the Colonial and Antebellum South.* Chapel Hill: University of North Carolina Press, 1999.

Gosse, Van. "As a Nation, the English Are Our Friends: The Emergence of African American Politics in the British Atlantic World, 1772–1861." *American Historical Review* 113, no. 4 (2008): 1003–28.

Gøbel, Erik. "The Danish Edict of 16th March 1792 to Abolish the Slave Trade." In *Orbis in orbem: Liber amicorum Jan Everaert,* edited by Jan Parmentier and Sander Spanoghe, 251–63. Ghent: Academia Press, 2001.

———. "The Danish Edict of 1792 to Abolish the Slave Trade." Unpublished conference paper, 2007.

Graham, Richard. *Great Britain and the Onset of Modernization in Brazil, 1850–1914.* London: Cambridge University Press, 1968.

Grant, Kevin. *A Civilised Savagery: Britain and the New Slaveries in Africa, 1884–1926.* New York: Routledge, 2005.

Gray, Denis. *Spencer Perceval: The Evangelical Prime Minister, 1762–1812.* Manchester: Manchester University Press, 1963.

Gray, John M. *A History of the Gambia.* London: Frank Cass, 1940.

———. *History of Zanzibar, from the Middle Ages to 1856.* London: Oxford University Press, 1962.

Green-Pedersen, Svend E. "The Economic Considerations behind the Danish Abolition of the Negro Slave Trade." In *The Uncommon Market: Essays in the Economic History of the Atlantic Slave Trade,* edited by Henry A. Gemery and Jan S. Hogendorn, 399–418. New York: Academic Press, 1979.

———. "Slave Demography in the Danish West Indies and the Abolition of the Danish Slave Trade." In *The Abolition of the Atlantic Slave Trade: Origins and Effects in Europe, Africa, and the Americas,* edited by David Eltis and James Walvin, 231–58. Madison: University of Wisconsin Press, 1981.

Gregory, George. *Essays, Historical and Moral.* London: J. Johnson, 1785.

Griffin, William D. "General Charles O'Hara." *Irish Sword* 10, no. 4 (1972): 179–87.

Grove, Richard H. *Green Imperialism: Colonial Expansion, Tropical Island Edens and the Origins of Environmentalism, 1600–1800.* Cambridge: Cambridge University Press, 1995.

Hague, William. *William Wilberforce: The Life of the Great Anti–Slave Trade Campaigner.* London: HarperPress, 2007.

Halévy, Élie. *England in 1815.* Translated by E. I. Watkin and D. A. Barker. London: T. Fisher Unwin, 1924.

Hall, Douglas. "Absentee Proprietorship in the British West Indies, to about 1750." *Jamaican Historical Review* 4 (1964): 15–35.

Hall, Neville A. T. *Slave Society in the Danish West Indies: St. Thomas, St. John, and St. Croix,* edited by B. W. Higman. Mona, Jamaica: University of the West Indies Press, 1992.

Hallett, Robin. *The Penetration of Africa: European Exploration in North and West Africa to 1815.* New York: Routledge and Kegan Paul, 1965.

Hamilton, Carolyn. *Terrific Majesty: The Powers of Shaka Zulu and the Limits of Historical Invention.* Cambridge, MA: Harvard University Press, 1998.

Hammond, J. L. Le B. *Charles James Fox: A Political Study.* London: Methuen, 1903.

Hancock, David. *Citizens of the World: London Merchants and the Integration of the British Atlantic Community, 1735–1785.* Cambridge: Cambridge University Press, 1995.

Harlow, Vincent. *New Continents and Changing Values.* Vol. 2 of *The Founding of the Second British Empire, 1763–1793.* London: Longmans, Green, 1964.

Haskell, Thomas. "Capitalism and the Origins of Humanitarian Sensibility." *American Historical Review* 90, no. 2 (1985): 547–66.

Hawthorne, Walter. "Nourishing a Stateless Society during the Slave Trade: The Rise of Balanta Paddy-Rice Production in Guinea-Bissau." *Journal of African History* 42, no. 1 (2001): 1–24.

Heintze, Beatrix. "Das Ende des unabhängigen Staats Ndongo (Angola): Neue Chronologie und Reinterpretation (1617–1630)." *Paideuma* 27 (1981): 197–273.

———, ed. *Fontes para a história de Angola do século XVII.* 2 vols. Wiesbaden: Steiner, 1985–88.

Heywood, Linda, and John Thornton. *Central Africans, Atlantic Creoles and the Foundation of the Americas, 1585–1660.* Cambridge: Cambridge University Press, 2007.

Higman, B. W. *Plantation Jamaica, 1750–1850: Capital and Control in a Colonial Economy.* Kingston: University of the West Indies Press, 2005.

———. *Slave Population and Economy in Jamaica, 1807–1834.* Cambridge: Cambridge University Press, 1976.

———. *Slave Populations of the British Caribbean, 1807–1834.* Baltimore: Johns Hopkins University Press, 1984.

———. "Slavery and the Development of Demographic Theory in the Age of the Industrial Revolution." In *Slavery and British Society, 1776–1846,* edited by James Walvin, 164–94. Baton Rouge: Louisiana State University Press, 1982.

Hilton, Anne. *The Kingdom of Kongo.* Oxford: Oxford University Press, 1985.

Hilton, Boyd. *The Age of Atonement: The Influence of Evangelicalism on Social and Economic Thought, 1785–1865.* New York: Oxford University Press, 1992.

———. *A Mad, Bad, and Dangerous People? England 1783–1846.* Oxford: Clarendon Press, 2006.

Hippisley, John. *Essays: I, On the Populousness of Africa.* London: T. Lownds, 1764.

———. "On the Populousness of Africa: An Eighteenth-Century Text." *Population and Development Review* 24, no. 2 (1998): 601–8.

Hochschild, Adam. *Bury the Chains: The British Struggle to Abolish Slavery.* London: Macmillan, 2005.

Hollingsworth, L. W. *Milango ya historia.* 3 vols. London: Macmillan, 1925–31.

Hollis, Patricia. "Anti-slavery and British Working Class Radicalism in the Years of Reform." In *Anti-slavery, Religion and Reform: Essays in Memory of Roger Anstey,* edited by Christine Bolt and Seymour Drescher, 294–318. Folkestone: Dawson, 1980.

Holmes, Timothy. *Journey to Livingstone: Exploration of an Imperial Myth.* Edinburgh: Canongate, 1993.

Holt, Thomas C. "Explaining Abolition." *Journal of Social History* 24, no. 2 (1990): 371–78.

Hopkins, A. G. "The 'New International Economic Order' in the Nineteenth Century: Britain's First Development Plan for Africa." In *From Slave Trade to "Legitimate" Commerce: The Commercial Transition in Nineteenth-Century West Africa,* edited by Robin Law, 240–64. Cambridge: Cambridge University Press, 1995.

Hopkins, Daniel. "The Danish Ban on the Atlantic Slave Trade and Denmark's African Colonial Ambitions, 1787–1807." *Itinerario* 25, nos. 3–4 (2001): 154–84.

———. "Danish Natural History and African Colonialism at the Close of the Eighteenth Century: Peter Thonning's 'Scientific Journey' to the Guinea Coast, 1799–1803." *Archives of Natural History* 26, no. 3 (1999): 369–418.

———. "Denmark's Prohibition of the Slave Trade and African Colonial Policy, 1787–1850." Unpublished conference paper, 2007.

———. "Peter Thonning's Map of Danish Guinea and Its Use in Colonial Administration and Atlantic Diplomacy, 1801–1890." *Cartographica* 35, nos. 3–4 (1998): 99–122.

Horowitz, Donald. *Ethnic Groups in Conflict.* Berkeley: University of California Press, 1985.

Howard, Allen M. "Nineteenth-Century Coastal Slave Trading and the British Abolition Campaign in Sierra Leone." *Slavery and Abolition* 27, no. 1 (2006): 23–49.

Hurvitz, Nimrod. "Muhibb ad-Din al-Khatib's Semitic Wave Theory and Pan-Arabism." *Middle Eastern Studies* 29, no. 1 (1993): 118–34.

Iliffe, John. *A Modern History of Tanganyika.* Cambridge: Cambridge University Press, 1979.

Ingrams, William Harold. *Zanzibar, Its History and Its People.* London: Witherby, 1931.

Inikori, Joseph E. *Africans and the Industrial Revolution in England: A Study in International Trade and Economic Development.* New York: Cambridge University Press, 2002.

———. *The Chaining of a Continent: Export Demand for Captives and the History of Africa South of the Sahara, 1450–1870.* Mona, Jamaica: University of the West Indies Press, 1992.

———. *Forced Migration: The Impact of the Export Slave Trade on African Societies.* London: Hutchinson, 1982.

———. "Slavery in Africa and the Transatlantic Slave Trade." In *The African Diaspora,* edited by Alusine Jalloh and Stephen E. Maizlish, 39–72. College Station: Texas A&M University Press, 1996.

Innes, Joanna. "Politics and Morals: The Reformation of Manners Movement in Later Eighteenth-Century England." In *The Transformation of Political Culture: England and Germany in the Late Eighteenth Century,* edited by Eckhart Hellmuth, 57–118. Oxford: Oxford University Press, 1990.

James, C. L. R. *The Black Jacobins: Toussaint l'Ouverture and the San Domingo Revolution.* London: Secker and Warburg, 1938.

Jennings, Judith. *The Business of Abolishing the British Slave Trade, 1783–1807.* London: Frank Cass, 1997.

Jochir sigendini magadiera [People who have lived brave lives]. London: Macmillan, 1951.

Johansen, Hans Christian. "The Reality behind the Demographic Arguments to Abolish the Danish Slave Trade." In *The Abolition of the Atlantic Slave Trade: Origins and Effects in Europe, Africa, and the Americas,* edited by David Eltis and James Walvin, 221–30. Madison: University of Wisconsin Press, 1981.

Johnson, E. A. J. *Predecessors of Adam Smith: The Growth of British Economic Thought.* New York: Prentice Hall, 1937.

Kakar, Sudhir. *The Colors of Violence: Cultural Identities, Religion, and Conflict.* Chicago: University of Chicago Press, 1996.

———. "Some Unconscious Aspects of Ethnic Violence in India." In *Mirrors of Violence: Communities, Riots, and Survivors in South Asia,* edited by Veena Das, 135–45. Delhi: Oxford University Press, 1990.

Kariuki, J. M. *"Mau Mau" Detainee: The Account by a Kenya African of His Experiences in Detention Camps, 1953–1960.* Nairobi: Oxford University Press, 1963.

Kaufman, Chaim D., and Robert A. Pape. "Explaining Costly International Moral Action: Britain's Sixty-Year Campaign against the Atlantic Slave Trade." *International Organization* 53, no. 4 (1999): 631–68.

Keirn, Tim. "Daniel Defoe and the Royal African Company." *Bulletin of the Institute of Historical Research* 61, no. 145 (1988): 243–47.

Kielstra, Paul Michael. *The Politics of Slave Trade Suppression in Britain and France, 1814–48: Diplomacy, Morality and Economics.* Basingstoke: Macmillan, 2000.

King, Kenneth James. *Pan-Africanism and African Education in East Africa.* Oxford: Oxford University Press, 1971.

Klein, Martin A. "Modern European Expansion and Traditional Servitude in Africa and Asia." Introduction to *Breaking the Chains: Slavery, Bondage, and Emancipation in Modern Africa and Asia,* edited by M. A. Klein, 3–36. Madison: University of Wisconsin Press, 1993.

———. "The Slave Trade and Decentralized Societies." *Journal of African History* 42, no. 1 (2001): 49–65.

Krise, Thomas W., ed. *Caribbeana: An Anthology of English Literature of the West Indies, 1657–1777.* Chicago: University of Chicago Press, 1999.

Labat, R. Père [Jean-Baptiste]. *Voyage du chevalier Des Marchais en Guinée, isles voisines, et à Cayenne en 1725, 1726 & 1727.* Amsterdam: Aux dépens de la Compagnie, 1731.

Lambert, David. *White Creole Culture, Politics and Identity during the Age of Abolition.* Cambridge: Cambridge University Press, 2005.

Lambert, Sheila, ed. *House of Commons Sessional Papers of the Eighteenth Century.* 132 vols. Wilmington, DE: Scholarly Resources, 1975.

Langley, J. Ayodele. *Pan-Africanism and Nationalism in West Africa, 1900–1945.* Oxford: Oxford University Press, 1973.

Lascelles, Edwin, et al. *Instructions for the Management of a Plantation in Barbados. And for the treatment of Negroes.* London, 1786.

Law, Robin. "An African Response to Abolition: Anglo-Dahomian Negotations on Ending the Slave Trade, 1838–77." *Slavery and Abolition* 16, no. 3 (1995): 281–300.

———. "Dahomey and the Slave Trade: Reflections on the Historiography of the Rise of Dahomey." *Journal of African History* 27, no. 2 (1986): 237–67.

————. "Further Light on Bulfinche Lambe and the 'Emperor of Pawpaw': King Agaja of Dahomey's Letter to King George I of England, 1726." *History in Africa* 17 (1990): 211–26.

————. "Here Is No Resisting the Country: The Realities of Power in Afro-European Relations on the West African 'Slave Coast.'" *Itinerario* 18, no. 2 (1994): 50–64.

————. "King Agaja of Dahomey, the Slave Trade and the Question of West African Plantations: The Embassy of Bulfinche Lambe and Adomo Tomo in England, 1726–1732." *Journal of Imperial and Commonwealth History* 19, no. 2 (May 1991): 137–63.

————. "Legal and Illegal Enslavement in West Africa, in the Context of the Trans-Atlantic Slave Trade." In *Ghana in Africa and the World: Essays in Honor of Adu Boahen,* edited by Toyin Falola, 513–33. Trenton, NJ: Africa World Press, 2003.

————. *Ouidah: The Social History of a West African Slaving "Port," 1727–1892.* Oxford: James Currey, 2004.

Law, Robin, and Kristin Mann. "West Africa in the Atlantic Community: The Case of the Slave Coast." *William and Mary Quarterly,* 3rd ser., 56, no. 2 (April 1999): 307–34.

Lecky, W. E. H. *A History of England in the Eighteenth Century.* 2 vols. London: Longmans, Green, 1892.

————. *History of European Morals.* London: Longmans, Green, 1884.

Lettsom, John Coakley. "Some Account of the Late John Fothergill." In *The Works of John Fothergill,* edited by John Coakley Lettsom. London: Charles Dilly, 1783.

Levene, Mark. Introduction to *The Massacre in History,* edited by Levene and Penny Roberts, 1–38. New York: Berghahn, 1999.

Levi, Primo. *The Drowned and the Saved.* Translated by Raymond Rosenthal. New York: Summit Books, 1988.

Lloyd, Christopher. *The Navy and the Slave Trade: The Suppression of the African Slave Trade in the Nineteenth Century.* London: Frank Cass, 1968.

Lofchie, Michael. *Zanzibar: Background to Revolution.* Stanford: Stanford University Press, 1965.

Loftin, Joshua Evans. "The Abolition of the Danish Slave Trade." PhD diss., Louisiana State University, 1977.

LoGerfo, James W. "Sir William Dolben and the Cause of Humanity: The Passage of the Slave Trade Regulation Act of 1788." *Eighteenth-Century Studies* 6, no. 4 (Summer 1973): 431–51.

Long, Edward. *The History of Jamaica.* 3 vols. London: T. Lowndes, 1774.

Lonsdale, John. "The Moral Economy of Mau Mau: Wealth, Poverty, and Civic Virtue in Kikuyu Political Thought." In *Unhappy Valley: Conflict in Kenya and Africa,* by Lonsdale and Bruce Berman, 315–504. London: James Currey, 1992.

Lorimer, Douglas A. "Black Resistance to Slavery and Racism in Eighteenth-Century England." In *Essays on the History of Blacks in Britain: From Roman Times to the Mid-twentieth Century,* edited by Jagdish S. Gundara and Ian Duffield, 59–70. Brookfield, VT: Avebury, 1992.

————. "Black Slaves and English Liberty: A Re-examination of Racial Slavery in England." *Immigrants and Minorities* 3, no. 2 (1984): 121–50.

Losi, John B. *History of Lagos.* Lagos: African Education Press, 1967.

Lovejoy, Paul. *Transformations in Slavery: A History of Slavery in Africa.* Cambridge: Cambridge University Press, 2000.

Lowe, John, Jr. *Liberty or Death: A Tract, by Which is Vindicated the Obvious Practicability of Trading to the Coasts of Guinea, for Its Natural Products, in Lieu of the Slave-Trade.* Manchester: J. Harrop, 1789.

Lyne, Robert Nunez. *Zanzibar in Contemporary Times.* London: Hurst and Blackett, 1905.

Lynn, Martin. "Consul and Kings: British Policy, the Man on the Spot, and the Seizure of Lagos, 1851." *Journal of Imperial and Commonwealth History* 10, no. 2 (1982): 150–67.

Madden, Frederick, and David Fieldhouse, eds. *Imperial Reconstruction, 1763–1840.* Vol. 3 of *Select Documents on the Constitutional History of the British Empire and Commonwealth.* New York: Greenwood, 1987.

Mamdani, Mahmood. *Citizen and Subject: Contemporary Africa and the Legacy of Late Colonialism.* Princeton: Princeton University Press, 1996.

Mann, Kristin, and Richard Roberts, eds. *Law in Colonial Africa.* Portsmouth, NH: Heinemann, 1991.

Manning, Patrick. *Slavery and African Life: Occidental, Oriental, and African Slave Trades.* Cambridge: Cambridge University Press, 1990.

Marks, Shula. "Patriotism, Patriarchy and Purity: Natal and the Politics of Zulu Ethnic Consciousness." In *The Creation of Tribalism in Southern Africa,* edited by Leroy Vail. Berkeley: University of California Press, 1991.

Martin, Eveline C. *The British West African Settlements, 1750–1821: A Study of Local Administration.* London: Longmans, Green, 1927.

———. "The English Slave Trade and the African Settlements." In *The Cambridge History of the British Empire.* Vol. 1, *The Old Empire, from Beginnings to 1783,* edited by J. Holland Rose, A. P. Newton, and E. A. Benians, 437–59. Cambridge: Cambridge University Press, 1929.

Martin, Rachel. "The Manchester Business Community and Antislavery, 1787–1833." PhD diss., University of Cambridge, 2002.

Martin, Samuel. *Essay upon Plantership, Humbly inscrib'd to all the Planters of the British Sugar-Colonies in America.* Antigua: T. Smith, 1750.

———. *A Short Treatise on the slavery of Negroes in the British Colonies.* Antigua: Robert Mearns, 1775.

Mason, Matthew E. *Slavery and Politics in the Early American Republic.* Chapel Hill: University of North Carolina Press, 2006.

———. "Slavery Overshadowed: Congress Debates Prohibiting the Atlantic Slave Trade to the United States, 1806–1807." *Journal of the Early Republic* 20 (Spring 2000): 59–81.

Masuzawa, Tomoko. *The Invention of World Religions, or, How European Universalism Was Preserved in the Language of Pluralism.* Chicago: University of Chicago Press, 2005.

Mathieson, W. L. *Great Britain and the Slave Trade, 1839–1865.* London: Longmans, Green, 1929.

Matthews, Gelien. *Caribbean Slave Revolts and the British Abolition Movement.* Baton Rouge: Louisiana State University Press, 2006.

Mazrui, Alamin, and Ibrahim Noor Shariff. *The Swahili: Idiom and Identity of an African People.* Trenton, NJ: Africa World Press, 1994.

McCaskie, T. C. "Cultural Encounters: Britain and Africa in the Nineteenth Century." In *The Oxford History of the British Empire.* Vol. 3, *The Nineteenth Century,* edited by Andrew Porter, 655–89. Oxford: Oxford University Press, 1999.

McConville, Brendan. *The King's Three Faces: The Rise and Fall of Royal America, 1688–1776.* Chapel Hill: University of North Carolina Press, 2006.

McCusker, John J. "The Economy of the British West Indies, 1763–1790: Growth, Stagnation, or Decline?" In *Essays in the Economic History of the Atlantic World,* edited by McCusker, 310–31. London: Routledge, 1997.

McDougall, E. Ann. "Discourse and Distortion: Critical Reflections on Studying the Saharan Slave Trade." *Outre-mers: Revue d'histoire* 89, nos. 336–37 (2002): 195–227.

McGowan, Winston. "African Resistance to the Atlantic Slave Trade in West Africa." *Slavery and Abolition* 11, no. 1 (1990): 1–29.

M'Leod, John. *A Voyage to Africa.* 1820. Reprint, London: Frank Cass, 1971.

Médard, Henri, and Shane Doyle, eds. *Slavery in the Great Lakes Region of East Africa.* London: James Currey, 2007.

Metaxas, Eric. *Amazing Grace: William Wilberforce and the Heroic Campaign to End Slavery.* San Francisco: HarperSan Francisco, 2007.

Midgley, Clare. *Women against Slavery: The British Campaigns, 1780–1870.* London: Routledge, 1992.

Miers, Suzanne. *Britain and the Ending of the Slave Trade.* New York: Longman, 1975.

Miller, Joseph C. *Way of Death: Merchant Capitalism and the Angolan Slave Trade, 1730–1830.* Madison: University of Wisconsin Press, 1988.

Miller, Peter N. *Defining the Common Good: Empire, Religion, and Philosophy in Great Britain.* Cambridge: Cambridge University Press, 1994.

Mintz, Sidney W. *Caribbean Transformations.* Baltimore: Johns Hopkins University Press, 1974.

Morgan, Philip D. *Slave Counterpoint: Black Culture in the Eighteenth-Century Chesapeake and Lowcountry.* Chapel Hill: University of North Carolina Press, 1998.

———. "Task and Gang Systems: The Organization of Labor on New World Plantations." In *Work and Labor in Early America,* edited by Stephen Innes, 189–220. Chapel Hill: University of North Carolina Press, 1988.

Morgan, Philip D., and Andrew Jackson O'Shaughnessy. "Arming Slaves in the American Revolution." In *Arming Slaves from Classical Times to the Modern Age,* edited by Christopher Leslie Brown and Morgan, 180–208. New Haven: Yale University Press, 2006.

Morton, Fred. *Children of Ham: Freed Slaves and Fugitive Slaves on the Kenya Coast, 1873 to 1907.* Boulder: Westview, 1990.

Mrina, B. F., and W. T. Mattoke. *Mapambano ya ukombozi Zanzibar.* Dar es Salaam: Tanzania Publishing House, 1980.

Mulcahy, Matthew. *Hurricanes and Society in the British Greater Caribbean, 1624–1783.* Baltimore: Johns Hopkins University Press, 2006.

Murray, David. *Odious Commerce: Britain, Spain and the Abolition of the Cuban Slave Trade.* Cambridge: Cambridge University Press, 1980.

Mwanjisi, Rungwe Kasanda. *Abeid Amani Karume.* Nairobi: East African Publishing House, 1967.

Namier, Sir Lewis, and John Brooke. *The House of Commons, 1754–1790.* 3 vols. London: Oxford University Press, 1964.

Nash, Gary B. *The Forgotten Fifth: African Americans in the Age of Revolution.* Cambridge, MA: Harvard University Press, 2006.

———. *Race and Revolution.* Madison: University of Wisconsin Press, 1990.

Needell, Jeffrey D. *The Party of Order: The Conservatives, the State, and Slavery in the Brazilian Monarchy, 1831–1871.* Stanford: Stanford University Press, 2006.

Newbury, Colin, ed. *British Policy towards West Africa: Select Documents, 1786–1874.* Oxford: Clarendon Press, 1965.

Newman, Richard S. *The Transformation of American Abolitionism: Fighting Slavery in the Early Republic.* Chapel Hill: University of North Carolina Press, 2002.

Nickolls, Rev. Robert Boucher. *Observations, Occasioned by the Attempts made in England to Effect the Abolition of the Slave Trade.* Kingston: G. Francklyn, 1789.

Nordenskiöld, August. *Plan for a Free Community upon the Coast of Africa.* London: R. Hindmarsh, 1789.

Nyakatura, J. W. *Abakama ba Bunyoro-Kitara.* 1947. Reprint, Kisubi: Marianum Press, 1999.

Observations on the Advantages which would arise to this country from opening a trade with the Coast of Africa: with a plan for the same by which the Slave-Trade may be Ultimately Abolished. Dublin, 1785.

Oldfield, J. R. *Chords of Freedom: Commemoration, Ritual and British Transatlantic Slavery.* Manchester: Manchester University Press, 2007.

———. *Popular Politics and British Anti-slavery: The Mobilisation of Public Opinion against the Slave Trade, 1787–1807.* Manchester: Manchester University Press, 1998.

O'Shaughnessy, Andrew Jackson. *An Empire Divided: The American Revolution and the British Caribbean.* Philadelphia: University of Pennsylvania Press, 2000.

———. "The Formation of a Commercial Lobby: The West India Interest, British Colonial Policy and the American Revolution." *Historical Journal* 40, no. 1 (1997): 71–95.

Pacheco Pereira, Duarte. *Esmeraldo De Situ Orbis.* Edited by Augusto Epiphânio da Silva Dias. Lisbon: Sociedade de Geografia, 1905.

Pagden, Anthony. *Lords of All the World: Ideologies of Empire in Spain, Britain, and France, c. 1500–c. 1800.* New Haven: Yale University Press, 1995.

Paley, Ruth. "After Somerset: Mansfield, Slavery and the Law in England, 1772–1830." In *Law, Crime and English Society, 1660–1830,* edited by Norma Landau, 165–84. Cambridge: Cambridge University Press, 2002.

Palmer, Colin. *Human Cargoes: The British Slave Trade to Spanish America, 1700–1739.* Urbana: University of Illinois Press, 1981.

Pandey, Gyanendra. *The Construction of Communalism in Colonial North India.* Delhi: Oxford University Press, 1990.

———. "In Defense of the Fragment: Writing about Hindu-Muslim Riots in India Today." *Representations* 37 (Winter 1992): 27–55.

———. "The Long Life of Rumor." *Alternatives: Global, Local, Political* 27, no. 2 (2002): 165–90.

Paquette, Robert L. *Sugar Is Made with Blood: The Conspiracy of La Escalera and the Conflict between Empires over Slavery in Cuba.* Middletown, CT: Wesleyan University Press, 1988.

Pearce, F. B. *Zanzibar: The Island Metropolis of Eastern Africa.* London: Unwin, 1920.

Peterson, Derek R. "Culture and Chronology in African History." *Historical Journal* 50, no. 2 (2007): 483–97.

———. "The Intellectual Lives of Mau Mau Detainees." *Journal of African History* 49, no. 1 (2008): 73–91.

Petterson, Don. *Revolution in Zanzibar: An American's Cold War Tale.* Boulder: Westview, 2002.

Piper, John. *Amazing Grace in the Life of William Wilberforce.* Wheaton, IL: Crossway, 2006.

Pitt, William. *The Speeches of the Right Honourable William Pitt in the House of Commons.* Edited by W. S. Hathaway. 2nd ed. London: Longman, Hurst, Rees, and Orme, 1808.

Pitts, Jennifer. "Boundaries of Victorian International Law." In *Victorian Visions of Global Order: Empires and International Relations in Nineteenth-Century Political Thought,* edited by Duncan Bell, 67–88. Cambridge: Cambridge University Press, 2007.

————. *A Turn to Empire: The Rise of Imperial Liberalism in Britain and France.* Princeton: Princeton University Press, 2005.

Porter, Andrew. "Trusteeship, Anti-Slavery, and Humanitarianism." In *The Oxford History of the British Empire.* Vol. 3, *The Nineteenth Century,* edited by Porter, 198–221. Oxford: Oxford University Press, 1999.

Postlethwayt, Malachy. *The African Trade, the great pillar and support of the British plantation Trade in America.* London: J. Robinson, 1746.

————. *Britain's Commercial Interest, Explained and Improved in a Series of Dissertations.* 2 vols. London: A. M. Kelley, 1757.

————. *The Importance of Effectually Supporting the Royal African Company of England.* London: M. Cooper, 1745.

————. *In Honour to the Administration: The importance of the African expedition considered: with copies of the memorials . . . the whole as planned and designed by Malachy Postlethwayt . . . to which are added, observations, illustrations, the said memorials.* London: C. Say, 1758.

————. *The National Advantage of the African Trade Considered being an enquiry, how far it concerns the trading interest of Great Britain, effectually to support and maintain the forts and settlements in Africa; belonging to the Royal African Company of England . . . with a new and correct map.* London: J. and P. Knapton, 1746.

Prakash, Gyan. "Writing Post-Orientalist Histories of the Third World: Perspectives from Indian Historiography." *Comparative Studies in Society and History* 32, no. 2 (1990): 303–408.

Prestholdt, Jeremy. *Domesticating the World: African Consumerism and the Genealogies of Globalization.* Berkeley: University of California Press, 2007.

Prothero, R. Mansell. "John Hippisley on the Populousness of Africa: A Comment." *Population and Development Review* 24, no. 2 (1998): 609–12.

Pybus, Cassandra. *Epic Journeys of Freedom: Runaway Slaves of the American Revolution and Their Global Quest for Liberty.* Boston: Beacon Press, 2006.

Radulet, Carmen, trans. and ed. *O cronista rui de pina e a "Relação do reino do Congo." Manuscrito inédito do "Códice Riccardiano 1910."* Lisbon: Comissão Nacional para as Comemorações dos Descobrimentos Portugueses, 1992.

Ragatz, Lowell J. *The Decline of the Planter Class in the British Caribbean, 1763–1833: A Study in Social and Economic History.* New York: Century, 1928.

Ramsay, James. *An Enquiry into the Effects of Putting a Stop to the African Slave Trade, and of granting Liberty to the Slaves in the British Sugar Colonies.* London: James Philips, 1784.

Ranke, Leopold von. "The Ideal of Universal History." In *The Varieties of History: From Voltaire to the Present,* edited by Fritz Stern, 54–62. 2nd ed. New York: Vintage, 1973.

Rashid, Ismail. "Escape, Revolt, and Marronage in Eighteenth and Nineteenth Century Sierra Leone Hinterland." *Canadian Journal of African Studies* 34, no. 4 (2000): 656–83.

Rathbone, Richard. "Some Thoughts on Resistance to Enslavement in West Africa." *Slavery and Abolition* 6, no. 3 (1985): 173–84.

Reese, Ty M. "The Drudgery of the Slave Trade: Labor at Cape Coast Castle, 1750–1790." In *The Atlantic Economy during the Seventeenth and Eighteenth Centuries: Organization, Operation, Practice, and Personnel,* edited by Peter A. Coclanis, 277–96. Columbia: University of South Carolina Press, 2005.

————. "Liberty, Insolence, and Rum: Cape Coast Castle and the American Revolution." *Itinerario* 28, no. 3 (2004): 18–37.

———. "Sheep in the Jaws of So Many Ravenous Wolves: The Slave Trade and Anglican Missionary Activity at Cape Coast Castle, 1752–1816." *Journal of Religion in Africa* 34, no. 3 (2004): 348–77.

Richardson, David. "The Ending of the British Slave Trade in 1807: The Economic Context." In *The British Slave Trade: Abolition, Parliament and People,* edited by Stephen Farrell, Melanie Unwin, and James Walvin, 127–40. Edinburgh: Edinburgh University Press, 2007.

———. "Shipboard Revolts, African Authority, and the Atlantic Slave Trade." *William and Mary Quarterly* 58, no. 1 (2001): 69–92.

Richardson, David, and Paul Lovejoy. "Trust, Pawnship, and Atlantic History: The Institutional Foundations of the Old Calabar Slave Trade." *American Historical Review* 104, no. 2 (April 1999): 333–55.

Roberts, Justin. "Working between the Lines: Labor and Agriculture on Two Barbadian Slave Plantations, 1796–1797." *William and Mary Quarterly* 63, no. 3 (2006): 551–86.

Robinson, Cedric. "Capitalism, Slavery and Bourgeois Historiography." *History Workshop Journal* 23, no. 1 (1987): 122–40.

Robinson, Donald. *Slavery in the Structure of American Politics.* New York: Norton, 1979.

Robson, Nicholas. *Hints for a General View of the Agricultural State of the Parish of Saint James, in the Island of Jamaica.* London: John Stockdale, 1796.

Rodgers, Nini. *Ireland, Slavery and Anti-slavery: 1612–1865.* Basingstoke: Palgrave Macmillan, 2007.

Rodney, Walter. "African Slavery and Other Forms of Social Oppression on the Upper Guinea Coast in the Context of the Atlantic Slave-Trade." *Journal of African History* 7, no. 3 (1966): 431–43.

———. *A History of the Upper Guinea Coast, 1545–1800.* Oxford: Oxford University Press, 1970.

Rogers, George C. "Letters of Charles O'Hara to the Duke of Grafton." *South Carolina Historical and Genealogical Magazine* 65, no. 3 (1964): 158–80.

Rotenstreich, Nathan. "The Idea of Historical Progress and Its Assumptions." *History and Theory* 10, no. 2 (1971): 197–211.

Ryden, David Beck. "Does Decline Make Sense? The West Indian Economy and the Abolition of the British Slave Trade." *Journal of Interdisciplinary History* 31, no. 3 (2001): 347–74.

Schama, Simon. *Rough Crossings: Britain, the Slaves, and the American Revolution.* New York: HarperCollins, 2006.

Schaw, Janet. *Journal of a Lady of Quality: Being the Narrative of a Journey from Scotland to the West Indies, North Carolina, and Portugal, in the Years 1774 to 1776.* Edited by Evangeline W. Andrews and Charles M. Andrews. New Haven: Yale University Press, 1921.

Schiller, Friedrich von. "The nature and value of universal history: An inaugural lecture (1789)." *History and Theory* 11, no. 3 (1972): 321–34.

Schwarz, Suzanne. "Commerce, Civilization and Christianity: The Development of the Sierra Leone Company." In *Liverpool and Transatlantic Slavery,* edited by David Richardson, Schwarz, and Anthony Tibbles, 252–76. Liverpool: Liverpool University Press, 2007.

Scott, Julius S. "Afro-American Sailors and the International Communication Network: The Case of Newport Bowers." In *Jack Tar in History: Essays in the History of Maritime Life and Labour,* edited by Colin Howell and Richard J. Twomey, 37–52. Fredericton, New Brunswick: Acadiensis Press, 1991.

Searing, James F. "No Kings, No Lords, No Slaves: Ethnicity and Religion among the Sereer-Safèn of Western Bawol, 1700–1914." *Journal of African History* 43, no. 3 (2002): 407–29.

———. *West African Slavery and Atlantic Commerce: The Senegal River Valley, 1700–1860.* Cambridge: Cambridge University Press, 2003.

Sharkey, Heather. *Living with Colonialism: Nationalism and Culture in the Anglo-Egyptian Sudan.* Berkeley: University of California Press, 2003.

Sharp, Granville. *Memoirs of Granville Sharp.* Edited by Prince Hoare. London: Henry Colburn, 1820.

———. "Memorandum on a Late Proposal to be Made on the Coast of Africa." In *An Account of the Constitutional English Polity of Congregational Courts,* edited by Sharp, 263–81. London: J. W. Parker, 1783.

Sheridan, Richard B. "Samuel Martin, Innovating Sugar Planter of Antigua, 1750–1776." *Agricultural History* 34, no. 3 (1960): 126–39.

Sheriff, Abdul. "Race and Class in the Politics of Zanzibar." *Afrika Spectrum* 36, no. 3 (2001): 301–18.

———. *Slaves, Spices and Ivory in Zanzibar: The Integration of an East African Commercial Empire into the World Economy, 1770–1873.* London: James Currey, 1987.

Shugerman, Jed Handelsman. "The Louisiana Purchase and South Carolina's Reopening of the Slave Trade in 1803." *Journal of the Early Republic* 22, no. 2 (2002): 263–90.

Sidbury, James. *Becoming African in America: Race and Nation in the Early Black Atlantic.* New York: Oxford University Press, 2007.

Simon, Reeva. "The Imposition of Nationalism on a Non-nation State: The Case of Iraq during the Interwar Period, 1921–41." In *Rethinking Nationalism in the Arab Middle East,* edited by James Jankowski and Israel Gershoni, 3–25. New York: Columbia University Press, 1997.

———. "The Teaching of History in Iraq before the Rashid Ali Coup of 1941." *Middle Eastern Studies* 22, no. 1 (1986): 37–51.

Skinner, Quentin. *Renaissance Virtues.* Vol. 2 of *Visions of Politics.* Cambridge: Cambridge University Press, 2002.

Smith, George. *Heroes of the Nineteenth Century: Nelson, Napier, Roberts, Livingstone.* London: Arthur Pearson, 1899.

Smith, Robert S. *The Lagos Consulate, 1851–1861.* London: Macmillan, 1978.

Smith, S. D. *Slavery, Family, and Gentry Capitalism in the British Atlantic: The World of the Lascelles, 1648–1834.* Cambridge: Cambridge University Press, 2006.

"Somerset's Case Revisited." *Law and History Review* 24, no. 3 (2006): 601–71.

Sparks, Randy L. *The Two Princes of Calabar: An Eighteenth-Century Atlantic Odyssey.* Cambridge, MA: Harvard University Press, 2004.

Spear, Thomas. "Neo-traditionalism and the Limits of Invention in British Colonial Africa." *Journal of African History* 44, no. 1 (2003): 3–27.

[Stephen, James]. *The Dangers of the Country: By the Author of* War in Disguise. London: J. Butterworth and J. Hatchard, 1807.

Stewart, Larry. *The Rise of Public Science: Rhetoric, Technology, and Natural Philosophy in Newtonian Britain, 1660–1750.* Cambridge: Cambridge University Press, 1992.

Stolow, Barbara, and Stanley Engerman, eds. *British Capitalism and Caribbean Slavery: The Legacy of Eric Williams.* Cambridge: Cambridge University Press, 1987.

Straus, Scott. *The Order of Genocide: Race, Power, and War in Rwanda.* Ithaca: Cornell University Press, 2006.

Summers, Carol. "Grandfathers, Grandsons, Morality, and Radical Politics in Late Colonial Buganda." *International Journal of African Historical Studies* 38, no. 3 (2005): 427–48.

Swan, James. *A Dissuasion to Great-Britain and the Colonies, from the Slave Trade to Africa.* Boston: E. Russell, 1772.

"Symposium on the Life and Writings of Eric Williams." *Journal of African American History* 88, no. 3 (2003).

Tattersfield, Nigel. *The Forgotten Trade: Comprising the Log of Daniel and Henry of 1700 and Accounts of the Slave Trade from the Minor Ports of England, 1698–1725.* London: J. Cape, 1991.

Taylor, Clare. "Planter Attitudes to the American and French Revolutions." *National Library of Wales Journal* 21, no. 2 (1979): 113–30.

Taylor, Eric Robert. *If We Must Die: Shipboard Insurrections in the Era of the Atlantic Slave Trade.* Baton Rouge: Louisiana State University Press, 2006.

Temperley, Howard. "Anti-slavery as a Form of Cultural Imperialism." In *Anti-slavery, Religion and Reform: Essays in Memory of Roger Anstey,* edited by Christine Bolt and Seymour Drescher, 338–50. Folkestone: Dawson, 1980.

———. "The Ideology of Antislavery." In *The Abolition of the Atlantic Slave Trade,* edited by David Eltis and James Walvin, 21–35. Madison: University of Wisconsin Press, 1981.

———. *White Dreams, Black Africa: The Antislavery Expedition to the River Niger, 1841–1842.* New Haven: Yale University Press, 1991.

Thornton, Henry. "General Outlines of a Settlement on the Tooth or Ivory Coast of Africa." In *The Papers of William Thornton,* edited by C. M. Harris, 38–41. Charlottesville: University Press of Virginia, 1995.

Thornton, John. *Africa and Africans in the Making of the Atlantic World, 1400–1800.* Cambridge: Cambridge University Press, 1992.

———. "The Demographic Effect of the Slave Trade on Western Africa, 1500–1850." In *African Historical Demography,* edited by C. Fyfe and D. McMaster, 2:693–720. 2 vols. Edinburgh: Centre of African Studies, University of Edinburgh, 1981.

———. "Early Kongo-Portuguese Relations: A New Interpretation." *History in Africa* 8 (1981): 183–204.

———. "As guerras civis no Congo e o tráfico de escravos: A história e a demografia de 1718 a 1844 revisitadas." *Estudos afro-asiáticos* (Rio de Janeiro) 32, no. 1 (1997): 55–74.

———. "I Am the Subject of the King of Kongo: African Political Ideology and the Haitian Revolution." *Journal of World History* 4, no. 2 (Fall 1993): 181–214.

Tomkins, Stephen. *William Wilberforce: A Biography.* Oxford: Lion Hudson, 2007.

Trouillot, Michel-Rolph. *Silencing the Past: Power and the Production of History.* Boston: Beacon, 1995.

Turner, David. *Fashioning Adultery: Gender, Sex, and Civility in England, 1660–1740.* Cambridge: Cambridge University Press, 2002.

Universities Mission to Central Africa. *East Africa in Pictures.* London: UMCA, 1900.

van der Veer, Peter. *Imperial Encounters: Religion and Modernity in India and Britain.* Princeton: Princeton University Press, 2001.

Vattel, Emmerich de. *The Law of Nations.* Rev. ed. London: G. G. and J. Robinson, 1797.

Verger, Pierre. *Fluxo e refluxo do tráfico de escravos entre o Golfo de Benin e a Bahia de Todos os Santos dos séculos XVII a XIX.* 1966. Translated from the French by Tasso Gadzanis. Rio de Janeiro: Corrupio, 1985.

Vernet, Thomas. "Le commerce des esclaves sur la côte swahili, 1500–1750." *Azania* 38 (2003): 69–97.

Vidal, Claudine. "Le génocide des Rwandais tutsi et l'usage public de l'histoire." *Cahiers d'études africaines* 38, nos. 150–52 (1998): 653–65.

Viswanathan, Gauri. *Outside the Fold: Conversion, Modernity, and Belief.* Princeton: Princeton University Press, 1998.

Waldstreicher, David. *Runaway America: Benjamin Franklin, Slavery, and the American Revolution.* New York: Hill and Wang, 2004.

Walker, James W. St. G. *The Black Loyalists: The Search for a Promised Land in Nova Scotia and Sierra Leone, 1783–1870.* Toronto: University of Toronto Press, 1976.

Walvin, James. *England, Slaves, and Freedom, 1776–1838.* Jackson: University of Mississippi Press, 1986.

———. *Slavery and British Society.* Baton Rouge: Louisiana State University Press, 1982.

Ward, J. R. *British West Indian Slavery, 1750–1834: The Process of Amelioration.* Oxford: Clarendon Press, 1988.

———. "The British West Indies in the Age of Abolition, 1748–1815." In *The Oxford History of the British Empire.* Vol. 2, *The Eighteenth Century,* edited by P. J. Marshall, 415–39. Oxford: Oxford University Press, 1998.

Ward, W. E. F. *The Royal Navy and the Slavers: The Suppression of the Atlantic Slave Trade.* London: Allen and Unwin, 1969.

Watson, Karl. "Capital Sentences against Slaves in Barbados in the Eighteenth Century: An Analysis." In *In the Shadow of the Plantation: Caribbean History and Legacy,* edited by Alvin O. Thompson and Woodville K. Marshall, 196–221. Kingston: Ian Randle, 2002.

Watts, David. *The West Indies: Patterns of Development, Culture, and Environmental Change since 1492.* Cambridge: Cambridge University Press, 1987.

Webb, Patrick. "Guests of the Crown: Convicts and Liberated Slaves on McCarthy Island, the Gambia." *Geographical Journal* 160, no. 2 (1994): 136–42.

Weinberg, Robert. "Anti-Jewish Violence and Revolution in Late Imperial Odessa, 1905." In *Riots and Pogroms,* edited by Paul Brass, 56–88. New York: New York University Press, 1996.

Whateley, Thomas. *Considerations on Trade and Finances of this Kingdom, and on the means of Administration, with Respect to the Great National Objects since the Conclusion of the Peace.* 3rd ed. London: J. Wilkie, 1766.

Wheeler, Henry. *The Slaves' Champion: The Life, Deeds, and Historical Days of William Wilberforce.* Green Forest, AR: New Leaf, 2007.

Wheeler, Roxann. *The Complexion of Race: Categories of Difference in Eighteenth-Century British Culture.* Philadelphia: University of Pennsylvania Press, 2000.

White, Luise. *Speaking with Vampires: Rumor and History in Colonial Africa.* Berkeley: University of California Press, 2000.

Whyte, Iain. *Scotland and the Abolition of Black Slavery, 1756–1838.* Edinburgh: Edinburgh University Press, 2006.

Wilberforce, Robert Isaac, and Samuel Wilberforce. *The Life of William Wilberforce.* London: John Murray, 1838.

Wilberforce, William. *Real Christianity: A Nation Was Blind until One Man Made Them See.* Edited by Bob Beltz. Ventura, CA: Regal Books, 2007.

Williams, Eric. *Capitalism and Slavery.* Chapel Hill: University of North Carolina Press, 1944.

Willis, Justin. "A Portrait for the Mukama: Monarchy and Empire in Colonial Bunyoro, Uganda." *Journal of Imperial and Commonwealth History* 34, no. 1 (2006): 105–22.

Wilson, Ellen Gibson. *Thomas Clarkson: A Biography.* Houndmills, Basingstoke: Macmillan, 1989.

Wood, Marcus. *Blind Memory: Visual Representations of Slavery in England and America, 1780–1865.* New York: Routledge, 2000.

———. "Packaging Liberty and Marketing the Gift of Freedom: 1807 and the Legacy of Clarkson's Chest." In *The British Slave Trade: Abolition, Parliament and People,* edited by Stephen Farrell, Melanie Unwin, and James Walvin, 203–23. Edinburgh: Edinburgh University Press, 2007.

Wright, Marcia. *Strategies of Slaves and Women: Life Stories from East Central Africa.* New York: L. Barber, 1993.

Wyndham, H. A. *The Atlantic and Slavery.* Oxford: Oxford University Press, 1935.

Yeros, Paris, ed. *Ethnicity and Nationalism in Africa.* Houndmills, Basingstoke: Macmillan, 1999.

Young, Arthur. *Political Essays Concerning the Present State of the British Empire.* London: W. Strahan and T. Cadell, 1772.

Zacek, Natalie. "Cultivating Virtue: Samuel Martin and the Paternal Ideal in the Eighteenth-Century English West Indies." *Wadabagei: A Journal of the Caribbean and Its Diaspora* 10, no. 3 (2007): 8–31.

Contributors

CHRISTOPHER LESLIE BROWN, professor of history at Columbia University, specializes in the history of eighteenth-century Britain, the early modern British Empire, and the comparative history of slavery and abolition. His published work includes *Moral Capital: Foundations of British Abolitionism* (2006) and, coedited with Philip D. Morgan, *Arming Slaves: From Classical Times to the Modern Age* (2006). He is now at work on a history of British experience along the West African coast in the era of the Atlantic slave trade.

SEYMOUR DRESCHER is University Professor of History and Sociology at the University of Pittsburgh. Among his writings are *From Slavery to Freedom: Comparative Studies in the Rise and Fall of Atlantic Slavery* (1998) and *The Mighty Experiment: Free Labor versus Slavery in British Emancipation* (2004). The latter was awarded the Gilder Lehrman Center's Frederick Douglass prize. He is currently completing a study on slavery and antislavery in global perspective for Cambridge University Press.

JONATHON GLASSMAN is associate professor of history at Northwestern University. He is the author of *Feasts and Riot: Revelry, Rebellion, and Popular Consciousness on the Swahili Coast, 1856–1888* (1995), which won the African Studies Association's Herskovits Prize. He is currently preparing a book on the rise of racial thought in colonial Zanzibar.

BOYD HILTON is professor of modern British history at the University of Cambridge and fellow of Trinity College. He is the author of several works on late-eighteenth- and nineteenth-century British history, including *The Age of Atonement: The Influence of Evangelicalism on Social and Economic Thought, ca. 1795–1865* (1988) and *A Mad, Bad, and Dangerous People? England 1783–1846* (2006).

ROBIN LAW is professor of African history at the University of Stirling, Scotland. He has for many years researched the precolonial history of West Africa, including its involvement in the Atlantic slave trade. Recent publications include *Ouidah, 1727–1892: The Social History of a West African Slaving "Port"* (2004) and, with Paul Lovejoy, *The*

Biography of Mahommah Gardo Baquaqua: His Passage from Slavery to Freedom in Africa and America (2001).

PHILIP D. MORGAN is Harry C. Black Professor of History at the Johns Hopkins University. He is the author of several works on the history of colonial British America, including *Slave Counterpoint: Black Culture in the Eighteenth-Century Chesapeake and Lowcountry* (1998), which won the Bancroft Prize. His current research concerns the history of race relations in Jamaica.

DEREK R. PETERSON teaches African history at the University of Michigan. He was formerly director of the Centre of African Studies at the University of Cambridge. He is author of *Creative Writing: Translation, Bookkeeping, and the Work of Imagination in Colonial Kenya* (2004), and coeditor of *Recasting the Past: History Writing and Political Work in Modern Africa* (2009). He is currently writing a book about the social history of patriotism in eastern Africa.

JOHN K. THORNTON is professor of history and African American studies at Boston University. His primary work has focused on the history of Africa (particularly Central Africa) and the African diaspora to the Americas in the sixteenth to eighteenth centuries. He is the author of *Africa and Africans in the Making of the Atlantic World* (1992; 2nd ed., 1998), *The Kongolese Saint Anthony* (1998), *Warfare in Atlantic Africa* (1999), and, most recently, with Linda Heywood, *Central Africans, Atlantic Creoles and the Foundation of the Americas* (2007), winner of the 2008 Herskovits Prize from the African Studies Association.

Index

BALISONG

The Lethal Art of Filipino Knife Fighting

Sid Campbell
Gary Cagaanan
Sonny Umpad

PALADIN PRESS
BOULDER, COLORADO

Balisong: The Lethal Art of Filipino Knife Fighting
by Sid Campbell, Gary Cagaanan, and Sonny Umpad

Copyright © 1986 by Sid Campbell, Gary Cagaanan, and Sonny Umpad

ISBN 13: 978-0-87364-354-2
Printed in the United States of America

Published by Paladin Press, a division of
Paladin Enterprises, Inc.,
P.O. Box 1307
Boulder, Colorado 80306 USA
+1.303.443.7250

Direct inquiries and/or orders to the above address.

Contents

To my loving sister, Janice Campbell Davis.

Sid Campbell

To my late Sifu, James (Jimmy) Lee, who opened my eyes; to my family, whom I live for; and to my parents, to whom I owe everything.

Gary Cagaanan

I wish to dedicate this book to my family; my children, Brian & Jackie; and to my friends and students who have supported all of my efforts.

Sonny Umpad

About the Authors

Sid Campbell, a sixth-degree black belt in Shorin-ryu karate, has been actively involved in virtually every facet of the martial arts for over twenty years. He began his early training in Okinawa under Grandmaster Shugoro Nakazato, 10th Dan and head of the Shorin-ryu Shorinkan (Kobayashi-ryu) Karate-Do.

Sid Campbell was one of the first Americans to introduce the Okinawan art of Shorin-ryu karate to the United States. He has taught over twelve thousand martial arts practitioners, introducing the martial arts to many law-enforcement agencies, fraternal organizations, clubs, recreation departments, schools, and organizations for the handicapped. He was one of the first martial arts instructors to teach the deaf and blind of the northern California area.

Campbell has been featured in many martial arts magazines, awarded the Presidential Sports Award for instruction to the military, and listed in Bob Wall's *Who's Who in the Martial Arts* and *Who's Who in Karate*. Campbell has also choreographed many action sequences for television and motion pictures, and written extensively on martial arts.

*   *   *

Co-author Gary Cagaanan is a police officer and has served as a defense tactics instructor for police in the greater San Francisco Bay Area. He is also a freelance writer and an avid practitioner of Visayan stick and blade combat.

Cagaanan began his martial arts training in the late 1960s, studying the world-renowned style of Kajukenbo, which he credits for his fundamental appreciation of conditioning and the ability to absorb punishment.

Cagaanan's interest in the martial arts enabled him to meet and train with practitioners of many styles. A significant turning point in his education was training with a student of the late James Y. Lee (better known as Jimmy Lee, Bruce Lee's training partner and head of Bruce Lee's Oakland Jeet Kune Do School), and eventually with Lee himself. While training with Jimmy Lee, Cagaanan also began studying boxing.

Cagaanan's martial training ceased for a time after the deaths of Jimmy and Bruce Lee, but now Cagaanan considers himself a reborn martial artist.

"I have found the Filipino martial arts to be fascinating," exclaims Cagaanan. "The facets of training and philosophy go hand-in-hand with jeet kune do principles. This is true especially of the Visayan style of stick and knife combat as taught by Sonny Umpad."

*   *   *

Co-author Sonny Umpad was deeply affected, as a small boy in the Philippine jungle, by seeing the skill with which an old *escrimador* (stick fighter) defeated a younger, stronger opponent.

When he was twelve years old, Umpad moved from the village of Bogo to the city of Cebu. In Cebu, survival among street toughs as well as the *escrima* masters of the Doce Pares and Balintawak Escrima Clubs encouraged Umpad's developing skills.

Umpad moved to San Francisco in 1969, where he continued his training in *escrima, kali,* and *arnis,* and began evolving a synthesis of these Philippine fighting arts.

In 1976, Umpad's twenty-six years' experience were refined to create the stick and knife fighting self-defense system called *corto kadena.*

Sonny Umpad teaches privately in the San Francisco Bay Area, halfway around the world from the home of the escrimadors who first introduced him to the art.

Acknowledgments

Special thanks to Ed Campbell, Warren Nelson, Sean Litton, and Donna and Gordon Lyda.

Sid Campbell

I am grateful to Max Pallan, Master Raymond Tobosa, Maestro Nick Mica, Jun Cauteverio, and the Doce Pares and Balintawak International Clubs in Cebu, Philippines. I want especially to thank my students, Richard Carny, Gary Cagaanan, Joe Olivarez of U.S. Karate Inc., and Chris Suboreau for their assistance in pioneering and teaching the Visayan style of corto kadena.

Sonny Umpad

1. Introduction

The individual who has pursued an avocation in the empty-hand combative sciences tends to believe that a knife or any hand implement, other than a firearm, is an extension of himself. The knife represents his intentions, his martial knowledge, and his physical actions. This assumption has some validity in some martial arts, but falls short of conveying the total picture of the combative sciences.

Many people perceive the empty-hand forms of combat as a way to show their ability to withstand pain, absorb abuse, and inflict their own fighting expertise on the adversary. This perception may be valid in unarmed combat, especially for those who believe they can take a punch in order to deliver a stronger one than the opponent's. But the individual who chooses to carry this philosophy over into knife fighting will quickly discover that taking a slash to give a slash will end in the hospital, or on a cold slab of marble.

Knife fighting is an exacting and highly refined science. It should not be construed as just a method of fighting while wielding a bladed instrument. The ultimate objective of this lethal science is to be so skillful with the knife that the adversary could not possibly inflict lethal harm on you; the knife fighter maintains complete control of the adversary, and neutralizes his aggressive actions.

Bladed combat has evolved over four hundred years in a country known worldwide for its skills in these little-known (but highly publicized) fighting arts: the Philippine Islands.

Many of the principles of knife fighting in this book are, or have been, well-kept secrets that have been passed down for generations in families whose members were expert stick and knife fighters in the Philippines. (Ferdinand Magellan, c. 1480-1521, the Portuguese navigator and discoverer, was slain by King Lapu-Lapu, who used the art of Philippine stick fighting to thwart Magellan's attempt to take over the 7,000-island chain.)

As a science, stick and knife fighting are similar in many ways, but knife fighting is generally reserved for the bold at heart, one who has proven his ability in stick fighting.

HISTORY

Long and colorful is the history of the arts of blade combat in the Philippine Islands. The islands were invaded by the Spanish early in the sixteenth century, but the invasion was met with fierce resistance. Most memorable was the fall of Magellan in 1521.

Resistance to the Spanish conquistadors continued as the Filipino warriors tried to expel the powerful Spanish Armada. They fought the Spanish forces, who wore metal-plate armor and used firearms, armed only with rattan sticks and spears. The eventual takeover of the Philippines by these invaders marked the beginning of some four hundred years of colonial rule by the Spanish.

Because of stringent Spanish control, the Philippine martial arts became a clandestine affair. Carrying any form of resistive weapon was prohibited, and neglect of this law was punishable by death. The Filipinos therefore disguised the practice of their combat arts in folk dances or religious plays known as *moro-moro*. The hardwood sticks (known as *bahi*) and the stalks of dried, hardened rattan, were incorporated into dance patterns that symbolized ritualistic farming and tribal ancestry. The preservation of the fighting arts, under this guise, was unknown to the Spanish, many of whom enjoyed the ritualistic ceremonies and colorful displays.

Despite the Spanish ban on the possession of bladed weapons, the Filipinos continued to develop their fighting styles, sometimes even incorporating warfare tactics used by the Spanish.

The early 1900s saw the end of Spanish colonialism, and the beginning of American domination of the Philippine Islands. That takeover was met with resistance similar to that experienced by the Spanish. The strongest resisters to the American occupation came perhaps from the Muslim Moros, of the southern Philippines. These fierce warriors, armed with sword-like weapons, battled the Americans with unexpected tenacity. Even when the Americans used rifles and handguns, the unrelenting retaliatory actions of the Muslim Moros were a serious threat to the American forces. The U.S. Marines got the nickname "Leathernecks" from the introduction of heavy leather, steel-reinforced collars to protect their necks from being slashed during these encounters.

The Filipino martial arts of *escrima, arnis,* and *kali* are enjoying a rebirth these days, because many elderly masters from the Philippines have begun to share their once-secret fighting arts with interested practitioners—particularly in the United States.

One of the more popular instruments associated with these Filipino martial arts is the "spiritually and physically blessed" *balisong.* The balisong, or butterfly knife, originated in the Batangas region of the Philippines, and so it is sometimes called *Batangas.* It is also referred to as the *Vientenueve,* or "twenty-nine," because, as legend has it, a great master in the blade arts could dispose of twenty-nine enemies with his butterfly knife.

The literal translation of the word "balisong" is "breaking horn" or "breaking song." The term "break" comes from the way the knife "breaks" open to expose the concealed blade. The word "song" usually refers to the rhythmic clicking sound the knife makes when it is artfully manipulated.

During and after World War II, the blades of the balisong knives were made out of scrap metal or from leaf-springs of old U.S. Army jeeps. Those knives were noted for their sturdiness while maintaining an incredibly sharp edge.

Often referred to as the "*nunchaku* of the 80s," the butterfly knife was introduced in America by soldiers returning from the Philippine Islands. Many Filipinos who emigrated to Hawaii and the continental United States taught the historical, traditional, spiritual, and technical aspects of these deadly knife arts.

Since its introduction to the Western world, the study of butterfly-knife discipline is flourishing. The many styles of butterfly fighting grow under the guidance of stick- and knife-fighting masters who have dedicated their lives to preserving the ancient heritage that evolved in the Philippine Islands.

PHILOSOPHY

The blade artist without philosophical conviction may be unsure of his spontaneous actions, and a victim of his own uncertainty. The balisong artist believes that a strong foundation in philosophical understanding is necessary to be truly effective as a knife fighter.

The balisong carries the unique historical and spiritual symbolism of the "triangular forces." The Filipino stick- and knife-fighting patriarch believes that the triangular forces affect all of the user's mental, physical, and spiritual actions with the balisong. These forces are known as *gunas* and represent the spiritual merging of the sentient, the mutative, and the static forces. According to ancient Vedic philosophy, these three forces manifest themselves as the source of creation, motion, or action, all of which are symbolic of the sacred qualities found in the study, practice, and use of the sanctified balisong.

In essence, to use this knife is to uphold the sacred belief that the butterfly knife is symbolic of the energy that originates from the combining of the triangular forces. It is essential that the practitioner fully understand that the balisong represents a purity of this ancient philosophy, and it must never be defiled. Many venerated Filipino masters of this art have intentionally avoided teaching the more advanced knife-fighting techniques because unappreciative protegés have violated this ancient Vedic philosophy.

The Visayan knife fighters, although they are highly skilled, remain rather anonymous and unassuming, because their early spiritual training taught humility of the knowledge and skills to take life. This modesty usually creates an illusion of someone lacking confidence or the ability to defend himself—an illusion that has sent more than one person to see his maker.

Modern-day Visayan knife fighters still use the ancient tactical wisdom, which may best be expressed in the ancient proverb, "Whatever is created will live, whatever lives will die, whatever dies will live again." Their actions and tactical knife-fighting strategies parallel those of the living creatures found in nature who fight for survival when left no alternative but to fight.

The natural survival philosophy of the Visayan knife fighter is one of peaceful coexistence with nature and its inhabitants. If it must actually come to knife fighting, the Visayan knife fighter, like other threatened animals, will not selectively choose a vital target and then strike. He attacks the closest target that poses a threat to his survival. For instance, the Visayan would attack the hand of a knife-wielding attacker. Accurately executed, this action forces the antagonist to make a choice between withdrawing and continuing his attack.

If the aggressor persists, the Visayan knife fighter will begin retaliating toward more critical areas of the attacker's anatomy. This tactic allows the opponent to make the withdrawal/continue choice again; the Visayan knife fighter only responds. This is a strategy typical of animals in nature.

The ultimate, retaliatory act of the Visayan knife fighter, provided the adversary has not heeded all of his warnings, is to take the final step of attacking the vital organs.

Specific techniques are used in Visayan knife fighting because it is a predominately defensive system. These techniques are based upon principles of survival that have endured countless thousands of years in the animal kingdom, and have been carefully studied and mastered by Filipino knife fighters.

PRINCIPLES

According to Visayan tradition, knife training comes only after the student is proficient in stick fighting. The longer sticks, or swords, have greater range, power, centrifugal strike force, and defensive ability than the shorter balisong.

The Visayan masters are concerned that the unprepared student may abuse knowledge of the knife-fighting arts. The balisong is concealable, can be used at close range, and can kill an unsuspecting person. Venerated knife masters therefore choose not to reveal deadly secrets to street punks or other unrespectable characters who might give this sacred art a bad name and reflect badly on the teacher.

Furthermore, Visayan knife-fighting masters believe that a short-handled blade is not fully effective unless the student is properly trained. A great deal of study and practice is necessary to achieve mastery; the trainee must be completely proficient in basic grips, footwork, rolls, the ability to flow from strike to strike *(amarras)*, basic slashes and cuts, and must have the correct mental attitude and discipline.

The Visayan style of knife fighting differs radically from other regional styles of Filipino stick and knife arts in that the Visayan master combines the characteristics of the individual with those of the knife, and creates a unique style to suit that individual.

The *corto kadena* is the fifth and final stage of basic training in Visayan knife combat. Only selected and carefully screened students of the system are taught the secrets that pertain directly to this inner wisdom, because of the seriousness of the training and the necessity for maturity, sound judgment, and a moral attitude in the student.

"Corto kadena" translates literally as "short, inside, chain or flowing" (corto) "movements" (kadena); it is more commonly interpreted to mean "inside-movement fighting."

The system itself differs from other methods in the emphasis on checking (touching and responding), evasion, angling, and the solid defensive shield created when the weapons are in motion. When the hand, arm, body, and weapon are synchronized, maximum acceleration makes possible a blinding blur of lethal motion in the eyes of the adversary.

The Visayan style incorporates offensive and defensive tactics that can be applied at all ranges, but close-range fighting and jamming (forceful intervention) techniques are preferred. When the *largamano* ("large or long hand") or long-range fighting principles are applied, they are used to destroy the opponent's timing, confuse and disorient him, and force him to respond to the greater-range techniques. Defensively, the Visayan stick and knife fighter creates a blinding blur of weapon motion that is compact and flows from one technique to another without hesitation. Even an unexpected interruption (interaction with the opponent) would not deter this whirlwind lethality. This unique fighting style, when incorporated with proper evasive and angling methods, creates a defense virtually impossible to penetrate with either hands or weapons.

The student begins with the three phases of basic training. The phases are: 1) the basic seventeen strikes (wide angles); 2) *ankla terradas* (anchor strikes); and 3) *abaniko terradas* (fan or short whipping strikes). After this training has been mastered, the practitioner pursues a study of *sinawali*, a regimented form of stick combat, to prepare for the deadly art of Visayan knife fighting.

You should now be forearmed with knowledge of this text. Each of the chapters will familiarize you with the skills needed for the next phase of training (provided you practice them seriously and learn them well). Refer to these principles as you progress, so you do not lose sight of your goals.

2. The Balisong Knife

According to several written sources, the structure of the balisong dates back to the latter part of the T'ang dynasty (c. A.D. 800). Since that time, the butterfly knife has changed little in actual design, but the materials of construction have advanced considerably.

Butterfly knives made before World War II were crude compared to the impeccably honed bladed weapons of Japan and China, but after all, the butterfly knives of the Philippine Islands were not designed to pierce armor, as the Samurai swords and Chinese weapons were. A butterfly knife could only slash through the light garments worn by the inhabitants of the humid Philippines.

During and after World War II, the balisong became more sophisticated. Junked or spare parts from army jeeps provided a higher quality steel, and ammo shells and brass munitions casings provided butt or pommel mountings that secured the end sections of the handles.

Today, a balisong can be very elaborate, with shiny mother-of-pearl handles, ingrained bone or deer antlers, polished and sharply honed blades, and so forth. But to the Visayan knife fighter, most of these cosmetic embellishments do little to increase the practical function of the butterfly knife.

The sharpness and design of the blade is the first concern—provided that the operating functions equal the design. To have a razor-sharp blade attached to an ill-functioning bifold handle would be just as bad as having an

9

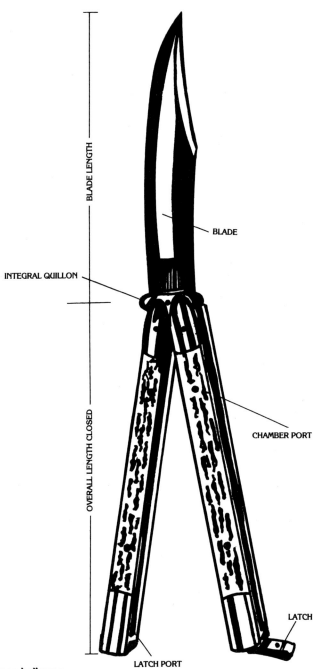

BLADE LENGTH

BLADE

INTEGRAL QUILLON

CHAMBER PORT

OVERALL LENGTH CLOSED

LATCH

LATCH PORT

Open balisong.

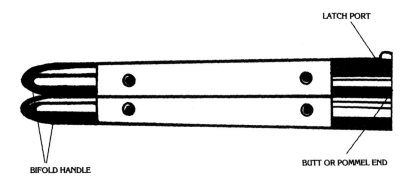

Balisong handle.

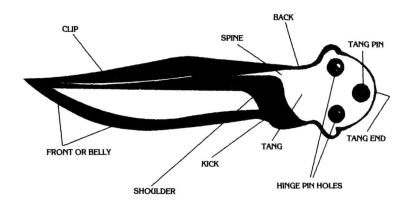

Balisong blade.

excellent breaking mechanism affixed to a poorly designed blade. Either way, the knife cannot operate at optimum performance level.

The opening and closing mechanism of a balisong should be built ruggedly. The tang pins and connecting rivets should be thick enough to permit years of use without wearing down. (A good graphite lubricant will enhance this durability.) Since the flipping can produce extreme wear and tear at these connecting points, most skilled knife fighters prefer pins made of good steel rather than brass or aluminum. The swiveling action should be smooth—this looseness affects the actual slashing and stabbing capabilities of the knife.

The handle should be thick enough to ensure that a firm grip can be maintained while the flipping techniques are being performed. (Some are so thin that the knife cannot be opened or closed without focusing attention on the manipulation—a distraction that is not needed in the art of knife fighting.) The handle should also be long enough so that when it is grasped in the center, both ends of the handle protrude at least one and one-half inches beyond the hand.

The latching mechanism is also critical in the operation of the butterfly knife. A sturdy, firm latch is much more effective than one that is designed to be loose, or has worked loose. A loose latch can disrupt the smoothness of flipping or repositioning actions, and it can dull the blade when it is turned inward toward the other bifold handle. The Visayan knife fighter usually prefers a latch with a tip that extends about one-eighth to one-quarter inch beyond the side of the handle. This permits him enough room to pop the latch quickly and easily when he needs to. Latches that are too short can make flipping the knife open difficult, and longer latches can hinder drawing the knife.

Many Visayan stylists have modified the tang pin (the pin that stabilizes and positions the blade when the knife is open) by attaching a flat section of thin metal to it. This strengthens the blade by forcing it against the forward ends of the bifold handles.

Most of the latch sections of butterfly knives are designed to fit into the handle section on the sharp side of the blade.

Although there are exceptions to this rule, the Visayan knife fighters prefer these original types. The latch position indicates which side of the blade is the cutting edge. When the knife is gripped on the side opposite to the latch, the possibilities of being cut with single-edged blades is minimized.

Many older Visayan knife fighters encourage the novice to dull the blade, because there is a real possibility of serious injury by gripping the knife on the wrong side of the latch, opening or closing the knife before the fingers are safely positioned along the handle, or being inattentive during flipping and catching maneuvers.

The quality of a butterfly knife will usually be reflected in the cost. Knives that are cheap will generally show shoddy workmanship. This should be your guide when selecting a butterfly knife that you want to last for years, because when learning the intricate techniques associated with the butterfly knife, it is better to become familiar with one knife.

It should be mentioned that laws in some areas limit blade length, and that double-edged knives are considered daggers and are prohibited in almost all the states.

3. Using the Balisong as a Fist Load

The balisong is ideally suited for alternative methods of self-defense because it can be opened and closed instantly. When the butterfly knife is in the chambered (closed) position, it has the same qualities as the *tabak maliit*—the short section of rattan or hardwood frequently used as a self-defense weapon in close-range combat.

One of the philosophical tenets of Visayan knife fighting is to use the minimum force necessary; the butterfly knife as tabak maliit (pocket stick) performs those less violent functions.

Many of these "fist-load" techniques can be employed in the same manner as most of the knife-fighting techniques, but the distance from the adversary may need to be several inches less. All the parrying, thrusting, striking, slashing, poking, ripping, and disengaging techniques can be employed. In addition, many hooking, choking, locking, pinching, and flailing techniques can be performed.

Everyday items that resemble the pocket stick or closed balisong—pen, pencil, comb, credit card, key ring, hair brush—can be converted into a self-defense tool. The Visayan knife fighter is always aware of this and does not hesitate to implement these tactics if he feels they best suit his immediate defensive needs.

By using the butterfly knife as a pocket stick together with his knowledge of anatomy, the fighter can strike the pressure points, causing temporary paralysis. Then with a quick flick of the wrist, he unchambers the butterfly knife and stands ready for immediate follow-up tactics. This unique dual purpose of the butterfly knife can be lethal, especially to someone who has exaggerated his own capabilities and has mistaken humbleness for lack of confidence.

Each of the illustrated striking areas can be attacked from many positions, using diverse hand and arm positions and incorporating various parts of the chambered butterfly knife. Do not limit your ability by limiting your creativity in using the butterfly knife as a fist-load weapon.

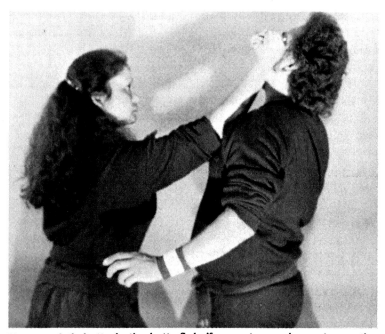

For a nonlethal attack, the butterfly-knife expert may choose to use the pommel section (butt end of the handle) to attack vulnerable areas such as the temple, eyes, throat, teeth, armpit(s), groin, ears, and solar plexus.

The tang strike, using the end where the connecting pin is located, is also used against nonlethal target areas. These types of fist-load techniques, because of the grip, allow the user to execute linear, direct strikes without having to reposition or modify the grip. They are also excellent techniques for buying time, when there is not enough time to flip open the butterfly knife to a front or back grip.

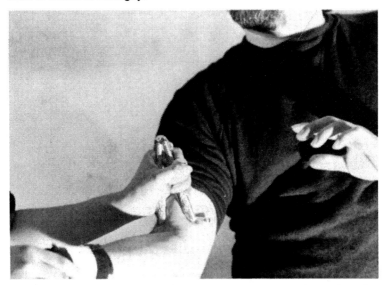

The pommel strike "pinch" technique can be used much like a vice grip. Once a target area is selected, both hands can apply pressure.

In this typical striking or punching maneuver, the butterfly knife merely provides additional reinforcement to the hand. By filling the hollow portion of the clenched fist, a more solid striking surface is achieved, thus increasing the impact potential.

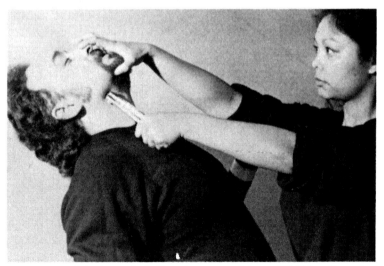

Any portion of the butterfly knife—the pommel, tang, bifold handle ends, or blade section—can be used to strike the pressure points. The Visayan knife fighter is taught early in his training that the pressure points are invaluable targets for inflicting pain, forcing the antagonist to release his grip, providing a warning of what could follow, or temporarily immobilizing the attacker.

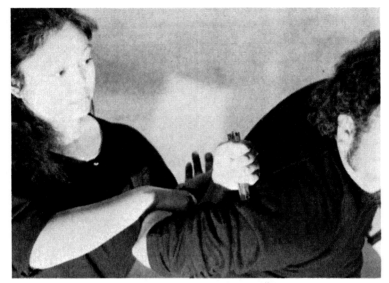

The butterfly knife can help apply additional force to a sensitive portion of the anatomy while close-range arm locks or other restraining techniques are applied.

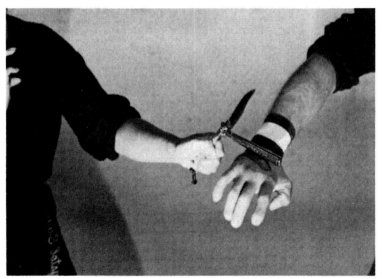

The butterfly knife can be used in a manner very similar to the ancient Okinawan weapon known as the nunchaku (two sticks connected by cord or chain). The butterfly knife, once it is flipped and spun, can generate speeds up to 150 mph and cause severe damage to the temple, eyes, or throat.

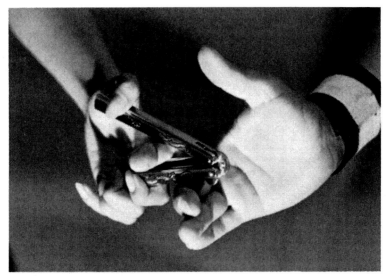

In the scissor technique, the butterfly knife is gripped in a preparatory position where each section of the bifold handle is held apart. Fingers, the nose, or ears can be quickly inserted between the handle and cutting edge of the blade.

The groin slam can be directed at an opponent directly facing the knife fighter, but it can also be directed behind if the knife fighter is surprised and attacked from the rear. The knife can be extracted from its concealed position and quickly slammed into the groin without forewarning the victim.

The open-blade fist load can be used (the pommel or tang end) when the blade is closed or when the blade is open (pommel end only) to attack any exposed target area of the adversary.

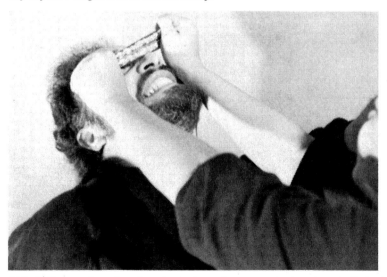

This strike requires that the wielder have firm control of each end of the handle. Although it can be used when the blade is open (more dangerous to the wielder), the Visayan knife fighter prefers to use it closed. These strikes are usually directed to areas such as the wrist (to break restraining grips), sensitive areas of the face and head, and the legs (to deflect low kicking attacks).

This fist-load strike is unique to the butterfly knife. It not only increases the range of the knife, but diminishes the striking surface of the handle section. This increases the amount of penetration that can be achieved when one of the bifold ends strikes the target area.

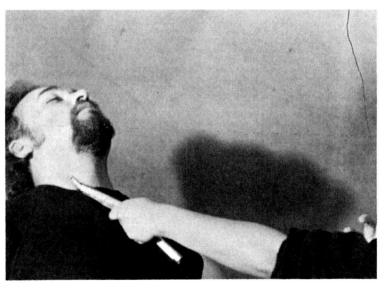

The latching mechanism, when placed at a perpendicular angle to the latching pin, can be used for raking or slashing attacks. Such attacks can temporarily disable the antagonist, permitting the knife fighter to regain the advantage.

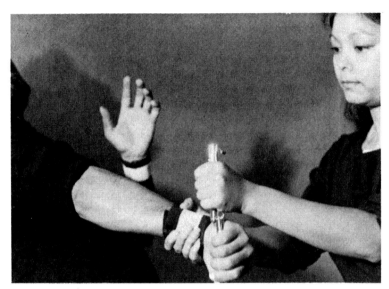

The arm-bar lock is used as a lever. If a portion of the knife (or blade) is grabbed, the wielder can release a portion of the handle while maintaining a grip on the opposite handle. By suddenly rotating the knife, the attacker will be forced to release his grip. If more force is needed, both hands and the upper body can be applied to the torquing action.

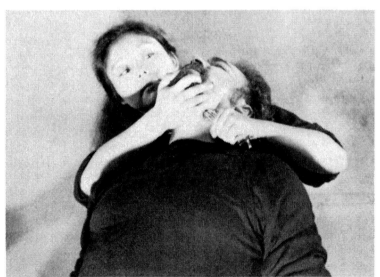

The tang gouge is applied with a penetrating, twisting motion. The tang portion of the folded, concealed blade is applied against such targets as the nostrils, ears, eyes, Adam's apple, and surrounding neck areas.

4. Concealing the Balisong

The Visayan art of knife fighting is based on the marriage of four integral facets of the science. Although each is a separate art and taught separately in this book, they complement and interact with each other. These four distinct arts are: 1) concealment; 2) gripping; 3) drawing; and 4) flipping.

The balisong is generally concealed. It is carefully placed so that the blade master knows the exact location and direction of the retaining lock, and the direction of the blade inside the handle (this is known because the typical balisong is designed so that when the knife is closed, the blade is facing the retaining lock).

Knowing these details, the Visayan master implements the gripping technique best suited to the circumstances and his needs—either a front or back grip.

After the handle has been gripped, drawing and flipping can begin. Flipping normally occurs when the end of the handle has cleared the pocket. Flipping usually brings the knife into action before the human eye can detect that the knife has begun to unfold, because the master is performing the flip while the knife is on the way to its target. Usually, this blur of motion is enough to deter the adversary, but if it becomes necessary, a few quick slashes, thrusts, and recovery maneuvers can usually force the antagonist to desist.

Concealment of the butterfly knife has long been a specialty among the Visayan blade masters. It is part of their art, and not merely hiding the blade from view.

Elements that affect drawing speed, diversionary tactics, accessibility, and the cuts and slashes that can be executed as the knife is being drawn must all be considered in regard to concealment. Concealment of the balisong is affected primarily by its size, design, and weight. Unless the balisong is modified to look like something else, it can be concealed virtually anyplace. The standard butterfly knife can be hidden in trouser, coat, or shirt seams; the leg portion of boots and high ankle shoes; a special pocket sewed into a garment; a shoe lining; folded in a sweat band, hat band, sleeve pocket, or behind a belt or pair of suspender straps; placed in the staff or handle section of a walking cane, a wallet lining, a purse strap or flap section of a handbag, a sock pocket, a pencil or pen case, a nail-file case, hollowed-out book spines, a rolled-up newspaper or magazine; attached to the inside of a watch or bracelet band, or even attached to a cord so that it dangles in a trouser leg or shirt sleeve.

Butterfly knives have been modified to look like a set of chopsticks in an open pocket, a pen and pencil set, a key ring, a comb case, a small case for spectacles or sunglasses, a pipe (a pipe bowl was temporarily affixed to one end of the handle), a custom-designed belt buckle, and even a very ornate necklace.

Accessibility, position of blade, posture of the fighter, mannerisms and casual gestures, urgency, secret intentions of the knife fighter, and distraction ploys all affect the draw and therefore the choice of place of concealment.

Naturally, time and timing also play a very important role in determining where and how the knife will be concealed. A Visayan knife fighter will spend countless hundreds of hours perfecting his drawing technique.

SPECIAL NOTE

It should be mentioned that possession of the balisong is a felony in several states. In these states there is an additional penalty for the concealment of such a lethal weapon. Usually the penalty for concealment greatly exceeds the penalty for possession. You should use your best judgment and act accordingly to ensure that your personal record remains clean and free of felony charges.

5. Gripping the Balisong

The Visayan knife fighter does not believe in a lot of elaborate gripping methods, because when actually engaged in a combative encounter, positive control must be maintained. A multitude of gripping methods only poses unnecessary complexities, might warn the adversary of your moves by specialized positioning, or make it impossible to maintain a broad range of offensive and defensive tactics.

The Visayan knife fighter believes in only two forms of gripping the knife. These are the front grip and the back grip, two direct, simple, and straightforward methods of grasping the knife handle that permit the user a broad range of applications.

Angulation is what enables the Visayan fighter to succeed with only two grips. Most specialized grips exist to position the blade so that a desired technique can be initiated. The Visayan knife fighter understands that either the front grip or the back grip can be used to achieve the same positions simply by rotating the wrist and arm. A quick flip, roll, turn, or a combination of the three make it possible for him to quickly achieve all of the diversity of the specialized gripping methods.

The butterfly knife is unique because of its flipping capability. The gripping and flipping techniques complement each other, and in many cases angulation is determined by rotating the wrist and arm while the hands and fingers grasp the knife.

Pay close attention to the thumb and index-finger

alignment before, during, and after flipping techniques have been executed. The final appearance of a front or back grip will not seem much different than a standard grip; it is how those positions were achieved that differentiate them from a typical thumb-over-wrapped-fingers method.

Mastering the basic gripping methods forms the foundation of the Visayan knife-fighting style. You must fully understand the sequences—how the fingers form the grips of the knife. Exactness in timing, coordination, and tension will affect every technique you learn with the balisong.

In the front grip, the handle is placed so that the hand is equally distant from the tang and pommel.

The fingers are then wrapped snugly around the bifold handle. Both sections of the handle should be forced tightly together so that the blade will not flex at the connecting pins.

The thumb is then wrapped around the handle.

The thumb overlaps the index finger. It is tensed until the desired tightness is assumed. The thumb should always be tense enough that the blade remains rigid and does not flex when direct tension is put on it. When the point of the blade extends out in front of the knife wielder, and the handle is gripped as described, this is known as the front grip.

To form the back grip, the handle is positioned in the palm so that the pommel is between the thumb and index finger.

The fingers are wrapped around the middle of the bifold handle.

The thumb is then wrapped around the handle, and the fingers are tightened on the handle.

The thumb is tightened around the wrapped fingers to apply more gripping force to the bifold handles. This is known as the back grip, where the knife is pointed in the opposite direction to the front grip.

In this grip variation, the knife is held in the front grip and the cutting edge of the blade faces up. This position is used for executing upward thrusts.

For this grip variation, the basic back grip is assumed with the cutting edge of the blade parallel to the arm. This position is often used when an arm grab or close-range slashing maneuvers are anticipated. This position is also a means of concealing the knife.

This back-grip variation is used for inside slashing, checking, and rolling techniques.

This front-grip variation is used in many rolling, stabbing, thrusting, slashing, and poking maneuvers. It also permits the wielder to extend his reach to perform intricate slashing maneuvers.

This back-grip variation is used for downward and overhead stabbing. When less lethal techniques are required, the wielder can use the knife as a fist load.

This modified front grip is used when knife repositioning is required while the knife fighter is in action. It can also be used for expediting a flipping technique without forewarning the adversary.

This modified front grip enables the wielder to execute lateral slashing techniques. Note that the blade is turned sideways.

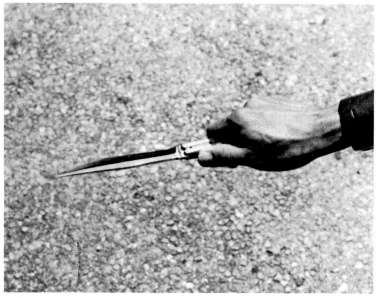

This is a reverse modified front grip, similar to the previous grip. It enables the wielder to execute lateral slashing maneuvers to the outside.

6. Drawing the Balisong

The balisong has many advantages over the typical pocket knife, or even the switch blade, when the user has mastered the gripping, drawing, and flipping techniques.

Typical pocket knives require both hands to open the blade. Of course, the more manipulation required to perform a given function, the longer it takes to do it. Variable length and strength of fingers and finger nails, strength of the spring mechanism, and exactness of positioning all may diminish the time it takes to open the blade and bring the knife into action. A switch blade, whether the side-handle mechanism or stiletto type, must be positioned so the button is comfortable before it is actuated.

When used properly by a skilled fighter, the balisong can make these knives seem archaic. Even fixed-blade knives that have to be drawn from a sheath can seem to be in slow motion compared to the butterfly knife wielded by a skilled Visayan knife artist.

In his hands, drawing happens so fast, it is virtually impossible to see the maneuvers unfold. One second the knife was completely concealed, and the next it is ready for fighting action. It seems to have come out of thin air.

Drawing the balisong is such a highly refined science because of the design of the knife. Since the blade is hinged to two separate handle sections and hidden inside the handle, one must master the flipping technique to open the knife. This skill prepares the user for the sophisticated drawing procedures, because every time the butterfly knife is flipped open or closed, the user becomes more familiar with the drawing technique and faster.

The drawing techniques presented in this chapter show you the most effective ways of marrying the four separate arts that form the foundation for learning the offensive and defensive techniques presented in later chapters. Pay especially close attention to the interaction of motion, distance, and timing needed to make the drawing technique complete. At first, you may feel clumsy, but with practice these maneuvers will become automatic, and you will get to the point where it will not be necessary to watch the knife unfold.

The right-side belt draw. The butterfly knife is suddenly exposed so that the hand can begin gripping the handle.

As soon as a basic front grip is made on the handle, an upward opening flip is implemented (see following chapter on flipping). The knife is now ready for action.

A typical Visayan ready position is assumed as the knife fighter waits to determine the course of action taken by his adversary.

The slide draw. The butterfly knife is ready for the slide draw. The tang end is exposed and pointed forward.

The hand subtly slides the knife out of its place of concealment. A basic forward flipping technique is then implemented while the knife is moving forward (see following chapter on flipping).

Opposite-side slide draw. The knife is concealed in the pants waist with the tang end pointing toward the back. The hand slides across (much in the same fashion as a cross draw) toward the handle while simultaneously lifting the shirt out of the way.

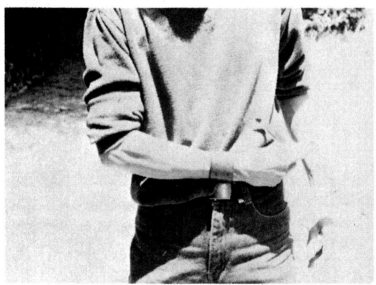

As the butterfly knife is extracted, a flipping technique is performed. Almost every flipping technique can be performed from this position (see following chapter on flipping).

The knife fighter is then poised to execute a cross slashing maneuver.

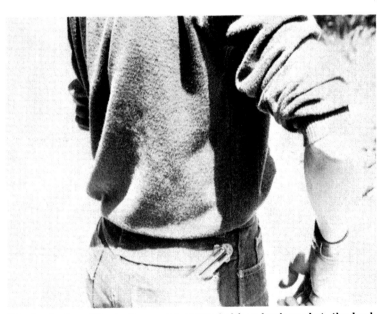

The back draw. The knife can be concealed in a back pocket, the back of the pants waist, or special knife pocket. The tang end of the knife should be exposed.

As the knife is extracted from the rear pocket, it is opened at the same time. This takes considerable practice to master, but it insures the fastest possible draw.

A flipping technique is then initiated (see following chapter on flipping), and the knife is gripped in the back-grip position.

7. Flipping the Balisong

The deadly butterfly knife of Visayas can be opened and closed without resorting to the slower two-hand methods used to chamber or unchamber the typical folding-blade knife. This process depends on gravity, precisely timed wrist-flipping action, and delicate finger manipulations, all synchronized.

The opening and closing of the butterfly knife must be perfected before one can proceed to the knife-fighting instruction. You should be able to manipulate the butterfly knife so that you can grasp it (using a proper grip), extract it (using a proper drawing technique), and flip it before a ready fighting attitude is assumed. Your ability in these skills, without having to give any thought to them or exert effort, will determine your readiness to proceed to the more advanced phases of Visayan knife fighting.

The flipping styles illustrated in this chapter are only the primary ways to chamber or unchamber the butterfly knife. From these fundamental operations there are many adaptations that can be construed. Use your imagination and the feel you develop through mastery of these basic techniques to create other flipping styles.

Many beginning butterfly-knife practitioners find it is best to pick up the knife every day and practice the opening and closing techniques. This is preferable to letting the knife sit for several days. Inherent feel with the butterfly knife will only be achieved through conscientious effort to develop ambidextrous skills—both hands should be able to manipulate the butterfly opening and closing procedures without having to look at the knife at all.

It is important to pay close attention to the captions on each photo, because opening and closing techniques take place so fast. Even strobe photography has difficulty in showing such high-speed movements.

When studying the instructional photographs 1) visualize the gravitational direction of the action; 2) observe the wrist flipping direction; and 3) study the finger manipulations. If the order of these actions is not carefully adhered to, it will make learning the flipping techniques very difficult, if not impossible.

Once one of the flipping techniques has been learned, return to the gripping and drawing techniques presented earlier, and attempt to apply them with the flip. (This way you will not bypass important techniques that are used in the later chapters.)

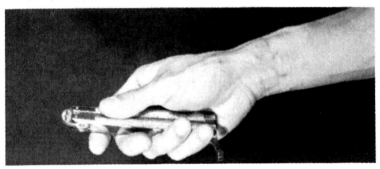

Back-hand wrist flip. Pop the latch with the little finger.

Flip the handle with the latch outward with a quick flip of the wrist. As the blade clears the gripped handle, reposition the fingers around the handle.

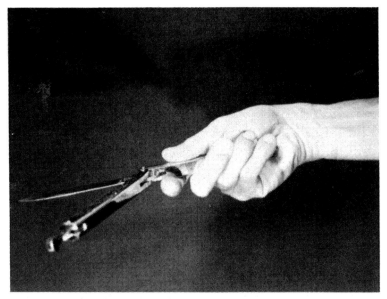

Rotate the handle a half turn counterclockwise (opposite direction if wielded with the other hand). This motion should be smooth and continuous.

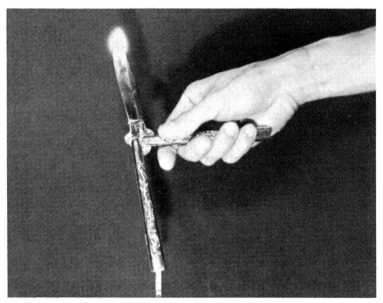

When the counterclockwise rotation assumes the position in the photograph, begin a back hand (toward your body), upward flipping action.

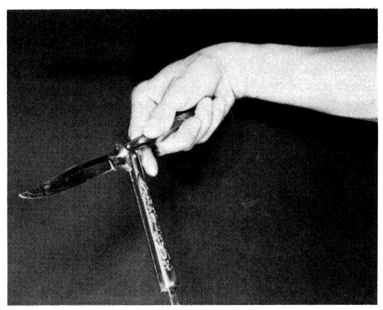

With a downward wrist motion, the weight of the loose handle is redirected toward the fingers.

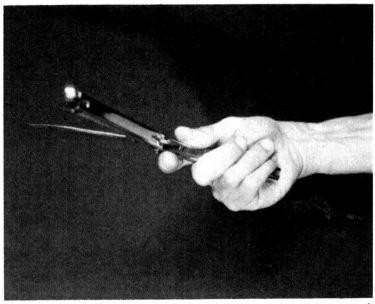

At that moment, an upward flip occurs, and the loose handle is returned to the waiting fingers.

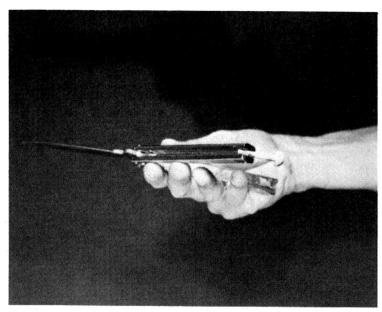

The fingers are then opened to receive the incoming handle. The grip is maintained with the meaty part of the thumb and the folded palm.

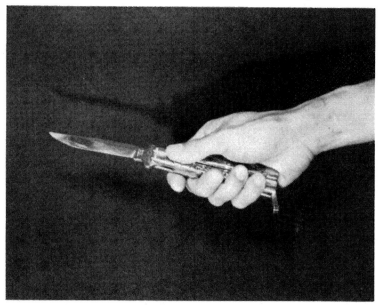

When the flip is completed, the fingers are repositioned around both sections of the bifold handle.

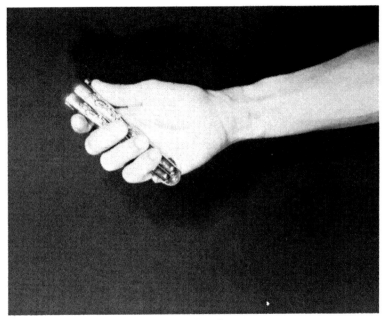

Back-grip flip. Pop the latch with the thumb.

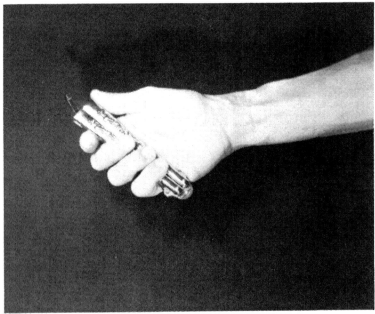

Shift the thumb slightly forward on the pommel end of the handle.

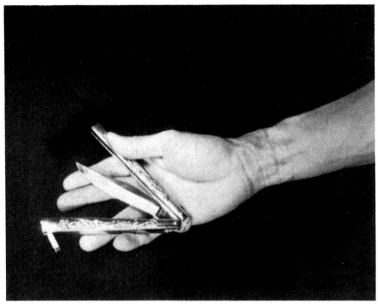

Release the fingers so the blade and handle drop downward, through the force of gravity combined with a slight downward flip of the wrist. The thumb and inner palm are used to secure the knife.

The blade and loose handle are flipped inward, toward you.

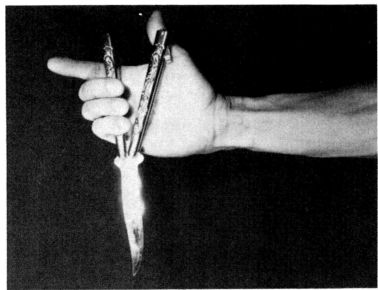

As the blade stops in the locked position, the loose handle continues upward. The entire maneuver is one smooth and continuous motion. The hand remains open to receive the incoming handle.

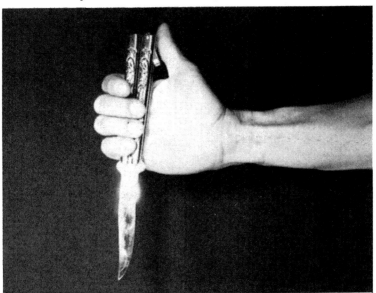

A loud clicking sound is heard when one handle hits the other. This is the signal to catch the knife—as you are not watching the procedure—with the fingers and wrap them around both handles.

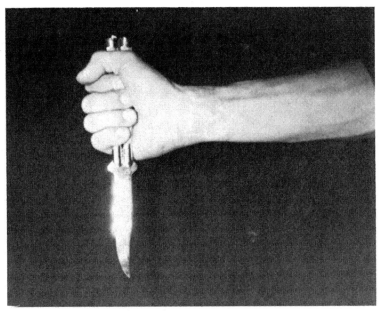

The thumb is quickly wrapped around the handles and the index finger, and the back-grip flip is completed.

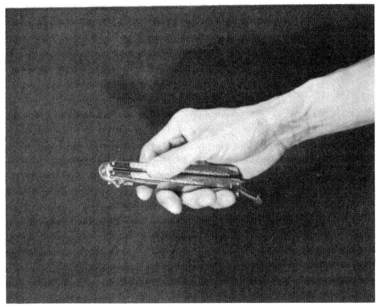

Snap-open flip. The latch is popped open with the little finger.

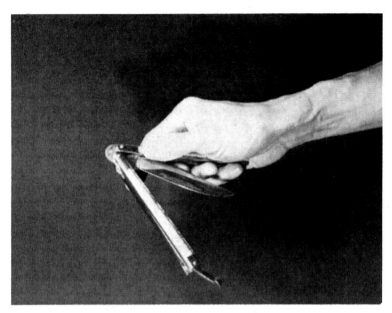

The fingers are released and the outer handle and blade are snapped open and away from the gripping hand.

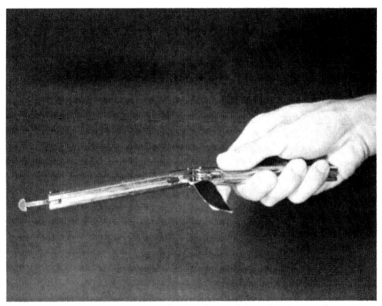

The snap movement forces the blade and handle to continue in a semicircular arc.

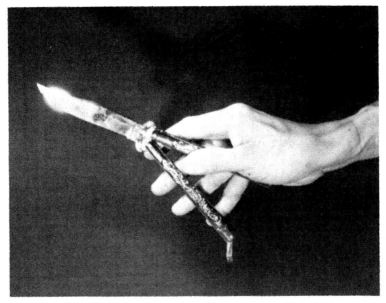

The gripped handle is then rotated clockwise (counterclockwise if the left hand is used). Simultaneously the fingers are opened to receive the incoming handle.

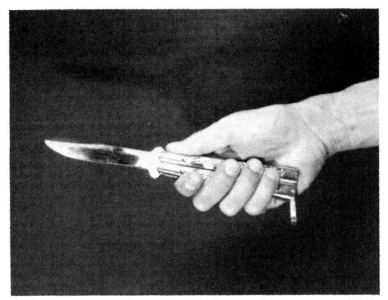

As the loose handle makes contact, the fingers quickly wrap around both of the bifold handles.

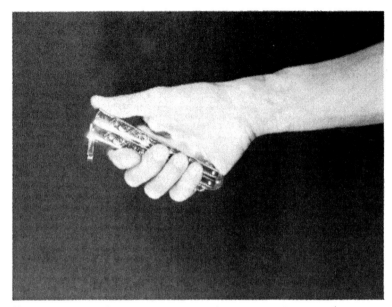

Reverse back-grip flip. A basic back grip is assumed with the knife handle. The latch is popped open with the thumb.

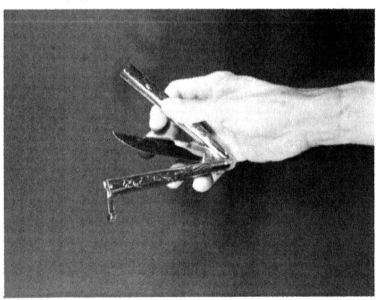

The bottom three fingers are released from the grip (the index finger and thumb maintain the grip on the knife). At the moment of the release, a downward flipping motion occurs.

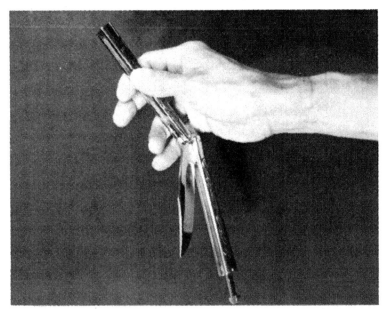

The blade travels downward toward the wielder at a rate of speed dependent on the strength of the flip.

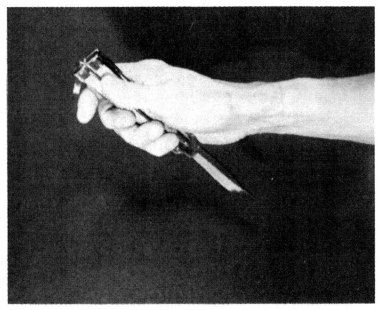

The fingers quickly release to permit the handles to make contact, and then regrasp the handles in the basic back grip.

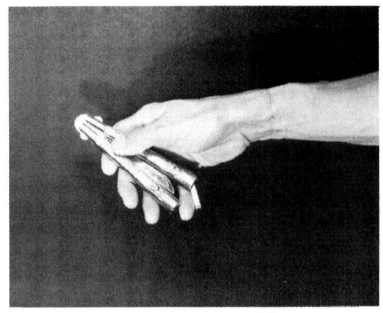

Upward flip. The latch is popped open with the little finger.

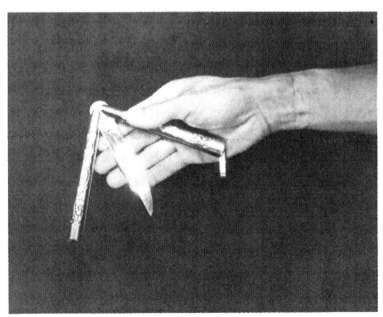

As the fingers are released from the grip, an upward wrist-flipping motion is initiated.

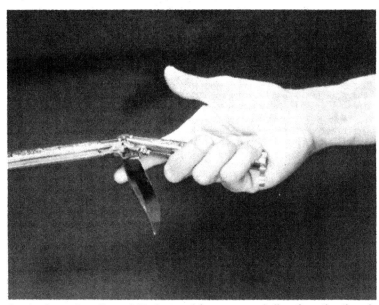

As the loose handle and blade travel in an upward direction, the thumb is released while the bottom three fingers grip the handle. The flip should be strong enough to override gravity.

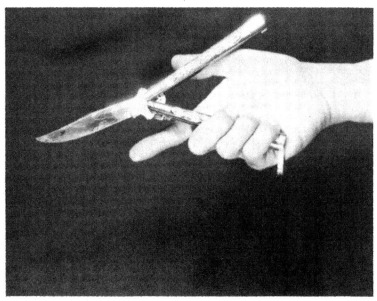

As the handle continues its movement upward and inward, the hand prepares to grip it.

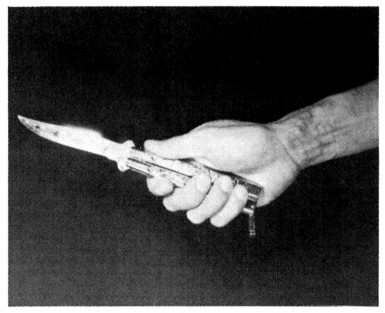

As the handles make contact, the fingers wrap around both of them.

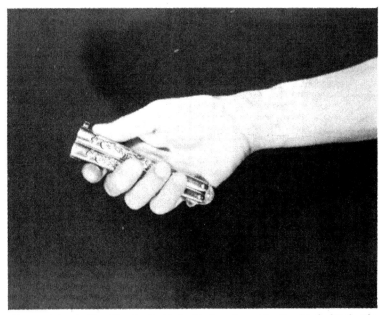

Outward back flip. The butterfly knife is gripped in the basic back-grip position.

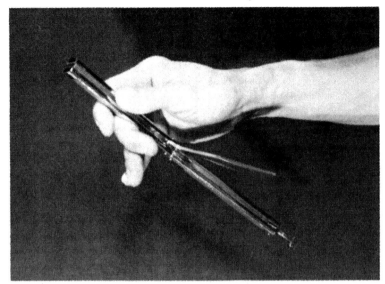

After the latch is popped open with the thumb, the butterfly knife is flipped horizontally inward and toward the outer side of the body. The bottom three fingers are simultaneously released to permit freedom of movement to the blade. The wrist flip must be strong enough to override gravity and propel the loose handle.

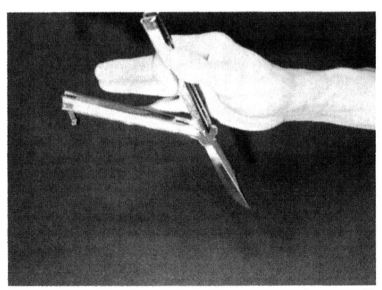

With the help of a slight upward wrist flip, the handle comes in contact with the fingers.

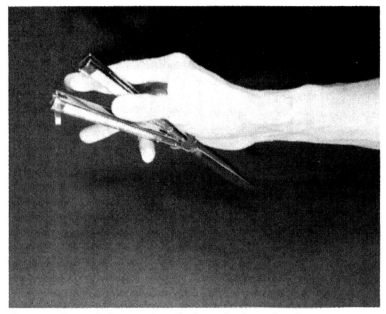

The open fingers help to retrieve the incoming loose handle.

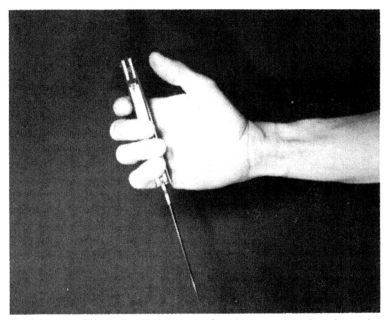

The hand may have to be slightly repositioned to accommodate the angle of return.

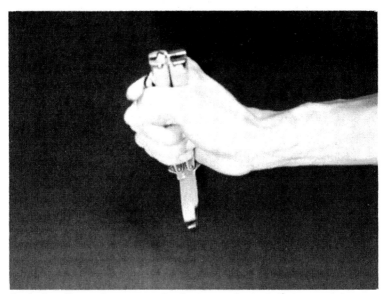

As the handles make contact, the fingers regrip the knife in the basic back grip.

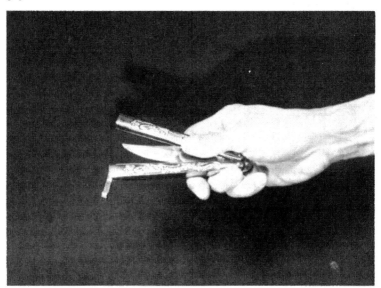

Airborne flip. This is an advanced technique that should only be attempted by the expert that has mastered all of the previous opening techniques. This technique can be useful for deceiving the opponent into thinking that the knife is going to be thrown. First, the knife is flanged, i.e., opened slightly with the thumb while the index finger spreads the bifold handles.

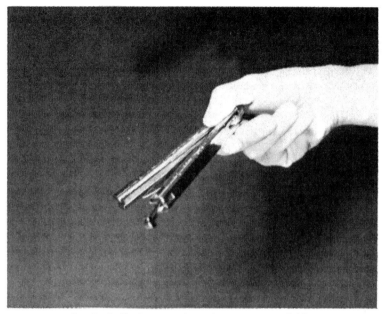

The thumb tilts the knife down as the wrist prepares to initiate an upward toss into the air.

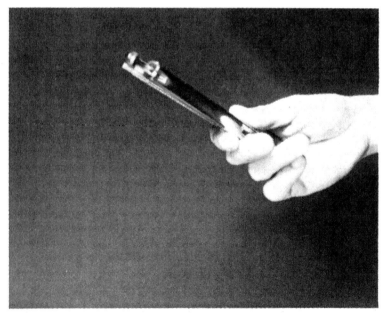

The wrist begins the upward flip.

The knife is released from the hand. Enough upward force must be applied so that the knife continues opening while the flip is taking place.

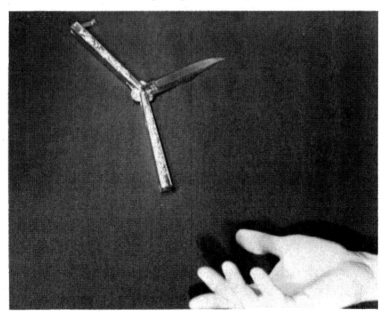

The knife continues to circle and open in the air.

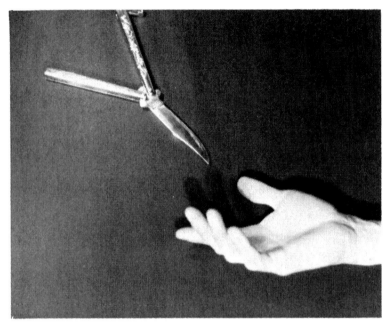

The knife opens further as it spirals through the air.

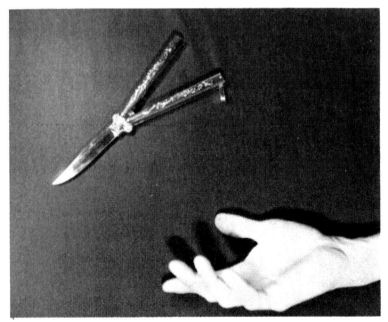

As the knife begins to descend, it has almost completely opened.

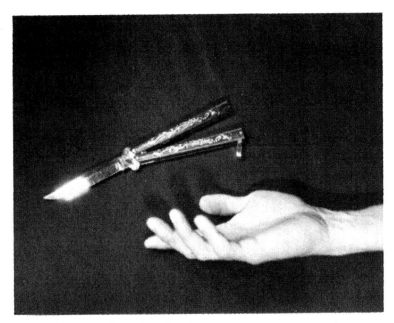

The knife falls into the waiting hand.

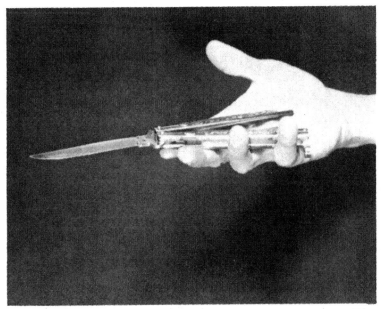

The knife lands squarely in the waiting hand. It may be necessary to adjust the hand and grip to catch the handles. Be careful not to catch the blade!

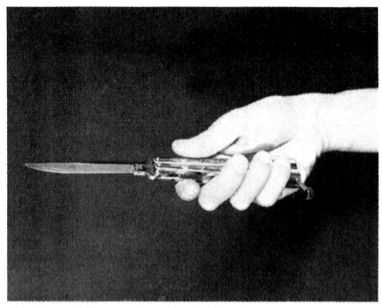

The airborne knife is caught and readied for action.

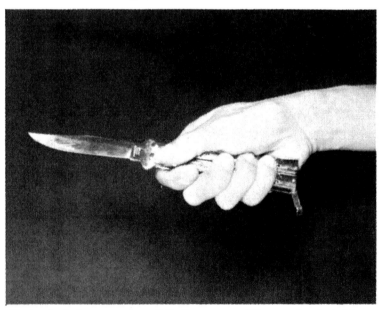

Closing techniques are essentially the reverse of the opening techniques. To begin this closing technique, the knife has been flipped and caught in a basic front-grip position.

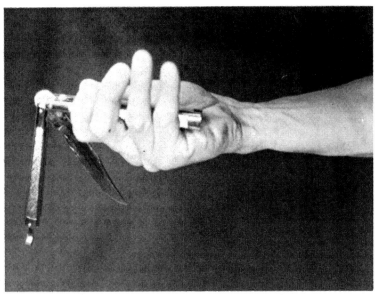

The wrist and knife are rotated clockwise, and the knife is allowed to fall open so that the handle and blade drop downward. Once the blade hits the locked position (when it cannot travel downward any further), the hand is in the position to flip the loose handle back upward.

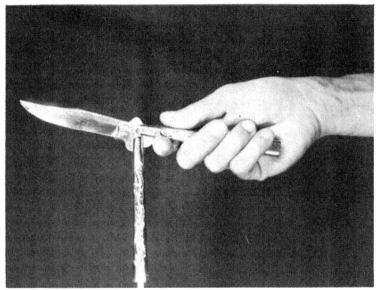

A quick upward flip initiates the necessary force to override gravity and set the blade and loose handle in an upward movement.

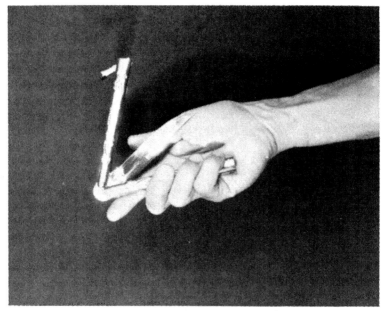

The blade and handle return to the closed position.

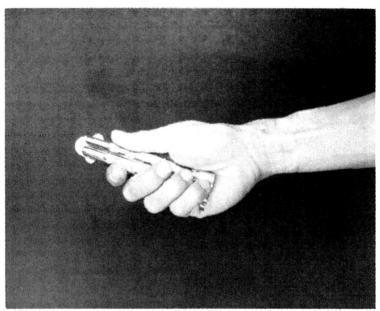

As the handles make contact, the fingers close around the incoming blade and loose handle, thus concluding the closing technique.

8. Fighting Stances

Unlike empty-hand combatants, knife fighters must be willing to improvise style and stance for the sake of personal safety.

Many novices, considering themselves excellent empty-hand fighters, insist on stances acquired through rigorous training in the stylized forms of pugilism—some even fail to realize the distinction between a lethal weapon and the bare fist. If they are defensive fighters and choose to remain immovable because of their ability to counterpunch, they will undoubtedly be slashed to pieces in a real knife fight. Then there are those of aggressive form, who concentrate so thoroughly on style that they create large openings in their defense—they, too, could be slashed to ribbons in a knife fight.

Never become so complacent or so set in a stylistic form that it cannot be altered to suit the specific situation. You must know yourself well enough to know how fast you can move and how agile you are; be capable of coordinating slashing, cutting, thrusting, ripping, blocking, checking, and fake moves with your foot work; be able to read the intentions of your adversary; be able to adjust movement or stance as the situation dictates; have a strong philosophical outlook on your skills and abilities; and always use fighting attitudes that are dictated by the actions or reactions of the opponent.

Visayan fighting positions are based on the particular fighting phase. There are certain attitudes (actions, expressions, postures) that are appropriate before, during, and after a confrontation. All the qualities like timing, speed, coordination, balance, and reflexes, must be applied to these ready-fighting attitudes. Do not worry about getting from one position to another, just use good judgment.

Ready-fighting postures must be performed on both sides. You do not want to be strong and comfortable on one side or in one direction, and weak and uncomfortable on the other.

Study the captions well and try to develop alternatives that could be used to supplement a specific fighting stance.* Visayan knife fighters always have three alternatives for each posture: one that could be used for moving in, one for remaining protected (just out of range of the adversary), and one for taking evasive action. All three directional attitudes should be stressed for one stance position. They too should be able to be performed on either side of the body and to either side. Do not rush this phase of training. If these stances are not mastered, it is doubtful you would ever get the chance to apply them in a real knife fight.

---

*In the photographs in this chapter and some of the following chapters, techniques are demonstrated with a large knife rather than the balisong. This is for the sake of viewing ease as it is sometimes difficult to discern the small balisong in photographs.

The crouch (preparatory phase). From this common posture, the Visayan knife fighter can maneuver quickly in every direction. Notice that the free hand is prepared to execute a checking movement.

The side step (preparatory phase). This posture is used when side stepping is anticipated. Using the "V" stance foot maneuvers (see page 81), they can also move omni-directionally. This ready-fighting stance is normally used when the adversary is at a distance that poses less of a threat to the knife fighter.

The slash position (preparatory phase). This posture is used at close and intermediate ranges when it may be necessary to move inside the opponent's position.

The low-level stalking posture (combat phase). This low-level stance is used to move in (and under) an attack.

The recheck posture (combat phase). This posture is used in less-threatening attacks.

The follow-up posture (post-combat phase). This posture is used after the knife fighter has demonstrated that he can defend himself. It displays caution while not appearing too threatening.

The resume posture. This posture is assumed when the knife fighter has determined that the fight must be taken further.

THE V STANCE

The "V" stance is a pattern of foot movement adaptable to every defensive and counteroffensive technique the fighter may use in combat. It is rare to find one specific stance that can provide all of the elements needed to defend against an opponent's range of tactics. Ideally, the trained knife fighter should be capable of assuming a wide range of stances, but he should also have a stance that can defend against a spectrum of adversaries.

The V stance is named for the pattern of the feet alternately moving from a centered, neutral position (regardless of which ready-fighting attitude the fighter has assumed). As the weight is shifted to one side of the V, a corresponding knife-fighting technique is executed. Then the forward foot returns to the neutral position (bottom of the V), and the opposite foot moves out.

To initiate the V stance, the feet face forward only slightly apart, with the knees slightly bent. The weight is equally distributed on each leg. The right foot steps forward at an angle to the right, with the weight distribution remaining 50 percent on each foot. The distance of the step can vary, depending on the reach of the opponent and the distance needed to counterattack.

The V stance makes it possible to execute either direct counteroffensive techniques to the inside of the opponent's center, or attacks to the left or right outer sides of the opponent. The enemy, through his offensive actions, determines the Visayan's direction. He can either move backward, to the base of the V, or he can move forward by traversing a diagonal. Offensively, defensively, or neutrally, the V stance affords the Visayan knife fighter the ability to resist aggressive force, or to flow with the actions of the antagonist.

Every technique taught in this book can be performed easily from this pattern, provided that the routine is practiced until you no longer have to give it conscious thought. Like a dance, your effort has to be instinctive so that intention is one with action.

The right foot is then retracted to the neutral, center position.

The left foot can then be slid out to the left (weight still equally distributed). The left foot is then retracted to the center position.

9. Checking and Knife Rolling

By relying solely on the knife and wrist and arm manipulations, knife fighters severely limit their capabilities.

Visayan experts, applying Filipino stick-fighting principles to knife fighting, practice the art of checking to double their knife-fighting capability.

Checking is a position, or state of readiness, in which the fighter uses his free hand in both offensive and defensive knife-fighting techniques.

Checking tactics are applied from a poised arm and free-hand position, in which the hand remains ready to guard; brace cutting actions; grab the opponent's weapon, wrist, arm, etc.; keep the adversary from grabbing, punching, striking, cutting, etc.; or prohibit him from continuing offensive or defensive actions.

As with stick fighting, Visayan knife fighters integrate checking with the actual knife manipulations themselves. All techniques are meant to be executed in one continuous motion, without pause or interruption between the slashes, blocks, checks, and counterstrike motions.

Checking manipulations are not randomly executed, but are highly refined systematic patterns of movement designed to intercept oncoming attacks and counter with the most appropriate slashes. The Visayan knife fighter learns many different patterns during his early training, when the stick(s) are being taught. By the time he has mastered the sticks, these checking actions are second nature. (A good reason for this! By that time, if he has not mastered the checking maneuvers, he could slash his own arms and wrists to ribbons while trying to inflict damage on his antagonist.)

When the sticks are used, as preparatory training for the knife, the Visayan artist tries to use checking to strike the training partner's stick. In actual combat he would strike the opponent's wrist, forearm, or elbows; and in cases of extreme closeness the balisong fighter would slash at the aggressor's organs. The checking techniques of the free hand would assist in opening up those areas if they were protected.

The Visayan knife-fighting artist believes that the most effective control and counterslashing can be achieved if the opponent's center is exposed. (It is very similar to the strategy used in chess: if the middle of the board is protected, the game can be won.) The Visayan butterfly specialist always keeps his middle (the area between the arms) protected while trying to expose the opponent's middle. The checking free hand assists in that effort while the butterfly knife is busy taking care of business. That is why the interactions between the blade-wielding hand and the free hand seem so intertwined.

A particular type of check can be used against a variety of attacks. All the checks can be performed in a pattern-like sequence from one check, if the motion remains continuous. Those patterns will correspond to the patterns of slashes that are found in the later chapters dealing with slashing and counterattacks. Observe these similarities closely. They help form the foundation of deadly Visayan knife fighting.

When learning the checking patterns, pay more attention to the free hand than the one wielding the blade. This way you will begin to appreciate the interaction between them. Remember that in many instances there could be no cutting action without checking. If the checking hand is ignored, there is an imbalance of activity, motion, and interaction between the arms.

VISAYAN KNIFE ROLLING

Knife- and wrist-rolling techniques of the Visayans are not

limited to knife fighters. In fact, the ancient Filipino stick-fighting arts like escrima and kali, as well as their modern derivatives, utilize the same techniques to elude and confuse the adversary, while providing the continuity to flow from one technique to another.

Knife rolling is an augmented wrist and knife manipulation in which the blade revolves in large, medium, or small circles, directed either forward or backward. All knife rolling techniques, regardless of arc size or directional travel, are designed to enhance the Visayan knife fighter's close- and mid-range fighting skills.

The rolling techniques make it possible, especially with short weapons like the butterfly knife, for the knife fighter to disengage a force intended to control his movement (usually arm, wrist, or hand grabs) by simply rotating the wrist as the tip and/or edge of the blade is forced into the antagonist's restraining arm. The following categories indicate the situations for which knife rolling is appropriate.

Disengagement

When the Visayan fighter has been restrained by an adversary, a quick circular roll with blade or stick can force the opponent to remove his grip.

Forceful intervention

Any push, grab, kick, slap, punch, or weapon attack can be thwarted before reaching the Visayan artist.

Positional changes

Wrist rolling combined with *pa-on* ("feeding" or feinting; see page 159) maneuvers can confuse the opponent.

Directional changes

Subtle rolls can change the weapon from a vertical to a horizontal direction, or vice-versa. They can also be used to connect ankla terradas (anchor strikes), abaniko terradas (short whipping strikes), and *pandol* (redirectional energy) techniques.

Checking and rolling

Checking and rolling is a method of blocking an attack while preparing the blade or stick for a quick counterattack. These combined tactics minimize the time it takes to follow up on an assault, allow a greater flexibility in slashing maneuvers, and diminish the possibility of the adversary blocking.

Psychology

When the rolling techniques are artfully executed, they can serve as a deterrent to the antagonist. In a series of quick rolling techniques, the blade often appears to be a blur of continuous motion, which can be a useful psychological weapon.

Power acceleration

Small rolls can greatly increase the speed of the weapon while drastically diminishing the wind-up time needed to strike. The faster the wrist is rolled the more velocity is accrued at the end of the knife or stick, and the greater the force at the time of impact.

Multiple cutting

The rolling maneuvers, when accurately directed, can be used with the striking (cutting and slashing) techniques, decreasing the time of multiple-cutting ploys, and allowing various angles to be achieved without repositioning the arm or body. This permits greater versatility for the Visayan fighter without alerting the opponent of his intentions.

Close-quarter combat

The tight circular moves can afford the fighter greater effectiveness at close ranges. The rolls enhance weapon velocity when space needed to gain acceleration is not available.

To begin a knife roll, the knife is gripped in a preparatory fighting position.

The grip is relaxed slightly as the wrist is rotated in a counterclockwise direction (clockwise if an opposite direction roll is desired). The thumb and index finger remain in permanent contact with the knife.

The knife continues (with the help of the wrist momentum) to circle in a smooth and uninterrupted path as velocity builds, so that impact will be increased.

The wrist continues to circle as the wrist is snapped toward the intended target. This roll should be one continuous motion.

Check-and-roll technique. The knife fighters are ready to engage.

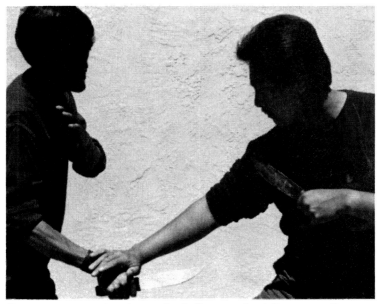

The opponent reaches in to check (i.e., touch, deflect, or redirect an assault).

With his free hand, the knife fighter quickly checks his opponent's extended hand to insure that a grab cannot be executed. At the same time, the knife-fighting expert initiates a knife roll to begin his own counterattack. This is the basic combination check-and-roll technique.

Before the opponent can withdraw his hand, the expert has determined his target, initiated the roll, and slashed by applying the final wrist snap.

Forward roll. The opponent attempts to check the knife-fighting expert.

Before the opponent knows what has happened, the expert executes a fast circular forward roll and slashes the extended hand.

If the antagonist persists, the expert immediately adds a checking maneuver while initiating another roll. He then slashes for the second time the opponent's outstretched hand.

Reverse roll. The knife expert has checked an oncoming attack.

Before the opponent's knife reaches its target, the expert shifts his weight to the opposite side (to keep the opponent guessing) and, at the same time, brings his knife under the opponent's outstretched arm. He then initiates a reverse cross-body roll.

He quickly twists the knife clockwise and uses the continued rolling motion to cut.

Lateral roll. This is either a forward or reverse roll executed in a side-to-side direction. Here, the opponent initiates a checking technique.

The knife-fighting expert begins to execute a reverse roll (to evade any checking and rolling on the part of his adversary or to slash the opponent's checking hand if it continues toward him).

The expert retracts his knife to his right side as the blade continues to travel in a lateral direction.

With a quick shift of the legs (using the Visayan V stance) the expert slashes the side of the opponent's face. The wrist snap of the rolling technique adds to the force of the slash.

Double roll. This roll is implemented when both hands hold knives, sticks, or other weapons. Both weapons can move in the same direction or in opposite directions. Here a simultaneous forward and reverse roll is demonstrated. The knife in the right hand begins a forward roll. The one in the left hand begins a reverse roll.

The rotations continue as speed and momentum are increased.

The knives have completed three-quarters of the 360-degree circle.

The double roll is completed. This technique not only increases dexterity, coordination, and familiarity with the weapon, but serves a very useful purpose when two weapons are wielded.

10. Visayan Knife Slashing

The Visayan knife-fighting master employs four types of cuts, each inflicting a varying degree of injury. The angle of the knife combined with the momentum of the body as it meets the target determines what type of cut will be executed.

The four kinds of cuts are slashes, stabs, rips, and gouges. By understanding the distinctions between the four types, you will be able to select the type that will be appropriate to the intensity of a given assault. The Visayan masters used an old adage, "The stronger and more intense the enemy would attack, the deeper we go with the knife."

Slashes

The slash is a surface cutting technique executed with a broad sweep parallel to the swing of the hand and arm. Slashes generally meet the target at a perpendicular angle, and are then drawn across it.

The range of these maneuvers is from several inches to more than six feet, depending on the amount of arm extension and/or body rotation. Slashes can be executed with equal efficiency from horizontal, vertical, and diagonal positions.

The body's momentum, sharpness of the blade, weight and size of the knife, and the protective garments worn by the adversary will all affect the penetration of the cut. A Visayan knife fighter always tries to use a razor-sharp, sufficiently weighted butterfly knife, and only attack exposed portions of the anatomy.

Since slashes are not deep cuts, they are used on arms, wrists, legs, and other less vulnerable parts of the antagonist's body for the purpose of thwarting and deterring. They can, however, be lethal when directed to the brachial or the radial artery. If the brachial artery is deeply slashed, the adversary can lose consciousness in thirteen to fifteen seconds, and die within two minutes. If the radial artery is severely slashed, there can be loss of consciousness in thirty seconds and death in about two minutes. Visayan knife fighters are acutely aware of this danger and only attack those areas as a last resort.

Slashes can also be used effectively as tactics of psychological warfare. The extremities and other areas of the human anatomy where the arteries are not close to the skin surface, when slashed lightly, can lose lots of blood without threatening life. A superficial slash to the forehead, for instance, can make the antagonist think he has been severely wounded, and in more cases than not, a knife fight comes to a sudden halt when the enemy sees his own blood flowing.

The Visayan knife fighter slashes to create and maintain distance between himself and the antagonist. A series of multidirectional slashes can deter the adversary just by posing a threat to his safety.

Stabs

To stab, the pointed tip of the blade is driven into the target at an angle.

Stabs are usually considered the most lethal kind of cut, especially if directed to the vital organs with a long enough blade. Most of the vital areas of the human anatomy are well protected by the skeletal structure, but Visayan knife fighters use tight, circular wrist and arm motions at points of the body that are not as well protected. Once access is gained, the stabbing cut is quickly redirected to the targeted organ.

There are two types of stabbing cuts. The first is known as a "full-committed cut," "coup de grace," or "death lunge" because of the forceful way it is administered to the vital organs. These committed strikes are used as a last resort.

The second type of stab is sometimes known as a "snake strike." These cuts produce punctures; the knife is then withdrawn quickly after the desired penetration is achieved. Snake strikes are not usually considered as lethal as the death lunge, but with calculated accuracy they can be deadly—thrust, for instance, into a neck artery, eye socket, ear, or under the sternum and into the heart.

The retracting action of this type of stab makes it ideally suited to the Visayan knife-fighting style. The strikes can be blended so intricately that the antagonist never even knows that a snake strike has occurred.

Snake strikes are implemented by speed jabbing. For a speed jab, the muscles of the knife fighter's arm and wrist must be relatively relaxed. (This allows for maximum acceleration, since the muscles are not tensed.) At the point just before penetration, the arm muscles are tightened to prepare for the impact, and when the knife blade is withdrawn, the muscles are retightened. Visayan masters use the speed jab only when they are sure they are in control, because if the opponent rushes at the wrong time, when the majority of the arm muscles are relaxed, the knife could be jarred from the hand.

Rips

When force is placed behind a blade in motion (as in a slash) and combined with angular perpendicular force (as in a stab), the cut is called a rip.

The rip employs a sawing motion. Exerted in one direction, it would simply puncture, but then the pull in the opposite direction tears the opponent's anatomical parts away.

The Filipino knife fighter uses rips to remove a gripping or restraining hand. They serve well to rip at the thighs or shins as a defense against kicks—the harder and more forceful the kick, the deeper and more severe the rip.

Rips can be lethal in cavities of the skeletal structure. The areas between the collarbone and the back of the upper rib cage are ideal locations for inflicting this damage at close ranges. Under the sternum can also be lethal, if the aorta or the lungs are punctured and torn open.

The human being goes through several phases when dying. When a massive amount of blood is lost (as in rip cuts), the individual loses his sight first before losing any other sense. Visual impairment is of prime importance to the blade artist: if the adversary cannot see you, the fight will soon be over.

Rips and stabs are both last-resort ploys. They are used only in a fight to the finish.

Gouges

A gouge is a stab with a twist. Like rips, gouges are for close range, and used when there are no alternatives.

Gouges can be used to disengage from an adversary, but they are slower than rips or slashes, and easier to see coming. Gouges to the upper torso with a wide twisting motion can destroy or severely damage a large portion of the internal organs and surrounding tissue. They can create internal hemorrhaging, which can lead to death.

VISAYAN KNIFE-CUTTING DO'S AND DON'TS

1. Do read your opponent's eyes for his intentions.
2. Do remain sure-footed and use V stepping movements.
3. Do use peripheral vision to see all of the adversary.
4. Do use continuous movement with hand and weapon.
5. Do use distraction to elude and fool the opponent.
6. Do use only strong and natural cutting and checking moves.
7. Do use the terrain (sun, ground, etc.) to your advantage.
8. Do use the range to your advantage.
9. Do use the philosophy and principles that suit the crisis.
10. Do know where the cutting edge of the blade is at all times.

1. Don't use fancy, out-of-control cutting techniques.
2. Don't let the knife stay in one position too long.

3. Don't react before accuracy is assured.
4. Don't take your eyes off the opponent.
5. Don't use fancy footwork while cutting.
6. Don't throw your knife at the adversary.
7. Don't get trapped in a position where you can't move.
8. Don't waste energy on techniques that are meant for another range.
9. Don't let the checking hand drop while changing positions.
10. Don't make a full-commitment movement when the opponent expects it.
11. Don't purposely cut into the bone or cartilage areas.
12. Don't rush the opportune moment to execute an accurate cut.

THE SEVENTEEN SLASHES OF DEATH

The seventeen slashes of death derive from Visayan-style stick fighting.

The seventeen "angles of attack" of escrima or kali can become literally "seventeen slashes of death" when rattan is substituted with one or two balisongs. The Visayan style of knife fighting converts the angles of attack of the stick-fighting art into the lethal art form of the slashes of death.

In this systematic pattern of carefully structured movements, seventeen smooth-flowing, continuous slashes artistically cross every vital area of the human anatomy. The seventeen sequenced slashes are a way for the practitioner to memorize the major, vital areas of the body, and a drill that can be practiced in a specified order, so the student can learn the seventeen basic strikes. In Visayan stick and knife fighting, the seventeen angles of attack are the first phase of study. In this phase, the student discovers that the slash patterns can be used with equal effectiveness as blocking maneuvers.

The seventeen basic slashes are learned first on the right-hand side of a left-handed student, and on the left-hand side of a right-handed student. This ensures that both the left and right sides get the same amount of training; ultimately this will mean that the Visayan fighter will be equally skilled with the left and the right hands.

Next, the beginning knife fighter is taught that this same sequence of slashes can be used to either the inside or outside of the adversary, so the knife fighter can utilize his skills in tactical situations without having to modify his natural style.

In the Filipino stick- and knife-fighting arts, there are countless possible combinations made possible by instantly rearranging the sequences so the techniques are responsive to the openings created by the previous blocking and/or attacking ploys.

Visayan knife-fighting experts categorize the four types of cuts into two styles when learning the basic seventeen angles of attack: the strike, which is a slash, and the poke, which is a stab.

The illustrations in this chapter outline the pattern of pokes and strikes. The order of these exacting sequences must not be altered or modified when they are being learned; to do so will diminish the natural follow-up feel. Begin at the first diagram, and master all the sequential slashes before proceeding to the next diagram. When they are all learned, you will have amassed the entire seventeen deadly slashes. This collective knowledge will make it possible to delve deeper into the various combinations of blocks and appropriate counters that correspond to the seventeen. Remember that the pattern must be learned with the hand you do not usually use if you are to achieve your ultimate dexterity. Both hands and both sides of the brain must become involved with this process. Do not take this advice lightly!

The basic seventeen slashes with a knife are all injurious, and many are fatal, depending on the depth of the cut and the force of the penetration.

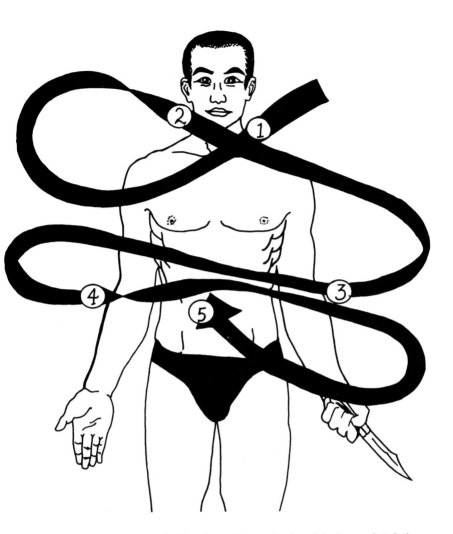

This diagram illustrates the first five strikes and pokes (slashes and stabs) taught in the Visayan knife-fighting art. They are presented from the perspective of a right-handed fighter. The directions would be reversed if the left hand was wielding the knife.

Refer to the lethal target illustration so that the slashes (strikes) and stabs (pokes) will correspond to the arterial locations of the anatomy. All of the slashes and stabs of the Visayan style are designed to attack these vulnerable areas.

The blade of the knife should be always positioned so that the front (or belly) portion of the blade is outward. This will take some practice when the wrist is rotated in the slashing patterns.

Memorize the entire pattern of slashes thoroughly. Remember that the entire sequence is designed to be performed in a swift and explosive fashion.

Strikes/pokes 6 through 8.

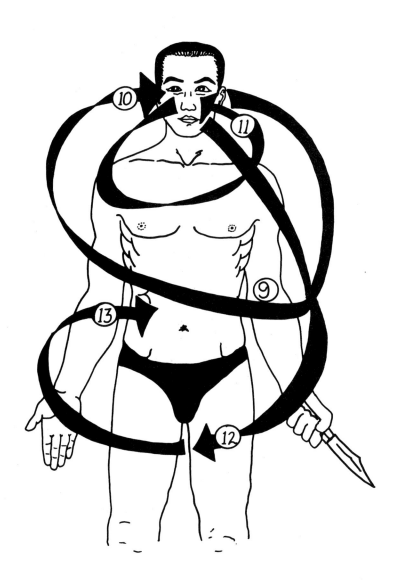

Strikes/pokes 9 through 13.

Strikes/pokes 14 through 17.

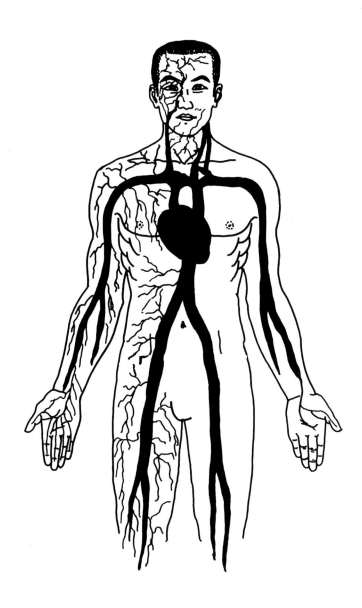

Lethal target diagram. The major arteries and veins are illustrated for the purpose of targeting these vulnerable areas.

The seventeen slashes demonstrated in the following photographs correspond to the seventeen slashes depicted in the anatomy drawings. The first slash is to the neck in a downward, diagonal direction. It is intended to sever the carotid artery and/or the jugular vein.

Slash 2 is to the neck on the opposite side.

Slash 3 is to the opponent's left inner arm. It is intended to sever the subclavian artery and/or vein.

Slash 4 is to the opponent's right inner arm.

The fifth move is a poke (stab) to the center of the torso. It is intended to puncture the lower aorta and/or the inferior vena cava artery.

Move 6 is a poke (stab) into the right eye.

Slash 7 is to the forearm.

Move 8 is a poke (stab) into the left eye.

Slash 9 is directed across the extended left arm, to cut the subclavian artery and/or vein. If the opponent's arms were positioned in a defensive block, the slash would cut the outer arm.

Slash 10 is across the head from the right side of the head to the left at eye level.

Slash 11 is across the head, starting on the left side.

For slash 12, the knife is turned slightly downward and directed in an arc across the left mid-thigh. It is intended to cut the femoral artery and/or vein.

Move 13 is a poke (stab) to the lower torso. It is intended to cut the aorta and/or inferior vena cava. Both supply the blood to the entire lower body.

For slash 14, the knife is reversed and drawn across the right thigh.

Move 15 is a poke (stab) into the lower abdomen.

For move 16, the knife is directed upward and then stabbed into the neck region. It is intended to cut the esophagus, left or right carotid artery, or jugular vein.

For move 17, the knife is circled downward and then the wrist is rotated and the knife brought upward to slash the top of the skull. Although a superficial cut, this final slash can cause massive blood flow, obscuring the attacker's sight.

11. Ankla Terradas

Ankla terradas is the second phase of Visayan training, introduced immediately after the practitioner has mastered the seventeen basic angles of attack and their defensive counterparts.

"Ankla terradas" in Visayan Filipino dialect translates literally to "anchor strikes." The term describes a way of increasing power and speed of a strike without drawing back the weapon (and thereby telegraphing your intentions) or extending the weapon-wielding hand and arm. This not only increases the time you have to perform a strike, but it enhances close-range fighting skills.

The secret of ankla terradas lies in the precise circular wrist action that occurs when a strike is executed. This exacting process can be performed much more easily with sticks—since they are longer and can be positioned so the free end can be forced under the forearm, under the armpit, etc.—than with shorter instruments, like the balisong.

In this action, the wrist generates a restrictive torque that is unleashed when the free end of the stick is released from its anchored position. When the stick is held under the armpit, or elsewhere, so that the free end cannot move freely as the wrist and arm torque, a tension is developed. At the time of the unleashing, the free end of the stick is directed violently toward its target. These anchor strikes accelerate from a stationary position to almost full velocity in a matter of milliseconds.

You must be able to perform the ankla terradas exercises with either hand. Do not be too concerned with accuracy at this point—that will come as your ankla terradas techniques mature. Concentrate on the principles of motion and the coordination between force generation and the release. The more wrist and arm torque applied before release, the more power. As your timing and coordination increase, so will your speed.

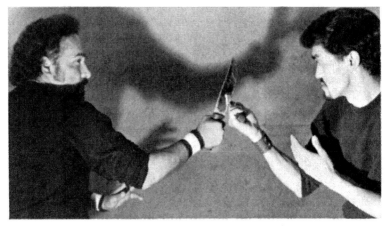

This ankla terradas technique should be mastered with sticks before knives are attempted. As contact is made with the opponent's knife, the wrist is tensed. This builds up a reserve of energy.

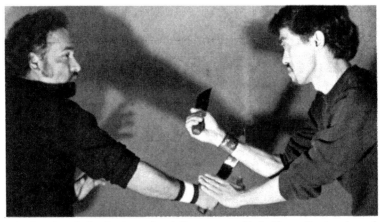

The free hand checks to redirect the opponent's knife as the tension of the knife hand is about to be released.

The wrist is violently unleashed. It is like a spring that has suddenly been released from a tightly coiled position.

The knife slashes into the opponent's exposed neck area. This entire sequence occurs before the opponent can blink his eyes.

12. Pandol

Pandol is a supplementary form of training that is used to harness the force of the opponent's energy and direct it back at him. Pandol teaches this skill through drills, usually with sticks, that encourage dexterity of both hands.

In Visayan corto kadena training, learning pandol immediately follows learning ankla terradas; pandol becomes easier to comprehend because of the wrist rotations and flexibility developed in ankla terradas.

The Visayan fighter can use pandol techniques to gain power. Thrusting his blade or stick into the force of the oncoming weapon, he rides the force of impact until an opening is created, and then, using a circular pattern of the wrist, redirects the opponent's weapon force in a new direction. In most cases, this redirected force is trajected right back into the enemy's exposed and vital target areas.

This action requires that the Visayan knife and stick fighter have a real feel for the sudden impact of an oncoming weapon, and that he know exactly when to redirect the impact before his weapon has absorbed the energy. If he is too late, he will have received the full power of the impact before it can be effectively redirected.

The fighter must have fast reflexes and know how to use small circular wrist motions. If the circular wrist actions are too large, the energy is absorbed before the power transfer can happen.

If the opponent's force is more powerful than expected,

it can have a shocking effect that is absorbed directly into the knife fighter's body. Obviously this will hamper his ability to respond. But when the timing corresponds with the moment of impact, the technique can provide the fighter with an excellent form of checking the opponent. In addition, this redirective effort can be used when an opponent is wielding two sticks or knives to form a second block to the weapon attack that may follow the first one.

Skillful Visayan knife and stick fighters develop the feel of pandol by practicing blindfolded. When they cannot see the oncoming weapon, they cannot anticipate its arrival. The feel and direction of the oncoming weapon must be evaluated by the strike—a determination that must be acquired through experience.

After the basic principles of pandol can be performed without looking, the student is ready to begin the angulation phase of pandol training. To redirect a weapon's energy from one angle to another without losing power, the wrist must be ready for sudden shifts in direction. As soon as the direction of the force has been determined, the fighter must know his wrist position, its turning capacity, the amount of space made available by the action, and where the return force is to be directed. Again, this art is based on experience. Nothing short of serious dedication will provide the student with this essential knife- and stick-fighting skill.

Study the examples of pandol, and try to apply principles introduced in the material on ankla terradas; they complement one another. The blindfold practice should be attempted only when you can safely control the absorption weapon and envision the exact location of the training partner, so that injury is not incurred.

The basic pandol drill will introduce the standard angles of redirection. Practice the drill with a training partner until it can be performed without thinking about what you are doing. The experience acquired through this training will further prepare you for actual knife sparring.

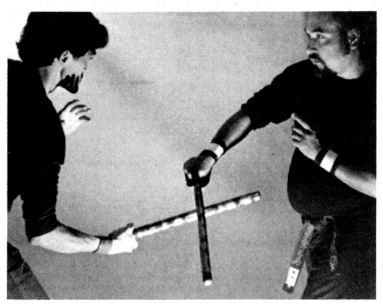

In the basic pandol drill, the opponent's downward force is directed against the top of the expert's extended stick (or knife).

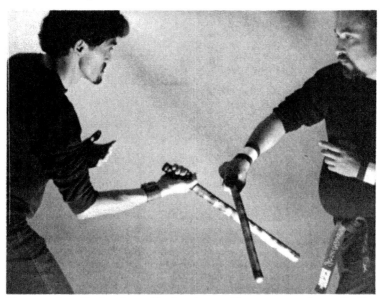

The expert suddenly relaxes the tension on his weapon and permits the opponent's weapon to penetrate, once he knows he's safely out of the line of fire.

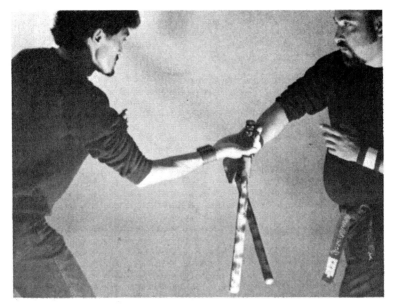

As he relaxes his wrist, the expert determines where he wants to redirect the force of the opponent's weapon.

The expert, combining his own energy with that of his opponent, strikes the extended hand. Striking the closest target is a basic technique of Visayan knife and stick fighting.

The blindfold pandol drill is an important sensitivity drill to develop a reflexive counterattack ability. This drill should first be practiced with sticks. Only when both partners are comfortable with the stick drill, should knives be used. Here, the blindfolded knife fighter feels his hand being touched by a foreign object (his opponent's hand).

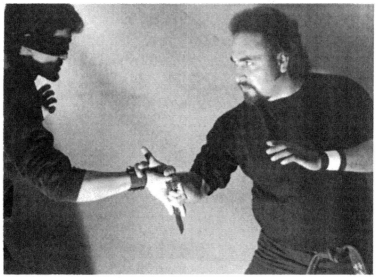

The knife fighter responds by rotating his wrist and absorbing the opponent's downward force.

The downward force is redirected into a slash to the opponent's wrist.

The slash severs the wrist muscles and tendons, thus preventing the opponent from continuing his attack.

13. Abaniko Terradas

"Abaniko terradas" literally translates to "fan or whipping" (abaniko) "strikes" (terradas). In the Visayan art of stick and knife fighting, this counteroffensive technique is introduced after the practitioner has mastered the ankla and pandol terradas. This third and shorter training phase combines anchor strikes, redirection strikes, and fan or whipping strikes.

Abaniko terradas can overcome any blocking tactic. The abaniko terradas destroy the opponent's defensive flow. The series of combination slashes and stabs are delivered to the vital areas that have been exposed, and the opposition must admit defeat.

The abaniko terradas are divided into two categories: the wide angle, and the close range. Wide-angle abanikos are designed to open up the opponent, and then the close-range abanikos are slipped in.

Combination abanikos are designed to interact with the checking, evading, and jamming ploys. The combinations illustrated in this chapter represent only a small fraction of the many possible combinations. If the natural feel and flow have been developed, it should not be difficult to develop your own particular amarras (series) that utilize the seventeen slashes of death. You should not proceed to the fourth phase of Visayan knife training, *sinawali,* until you have developed three or four dozen sequences. Each series should include a minimum of four or five different slashes and stabs. Remember that the wide-angle defensive abanikos should precede the smaller, close-range ones.

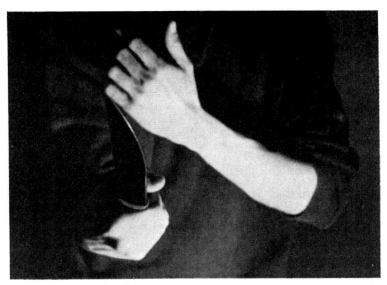

The abaniko terradas drill is intended to broaden and increase your knowledge of the ways that the knife and stick can be manipulated at extremely close ranges. Wrist action, ankla terradas (anchor strikes), and pandol (redirective methodology) are prerequisites for beginning this third phase of training. This drill should be mastered with both the left and right hands. To begin, the knife should be held out in front of you.

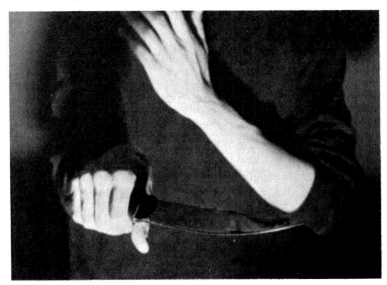

Perform a tight circular motion with the wrist in a counterclockwise direction. Continue the motion in a smooth counterclockwise manner.

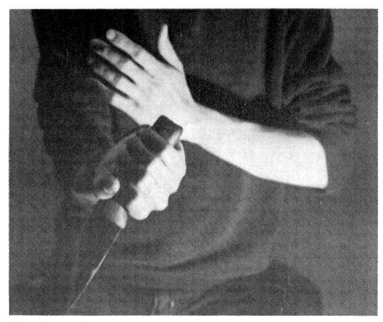

The wrist rotation continues.

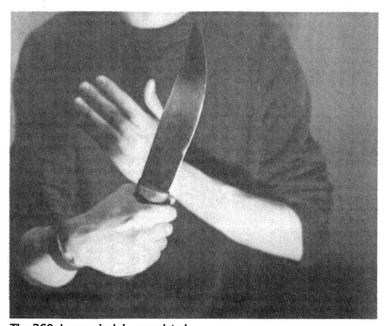

The 360 degree slash is completed.

The wrist is then tilted down and a clockwise wrist rotation is initiated. There should be no stops between direction changes; motion should be smooth and continuous.

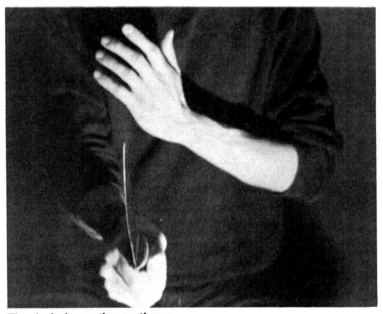

The clockwise motion continues.

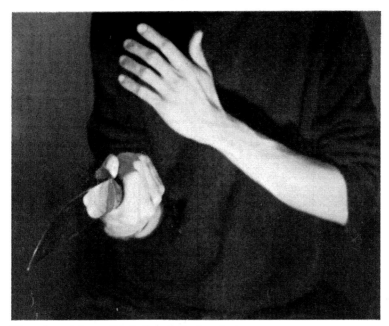

There is no interruption in the clockwise slash.

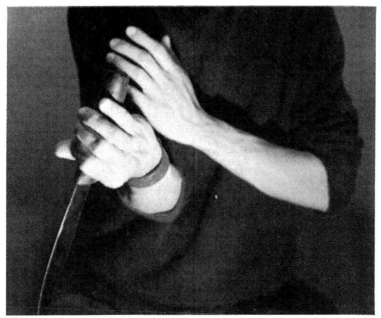

At the end of the rotation, the knife points down with the blade facing out.

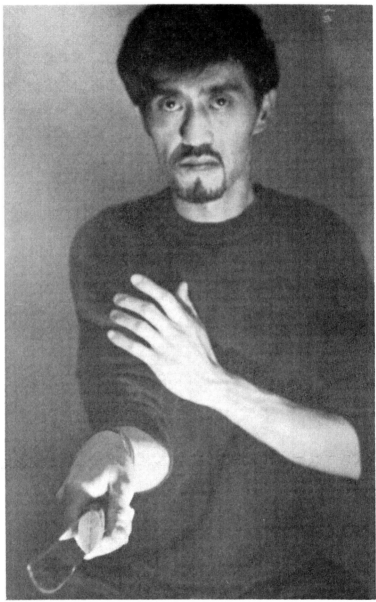

The wrist is then forcefully flicked in a counterclockwise direction. Whether a stick or knife is used, every portion of the arc can be used for striking, slashing, etc. The moves can also serve to deflect oncoming attacks, disengage grabbing maneuvers, and create illusions to confuse the opponent as to the intentions of the user.

14. Sinawali Training

At this fourth phase of training, the stick fighter training to use his butterfly knife in a real fighting encounter must realize that each phase of training must be carefully mastered before the next level is begun. At this level of training, many of the previous phases are reintroduced under practical (as opposed to the earlier, theoretical) circumstances. The first three phases stressed wide movements (the trainee will begin to understand that many of the same principles will exist), except now the techniques will be tighter, corto kadena movements (short, inside movements), which typify the Visayan stick-and knife-fighting arts.

This fourth phase of training will stress essential knife- (or stick-) fighting elements such as understanding and being able to use basic angles and proper body mechanics to enhance the fighting techniques. In addition, the trainee is taught to use economical movement and develop faster reflexes by tightening the maneuvers and using smaller, but stronger moves against the blocking and countering opponent. The practitioner must either achieve these qualities or fall victim to his own slowness.

These shorter movements are taught by the Visayan master using a training method called *sinawali* ("weaving"). The term comes from the analogy to cloth: the weave of one fiber (fighter) is precisely related to the angle, direction, and relationship of the other fiber (his opponent).

Sinawali, as the beginning form of fourth-phase training,

has three types: the single sinawali (single stick, hand, or knife), the double sinawali (the double stick, hand, or knife), and the reverse sinawali (the techniques are altered to broaden the ways in which they can be applied).

All sinawali is practiced with a training partner, and the interplay between partners must be approached with serious concern, since the trainees will eventually work with razor-sharp butterfly knives.

The initial moves and counters must be performed precisely for the prescribed set to progress. Any changes or alterations invalidate the two-person format. The sets, because they are so well-designed and clear, give the practitioners immediate feedback if the movements have been done correctly. To execute the two-person format, each fighter must be aware of the attacking move, where the target (opening) is, and how the move will strike; only in this way can the defender respond to the attacker. Each move elicits a response from the training partner.

Each move-response pattern has a different target in the high, middle, or low sections of the anatomy. This applies not only to close-range, frontal movements, but to the whole body, which should be viewed as a spiral, always turning and moving to and from the inner to outer sides.

As the offensive partner strikes at one target, the defensive partner blocks or counterattacks in order to create an opening in the partner's defense. Each student must continually attempt to find the opponent's exposed targets while keeping his own protected—an art acquired by learning the anchor strikes, in which the elbows remain close to the body.

Agility, timing, balance, V styles of footwork, knowledge of pa-on, abaniko terradas, ankla terradas, and pandol, in addition to a keen concentration, are all essential to performing the sinawali. In order to respond quickly and accurately, these responses must become second nature; there is not time when practicing a sinawali two-man exercise to think about a move. If the exchanges were real, which eventually they will be, thinking about a move would result in a casualty.

You should find a serious and enthusiastic training partner to help you master the sinawali drills—of course you will be helping him achieve the same level of proficiency at the same time. The moves of a sinawali drill alternate between the two partners, and as the forms progress, roles should be reversed, so that both offensive and defensive moves are mastered.

It should only be after the hands and stick sinawali arts have been fully learned that the more deadly blade sinawalis be attempted. Blade sinawali movements are much closer, more precise, and much, much quicker, but use the same principles as the hand and stick sets.

Once the single-stick sinawali drill is mastered, the same methodology can be applied to the knife. The first strike is initiated by the left partner. Note the positions of the free hands.

The left partner retracts his weapon and prepares for his second assault.

The attack is blocked and a check is initiated.

Disengagement occurs.

A side strike initiated by the left partner is quickly blocked. This short drill can be continued indefinitely. Once both partners are familiar with the routine, they should switch sides.

15. Defenses, Combinations, and Tricks

The Visayan knife-fighting expert has options for defense usually neglected during combat by a less skilled fighter; these are due to his intense training and long experience. The Visayan knife fighter is highly skilled in all seven of the defensive options, and knows when and where to apply them.

The seven primary defense options the Visayan master has at his disposal include, but are not limited to:

1. Evading the attack completely.
2. Evading the attack while executing a counterattack.
3. Intercepting the attack.
4. Intercepting the attack and then counterattacking.
5. Jamming or neutralizing an attack and then counterattacking.
6. Cutting, slashing, or ripping away a restraining maneuver, if the adversary has penetrated to close range.
7. Applying an offense after the aggressor has initiated an attack.

Circumstances; the opponent's actions, reactions, and positioning; type of aggression; quickness and skill of the adversary; and your own expertise will all play a vital role in determining which type of defense tactic to apply in a given situation. If one of the seven defenses does not work as you had planned it, do not attempt to use the same one again. As the old Visayan Filipino knife fighters say, "Always be unpredictably unpredictable."

Defense 1. Evading an attack completely. The attacker has made a broad slash at the knife expert.

The attacker begins to prepare another assault.

As the attacker lunges forward, the expert quickly sidesteps to avoid contact.

As the attack extends forward, the knife master shifts to the opposite side to avoid the assault.

Defense 2. Evading the attack while executing a counterattack. The attacker has executed a diagonal slash, which the expert evades while maintaining close enough range to counterattack.

The expert performs a check (in this case, a grab) with his free hand against the opponent's weapon hand.

The blade master places the butterfly blade against the attacker's neck, and the attacker is "persuaded" to drop his weapon.

Defense 3. Intercepting an attack. The attacker begins his assault by executing a lunge with his free hand.

The blade master responds to the feint by neutralizing the maneuver with a check.

The attacker then presses inward with the knife attack. The knife fighter expects this and sidesteps to the other side of his opponent.

The blade master turns his knife to the side so as not to seriously harm the antagonist, but to demonstrate that he could have easily slashed the arm to the bone.

Defense 4. Intercepting the attack and then counterattacking. The attacker slides in and executes a close-range low-level stab. It is immediately intercepted by the blade edge of the knife fighter's knife held in the back-grip position.

The expert slashes along the opponent's extended arm while simultaneously bringing his free hand into play.

The free hand quickly grabs the adversary's arm before he can remove it.

The knife master redirects his blade upward toward the opponent's neck for the counterattack.

Defense 5. Neutralizing an attack and then counterattacking. As the opponent attacks, the knife expert moves in and checks the lunge while cutting the opponent's arm.

While keeping his free hand in contact with the opponent's weapon hand, the knife expert executes another slash, this time to the upper forearm.

As the attacker attempts to disengage, the expert continues to slice at the arm being retracted.

Defense 6. Breaking a restraining maneuver. The knife fighter's weapon arm is grabbed.

The knife fighter quickly executes a clockwise wrist roll and places the blade along the opponent's arm.

A wrist snap (pandol technique) forces the antagonist to release his grasp, while simultaneously, the knife fighter slashes the wrist. He swiftly follows with one of the seventeen slashes of death.

Defense 7. Applying an offense after the aggressor has initiated an attack. As the adversary executes a low-level attack, the knife fighter slides his leg out of the way of the attack.

As the antagonist begins to redirect his attack, the expert shifts position and checks the attacker's hand.

The expert quickly counterattacks by slashing the exposed arm of the adversary.

The counterattack is continued with a more lethal slash to the exposed neck of the victim.

LETHAL SLASHING COMBINATIONS

The Visayan knife masters call slashing combinations "amarras." Amarras can be an effective offense, but the philosophical tenets of the Visayan knife fighter dictate that they should be used only for retaliatory purposes.

This lethal combative art emphasizes a natural, flowing continuum. Because of this fluidity, you must study how the techniques are combined. If you ignore the connecting movements in favor of the slashing or poking techniques, you will have missed the object of the training.

Referring to the chapter on the seventeen slashes of death and applying those skills will make learning lethal slashing combinations easier. Also, the abaniko terradas and pandol chapters will be useful in helping to achieve the fluidity you need.

You can create these combinations yourself, remembering that the continued flowing action must be maintained. Emphasize logical positioning, inherent feel of the weapon, positioning relative to the opponent or training partner, and technique.

Do not get so elaborate in designing combination sequences that you lose track of reality. Remember that the opponent's actions are going to be the primary prompt to your actions. You can't think, but must feel a combinational remedy to suit a particular situation. Do not memorize a sequence and attempt to apply it to an ideal situation—there will never be an ideal situation.

VISAYAN KNIFE-FIGHTING TRICKS

After the knife-fighting student has mastered sinawali, he is introduced to pa-on. Some consider these ploys devious, but Visayan masters consider them tools of the craft, and find the butterfly knife well-suited to this dark side of their art.

Pa-on translates literally as "feeding," indicating the way the Visayan master lures his unsuspecting foe into his web of illusion. He feeds the adversary a false maneuver, which the adversary is forced to accept, or become a victim of his own nonacceptance.

While a fist fighter may attempt to deceive by absorbing the opponent's punches, strikes, or kicks to dish out in turn his own brand of devastation, the knife fighter will not take the risk of getting stabbed in a vital organ or slashed across the neck in order to inflict a similar type of injury on the adversary. This is one of the primary reasons for pa-on. The level of intensity of knife fighting itself will generally dictate the actions or reactions of the adversary. Visayan masters use this psychology in pa-on ploys.

Pa-on is similar to the old "bait and switch" sales trick, where one thing is advertised and another is offered when the "sucker" arrives. There are many ways to implement this trick in the art of knife fighting, but the concept remains the same regardless of the ruse used.

Because of the Visayan philosophy and principles of knife fighting, the Visayan fighter would never provoke a fight by taking the offensive role; this minimizes the possibility of falling victim to his own pa-on ruse. A fight with another fighter of the same philosophy would end in a stand off; both would be better off, since there would not be any bloodshed, or need to use their deadly art.

In one of the most common pa-on tactics, a simple fake attack is initiated to force a reaction from the enemy. The reaction tells the knife fighter of the opponent's immediate plans, and also indicates how swift, how smart, and how effective the enemy could be if the fight lasted longer than a few seconds.

An individual without a philosophy to guide his action can be deceived easily by creating an intentional opening to "feed" him. If he thinks his offensive actions can be successful, even given highly adverse conditions, he may initiate them, and the Visayan knife fighter is skilled at providing openings large enough to tempt even the most skeptical antagonist. Once the unwise adversary begins his offense, the Visayan fighter knows what to expect, when to expect it, and how to retaliate.

The Visayan fighter can employ false offensive ploys designed to make the opposition counterattack. When the counterattack comes within range, he begins counteroffensive tactics to intercept or block the assault. When the knife fighter has mastered the art of pa-on, he will be able to plan three to five movements in advance.

Pa-on techniques elevate the practitioner's awareness level. Under critical conditions, speed, power, reflexes, and control must complement the awareness of the knife fighter. This mental-physical relationship must be such that the practitioner is always aware of the reality of the situation. Perhaps that is why the Visayan knife-fighting expert becomes almost religiously devoted to his art.

The following pa-on techniques are only a few of the many diversionary ploys used by Visayan knife fighters, but by using the principles found throughout the text, you can adapt to many actual situations. You should always realize, however, that knife fighting is a deadly serious business and that there is no room for theoretical misappropriations of sound pa-on strategies.

Drawing

The Visayan knife fighter uses drawing to create an opening in his defense, which is used to coerce the enemy into taking a chance, and attacking the opening. When the attack is initiated, the Visayan fighter quickly closes the opening, simultaneously counterattacking.

Force feeding

The force feeding tactic is used to upset the antagonist's rhythm and cause him to counterattack. The Visayan knife fighter attacks the opponent from a mid-range distance. The adversary has several options available to him, and the Visayan reacts according to the actions taken by his victim. If he decides to check the false attack, the Visayan will check and counterattack. If the adversary evades, the knife fighter prepares an aggressive counterploy and proceeds with his original strategy. If the enemy does not react at all, it may be because he is aware of pa-on. If that occurs, the butterfly technician may opt to use another ruse.

Side feeding

Side feeding is used to force the opponent into committing his weapon to the frontal or leading position in relationship to the enemy. (This may be done by drawing the enemy in with another ruse.) The Visayan knife master retaliates to the strong side (the side wielding the weapon) by moving in and attacking the closest portion of the adversary's body, and if the weapon is the closest object, he attacks that as he continues to move in.

Inside feeding

After a draw feed is initiated and the enemy responds to it, the Visayan knife master may opt to feed to the center of the opponent's body. By continually faking cuts and opening up the adversary, the portions of the anatomy between the arms are attacked with some or all of the seventeen basic slashes of death.

The break-rhythm feed

If the opponent has a well-controlled rhythm, the Visayan may opt to vary his own rhythm to upset that of the opponent. By making faking gestures with his force feeds, and using the V stance, he will force the opponent to make an unprepared attack, and the Visayan initiates inner or outside counterattacks.

The multi-feed ruse

This is a tactic in which the Visayan continually executes a series of false force feeds to make the enemy execute an attack. Rather than focusing on the feints themselves, the knife fighter will remain alert to the instant the antagonist attacks, when he will employ a counteroffense technique.

The student of Visayan knife fighting is not permitted to begin using the art of pa-on until he has fully comprehended the distinction between play and reality. For that reason, he is trained in a modified version of real knife fighting, in which practitioners use drills that reflect real knife-fighting tactics. They may be introduced to rudimentary pa-on tactics, depending on their maturity and skill levels. (Even then they are practiced under controlled conditions.) Pa-on practice is a prelude to actual *sumrada* (sparring) that every Visayan knife fighter must learn before he can be considered skillful with the lethal butterfly knife.

16. Knife Fighting on the Streets

The Visayan balisong expert knows that most street-wise punks act with a brashness induced by drugs or lack of confidence, or out of desperation for money or other valuables, all of which indicate a lack of control or discipline.

The Visayan knife fighter is prepared to deal with such confrontations physically, mentally, and emotionally. When it becomes impossible to avoid a volatile situation, the Visayan fighter has no reservations about using his lethal skills. The attitude of the well-prepared knife fighter is the same on the street as it is in a more peaceful environment.

The Visayan fighter has no reservations at all about his actions, because he has already affirmed his belief in Visayan philosophy and principles. He knows that if he has to think about his actions once, his personal safety has been threatened, and chances are it will be too late to defend himself.

While most people are horrified at the sight of a knife pulled against them on the street, the Visayan knife fighter feels right at home. He has spent thousands of hours engaged in close-range knife-fighting practice, and having had a razor-sharp butterfly knife come within fractions of an inch of his vital areas strengthens his ability to remain calm.

The techniques, principles, and tactics of street fighting remain within the traditionalized style of Visayan knife play. The environment may change, the form of weaponry may change, but the art of knife fighting remains the same.

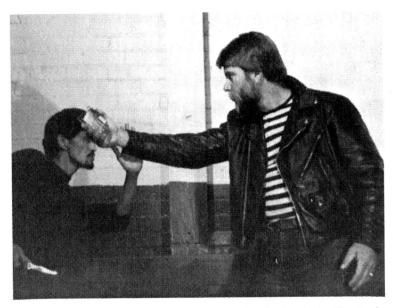

Technique 1. The butterfly knife vs. a broken bottle. As the bottle attack
is initiated, the knife expert checks the attack with his free hand while
sidestepping the brunt of the antagonist's force.

The knife fighter attacks the closest target, i.e., the wrist of the hand
wielding the broken bottle.

Then a quick slash to the inner arm is executed since the antagonist has not yet dropped his weapon.

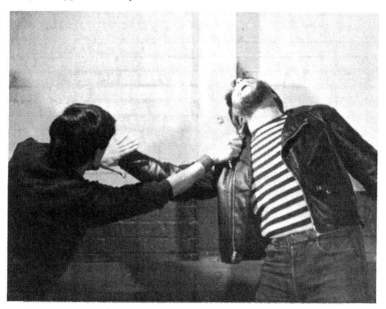

The knife fighter executes a superficial slash to the meaty part of the neck. This entire technique is executed in about one and one-half seconds.

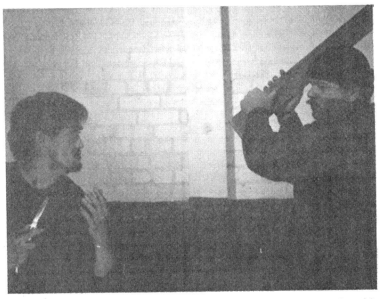

Technique 2. The butterfly knife vs. the stick. The aggressor attacks with a powerful overhead swing.

The knife fighter avoids the attack by sidestepping while preparing to use his butterfly knife. He attacks the closest possible target, the upper forearm of the antagonist.

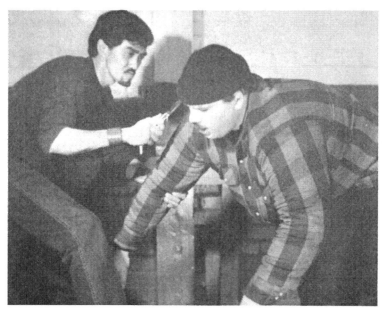

Before the antagonist can recover, the knife fighter grabs the antagonist's right arm.

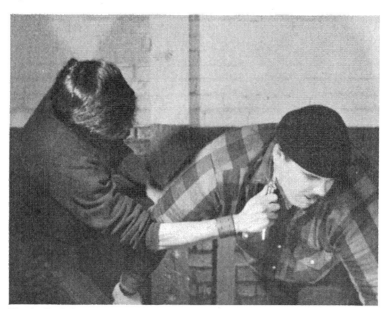

The knife fighter can now intimidate the antagonist by holding the blade of the butterfly knife to his neck.

Technique 3. The butterfly knife vs. the overhead club assault. The adversary initiates an overhead assault.

The knife fighter swiftly moves inside, and out of the path of the weapon. This strategy is based on moving in to the opponent's range rather than evading the attack. Simultaneously, the butterfly knife slashes into the veins on the inner arm near the elbow.

Using a modified pandol strike, the knife fighter redirects the blade to the opposite side and slashes along the outer arm.

Still moving to the inside of the adversary's position, the knife fighter executes a lethal slash to the artery on the side of the neck.

Technique 4. The butterfly knife vs. the lunging club assault. The antagonist tries to knock the knife out of the knife fighter's hand.

The knife fighter quickly circles his arm around the assault before it can strike his hand.

The knife fighter focuses on the exposed inner wrist where the artery is located.

The circular motion of the knife continues downward as the blade slashes the artery on the inner wrist.

Technique 5. The butterfly knife vs. the chain. As the chain is airborne, the knife expert sidesteps using the V stance and shifts his weight to the side, avoiding the path of the chain.

The knife expert grabs the adversary's arm with his free hand before the chain's momentum has subsided.

Still checking the attacker's weapon arm, the knife expert stabs him in the upper arm, traumatizing the muscles that control the wielding of the chain.

Technique 6. The butterfly knife vs. a larger knife. As the attacker executes a diagonal downward slash with the larger and longer machete, the butterfly-knife master moves under and around the attack.

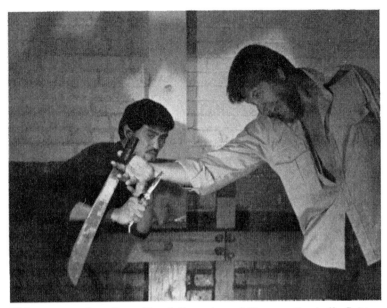

Rising up on the other side of the antagonist's arm, the knife fighter coordinates his rise with an upward cutting motion against the attacker's wrist. By severing the wrist tendons, the attacker loses control of the machete.

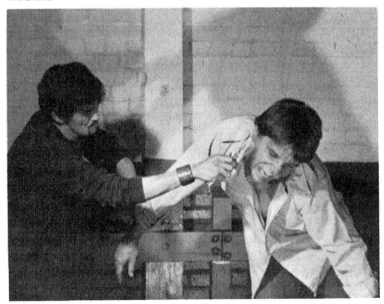

A second counterattack is directed to the ear.

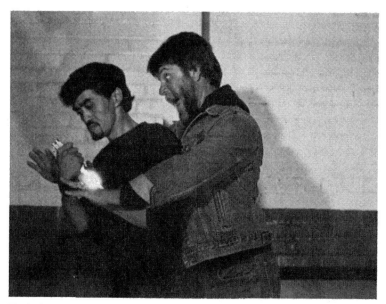

Technique 7. The butterfly knife vs. a rear bear hug. As soon as the knife fighter is gripped from behind with a bear hug, he stabs the antagonist's left hand, the closest accessible target.

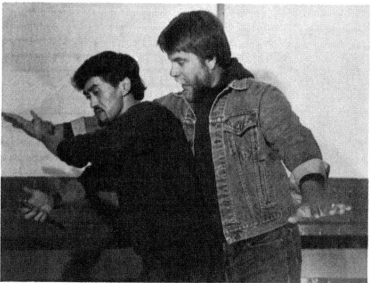

As the adversary retracts his injured hand, the knife fighter shifts his weight using the V stance and attempts to break free and get out of the attacker's range.

With a quick swiveling motion, the knife fighter frees himself and stabs the attacker in the side.

Technique 8. The butterfly knife vs. a kick and punch combination. The adversary executes a front thrust kick toward the knife fighter's groin. The knife fighter stabs the attacker's inner thigh, while simultaneously using a low-level block (a checking maneuver) against the leg.

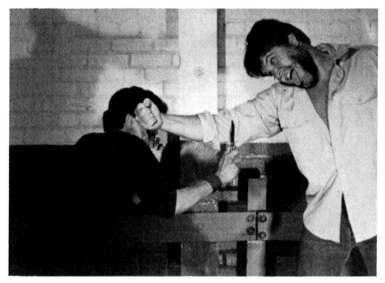

With the injured leg out of the action, the antagonist continues his assault with a closer-range attack—a punch to the knife wielder's head area. The knife fighter shifts his head out of the way while slashing the antagonist's inner arm with the butterfly knife. Within a fraction of a second, he slashes into the inner arm with the butterfly knife.

While the punching hand of the opponent is controlled by the knife fighter's checking maneuver, he places the point of the knife against the opponent's neck to force him to stop his attack.

17. The Balisong, the Law, and You

The laws pertaining to knives vary from state to state, and from city to city. Some are more restrictive than others. Since the enacted laws in the state of California (and New York) are very stringent in this respect, they may be used as a basic guideline for selling, possessing, and using the butterfly knife. Other states have similar regulations (though many are not as technically explicit as California or New York); check with your local police department to determine the laws which affect owning, carrying, or using such a weapon.

California prohibits a long list of weapons, many of them bladed. It is noteworthy that the balisong is not on that list. However, in Los Angeles and other major metropolitan areas in California, double-edged bladed instruments are considered daggers and are illegal, as are knives that have a blade length of six inches or more. In New York, and many other states, blade length should not exceed four inches. These should be determining factors when purchasing a butterfly knife locally or through the mail.

In many states the penalty for concealing a bladed instrument is greater than the penalty for possession. Many of these statutes state that "fixed blades" or a "folding bladed" knife that exceeds a certain length must be openly displayed, and most approved carrying methods involve the use of a sheath or other carrying device on a belt. There are exceptions to this rule.

The balisong should be carried, used, and displayed with good sense. Flaunting your technique can provoke a stranger to report you to the local authorities. Use discretion when opening your balisong. Do it as you would any other folding knife, and use both hands. This will discourage people from thinking that you are a knife-fighting expert, and will possibly prevent you from getting in a lot of trouble with the police.

18. Conclusion

An instructional text cannot fully convey the many nuances of the beautiful butterfly knife, but it is the sincere desire of the authors that enough knowledge was presented here to take you to the advanced stages of this timeless art. If we provided you with a purpose for learning, a reason for practicing, and the inspiration for mastering "the deadly butterfly of Visayas," then our collaborative effort as martial authors has not been in vain.

The ultimate experience will undoubtedly come when you have sought out a qualified instructor in these ancient Filipino martial arts, and we wish you the best of luck on your journey.

Glossary

abaniko (a-bon-ee-ko) whipping or fan strikes.

amarra (ama-ra) striking technique.

ankla (ank-la) anchor, grip.

anting-anting (aunting-aunting) amulet said to give fighters invincibility and strength.

baraw (ba-rao) knife.

baston (bas-ton) stick (Tagalog dialect).

Batangas (Ba-tang-gas) region of the Philippines where the balisong originated; another name for the butterfly knife.

corto (coor-toe) short, or inside.

dinongabai (dee-nong-ga-buy) literally, knife fight; a drill for hand sensitivity.

doble (doob-lay) double or double knife/stick.

doble kada (doob-lay-kaw-dah) double sticks or the use of two sticks.

garote (gaw-ro-tee) stick (Tagalog or Visayan dialect).

ginonting (ge-noon-ting) scissor-type block.

gonting (gon-ting) scissors block.

guru (goo-roo) instructor.

hiwa (hee-wa) to cut.

kadena (kah-dee-na) chain movement.

largamano (larga-mah-no) long-range combat, broad movement.

maestro (mice-tro) master instructor.

olisi (o-lee-see) stick.

orasyon (oras-yon) prayer to give fighters the fighting spirit and strength for combat.

oway (o-why) rattan.

pandol (poon-dole) literally, to stamp or stamping; principles of redirecting force.

sagang (sa-gaang) blocking.

sayaw (sa-yow) dance or form of movement.

sinawali (sin-knee-wah-lee) series of exercise movements that prepare the student in the use of one or two sticks.

solo (so-low) single or single knife/stick.

sumrada (soom-rah-dah) sparring.

terradas (ter-rah-dos) strike or striking.

tosok (too-suk) to poke.

vientenueve (bine-tee-nu-eh-veh) literally the number 29; a particular type of balisong.